Business Policy and Strategy
Concepts and Readings

Business Policy and Strategy

Concepts and Readings

DANIEL J. McCARTHY, D.B.A.
Professor of Management

ROBERT J. MINICHIELLO, D.B.A.
Professor of Marketing

JOSEPH R. CURRAN, Ph.D.
Associate Professor of Accounting

All of Northeastern University

1975

RICHARD D. IRWIN, INC. Homewood, Illinois 60430
Irwin-Dorsey International London, England WC2H 9NJ
Irwin-Dorsey Limited Georgetown, Ontario L7G 4B3

First Printing, May 1975

ISBN 0-256-01680-1
Library of Congress Catalog Card No. 74–31601
Printed in the United States of America

Preface

THIS TEXT contains the material for a course in business policy at the undergraduate level, the graduate level, or for practicing managers. It may also be combined with selected cases from the Intercollegiate Case Clearing House, with a case book such as *Policy Formulation and Administration* by Smith, Christensen, Berg, and Salter, or with a computer game or simulation in the area of business policy or general management.

The authors have noted that most books on business policy are primarily case books and that there has existed the need for detailed text material in the field. This book supplies that material and enriches it with important readings which aid in presenting the conceptual foundations of this field of study.

In recent years, the subject of business policy has become a required course in the curriculum of all undergraduate and graduate programs in business, management, and administration. Although there is no agreement on the "best" way to conduct such courses, many instructors begin by developing a framework useful to the study. Cases and or simulations are then utilized to apply the framework to particular situations. This book develops in detail a framework for the formulation and implementation of strategy for business and other organizations. Utilizing both text and readings, the formulation phase of strategy, and the implementation phase, are examined and explained in depth, a feature which the authors believe is much needed. Depending upon the preferences of individual instructors, this book may be combined with cases or other appropriate vehicles to allow students opportunities to apply the concepts developed. The authors believe that business policy is now at a stage where both a body of knowledge and a useful framework exist for students and managers to master if they are to understand the management of total organizations.

The conceptual material of this book is applicable to the study of policy and strategy in business and nonbusiness organizations. The text, in explaining concepts, provides numerous examples in both business and nonprofit settings. The job of top executives or general managers is analyzed through the use of a strategy framework. The early chapters of the book examine the concepts that underlie strategy, considering in depth the total organization and its parts as well as the environmental forces that affect all organizations, business and nonbusiness.

Organizational objectives are discussed in a chapter which includes as well an analysis of personal values and objectives in policy and strategy formulation. The formulation of strategy is then covered in depth both as to the process involved and as to the concepts that underlie this vital task of general managers.

The implementation of strategy is the focus of the several chapters covering organizational structure and behavioral considerations, planning, and the budgeting and control processes. The authors believe that the detailed analysis of these topics and the way in which the text weaves them into the fabric of the strategy framework is a major contribution of this book.

In all chapters, text material is supplemented with highly relevant readings which examine narrower topics in depth, and which are accompanied by pointed questions to focus attention on critical issues.

Although there is no standard format for a course in business policy, virtually all such courses study the job of general managers or top executives of organizations. The skills required to perform well in such jobs whether in business or nonbusiness organizations are examined. Emphasis is placed upon the conceptual understanding and skill required of these managers, their need to understand total organizations, and the requirement that they plan for the future of these organizations. It is this conceptual view that is enhanced by an understanding of the framework of strategy, and it is this view that this book seeks to develop in students and managers.

April 1975

DANIEL J. McCARTHY, D.B.A.
ROBERT J. MINICHIELLO, D.B.A.
JOSEPH R. CURRAN, PH.D.

Contents

1. **The Study of Policy and Strategy**   1

Policy and Strategy as Top-Management Functions: *An Integrative Function. Setting Goals and Objectives. Formulating Major Policies and Plans. Providing and Organizing the Resources of the Organization. Implementing and Controlling. Problems, Opportunities and Decisions. The Conceptual Point of View. Training for Top Management.* The Case Method of Instruction and Its Objectives: *The Role of the Student. The Role of the Case Method Instructor.* Relationship between the Case Method Approach and this Book for the Study of Business Policy. Plan of the Book.

     READINGS

        1.   Business Policy: Goals, Pedagogy, Structure, Concepts,
            Ram Charan, 14
        2.   Tomorrow's Management: A More Adventurous Life in a
            Free-Form Corporation, *Max Ways,* 25
        3.   Because Wisdom Can't Be Told, *Charles I. Gragg,* 39

2. **Introduction to Organizational Strategy**   48

The Meaning of Organizational Strategy. Utility of Strategy. The Strategic Process. Formulation of Strategy and Major Elements within Strategy: *Strategic Objectives. Product-Market Scope as a Major Element within Strategy. Allocation of Resources, Risk Horizons, Time Horizons.* Implementation of Strategy. Evaluation of Strategy. Summary.

     READINGS

        4.   The Critical Role of Top Management in Long-Range Planning,
            George A. Steiner, 63
        5.   Shaping the Master Strategy of Your Firm,
            William H. Newman, 76
        6.   Corporate Strategy: Design and Implementation (A Slide Presentation), *Robert H. Caplan III,* 95

3. **Resource Profile: Assessment of Internal Strengths and Weaknesses**   106

Objectives and Results of Comprehensive Analysis. The Role of Internal Analysis in Evaluating and Formulating Strategy. The Process of Analysis. Internal Areas for Analysis. Analyzing Management, Departments, and Functions: *Management. Finance and Accounting, Marketing, Production, Manufacturing, and Engineering. Research and Development. Other Areas.* The Human Side of the Enterprise. Top Management Viewed in Perspective. Summary.

READINGS

7. How to Evaluate a Firm, *Robert B. Buchele,* 132
8. The Capability Inventory: Its Role in Long-Range Planning, *E. Kirby Warren,* 154

4. **The Search for Opportunity: Assessment of the External Environment**   172

Introduction. The Need for Appraisal of the Environment. The Major Environmental Forces. Technological Forces. Sociocultural and Psychological Forces. Legal-Governmental Factors. Economic Factors. Industry Structure and Practices—Competition. On Appraising the Environment. Summary.

READINGS

9. If You're a Businessman, This Chart May Be the Shape of Your Future, 193
10. Evaluating Signals of Technological Change, *James R. Bright,* 202

5. **Objectives—Organizational and Personal**   218

Introduction. The Need for Objectives: *Essential to Strategic Planning. Defines the "Reason for Being" of an Organization.* The Nature of Objectives: *Achieving—Becoming—Attaining. The Personal Dimension. Levels of Objectives: Strategic to Operating. Hierarchy of Objectives. An Illustration of the Hierarchy.* The Personal Dimension of Objectives: *Influence of Personal Values and Needs on Organizational Objectives.* Management by Objectives. Social Responsibility as an Objective. Balancing Objectives: *Needed in Strategy Formulation and Implementation. A Basis for Evaluating Management and Strategy.* Summary.

READINGS

11. Personal Values and Corporate Strategy. *William D. Guth* and *Renato Tagiuri,* 233
12. A Fresh Look at Management by Objectives, *Robert A. Howell,* 248
13. The Social Responsibility of Business Is to Increase Its Profits, *Milton Friedman,* 258

6. **Identifying, Evaluating, and Formulating Strategy**   265

Introduction: *Organizing for Strategy Development. An Illustration of Roles in Strategy Development. Emphasis on the Present Strategy.*

Previous Chapters as Foundation for Strategy Development. Identifying the Present Strategy: *Areas for Analysis in the Identification Process. Maytag Company.* Evaluating the Present Strategy: *Criteria for Evaluation.* Rationale for the Existing Strategy: A Criterion for Evaluation: *Values of Managers and Owners. Taking Advantage of Market Opportunities. Taking Advantage of Organizational Competence. Combination of Reasons.* Considering Change in the Strategy: *The Gillete Company.* Changing the Strategy: Strategy Formulation: *Value of Analyzing the Present Strategy. Limitations of Analyzing the Present Strategy. Importance of External Factors. The Need to Consider All Elements. The Importance of Balance.* Summary.

READINGS

14. Construction of a Business Strategy, *Bruce D. Henderson,* 289
15. The Science of Strategy-Making, *Henry Mintzberg,* 293
16. How to Evaluate Corporate Strategy, *Seymour Tilles,* 310
17. Formulating Strategy in Smaller Companies,
    Frank F. Gilmore, 329

7. **Implementing Strategy: Organizational Structure and Behavior**   346

Introduction. Importance of Implementation. Elements of Implementation: Securing, Organizing, and Directing the Utilization of Resources. Interrelated Activities and the Art of Management. Organizational Structure and Strategy Implementation. Organizational Behavior and Strategy Implementation. The Process of Organizing: A Dilemma in Implementing Organizational Strategy: *Breaking down the Tasks to Be Performed. Coordination toward the Overall Goal. Dilemmas and Some Examples. Other Elements of the Process. Principles and Situational Analysis. Communications and Information.* Analyzing and Changing Organizations: A Challenge in Strategy Implementation: *Emphasis on the "Going Concern." Structural Aspects of Change. Behavioral Aspects of Change. Need to Consider All Aspects When Implementing or Formulating Strategy.* Implementation, Interrelationships, and Leadership. Summary.

READINGS

18. Strategy and Structure ("Some General Propositions"),
    Alfred D. Chandler, Jr., 369
19. Organizational Structure and Multinational Strategy,
    Lawrence E. Fouraker and *John M. Stopford,* 379

8. **Implementing Strategy: Planning and Budgeting**   394

Introduction. The Planning Process: *Objectives, Strategic Planning, and Period Planning.* Implementing Plans. The Budgeting Function: A Management Approach: *The Kinds of Budgets. The Advantages of Budgeting. Disadvantages of Budgeting.* Implementing Strategy through the Budgeting Process: *Planning Element of the Budget. Coordination Element of the*

Budget. Control Element of the Budget. Replanning Element of the Budget. Summary.

READINGS

20. Selection of a Framework, *Robert N. Anthony*, 411
21. The Planning Dilemma: There Is a Way Out, *James S. Hekimian* and *Henry Mintzberg*, 428
22. Using the Systems Analyst in Preparing Corporate Financial Models, *Daniel J. McCarthy* and *Charles A. Morrissey*, 442

9.   Implementing Strategy: Control and Motivation   454

Introduction. Perspective on the Budget and Control: *Relationship of Control to Strategy.* Control, Responsibility, and Reporting. Control and Exception Reporting. Motivational Considerations. Relationships among Strategy, Plans, Control, and Motivation: A Case Study: *The Burnside Division.* The Planning Concept Illustration. Summary.

READINGS

23. Do Management Control Systems Achieve Their Purpose? *Douglas McGregor*, 470
24. Motivation and Coordination in Management Control Systems, *Charles T. Horngren*, 484

chapter 1

The Study of Policy and Strategy

Policy and Strategy as Top Management Functions
  An Integrative Function
  Setting Goals and Objectives
  Formulating Major Policies and Plans
  Providing and Organizing the Resources of the
    Organization
  Implementing and Controlling
  Problems, Opportunities, and Decisions
  The Conceptual Point of View
  Training for Top Management

The Case Method of Instruction and Its Objectives
  The Role of the Student
  The Role of the Case Method Instructor

**Relationship between the Case Method Approach and
  This Book for the Study of Business Policy**

Plan of the Book

Readings

A TOP MANAGEMENT JOB is the aspiration of many: the student who struggles to learn; the graduate just launching a career; the young executive on the rise; and the experienced executive reaching for the top. Some will achieve the aspiration; many will not.

Luck, chance, personal influence, and bad judgment may place in top-management positions some who are not qualified for such a challenge and deprive others who may be very well qualified. Likewise, some of those apparently most qualified will fail, while others with less impressive credentials will act with great success.

Many who achieve a top-management position will do so in the business world. But an increasing number will become top managers of other institutions: schools, hospitals, foundations, governments, and so forth. The skills needed to be an effective top executive in these fields are essentially the same as those needed in business. Thus the concepts and approaches included in this book, developed primarily in a business setting, are recommended also to those who aspire to high managerial achievement in other areas.

The principal target of this book is the top-management aspirant who is still a student in the formal sense. Thus, the book is designed essentially for the advanced student of business management. However, practitioners who have not experienced recent training in administration will find much that is useful in these pages. This first chapter will introduce some of the essential elements of the top manager's job that are concerned with strategy and policy considerations. Subsequent chapters will analyze these aspects of top management's work in depth. Methods of training top-management aspirants will also be discussed in this introduction.

POLICY AND STRATEGY AS TOP-MANAGEMENT FUNCTIONS

In recent years the concept of corporate strategy has been utilized as a framework to explain many important facets of the job of top management. Essentially, strategy considerations encompass deciding (a) what a company is to be; and (b) how it is to become what it is to be. In effect, strategy includes the goals and major policies of the organization.[1]

The idea of strategy has developed into a useful vehicle by which to consider critical elements of the job of top managers. The concept of strategy has been considered to incorporate various activities including the *identification* of strategy; the *determination* or *formulation* of strategy; the *implementation* of strategy; the *evaluation* of strategy. Thus these tasks encompass a vital portion of the job of top management. However, top-management personnel are typically most concerned with identifying and formulating strategy, and with planning for and initiating its implementation. Usually, the actual implementation process is carried out by all members of the organization. Top-management and lower levels in varying degrees are vitally involved in the continuous evaluation of the chosen strategy. The specific approach to strategic tasks and the particular involvement of top management, however, does differ depending upon the size of the organization.[2]

---

[1] S. Tilles, "How to Evaluate Corporate Strategy," *Harvard Business Review*, July–August 1963, p. 112.

[2] For a full discussion of this point, see F. F. Gilmore's article included in the readings of this book (Chapter 6), "Formulating Strategy in Smaller Companies," *Harvard Business Review*, May–June 1971.

An Integrative Function

"Dealing with the total enterprise provides challenges and opportunities which do not exist in the management of a single part."[3] The chief policy maker of the organization must consider as a totality all aspects of its business, including those which affect the organization from within and without. Not only must he or she be informed about all facets independently, but further he must analyze each, and then pull together all relevant aspects in a form meaningful to the guidance of the organization. Decisions must be made utilizing the integrated and analyzed information. The monumental complexity of this task, of course, increases almost geometrically as an organization grows in size.

How is this integrative aspect of the executive function accomplished? It is accomplished principally through the function of setting goals or objectives; framing major plans and policies to accomplish these goals; providing and organizing the resources needed to achieve the purposes; and carrying out the necessary activities to see that the organization accomplishes its various purposes.

Setting Goals and Objectives

Barnard has explained that the executive is "to formulate and define the purposes of the organization."[4] In analyzing this task, it becomes apparent that here is the source of inspiration from which flows the life of the organization. It is at this stage that a decision is made as to what the entity is to be, or expressed differently, what business the company is to pursue.

Unless a fully conscious and realistic decision is reached in this area of objective definition, management can never know if it is doing what it might do best, doing what it wants to do, or doing all that it may be capable of doing. Strategy formulation is concerned primarily with this most crucial aspect of organizational purpose.

Formulating Major Policies and Plans

The management which succeeds in establishing the major purposes of its organization will not even have completed this important step when it will already be asking how to achieve these ends, in what order, and over what periods of time. It will become quickly involved in the policy

---

[3] Robert L. Katz, *Cases and Concepts in Corporate Strategy* (Englewood Cliffs, N.J.: Prentice-Hall, Inc., 1970), p. 7.

[4] Chester I. Barnard, *The Functions of the Executive* (Cambridge, Mass.: Harvard University Press, 1938), p. 215.

making and planning needed to steer its way on the road to achieving the objectives that have been established.

Although a tremendous amount of detail and data will eventually be generated and utilized in making policies and plans, the top-management team will most likely be concerned only with the most basic of these.

Providing and Organizing the Resources of the Organization

Strategy formulation as described thus far has suggested a process quite intellectual in nature. It has required an analytical view and a conceptual and integrative ability on the part of top managers to visualize the potential and direction of the enterprise. The process of providing and organizing resources is similar but it further moves toward action, and toward the implementation of strategy.

Initially, organizing resources, human, financial, and physical, is an exercise in logic with the basic objectives and strategy of the company always in mind. Soon though, as decisions are made, actions must be taken, money must be raised, buildings built and people hired, or sometimes let go. All of these resources must be organized in a fashion which best serves the purposes of the organization. Organizational structure, once determined, is usually slow to change and basic changes should be most meaningfully coordinated with the organization's strategy.

Implementing and Controlling

The line betwen formulating and implementing is truly a fine one, and in practice it often seems that one hardly exists. Implementation, however, is concerned more with the day-to-day activity by which purpose is accomplished, resources are utilized, activities are directed, results are monitored, and operations are controlled. The heart of this phase of the management process is communication and information. Whether verbal or written, whether figures, words, or symbols, whether formal or informal, the information which is generated in and around the activity of the business is what enables the executives to direct and control the organization toward the achievement of corporate goals. It is often, too, the communications of the top executives which motivate the people of the enterprise, or which fail to do so.

Problems, Opportunities and Decisions

Two activities take a major part of any top manager's time. Discovering the important problems, issues, or opportunities, to which his time should be devoted is the first; the second is solving these problems by making the appropriate decisions, or selecting the most appropriate opportunities. Both can be most intelligently and ably handled if viewed within the structure of an organization's strategy.

It is important here in recognizing problems to emphasize again the integrative nature of the top-management job. Problems which gain attention at this level are complicated, multidimensional, and have major ramifications for the organization, and perhaps beyond the organization. And these problems seem to be endless. They arrive before the executive from many sources and the supply never diminishes. The same applies to opportunities but often these are harder to recognize.

The first job for managers then, is to decide what problems or opportunities most warrant their attention. This may not appear at first blush to be of such enormous import, but one major study has found it to be critical.[5] Considering such issues and opportunities in the light of the organization's strategy will be of immense help to the executive facing them. If the problem or opportunity is worthy of consideration, the executive must gather all needed information at a cost of time and money, decide how much is enough and proceed to "solve the problem," or "capitalize upon the opportunity." Again, this response will very often be most appropriate if it is made in light of strategic considerations.

Much of the solution on the part of the chief executive may be in a short statement, memo, or telephone call by which he or she communicates his decisions. Actually this decision will probably only start the mechanism toward the solution. Yet these decisions at the top are the source of direction for the enterprise, and lead to countless other decisions within the overall organization. This never-ending process makes it critical that an understanding of the corporate strategy is found at the various levels within the organization. Without such a common denominator, there is far less probability of coordinated action at all levels toward corporate goals.

The Conceptual Point of View

From the foregoing brief analysis of strategic aspects of the top executive job, it should be apparent that the individuals who fill these positions or aspire to do so, as well as those who would meaningfully study this field, must develop a point of view indispensable to understanding what is involved. That point of view must involve the nature of conceptualization, that special facility of abstractly constructing and viewing ideas and operations as a totality.

The ability to sense what information is needed and appropriate, and how it should be ordered to facilitate understanding assumes an analyt-

---

[5] W. F. Pounds, "The Process of Problem Finding," *Management Review*, Fall 1969.

ical and, where feasible, even a scientific approach to knowledge, problems, and decisions. Yet, the exercise of informed judgment retains the essential qualities of an art which has no claims on certainty. The best use must be made of all knowledge, skill, and abilities to exercise judgment, to arrive at conclusions, and to make decisions, while recognizing the uncertainty involved in the entire process.

A major purpose of this book is to assist in the development of this point of view by providing the concept of strategy as a framework within which to consider the crucial aspects of the top executive job. Knowledge will be made available in the text and readings. But beyond this, the vital requirement is involvement for the student, or practitioner, in order to test his knowledge and framework, and to develop the analytical and conceptual skills so vitally required in this important area of activity.

Training for Top Management

In the authors' opinion, a most practical pedagogical approach for training top-management aspirants is the study of the conceptual material presented in this book, supplemented by the readings provided, and combined with rigorous exposure to a variety of challenging business policy cases or other types of simulated experiences. Study of textual materials and suggested readings alone is not sufficient training for prospective top managers. It is essential to become involved in the kinds of situations that are the working lives of top executives. One must practice defining problems, clarifying issues, analyzing data, forming conclusions, setting objectives, formulating strategy, establishing alternatives, predicting consequences, and developing programs of action. The analysis of business policy cases provides much of the needed practice, as does involvement in other appropriate real or simulated situations such as policy "games."

Students can be trained only to a certain point by being told by the author or lecturer. Gragg's article reproduced in this book is the classic exposition of this idea. Top executives are not just recipients of information. They have to analyze it and decide what to do about it. The study of cases requires students to analyze situations and decide what to do—invaluable training for the top-management aspirant.

Although this introduction considers primarily the case method for training prospective top managers, other useful supplementary techniques may be employed, such as roleplaying, computerized business games, the incident approach, or the in-basket technique. These methods and others provide experiences similar or supplementary to cases at varying costs of time and money and with varying degrees of effectiveness. But given the present state of development of pedagogical techniques, it is the position of the authors that the case approach is the most available, practical, and useful method for training managers.

THE CASE METHOD OF INSTRUCTION AND ITS OBJECTIVES

It has been written that "the case method is a complex method of instruction which stubbornly refuses to stand still to be photographed."[6] This statement captures the dynamic nature of this method of instruction. But despite the absence of pictures, several users and observers have described and analyzed the case approach. Stated most simply, the basic mission of the case method of instruction is the training of students to think for themselves. One experienced case teacher has described the goals of case method instruction as follows:

> The maximum goal of the case method is the development of a mind which has superior ability to transfer its powers from familiar types of problems to new ones. Persons with such minds also need the power to explain to others what is going on, that is to verbalize their thinking. In contrast, as a minimum goal, most teachers of the case method would accept "direct learners," that is to say persons who can be observed to deal intelligently with the problems they face, although they are not able to explain the thinking process they have gone through. It is supposed that these students have an ability to generalize and transfer inarticulately without verbalization![7]

Hunt further restated these goals more fully as follows:

1. The power to analyze and to master a tangle of circumstances by selecting the important factors from the whole set of facts and by weighing their importance in context.
2. The ability to utilize ideas to test them against the facts of the problem, to throw both ideas and facts into fresh combinations, thus discovering ways which make them appropriate for the solution of the problem at hand.
3. The ability to recognize a need for new factual material or the need to apply technical skills to a problem, and the ability to assimilate such facts and skills as are needed for the solution of the problem at hand.
4. The ability to use later experience as a test of the validity of the ideas already obtained, with flexibility to revise goals and procedures as experience is deepened.
5. The ability to communicate to others in a manner which induces thought.
6. The ability to use ideas in theoretical form. That is to say, one should be able to create a coherent structure of generalized propositions from his problem-solving experience.

---

[6] Albert H. Dunn, III, "Basic Characteristics of the Case Method," in *The Case Method at the Harvard Business School,* ed. Malcolm P. McNair (New York: McGraw-Hill Book Co., 1954), p. 92.

[7] Pearson Hunt, "The Case Method of Instruction," *Harvard Educational Review,* Summer 1961.

7. The ability to attain the goal simply, completely, and without any more waste than is necessary in any thinking about an unfamiliar problem.[8]

These powers and abilities comprise the skills needed by top managers if they are to be effective in carrying out the tasks described previously. But these skills can only be learned by practice, and short of a trial-and-error kind of learning through the school of experience (a very lengthy and sometimes costly process), by a kind of practice the case method involves. For as Gragg wrote:

> It can be said flatly that the mere act of listening to wise statements and sound advice does little for anyone. In the process of learning, the learner's dynamic cooperation is required. Such cooperation from students does not arise automatically, however. It has to be provided for and continually encouraged. . . .
>
> It would be easy to accept the unanalyzed assumption that by passing on, by lectures and readings, to young men of intelligence, the accumulated experience and wisdom of those who have made business their study, the desired results could be achieved. . . . This assumption, however, rests on another decidedly questionable one: namely, the assumption that it is possible by a simple process of telling to pass on knowledge in a useful form. This is the great delusion of the ages. If the learning process is to be effective, something dynamic must take place in the learner."[9]

The dynamism that Gragg cites as the key desideratum in learning is an essential part of the case method process of educating prospective top managers. Another noted teacher has described this process as a kind of education that "must afford the training to enable the individual to meet in action the problems arising out of new situations of ever-changing environments; education that consists of 'acquiring facility to act' in the presence of new experience."[10]

The Role of the Student

The case method of instruction by its inherent nature provides students with the vital kind of training needed for administrative competence. Students assigned a case are actually given a body of material typically consisting of facts (quantitative and qualitative) regarding an enterprise

---

[8] Ibid.

[9] Charles I. Gragg, "Because Wisdom Can't Be Told," in *The Case Method at the Harvard Business School,* ed. Malcolm P. McNair (New York: McGraw-Hill Book Co., 1954).

[10] Arthur S. Dewing, "An Introduction to the Use of Cases," in *The Case Method at the Harvard Business School,* ed. Malcolm P. McNair (New York: McGraw-Hill Book Co., 1954), p. 2.

and various facets of its operation and environment, as well as the opinions, beliefs, assumptions, aspirations of various people identified in the case, i.e., executives and employees of the company, competitors, consultants, industry experts, researchers, and so forth.

The students, in preparing for class, are expected to master the facts, to draw conclusions from the facts, and to develop a program of action for the enterprise. Then in class students are expected to participate in a discussion of the case in which they present and defend their own views and/or critically appraise the views of others.

This total process is focused on two simple questions: What should the management of the company do? Why? However, the process of arriving at answers to these questions involves the student in a most demanding mental exercise; the challenge of exercising judgment and formulating workable decisions. For often the problems in a case, especially a business policy case, are not clearly perceived: frequently there is conflicting evidence and opinion; there may be several feasible alternatives, some not explicitly stated in the case; there may be a matter of urgency forcing a decision in the face of insufficient data; and the possible moves of competitors or future economic conditions may present complicating uncertainties.

But wrestling with these conditions is what top-management personnel are paid for and as Gragg has said, "the time inevitably arises when young people must engage in practical action on their own responsibility. . . . The serious student gets the essential background for responsible decisions without the risks to himself and to his firm which are inseparable from amateurish action. The student is led to active consideration of a tremendous number of diverse and related real situations which it would take him at least a lifetime of experience to encounter, and he is thus given a basis for comparison and analysis when he enters upon his career of business action."[11]

In addition to the mental development and training that the case method develops in students, there are other benefits. After students have studied the case situation and decided what they would do and why, they must come to class to participate in a discussion of the case. This requirement deepens the students' involvement in the case situation. It forces the students to be prepared to make an oral presentation of their position; to be prepared to answer the questions and counterarguments of other students or of the instructor; to develop the open-mindedness to recognize shortcomings in their own analysis or program of action; and to develop the flexibility to revise their position and program after reflecting upon the contributions of others.

Consequently, the student also develops the skill of being able to

---

[11] Gragg, "Because Wisdom Can't Be Told," pp. 8, 14.

participate effectively in a discussion of an important business problem. The communication and human relation skills so fostered are also essential to eventual administrative success.

The Role of the Case Method Instructor

The preceding discussion of the value of case method instruction and the particular benefits to students assumes a particular teaching approach. While there are many different personal teaching styles, and probably no two case instructors handle a class in the same manner, case method instruction in the field of business administration as advocated by the authors is characterized by the basic approach originally developed at the Harvard Business School but now employed by many instructors at countless institutions. Required is an environment in which a tough-minded analysis of a case is carried out by the class under the guidance of the instructor.

Thus, the authors are not suggesting the type of classroom situation in which the class merely reads the case assigned and the instructor essentially lectures on the case, suggesting how a certain policy or decision is wise or unwise in his opinion, and concluding with the instructor's recommendations for the company. In contrast, the burden should be placed upon the students to analyze the case, to discuss the relevant issues and to decide what should be done. However, a consensus by the class regarding appraisal and action is not necessarily an objective. As one teacher has written: "There should not be a single problem in use which is not capable of at least two intelligent solutions, and it would be surprising if any group of experienced businessmen could offer an unequivocal solution with unanimous accord to anyone of them."[12]

Effective case discussion requires a very skilled instructor. One such instructor has written of the case teacher that "at first glance his duties seem less onerous than those of a lecturer in the main stream of educational tradition." But after discussing in detail the duties and responsibilities of the case teacher, Andrews concludes: "In the face of these large requirements (placed side by side with the limiting fact that faculty members must be recruited from the human race), I think it is fortunate that the skills demanded are not beyond the range of skills which can be learned."[13]

Students often request the instructor's "answer" to a case. Sometimes they feel frustrated by a particularly difficult decision or are seeking

---

[12] Dewing, "An Introduction to the Use of Cases," p. 3.

[13] Kenneth R. Andrews, "The Role of the Instructor in the Case Method," in *The Case Method at the Harvard Business School*, ed. Malcolm P. McNair (New York: McGraw-Hill Book Co., 1954), p. 98–99. Those interested in a superb discussion of the role of the instructor in case method teaching are advised to read Professor Andrews' essay in full (pp. 98–109).

confirmation of the "correctness" of their own decisions. Usually they are curious to know what the instructor thinks. The authors' position on this often debated issue in pedagogical technique is to refrain from providing students with "answers" to cases, although providing helpful insights can prove valuable. An especially illuminating discussion of this issue and some other requests made by students of a case instructor was written by Joseph C. Bailey, Professor of Human Relations, following a long discussion with one of his classes at the Harvard Business School.[14]

RELATIONSHIP BETWEEN THE CASE METHOD APPROACH AND THIS BOOK FOR THE STUDY OF BUSINESS POLICY

From the above discussion of the case method, it should become apparent why this vehicle is an especially useful and practical approach to the study of business policy which is essentially the study of the top-management job, its functions, relationships, demands, and complexities. But more than cases are required in this study.

Although widely utilized and highly valuable, the case method alone is not sufficient today for the best accomplishment of the objectives of most courses in business policy. The course should seek to provide useful knowledge and generalizations about the subject of strategy and aspects of the top-management job. The development of a conceptual point of view or framework with which to view overall situations and their interrelated parts is also an important objective. There is much to be learned by students of management, even including what some would hold to be "principles" of management. But this information is quite inert until it is considered or utilized in a real or simulated situation. It is this application of "principles" to the "real world" or simulation of the real world that transforms information, theories, and principles into meaningful aids for learning and doing. Without applications in real or simulated situations, business theory can be very difficult for students to appreciate. Thus it is expected that this book will be utilized with reproduced cases such as those available from the Intercollegiate Clearing House, with a published casebook, or with simulations such as business "games."

If the primary reason for the study of business policy is to produce practitioners and decision makers, this emphasis on application is as required as is the understanding of concepts and ideas. Particularly in the field of policy, although also important to various functional areas, it is necessary to "get involved" in the problems, analyses, and decisions. Because it is so difficult for the student in the abstract to really understand the complexity of higher level management problems and decisions, it is

---

[14] Joseph C. Bailey, "A Classroom Evaluation of the Case Method," on file at Baker Library, Harvard Business School.

imperative that he get some "feel" for them. Simply stating that the top manager sets objectives, establishes long-range plans, and reviews the overall performance of the organization may be a beginning at job definition. But the very nature of these top executive functions is rather difficult to grasp by explanation and theory alone. The ideas presented in this book are helpful to students in building a valuable background of tools and knowledge, but it is the premise of the authors that expository material alone could never totally succeed in giving a student a full understanding of business policy or the strategic elements of the top-management job. Thus this book is viewed as a companion to cases and other vehicles that are meaningful, practical, inexpensive and available. The textual material of this book, however, is also meant to provide a framework for students of business policy who may be employing their skills in the real world. For this reader, his or her own organizational situation provides a real live case.

The best learning usually takes place in this field when one faces practice armed with useful theory and equipped with a point of view with which to confront situations. An instructor in teaching business policy generally employs an implicit framework within which he views cases and similar situations. Should not the student also have a framework to utilize as an important learning aid? This premise does not say that "answers" are provided. It contends only that students should be provided with the material of the field, including any available theory, to utilize in the analytical and decision-making processes as they deal with real situations. The "field" of policy has been developing and this text material is meant to provide students with a useful approach for viewing policy situations in organizations. It is a framework to be utilized, and hopefully will make observed situations more meaningful to the student who views them as policy situations demanding analysis and decisions.

Because much has already been published in the various areas encompassed by corporate policy, this book includes as readings what the authors consider to be some of the most useful material available. Consideration of cases and simulations can be made more meaningful when those discussing such situations can refer to ideas and theories which illuminate the individual situation under discussion. Because of the importance, then, of exposing students to published knowledge in the policy field, readings have been included which are appropriate to the subjects of the various chapters.

PLAN OF THE BOOK

The chapter topics and related readings are organized to present the identification and formulation of strategy within Chapters 3, 4, 5, and 6 and major aspects of strategy implementation in Chapters 7, 8, and 9.

In the following chapter, the concept of strategy is introduced and discussed in depth to provide a full understanding of this concept. Chapters 3, 4, and 5 consider the internal and external situations of an organization. The internal view focuses upon organizational resources and develops an approach for analyzing a firm's internal profile. The external view appraises the range of considerations which must be considered when analyzing the environment of the organization. Chapter 5 covers the nature of objectives, the various kinds of objectives, and major factors that influence objectives such as the personal values of decision makers.

Strategy formulation and development depends upon the major areas of internal profile, external environment, and objectives as inputs. Thus, Chapter 6 demonstrates how the internal profile of resources, the external environment, and personal objectives and values all come together in the formulation of corporate or organizational strategy. Furthermore, the chapter allows the student to see how paramount these same three considerations are in the evaluation of corporate strategy.

The last three chapters consider the implementation of strategy which is a necessary ingredient if the entire strategic process is to be understood. Three traditional management tasks of organizing, planning, and control are viewed as processes which are critical to the implementation of strategy within an organization.

In summary, this book is a book about organizational policy which provides information about the elements which together make up the area of study generally encompassed under the "umbrella" of policy. These are the identification of strategy, the formulation and implementation of strategy, and the evaluation of strategy. The book is meant to provide insight into the field of policy by providing text and important related readings. Although not a casebook, it is expected that this book will be utilized in conjunction with cases or simulations when it is used in a policy course. When utilized by a practitioner of business the theory and information should be most meaningful to the reader when related to his or her own particular organizational situation.

1. Business Policy: Goals, Pedagogy, Structure, Concepts[*]

RAM CHARAN

PART I

BUSINESS POLICY (usually referred to around the School as "Policy") is the only compulsory course in the second year of the MBA Program. The importance attached to Policy by the Faculty is evident from the fact that it *is* required of all MBA candidates.

Policy is distinguished by its concern with what is relevant and critical to the enterprise as a whole. It deals with the problems and processes of top management which is the agency responsible for the short- as well as the long-run viability of the *total enterprise,* its relationship to the environment, and its effectiveness in fulfilling its purpose.

The course draws from and builds on all the first-year required courses: Marketing; Production; Finance; Managerial Economics, Reporting, and Control; Planning and the Business Environment; Human Behavior in Organizations; Organizational Problems; and Written Analysis of Cases. Learning functional knowledge for its own sake is not enough; it must have a focus to be meaningful and operational. Policy provides this focus; it integrates the relevant content of the functional disciplines within the context of the "organizational purpose."

In recent years, the course has seen an accelerated pace of evolution in terms of its conceptual framework and structure. The following discussion is an attempt to describe Policy as it stands today—goals, pedagogy, structure, and concepts. The ideas presented are largely a product of several decades' work by the Business Policy Faculty.

---

[*] Ram Charan, "Business Policy: Goals, Pedagogy, Structure, Concepts," *Harvard Business School Bulletin,* July–August and November–December 1966. Reprinted with permission of the publisher.

Policy Goals

The basic goal is to encourage the student to cultivate attitudes, skills, and knowledge pertinent to top management. In the abstract form, the student is encouraged to develop an attitude toward broadening his perspective. To be able to formulate a viable strategy he must be capable of seeing the forest for the trees. He must analyze carefully the impact of issues in several dimensions. He should realize explicitly what he can achieve, what he cannot, and to what degree. The student must gear the goals of his specialty to the broad perspective of the total entity, constantly cultivating the willingness and toughness (not inflexibility) to face multidimensional problems. He then must take responsible action, even if complete information cannot be obtained.

The student is encouraged to reevaluate the traditional economic goal of the corporation, i.e., profit maximization. He is to formulate a multidimensional, not simply economic, set of goals within the context of perceived social and national needs. At a higher level of abstraction, this set of goals need not necessarily be acceptable to other elements in the society. But he must actively articulate the corporate goals rather than let them be passively misunderstood by the disapproving elements in the society. In a nutshell, his attitudes should broaden from being that of a simple economic man to that of a "responsible citizen" who provides economic services.

An even more basic Policy goal is that of fostering integrative, adaptive, and creative skills. The student draws upon various disciplines to resolve issues that are critical to the company. But mechanistic integration of several functional areas—finance, marketing, or manufacturing—is not enough. He must look into the surroundings of the entity. He must change, influence, or adapt the company to the environment. Above all, creative ability must come into play, not only in generating alternatives that passively match the external opportunities and the internal needs of the business, but also in actively shaping the external environment. Need for thorough logic lies at the heart of the process of cultivating these skills.

The above attitudes and skills cannot be developed in a vacuum. It is necessary for the student to be familiar with the practical problems and responsibilities of top management in a variety of situations. To help sharpen his attitudes and skills, he learns how practitioners and academicians have looked at the variety of these problems and issues. He discovers concepts which can help in his corporate strategy, to devise a plan of action to attain the strategy, to create mechanisms for evaluating progress, and to take corrective action when necessary.

Generalities from the literature could be useful. But when coming to a specific decision, the complexity of each situation is unique. "Unidimensional general principles" can hardly be the panacea for specific top management problems.

The choice of Policy goals reflects the point of view of the practitioner. Policy emphasizes breadth over depth. It focuses more on skills and attitudes than on techniques and functional knowledge. Its approach is to train a "generalist" rather than a "specialist." The "generalist" approach is appropriate to the point of view of the practitioners because inadequate or contaminated data and the contaminated complexity of multidimensional problems of top management defy the neatness and simplicity of assumptions inherent in alternative approaches such as that of mathematical theory. This does not mean that the Policy course ignores their contribution; rather, it attempts to weave their relevant elements into a "purposeful whole."

Pedagogy

The Policy goals, particularly the attitudes and skills to be cultivated by the student, can hardly be achieved by the conventional "lecture method." The cultivation of these skills requires practice and drill in a variety of actual problems of general management. The Policy course, therefore, uses the case method as a teaching vehicle to emphasize the analytical decision-making approach. Through the process of identifying and comparing conceptual uniformities, categorizing experience, and weaving one situation with another, the student discovers useful concepts and generalizations. This case approach is necessarily supplemented by readings of excerpts from textbooks and articles, and by the instructor's additional knowledge and experience.

In the class discussion, the student assumes the responsibility of a general manager, makes necessary judgments, presents a logical analysis, and recommends a course of action including plans to carry it out. He must defend this course of action before his peers, acquire the additional experience of the class, assimilate the arguments of disagreeing students, cultivate skill in asking pertinent questions, and be ready to modify his recommendations, if necessary.

The student's learning process is further supplemented by frequent written reports. These reports provide the student an opportunity to develop a deeper understanding of the relevant concepts in addition to a thorough analysis of the assigned case.

Cultivation of skill in asking pertinent questions is probably the most painstaking of these processes. Such skill will prove its value in helping the student in distinguishing the relevant from the irrelevant, the important from the trivial, and in understanding explicitly the nature of the implicit assumption in compound questions. For example, the compound question, "When are you going to stop beating your wife?" assumes that the subject has been beating his wife—probably continually, periodically, or frequently. However, this assumption must be examined before answering the question. What is even more important for the student is learning to recognize, and to say so, when he does not have the answer to a pertinent question.

Pedagogical effectiveness is largely a function of the case material, the structure of the course, and the instructor. For a given group of students the instructor is a major variable. He is to determine the degree of toughness he must exercise in demanding that students present their arguments with vigor and logic. He has some flexibility in sequencing the cases and concepts within a segment of the course. Instructors can and do enrich the course with their personal experience and maturity.

Because a majority of students are not familiar with top management problems, occasional mention of the instructor's personal experience is helpful. More importantly, the instructor's penetrating questioning in the class discussion does reflect the degree and quality of his incision into the case, his view of what appears to be relevant for top management, and his capacity to structure the discussions and to relate issues and concepts to the core of the course. The quality of questioning, the skill in relating the various concepts and segments of the course, the ability to stretch the imagination of the student beyond the case and the classroom into the real world, and the total involvement of the instructor have a marked impact on the student. These are the determinants of the *degree* of the instructor's effectiveness.

It should now be clear that there is more to pedagogical effectiveness than simply the use of the so-called "case method." From school to school and within a school the degree of effectiveness of a given group of cases will vary. For the case method to be effective, the selection and sequencing of the cases and an understanding of the level of capability and time constraints on the students are also important.

The Policy Theme

The "concept of corporate strategy" is the underlying theme in the Policy course. The word strategy has several meanings in different contexts. We define it as "the pattern of objectives, purposes, or goals and major policies and plans for achieving these goals, stated in such a way as to define what business the company is in or is to be in and the kind of company it is or is to be."[1]

Our definition of strategy has multidimensional aspects. It includes the

---

[1] E. P. Learned, C. R. Christensen, K. R. Andrews and W. D. Guth, *Business Policy: Text and Cases* (Homewood, Ill.: Richard D. Irwin, Inc., 1965).

definition of the product functions, the product-market-distribution channel relationship, the nature of financing and the degree of risk inherent in it, and finally the character, the size, and the kind of organization which is to be the medium of achievement. Obviously, each dimension or component of the strategy should be consistent. Change in any one component should be enough reason for review of the total strategy. Despite the lack of explicitness, a strategy—or lack of strategy—can readily be deduced from the firm's current behavior.

The distinguishing characteristic of entrepreneurs is their capacity to recognize and create opportunities and, explicitly or implicitly, to formulate a corporate purpose. The process of strategy formulation is not, however, entirely intuitive or inherent in any one type of human being. This process can be partly learned from practitioners and transferred to students.

The determination of corporate strategy is the basic task of an organization and its top management. Themes such as Economic Theory of the Firm are of little help in learning or transferring the process of determining corporate purpose. Such theories ignore the basic purpose as given.

The Policy Structure and Concepts

Because of multidimensional aspects of the process of general management, it is convenient to categorize the course into several related but interdependent conceptual segments and subsegments so that each will build upon the preceding one. The MBA Policy course is divided into two segments: (1) determination of corporate strategy and (2) implementation of that corporate strategy.

It is important to note at the outset that the two segments in business life are seldom static or isolated from each other. Intense intellectual activity really takes place when one has to formulate and implement a revised strategy, and, at the same time, "keep the ship afloat."

PART II

As noted at the end of Part I, the multidimensional aspects of the process of top management make it convenient to categorize the course into several related and interdependent conceptual segments and subsegments so that each will build upon the one preceding. The MBA Policy course is divided into two segments: (1) determination of corporate strategy and (2) implementation of corporate strategy.

In this connection it may be worthwhile to reemphasize the fact that in actual business the two segments are seldom static or isolated one from the other. It is a real challenge to formulate and implement a new strategy on the one hand, while on the other hand attending to the current details which "keep the ship afloat."

Determination of Corporate Strategy

The core of this segment is the choice of a *viable* strategy in the context of the firm's environment. This segment is further divided into: analysis of environment and selection of *economic alternatives* which will match the corporate resources and character at a risk commensurate with the profit and viability which the alternatives offer. This choice is further narrowed to reflect the management's *"controlling" personal values and aspirations.* Finally one chooses a strategy that is also acceptable to the management as *moral and socially* responsible. Any choice that is inconsistent with any of the above must force the strategist to search again, alter one or more parameters, and generate alternative strategies that will *at least* satisfy the above constraints (see chart below).

Environment and Economic Strategy. Analysis of environment involves the examination and detection of international, national, political, social, economic, and technological trends relevant and critical to the corporation. The student is to judge and project the critical short- and long-run trends, assess their composite effect on corporate purpose, and detect which external constraints he can influence. It is important for him to assess both opportunity and risks inherent in these trends.

Identification of feasible economic opportunities involves the assessment of corporate strengths and weaknesses, e.g., managerial, marketing, production, and financial skills. Over a period of time an organization develops a character. It cultivates some distinctive competences that may be reflected in terms of marketing, product, quality, precision, human resources, and leading the industry in research, and so on. The student is to face the issue; what is the nature of the organization to be and how can the company's distinctive competence be mobilized to take fullest advantage of its environmental opportunities?

A series of cases about a particular industry helps the student to gain insight in the variety of strategies followed by companies within the same industry, within the same environment, and within the same time span. For example, the typewriter industry series contains: (1) a note on the industry as a whole, including total market data, market share where possible, domestic and foreign price structure, imports and exports, technological developments before and after World War II, the trends in product design and what the industry leaders think of the future; and (2) a number of cases on three major competing typewriter companies, including their strategies and strategists, product line, markets, internal resources, and future plans.

Within the same period of time, the three companies reacted differently. Within the context of trends deduced from the industry note the student must make specific strategic recommendations for each company in question. Strategic recommendation for one company may differ from others. For example, following the industry leader could be disastrous for another company.

The student gains insight into a variety of strategists, their dominant traits, and the effects of dissension within the managerial groups on the choice of a strategy. The dominant-personality traits are a factor, probably a major one, in the choice of a strategy, but they are not a substitute for organizational leadership.

Personal Values and Aspirations. People at the helm of the organization have explicit or implicit personal aspirations and values. These are usually multiple in nature. Relative ranking of these values may change, even though they remain interdependent and, frequently, internally inconsistent. Although difficult to measure and rank, the personal values of those who are in "control" of the organization have a significant bearing on the choice of strategy.

The student, therefore, further narrows the choice of economic alternatives to those which will also meet the multidimensional constraints of personal values and aspirations. For example, managers will choose high-risk strategy because they can, and feel they must, cope temperamentally with its attendant gyrations. A student recommendation that does not account for this kind of personal value can hardly be acceptable to this kind of management.

While concepts regarding personal values are provided for the student through text material, emphasis is placed on his explicit definition and ranking of personal value parameters. Achievement of the highest-ranking

Stages in Policy Development (a conceptual representation of the process of formulating corporate strategy)

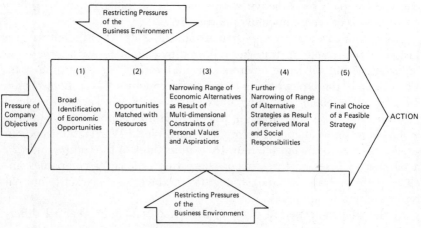

parameter does not necessarily mean that the lowest-ranking value can be completely ignored.

Moral and Social Responsibility. Traditionally, the role of a businessman is recognized by the economist as that of a profit maximizer. But, above all, he is a citizen of the society in which he lives. Should his role be broadened from that of an economic man to that of a "responsible citizen providing economic services" within the context of perceived moral, national, and social goals? Should he actively participate in shaping the attitudes of the society of which he is a member or merely take a reactive role seeking to counterbalance the increasing importance of powerful pressure groups such as labor? Examination of these issues is important irrespective of whether the manager is at the helm of a public or a private sector organization.

The student is exposed to issues ranging from personal expression on public matters to the desirability of trading with national enemies. Should he be entirely responsible to the shareholders or should he be a mediator to resolve his possibly conflicting obligations to public, to consumer, to creditor, and to competitor?

There are few techniques or well-accepted answers to these issues. Probably each situation will be unique. A student broadens his perspective by listening to the various viewpoints of his peers, and instructors. He gains insight into what is already written by well-known defendants of this dimension in the corporate setting. Beyond the collection of factual knowledge, each student must develop his own framework, his own philosophy. Criticism of almost all his decisions along this dimension would be inevitable. The question is whether he can successfully articulate and defend his philosophy.

Thus, the segment Determination of Corporate Strategy has three major categories: formulation of economic strategy, personal values and aspiration, and moral and social responsibility. Each category is multidimensional in nature. It is, indeed, an intellectual challenge for anyone to formulate a viable strategy that is acceptable and that satisfies the multiple constraints.

Implementation of Corporate Strategy

The core of this segment is the choice of an "internal mechanism"—an organizational structure, organizational processes, and pattern of leadership—that will help accomplish the chosen strategy.

Structure. The choice of an organizational structure involves (1) the relative ranking of key tasks of the strategy; (2) the assessment of the competence, working styles, and commitment of key people; (3) the determination of a hierarchical structure including the distribution of formal authority and the design of an information system that will permit the reintegration of subdivided tasks. The structure must be sensitive to the inevitable changes in environment and thus be capable of effecting probable change in strategy.

Concepts and issues regarding the structure are discussed, such as: (1) "management by objectives"; (2) economy of specialization through grouping like activities; (3) limitations, prerequisites, and implications of centralization and decentralization; (4) assignment of responsibility with or without commensurate authority; (5) "product-manager" concept; (6) impact of growth on changes in the relative ranking of key tasks and in the role of the chief executive; (7) problems of transition in replacing key people that may necessitate change in structure or even strategy.

Considerable literature and research on these concepts and others related to structure, both in descriptive and in normative form, are available. However, concepts, singly or in groups, seldom fit the needs of actual administrative realities of life. Modification of one or more concepts and new ways of structuring the organization may have to be developed to satisfy a unique situation.

Processes. The function of the "chosen organizational process" is to influence the organizational behavior for a given strategy and structure. "Organizational process" is further divided into three categories: motivation and incentives, standards and measurement of performance, and a system of restraint and control. Each of them is multidimensional and interdependent. The design and actual operation of the data communication system lies at the heart of these processes. The current development in the area presents a wide variety of tools from which to choose in order to influence organizational behavior.

Contrary to the usual belief, any one of the above categories would seldom be sufficient in accomplishment of purpose. A balanced blend of these tools is more likely to prove successful. None of the concepts or tools developed by one set of folklore specialists is innately any better than those developed by the other set of specialists. A considerable skill in the selection and application of these tools to specific situations must be cultivated.

In the framework of motivation and incentives influencing some aspects of organizational behavior, the student examines issues such as: the need for multiple criteria to determine compensation; the relative power and kinds of financial and nonfinancial incentives; and the need for keeping a simple relationship between compensation and the assigned purpose.

In terms of standards and measurement of performance, the student examines the need for multiple criteria and recognizes the pitfalls of using a single quantitative indicator. He sees the importance of appraising subordinates in terms of their effectiveness in facing unknown problems rather than simply in terms of how well they are meeting their budgets.

And, he examines the degree to which reliance on the criteria can be substituted for personal supervision and involvement of the superior.

Organizational behavior is also influenced through the systems of restraint and control. The student examines the need for integrating informal, social controls with the formal control; the latter could emphasize short-run performance and possibly lead to unethical practices. Control systems could encourage or inhibit innovation, risk-taking, and management development.

However, the better the choice of people and structure the simpler the relationship between the organizational processes and the corporate purpose is likely to be. The development of people should therefore not be left to chance. Planned development should be undertaken in terms of multiple requirements of strategy. It may require new kinds of training, jobs, and emphasis on purpose rather than procedure.

The student is exposed to a variety of general manager's roles as an architect, promoter, and defender of strategy,[2] an institutionalizer of the neutral polity of the people, and conciliator of conflicts and needs of the organization. At a highly personal level, he personifies purpose rather than power. His style must be congruent with the ends sought. The need for conscious planning increases according to the growth in size and diversity of the business.

Finally, this segment allows the student insight into the deeper complexity of formulation and implementation of change in strategy. He is exposed to issues such as: problems of transition; problems in structuring mammoth international corporations where most key tasks defy neat compartmentalization; place for long-range planning; the impact of change in incentive systems; problems and ways of integrating and structuring new acquisitions; and resolving the conflicting corporate and divisional goals.

It is in the area of implementation of corporate strategy that a major proportion of so-called "organization principles" or "principles of administration" have evolved in the last half-century. As the reader might appreciate from his knowledge of the literature, the above cannot purport to be a complete list of the concepts and issues of this segment.

Broad Framework Is Essential

Admittedly, the present course does not present a theory of management that can match the rigor of traditional academic theories. As Professor Kenneth R. Andrews, Policy area chairman at the Harvard Business School, rhetorically asks, "How do you specialize in generalities?"

The approach presented here provides a focus for explicit recognition

---

[2] Ibid.

of significant parameters, a focus for synthesizing and integrating relevant contributions from various disciplines, and a framework for categorizing problems, processes, and research concepts. Obviously, much of the work is empirical. But the twentieth century has witnessed significant progress in the conceptual distillation of the empirical experience of both the academicians and the practitioners.

The process of general management as we visualize it has little to do with categories such as the public or private sectors. We define corporate purpose broadly and in conceptual terms. In the private sector, corporate purpose would probably have profit, growth, market share, or product development as one or more of the indicators of its accomplishment. So could a public sector corporation, but the indicators need not be the same.

To be sure, there would be differences in the nature and significance of parameters between and within both the public and private sector corporations. But an organization that drifts without a specific purpose and without the indicators of its accomplishment could hardly be developed into a viable institution; it will be simply a conglomeration of resources.

This course may be disappointing to those who expect to learn and accumulate factual knowledge, principles of management and organization, or what one entrepreneur and professional manager once called the bag of tricks. This, however, is not the prime objective. The emphasis is on the cultivation of skills, attitudes, and assimilation of relevant concepts. The more they are cultivated, the more transferable they become to a wide variety of activities.

Finally, to quote Professor Andrews once again, "The Policy course provides a broad framework. It is an orderly way of comprehending the total world of the top management." It is the beginning and, indeed, this is the first step we should take.

STUDENT REVIEW QUESTIONS

1. What are the goals of a course in Business Policy, according to Charan?
2. What is meant by a "multidimensional set of goals" for an organization?
3. How does Charan distinguish between "determination" of strategy and "implementation" of strategy?
4. What are the various "stages" in policy development?
5. Discuss in the context of Business Policy the significance of the question attributed to Professor Andrews, "How do you specialize in generalities?"
6. Do Charan's ideas on strategy apply to nonprofit organizations, in your opinion?

2. Tomorrow's Management: A More Adventurous Life in a Free-Form Corporation*

MAX WAYS

WHAT industrialization was to the nineteenth century, management is to the twentieth. Almost unrecognized in 1900, management has become the central activity of our civilization. It employs a high proportion of our educated men and determines the pace and quality of our economic progress, the effectiveness of our government services, and the strength of our national defense. The way we "manage," the way we shape our organizations, affects and reflects what our society is becoming.

The essential task of modern management is to deal with change. Management is the agency through which most changes enter our society, and it is the agency that then must cope with the environment it has set in turbulent motion. To carry out its active social role of adaptation, management itself, therefore, must be adaptable. Already the nature of management has undergone drastic alterations. As it stands today on the threshold of the final third of its first century, modern management seems pregnant with another metamorphosis. It is now possible to see in outline the shapes toward which the next generation of management will tend.

One of the more obvious questions of the last ten years has been whether the number of management men will continue to expand faster than the economy. Will many of the millions now pouring forth from the universities find that management is a contracting job market in which they will be surplus? The question is currently linked with predictions about the computer revolution. Without doubt, computers have taken over some work formerly done by middle management, and are capable of taking over much more. But this fact is only a part of the whole busy

---

* Max Ways, "Tomorrow's Management: A More Adventurous Life in a Free-Form Corporation," *Fortune* magazine, July 1966. Copyright 1966 Time Inc.; reprinted by special permission.

scene. Management is still expanding and probably will continue to expand as *new* tasks are created. Indeed, the new information technology represented by computers is one of the important factors creating the new tasks.

A less obvious question raised by the computers bears on the character, rather than the size, of future management. Will instant access by top management to operational information reverse the trend toward managerial decentralization, which has had the salutary effect of giving more independent scope to more people? It is easy to think of examples where authority now dispersed might be efficiently reconcentrated at the top with the aid of computers. But such reconcentration is not the main trend in organization today. Since the new information technology began coming into use in the Fifties, the trend toward decentralization has probably been accelerated, indicating that there were better reasons for decentralization than the lack of instant information at headquarters. Computers *can* be used to reinforce either a centralizing policy or its opposite; the probability increases that decentralization will in the coming decades be carried to lengths undreamed of ten years ago.

Much more is involved in these issues than the relative short-run efficiency of men and computers. One can even accept the prediction that the computer revolution will prove to be a more important development than the industrial revolution, and yet see both industrialization and computerization as *details* in the still broader sweep of a historical era wherein men for the first time deliberately organized their civilization around the processes of social change. In this larger context, both practitioners of management and academic observers of it are developing radically new ideas about what it should and will become. Some of these projections are the more surprising because modern management, in its brief history, has been widely misunderstood. Actual management is already decades ahead of the popular myths about how it works.

THE STAND-INS FOR MR. LEGREE

Assets, they say, make men conservative. Because language, incomparably the greatest of mankind's social assets, changes slowly, we are forced to describe the new and unfamiliar in terms drawn from the old and familiar. Since some change occurs in any period there is always a lag between actuality and the past-bound words we use to describe it. Where change is slow or is confined to a narrow segment of life, this language lag does no great harm. In the fast-changing twentieth century, however, the language lag causes untold confusion.

Corporations, government agencies, and scientific institutes are really quite different from tribes, families, armies, feudal estates, and monasteries, but our ideas of the newer organizations are distorted by an anachronistic vocabulary drawn from the older group. Business leaders of the late nineteenth century were called "captains of industry" or "robber barons." Government bureaus have "chiefs." Many present-day organizations still think they operate by "chains of command." From one point of view, management stands in the place of "the owner," a historically familiar figure; it is easy to slip into the habit of talking about a company as if it were merely a complicated kind of plantation with hundreds of "overseers" substituted for Mr. Legree.

As late as the 1920s some American law schools were handling what little they had to say about the internal life of corporations under the rubric of "the law of master and servant." The very word "manager" suggests—even more strongly than "management"—that the basis of the activity is power over other men. (In the 1950s, General Electric recognized that a large proportion of the people in management did not, in any literal sense, "manage." G.E. began to speak of management as made up of two groups: managers and "functional individual contributors." The number of "fics," who may be physical or social scientists, lawyers or public-relations experts and who are often future managers or ex-managers, is increasing in nearly all large companies.) In short, the early image of the corporation was heavily loaded on the side of authoritarianism because the early vocabulary pertaining to management came from the patriarchal family, from military organization, from legal concepts of ownership, and from memories of the feudal hierarchy.

Upon this primal image of the corporation some less antique but equally misleading concepts were then superimposed. The science of economics developed in the nineteenth century when the public had become familiar with mechanical principles. Both classical and Marxist economics leaned heavily on mechanical analogies. The economists' model still in service today is a machine. Since humanity is that element in economics least susceptible to mechanical treatment and prediction, economics tends to suppress the human factors. "Economic man" is the most oversimplified of all views of our otherwise interesting species. Man's astounding capacities must be expressed in erglike units, man's even more astounding appetites must be reduced to chilly abstractions resembling Newton's gravitational pull, and man's most profound uncertainties must be ignored because they cannot be quantified. This dehumanized economists' model of the total economy, recast in compact form, merged with the older authoritarian myth of the corporation. The resulting popular image: a kind of life-with-father, automated.

BUREAUCRACY AS A MACHINE

Early in the twentieth century the great German sociologist Max Weber, noting common elements in business organizations, government bureaus, and the Prussian military structure, called the new organizational form "bureaucracy." In a bureaucratic system, public or private business was carried out "according to *calculable rules* and 'without regard for persons.'" Functionaries with specialized training learn their tasks better by practice. "Precision, speed, unambiguity . . . unity, strict subordination, reduction of friction—these are raised to the optimum point in the strictly bureaucratic administration, and especially in its monocratic form." Weber said the new form was succeeding because the "bureaucratic mechanism compares with other organizations exactly as does the machine with the non-mechanical modes of production." Around the same time, Frederick W. Taylor in the U.S. promulgated "scientific management" in which workers were regarded as parts of a corporate machine, the excellence of which was to be measured, of course, by its "efficiency."

It is against this persistent image of dehumanized modern organization that students today react with the sort of castration phobia expressed in the picket-sign slogan: "I am a human being; do not fold, bend, or mutilate." This fear and defiance of modern organization appears in scores of novels and plays, which restate Charlie Chaplin's *Modern Times;* the myth is the root of many anti-business (and some anti-government) attitudes; it even pervades management itself, souring fruitful careers with the sense that life is being sacrificed to a domineering and impersonal organization. The man who says, "I am a cog" does not thereby become a cog—but he may become an unhappy and "alienated" man.

BEYOND EFFICIENCY LIE THE HUMAN QUALITIES

Whatever of truth there once was in the myth of the modern organization as a tyrannical machine has been diminishing for fifty years. The myth never took account of the modern organization's essential involvement in change. As this involvement has deepened, reality and myth have drifted further apart. Around 1900 there was many a one-product manufacturer with a stable technology and a well-defined, reliable market. Such a company could increase its efficiency by routinizing more and more of its decisions into what Max Weber had called "calculable rules." Companies in this situation are exceedingly rare today. In the Sixties, a typical company makes scores, perhaps hundreds or thousands, of products, which it knows it will soon have to abandon or drastically modify; it must substitute others selected from millions of possibilities. Most of the actual and possible products are affected by rapidly changing techniques of production and distribution. Present and prospective markets are enticingly expansive, but fiercely competitive, loosely defined, and unstable.

In this situation, a company cannot be rigidly designed, like a machine, around a fixed goal. A smaller proportion of decisions can be routinized or precoded for future use. The highest activity of management becomes a continuous process of decision about the nature of the business. Management's degree of excellence is still judged in part by its efficiency of operation, but much more by its ability to make decisions changing its product mix, its markets, its techniques of financing and selling. Initiative, flexibility, creativity, adaptability are the qualities now required—and these are far more "human" than the old mechanical desideratum, efficiency.

The institutional system of the Soviet Union has been rigidly organized on the old bureaucratic model. Central authority fixes a definite goal, whether an increase in steel production or a vehicle to reach the moon. Material and human resources are mobilized around that goal. In terms of sheer efficiency certain aspects of the Soviet system work well. Yet we are right in regarding the U.S.S.R. as a "backward" country, and certain Russian leaders are justified in their recent efforts to move toward a more flexible and decentralized system. . . . To cope with a very fluid technological and social environment such as that of the U.S., Soviet management would need much greater emphasis on the specifically human qualities.

Even U.S. governmental institutions, which are years behind our corporations in the evolution of management, are now using flexible approaches inconceivable in the U.S.S.R. The U.S. has consciously embarked on a huge effort to improve the quality of education without defining in any but the vaguest terms what that "improved" quality might be. We assume that through a highly decentralized educational system we may be able to grope our way "forward," step by step, forming new values and new targets as we proceed from choice to choice. In a similar spirit, we have begun an effort to improve the Appalachian region without knowing in advance what we want Appalachia to become. We have no centrally designed plan for Appalachia, but we believe that if the effort is "well managed," in the new (nonbureaucratic) sense of that phrase, a livelier Appalachia may result from the federal government's stimulation of changeful decisions by individuals, communities, and organizations in Appalachia. It is impossible to imagine the U.S.S.R.— or any other organization formed along the old authoritarian, machine-like lines—generating organized activity without first defining "the task."

MANAGEMENT AND CHANGE NEED EACH OTHER

U.S. corporations are pioneering the movement toward the new style of management because they are more heavily engaged than any other category of organization on the frontiers of actual social innovation. It is true, of course, that the main base of modern innovation lies in scientific discovery, most of which is—and all of which could be—carried on inde-

pendently of business organizations. But the mission of science is to discover new truth; it is not organized to perform the additional and very
different work of transforming discoveries into technological inventions;
still less is it organized for the third stage of introducing these inventions
into actual use. Usually, scientific discovery is the product of concentrated specialization in a field of study. Innovation, on the contrary, almost always requires various kinds of specialized knowledge drawn from
many fields. One of the primary functions of modern management is to
assemble various skills and coordinate them in production.

Science and technology, which make possible an ever increasing range
of products and services, do not tell us which of these to produce. So
another task of management is to mediate between the evolving wants of
society and the evolving abilities for satisfying those wants. This mission,
performed within a competitive market system, also requires many kinds
of specialized knowledge—e.g., market research, cost analysis—and very
complex and delicate coordination. The whole process is suffused—as
science is not—with questions of *value,* questions of whether the corporation and its customers want A rather than B. The judgments of management are relative and they are often intuitive—i.e., based upon incomplete
and perhaps unreliable information. Management's hunger for knowledge
on which to base decisions becomes ever stronger, but is fated to be forever unsatisfied. The advance of knowledge does not reduce the remaining body of ignorance because "possible knowledge" is not a finite
quantity. In practical affairs, as in science, the more we learn the more
questions confront us. Innovation does not wait until risk of failure has
been eliminated by complete knowledge; in an era of radical change,
management cannot be designed to work like a machine on the assumption that the goals and conditions that determined its design will remain
constant.

Although statistical comparisons are impossible, it is almost certainly
true that the numbers employed in "management" have been growing
more rapidly than the total economy during the past fifty years. If we
apply the old bureaucratic machine standards of efficiency we are led to
suppose that the vast increase in the numbers of management men represents the wasteful working of Parkinson's Law. But if the prime mission
of management is to deal with change, then the size of management
should be roughly proportionate to the rate of innovation rather than to
the amount of physical output. This explains why the U.S. needs a propor-
tionately larger managerial force than the less lively economy of the
U.S.S.R. For years it has been obvious that in numbers and in quality
British management was inferior to that of the U.S. and that Britain was
not educating nearly enough men to fill its assumed management need.
Yet no acute British "shortage" of management personnel exists in the
sense that the market there places a very high price in money or prestige

on management men; in fact, during the past twenty years a high proportion of men with the kind of training regarded as needed in management
have emigrated from Britain, feeling their abilities to be in surplus in a
relatively stagnant society. To take a more extreme example, the African
nation of Gambia, which produces very few managerial types, would be
the world's worst place to look for a job in management.

It appears that the need for management cannot be calculated on a
simple supply-and-demand basis, because management creates change
and change creates the need for management. As the "inventory" of management people in a society rises (in quantity and quality) the demand
for still more management rises with it; or, to put it another way, the rate
of innovation and the managerial function are interdependent. Except on
a short-range basis or in respect to specific categories of management
work, it is pointless to talk about a "shortage" or a "surplus" of managers.

Seen in this perspective, the computer revolution, by powerfully enhancing management's effectiveness in dealing with change, should have
the long-range effect of increasing demand for management men. U.S.
experience to date seems to support this theoretical expectation. Recruiting for management (of both managers, strictly so-called, and of such
"functional individual contributors" as scientists, engineers, accountants)
has never been more active, as any reader of newspaper advertisements
is aware. More significantly, corporations are making increasing efforts to
identify early the men with a high management potential, to train them
rapidly, and to promote them to jobs of greater responsibility. This
tendency seems especially marked in companies that have been quick to
make use of computers. Probably the new information technology has had
the effect of breaking bottlenecks that had restrained these companies
from generating innovation and coping with the changing environment.

BACK TO THE FAMILY FIRM?

Not everyone expected this expansion of management. In 1958, when
the computer revolution was young, two respected observers of management, Harold J. Leavitt and Thomas L. Whisler, wrote for the *Harvard
Business Review* a much-discussed article entitled "Management in the
1980's." The article made a persuasive case for the proposition that the
new information technology would reverse the trend toward decentralized and "participative" management. Leavitt and Whisler said: "In one
respect, the picture we might paint for the 1980's bears a strong resem-
blance to the organizations of certain other societies—e.g., to the family
dominated organizations of Italy and other parts of Europe, and even to
a small number of such firms in our own country. There will be many
fewer middle managers, and most of those who remain are likely to be
routine technicians rather than thinkers." At the end came this portentous

note: "We may have to reappraise our traditional notions about the worth of the individual as opposed to the organization."

Seven years later, with much more evidence to draw upon, H. Igor Ansoff, professor of industrial administration at Carnegie Institute of Technology, wrote for the *Harvard Business Review* a sort of answer to Leavitt and Whisler. In "The Firm of the Future," Ansoff said that the right question was not what the new information technology would do to management but "how will the manager use these extraordinarily powerful tools in furthering the objectives of the firm in its environment of the future." Since "the forces which will shape the future firm are already at work . . . the shape of the firm in the 1980's . . . need not be perceived dimly through a crystal ball [but] can be sketched by analyzing and projecting from the present." He listed three trends in the business environment: (1) *product dynamics*—"the life cycles of products will become shorter"; (2) *Market dynamics*—"as superior technology displaces it from its traditional markets, the firm has to fight back by looking for new pastures" and the growing internationalization of markets will add to the competitive "turbulence"; (3) *firm and society*—governmental and social limits on the firm's behavior will increase so that "its search for profit will be strongly affected by an awareness of social consequences." The firm of the future would be able to program many of its activities, thus releasing management to deal with the increasing load of "non-programmable" decisions that would confront it in the new environment.

The manager to match these formidable new conditions would be "broader gauged than his present counterpart." He would need a grip on the firm's technology, but he would also have to deal with problems on "a combined economic-political-cultural level." The new environment would call for more managerial skill in human relations. "Increasing importance will be placed on the manager's ability to communicate rapidly and intelligibly, gain acceptance for change and innovation, and motivate and lead people in new and varying directions." Ansoff was not worried that management might be made obsolescent by new information technology. "The manager of the future will need all the computer help that he can get in coping with the greatly increased complexity of his job."

"MAN IS A WANTING ANIMAL"

The fluid business environment of the future will demand not only a different kind of manager but a different organizational structure. Management's need to keep redefining "the nature of the business" applies not only to the product mix but also to the internal arrangements of the organization. One reason why men and their organizations may fail to adapt is that they cling to erroneous ideas about themselves and/or their situation. The late Douglas M. McGregor, of the Sloan School of Management of M.I.T., believed that the evolution of organizations was being retarded by a set of erroneous beliefs about man and his work which he called Theory X. The average man dislikes work, according to Theory X, and must therefore be coerced, directed, and controlled. He can be made to contribute to the achievement of organizational objectives only by a threat to the supply of his physiological needs. He seeks security and wishes to avoid responsibility for decisions. The old idea of authoritarian, paternalistic organizations fits Theory X; it is better for all concerned if power can be concentrated in the exceptional men at the top, who like responsibility.

Today men respond to certain stimuli that McGregor wrapped in a proposition called Theory Y. They take for granted the fulfillment of their basic material needs. "A satisfied need," McGregor said, "is not a motivator of behavior. Man is a wanting animal, [and his] needs are organized in a series of levels—a hierarchy of importance." A man whose stomach is satisfied by a secure supply becomes conscious of needs at a higher level. He seeks to feed his ego, which is more insatiable than any stomach, and to achieve a richer sense of his own identity. Many of these higher wants can best be satisfied by the kind of work that has a substantial content of intellectual activity and moral choice. Our society is by no means affluent in providing work of this sort, but more and more men in the professional and managerial category are finding their highest rewards in responsible work itself rather than merely in their pay.

Obviously, an organization based on the assumptions of Theory Y will array itself very differently from the old pyramid, where as much authority as possible was concentrated at the top. A Theory Y corporation would *prefer* to distribute responsibility widely among its managers, even if decision making could be centralized without loss of efficiency. A Theory X organization wants each individual to perform reliably the function assigned to him in the design of the total machine; a Theory Y organization wants an individual to be involved consciously in the relations between what he does and what others are doing; it wants him to seek ways of improving those relations in terms of his own expanding goals and the changing goals of the organization; it wants the individual to participate in setting goals for himself and for the organization.

FAREWELL TO FAUST

What McGregor did was to put a solider and more "human" base under older theories of "participative" management, which had slopped over into the dubious proposition (derisively referred to as "the contented-cow psychology") that the way to make workers efficient was to make them happy. McGregor's Theory Y allows plenty of room for discontent and tension; it provides, however, a realistic way to reconcile the needs of the individual with the objectives of the organization. The individual is no longer seen as entering a corrupt Faustian barter in which he abandons his "soul" in exchange for material satisfactions and power—a deal that will become increasingly repugnant to the more highly educated men that management will require. In short, the kind of management called for by Ansoff's projection of the future business environment could be provided under Theory Y much better than under Theory X.

Warren G. Bennis, McGregor's successor as chairman of the Organization Studies Group at M.I.T., asserts in a recent book, *Changing Organizations,* that during the past decade "the basic philosophy which underlies managerial behavior" has made a fundamental shift in the direction of Theory Y. Bennis discerns the philosophic shift in three areas:

1. A new concept of man, based on increased knowledge of his complex and shifting needs, which replaces the over-simplified, innocent push-button idea of man.
2. A new concept of power, based on collaboration and reason, which replaces a model of power based on coercion and fear.
3. A new concept of organizational values, based on humanistic-democratic ideals, which replaces the depersonalized mechanistic value system of bureaucracy.

Bennis is quick to say he does not mean that these transformations "are fully accepted or even understood, to say nothing of implemented in day-to-day affairs." But "they have gained wide intellectual acceptance in enlightened management quarters . . . have caused a tremendous amount of rethinking on the part of many organizations, and . . . have been used as a basis for policy formulation by many large-scale organizations." The shift in philosophy and the practical predicaments arising out of twentieth-century changes in the environment support one another in encouraging management to accelerate its own evolution. Business organizations, Bennis believes, are leading the way in replacing the old "bureaucratic mechanism," which was "capable of coordinating men and power in a stable society of routine tasks [but] cannot cope with contemporary realities."

ASSETS NOT ON THE BALANCE SHEET

The business scene of 1966 shows substantial evidence to support this view. Some of the evidence lies in what business leaders are saying, and some in what they are doing. One significant change is the increasing sense that management is the chief asset of the corporation rather than an overhead expense. "Investment for modernizing plant and equipment is often wasted unless there is a corresponding investment in the managerial and technical talent to run it," says M. J. Rathbone, former board chairman of Standard Oil (New Jersey). He notes that the valuation of a corporation's securities is based more upon appraisals of the quality of its management than upon the corporation's inanimate assets.

Many advanced companies engage in "total career development," a conscious policy of maximizing managerial quality over the long run by balancing the old criterion of finding the best man for the job with some consideration of the best job for the development of the man. This policy is pursued even where it results in some short-run sacrifice of efficiency. Sears, Roebuck has for many years carried on an elaborate effort to identify as early as possible those individuals who have a high potential for development, and to measure as accurately as possible how they respond to various kinds of managerial challenges. Polaroid has taken a further step in the Theory Y direction; instead of having its top management planning the paths for executive careers, Polaroid uses a "posting system" in which its men are encouraged to compete for forthcoming job vacancies. General Electric's intense concern with the development of managers includes the belief that the man himself sets the objectives for his career and that the company must make an organized effort to keep open the means by which an individual can broaden his responsibilities, along lines he chooses himself.

The concern for broadening responsibilities goes all the way down to men recently recruited from college. Companies have noted with alarm that many young people, recruited after considerable effort, quit in the first year or two. The pay may be satisfactory, but they complain that their jobs are "too routine," or "not demanding enough." To meet this criticism, some companies are giving trainees jobs in which they can make costly mistakes. "There is no justification left for prolonged training procedures that prevent people from taking responsibility," says Frederick R. Kappel, chairman of A.T.&T. "There is no excuse for the timid doling out of oversupervised little jobs that allow a person no opportunity to show what he can do." Noting that many youngsters find business goals "too narrow" to fire their imaginations, Kappel counters with a broad one: In the "interaction of science and society," he says, "it is the goal of business management to translate discovery into use. Our job in industry is to assimilate the scientific revolution in such a way that practical values will flow to the public, to society at large, in the most orderly and economical way."

THE WHITE SPACE BETWEEN THE BOXES

The structure of science is loose-jointed, non-pyramidal, non-authoritarian. The same adjectives apply to the structure of modern "society at large." Working between science and society, two fluid and unpredictable worlds, corporations must not let their own structure petrify.

Companies alert to the danger, therefore, have set up continuous reviews of their organization charts. At least one company goes so far as to engage in periodic shake-ups, just to keep its structure from "freezing." A more intelligent way is represented by those companies (including U.S. Rubber and Kimberly-Clark) that have set up permanent analytical staffs to find out how parts of the company actually relate and figure out how they ought to relate. In the search for more flexible structures the old distinctions between staff and line and the old walls between specialists and between departments tend to blur. "The interesting part of the organization chart," says one management consultant, "is in the white space between the boxes. That's where the real activity goes on."

The organizations now evolving on the beliefs of Theory Y represent a shift from a mechanical to an organic model that confronts managers with more subtle and complex challenges. How, for instance, is the unity and coherence of the organization to be maintained in an evolving freeform structure of mobile individuals?

Transitionally, a lot of authority is still concentrated at "the top," but it exists as a reserve to deal with crisis, major internal conflict, and the fundamental decisions affecting the whole organization that cannot, under present conceptions, be made elsewhere. Some management analysts, searching for the shape of the future, are looking intently at large, diversified corporations whose divisions and subdivisions are now competing actively against one another within a loose corporate framework. Can this internal competition be stepped up by rewriting the rules of the game and improving the scoring system? If "the market" is a good way to organize the economy as a whole, why not deliberately make the corporation's internal structure more market-like? At present, the resources of the firm tend to flow toward those divisions where the return on investment has been highest; this "rule" may put too much emphasis on the past. Accountancy, concentrating on the record of what has happened, has not paid enough attention to projecting comparisons between the probable future prospects of several divisions of a company. The Defense Department's work in projecting the comparative cost effectiveness of different weapon systems not yet in being has given business a powerful impetus in the direction of a new kind of accountancy oriented toward the future. Computers, by simulating the results and cost of competing projects, can be of immense help in this kind of accountancy.

Thinking along the lines of an internal corporate market, Professor Jay Forrester of M.I.T. wants companies to get rid of the familiar budget centers, replacing them with profit centers. The budget-center system sets up a conflict between those groups (production, sales, research, etc.) whose interest is to spend and those groups whose function is to restrain spending, such as the controller's office. Because such conflicts can be resolved only at the top of the corporation, the budget-center system perpetuates the authoritarian form of organization. Internal profit centers, on the contrary, demand self-restraint because no group has an interest in spending, as such, or in saving, as such. Every group has an interest in the difference between them—i.e., profit.

Forrester would also break up such central services as purchasing and drafting rooms. Created in the name of efficiency, they can result in "internal monopolies" that tend to become somnolent and unresponsive to the need for change. Moreover, they confuse the accounting system within which internal competition is conducted. The economies of scale that they are supposed to produce are not worth what they cost in deadening the initiative and responsiveness of the corporation.

THE INDEPENDENT PROFESSIONALS

The substitution of structures in which more people exercise self-control fits with the broadest trends in modern society. Professor Bennis believes that "democracy is inevitable" because it "is the only system which can successfully cope with the changing demands of contemporary civilization." By democracy, Bennis means "a climate of beliefs" including "full and free communication, regardless of rank and power; a reliance on consensus, rather than . . . coercion or compromise, to manage conflict; the idea that influence is based on technical competence and knowledge rather than on the vagaries of personal whims or prerogatives of power; [and] a basically human bias, one which accepts the inevitability of conflict between the organization and the individual but which is willing to cope with and mediate this conflict on rational grounds."

Not everybody would use the word democracy to describe this set of beliefs, but the contrast between this "climate" and that of the authoritarian machine-like organization is clear. It is also clear that the actual trends in U.S. management are moving in this direction and not back toward the shape forecast by Leavitt and Whisler, "the family dominated organizations of Italy and other parts of Europe."

"Professionalism" is here to stay a while. The scientist, engineer, and lawyer are indispensable to management and so are "professional" communicators and others whose skill lies in the coordination and leadership of specialists. The professional man in management has a powerful base of independence—perhaps a firmer base than the small businessman ever had in his property rights. The highly trained young man entering management today can look for corporate aid in enhancing his competence and hence his base of independence. He need not aspire to becoming *the* top officer of the firm, who holds the only "human" job in an organization conceived on the old line of a machine with all its decision-making initiative concentrated in the "operator" at the top. Today's management recruit can—and, in fact does—have the more rational and less frustrating ambition of a life of ever widening responsibility and choices. The prospect for a managerial career today is more adventurous than it ever was, because by the year 2000 there will be hundreds of thousands, perhaps millions, of Americans, whose influence on the quality of life in their more fluid society will be greater than that of any past "captain of industry."

STUDENT REVIEW QUESTIONS

1. What does the author mean when he says, "The way we 'manage,' the way we shape our organizations, affects and reflects what our society is becoming"?
2. What are the shortcomings of the "economic man" concept, and what misunderstandings has this idea generated on the part of some managers and theorists?
3. Discuss the author's view of what constitutes the "highest activity of management."
4. What effects will the computer have on the manager's job, according to the author? What has your own experience shown you regarding the effects of the computer on management?
5. Ways makes some observations and recommendations concerning the top manager's job as of 1966. Do you think his ideas are valid today, and in what ways are they valid or invalid?

3. Because Wisdom Can't Be Told*

CHARLES I. GRAGG

So he had grown rich at last, and thought to transmit to
his only son all the cut-and-dried experience which he
himself had purchased at the price of his lost illusions;
a noble last illusion of age. . . .

———*Balzac*

IT CAN be said flatly that the mere act of listening to wise statements and
sound advice does little for anyone. In the process of learning, the
learner's dynamic cooperation is required. Such cooperation from students does not arise automatically, however. It has to be provided for and
continually encouraged.

Thus, the key to an understanding of the Business School case plan of
teaching is to be found in the fact that this plan dignifies and dramatizes
student life by opening the way for students to make positive contributions to thought and, by so doing, to prepare themselves for action. Indeed, independent, constructive thinking on the part of students is essential to the sound operation of the plan. This result is achieved in two ways.

In the first place, students are provided with materials which make it
possible for them to think purposefully. For the benefit of those unfamiliar
with Business School cases, it is merely necessary to explain that, as now
used, a case typically is a record of a business issue which *actually* has
been faced by business executives, together with surrounding facts,
opinions, and prejudices upon which executive decisions had to depend.
These real and particularized cases are presented to students for considered analysis, open discussion, and final decision as to the type of
action which should be taken. Day by day the number of individual business situations thus brought before the students grows and forms a back-

* Charles I. Gragg, "Because Wisdom Can't Be Told," *Harvard Alumni Bulletin,*
October 19, 1940, pp. 78–84. Copyright 1940, Harvard Bulletin, Inc. Reprinted with
permission.

log for observing coherent patterns and drawing out general principles. In other words, students are not given general theories or hypotheses to criticize. Rather, they are given specific facts, the raw materials, out of which decisions have to be reached in life and from which they can realistically and usefully draw conclusions. This opportunity for students to make significant contributions is enhanced by the very nature of business management. Business management is not a technical but a human matter. It turns upon an understanding of how people—producers, bankers, investors, sellers, consumers—will respond to specific business actions, and the behavior of such groups always is changing, rapidly or slowly. Students, consequently, being people, and also being in the very stream of sociological trends, are in a particularly good position to anticipate and interpret popular reactions.

In the second place, the desired result of student participation is achieved by the opening of free channels of communication between students and students, and between students and teachers. The confidence the student can be given under the case system that he can, and is expected to, make contributions to the understanding of the group is a powerful encouragement to effort. The corollary fact that all members of the group are in the same situation provides the student with exercise in receiving as well as in giving out ideas. In short, true intercommunication is established.

In these facts lies the answer to the unique values of the case system, and from these facts also arise certain difficulties encountered in its use. It is not easy for students to accept the challenge of responsible activity in the face of realistic situations. Nor is it always easy for teachers to preserve the needed open-mindedness toward their students' contribution. Nevertheless, the very existence of the assumption, implicit in the case system, that students are in a position to and will exert themselves to think with a lively independence toward a useful end in itself provides a real stimulus. By the same token, the stage is so set as to simplify the teacher's task of encouraging students to participate actively in the process of learning. The students are given the raw materials and are expected to use them. The teacher, for his part, has every opportunity and reason to demonstrate an encouraging receptivity as well as to inform and guide.

Thinking out original answers to new problems or giving new interpretations to old problems is assumed in much undergraduate instruction to be an adult function and, as such, one properly denied to students. The task of the student commonly is taken to be one chiefly of familiarizing himself with accepted thoughts and accepted techniques, these to be actively used at some later time. The instruction period, in other words, often is regarded both by students and by teachers as a time for absorption.

Thus many students entering graduate schools have become habituated to the role of the receiver. The time inevitably arrives, however, when young people must engage in practical action on their own responsibility. Students at professional school have a little time, at the [Harvard] Graduate School of Business [Administration] two years, to achieve the transition from what may be described as a childlike dependence on parents and teachers to a state of what may be called dependable self-reliance.

If the hearts of the young men entering a graduate school of business administration could be clearly read, it is likely there would be found in many a cherished hope that upon graduation they would find positions of authority and power awaiting them. This is a carefully guarded hope, because for some reason there is a general feeling that it is an unseemly one for young men to harbor. Yet, although the students who possess this hope may be said to be unrealistic under conditions as they exist, they cannot be said to be other than logical. For if a young man more or less permanently is to occupy a humble position in the business hierarchy, he can make better use of two years of his time than spending it at a school of business administration. The apprentice system is open to the young man who wishes to enter business in a fuller way than it is to the young man who seeks to work in the field of law or of medicine, for example. Except in a few instances, such as the plumbing and electrical trades, there are no restrictions similar to those imposed by bar or medical examinations as to who can start in business. And, if a young man who is to spend his life as a salesman, floorwalker, clerk, or minor official has several years to devote acquiring background, he is likely to find that study of sonnets, or operas, or fishing, or philosophy will be more sustaining to his soul than a broad knowledge of business operations.

The work of a graduate school of business consequently must be aimed at fitting students for administrative positions of importance. The qualities needed by businessmen in such positions are ability to see vividly the potential meanings and relationships of facts, both those facts having to do with persons and those having to do with things, capacity to make sound judgments to others so as to produce the desired results in the field of action. Business education, then, must be directed to developing in students these qualities of understanding, judgment, and communication leading to action.

Furthermore, since young men who contemplate entering a graduate business school customarily have an alternative opportunity to enter business immediately, the business school must be able to do more for its students than could be accomplished in a corresponding period of actual business experience. Formal professional education necessarily postpones the time of responsible action. Yet a principal object of professional education is to accelerate the student's ability to act in mature fashion under conditions of responsibility. A young man who completes a professional course is expected to demonstrate a more mature judgment, or to demonstrate mature judgment at an earlier period, than the young man who enters upon a career of action without benefit of formal training. The presumption in this situation obviously must be that it is possible to arrange programs of training in such a way as to do more than offset the effect of prolonging the student's period of ostensible immaturity.

It would be easy to accept the unanalyzed assumption that by passing on, by lectures and readings, to young men of intelligence the accumulated experience and wisdom of those who have made business their study, the desired results could be achieved. Surely, if more or less carefully selected young men were to begin their business careers with the advantage of having been provided with information and general principles which it has taken others a lifetime to acquire and develop, they might be expected to have a decided head start over their less informed contemporaries.

This asumption, however, rests on another, decidedly questionable one: namely, the assumption that it is possible by a simple process of telling to pass on knowledge in a useful form. This is the great delusion of the ages. If the learning process is to be effective, something dynamic must take place in the learner. The truth of this statement becomes more and more apparent as the learner approaches the inevitable time when he must go into action.

We are all familiar with the popular belief that it is possible to learn how to act wisely only by experience—in the school of hard knocks. But everyone knows that, from a practical point of view, strict adherence to the literal meaning of this belief would have a decidedly limiting effect upon the extent of our learning. Time is all against it. So we all try to tell others what we know or what we think we know. A great part of our educational system, perhaps necessarily, rests on this basis. It is the simple, obvious way of passing the torch of culture from hand to hand.

Entirely aside from the seemingly sound logic of this course, there exists a natural and strong tendency for people to tell others what is what —how to think, or feel, or act. Often this tendency seems, to the one having it, like an urge to duty. A friend of ours, for example, may remark that he is worried because he doesn't seem to be getting anywhere with the president of the company. "He doesn't seem to know I'm around," our friend explains. Ah ha! We know the answer to that one and will tell our friend how to solve his problem. "Look here, old boy, the trouble with you is you are too shy. Just speak up, loudly and firmly. Tell him what's what. The old buzzard won't ignore you then!"

It is possible that our desire to pass on our knowledge springs in part from the fact that such activity places us, for the time being, in the superior position. From our earliest beginnings there have been people around to tell *us* what to do, to pass on to us their experience and wisdom. There is no little gratification in turning the tables. For a while we will be the parents and someone else can be the child. It is only necessary to listen to a six-year-old lecturing a three-year-old to see vividly the strength of this urge.

Teachers, since it is their avowed objective to extend the knowledge boundaries of others, are particularly beset by the temptation to tell what they know—to point out right paths of thought and action. The areas in which their help is called for are ones they have penetrated many times. They have reflected, presumably, upon their subjects from all angles. They feel that they know the answers and, with unselfish abandon, they are willing to tell all. Their students thus will be saved all the time and effort it would have taken them to work things out for themselves, even granted they ever could work out such excellent answers.

Yet no amount of information, whether of theory or fact, in itself improves insight and judgment or increases ability to act wisely under conditions of responsibility. The same statistical tables covering all aspects of a business may be available to every officer of the organization. Nevertheless, it does not follow that it makes no difference to the business which officer makes the decisions. Likewise, the whole body of generally accepted business theory may be equally familiar to all executives, yet the decisions reached by the various individuals are unlikely to be the same or to have equal merit.

We cannot effectively use the insight and knowledge of others; it must be our own knowledge and insight that we use. If our friend, acting solely on our advice, undertakes to tell the president what is what, the chances are he will make himself conspicuous but not impressive. For him to use our words effectively, granted our diagnosis of the situation is sound, they must become his own through a process of active thought and feeling on his part. Then, if he agrees with us, he will be able to act as we suggest, not on our advice, but from his own heart. The outstanding virtue of the case system is that it is suited to inspiring actively, under realistic conditions, on the part of the students; it takes them out of the role of passive absorbers and makes them partners in the joint processes of learning and of furthering learning.

The case plan of instruction may be described as democratic in distinction to the telling method, which is in effect dictatorial or patriarchal. With the case method, all members of the academic group, teacher *and* students, are in possession of the same basic materials in the light of which analyses are to be made and decisions arrived at. Each, therefore, has an identical opportunity to make a contribution to the body of principles governing business practice and policy. Business is not, at least not yet, an exact science. There is no single, demonstrably right answer to a business problem. For the student or businessman it cannot be a matter of peeking in the back of a book to see if he has arrived at the right solution. In every business situation, there is always a reasonable possibility that the best answer has not yet been found—even by teachers.

Exercise of mature judgment obviously is inconsistent with a program of blindly carrying out someone else's instructions. Moreover, no matter how worthy those instructions may be, they cannot cover every exigency. Tommy's mother says: "On your way home from school never cross the street until the policeman tells you to and, when he does tell you to, run." Perhaps one day no policeman is there. Is Tommy to wait forever? Or, perhaps a driver fails to observe the policeman's signals. Is Tommy to dash under the speeding wheels?

So far as responsible activity in the business world is concerned, it is clear that a fund of ready-made answers can be of little avail. Each situation is a new situation, requiring imaginative understanding as a prelude to sound judgment and action. The following sad limerick, aimed at describing what might happen to business students without benefit of cases, has been contributed by a friend who prefers to remain anonymous.

> A student of business with tact
> Absorbed many answers he lacked.
>   But acquiring a job,
>   He said with a sob,
> "How *does* one fit answer to fact?"

A significant aspect of democracy in the classroom is that it provides a new axis for personal relationships. No longer is the situation that of the teacher on the one hand and a body of students on the other. The students find their attention transferred from the teacher to each other. It is not a question of dealing more or less *en masse* with an elder; it is a question of dealing with a rather large number of equals and contemporaries whose criticisms must be faced and whose contributions need to be comprehended and used. Everyone is on a par and everyone is in competition. The basis is provided for strong give and take both inside and outside the classroom. The valuable art of exchanging ideas is cultivated, with the object of building up some mutually satisfactory and superior notion. Such an exchange stimulates thought, provides a lesson in how to learn from others, and also gives experience in effective transmission of one's own ideas.

Under the case system, the instructor's role is to assign the cases for discussion, to act as a responsible member of the group delegated to provoke argumentative thinking, to guide discussion by his own contributions and questions toward points of major importance, and, if he chooses, to take a final position on the viewpoints which have been threshed out before him. The more powerful are the student arguments, the heavier is the burden on the instructor; he must understand and evaluate each contribution, many of which are new to him, regardless of how thoroughly he has studied the cases or how many times he has used them with previous classes. To the instructor, every class meeting is a new problem and a new opportunity both to learn and to help others to learn. The important question under these circumstances is not whether the student pleases the instructor, but whether he can either support his views against the counterattacks and disagreements of others in the group or, failing to do so, can accept cooperatively the merits of his antagonists' reasoning.

For both teachers and students, the disciplines of the case method of learning are severe. Sometimes the shock is devastating to young men who previously have been dominaed by patriarchal instructors and thus have been faced merely with the relatively simple task of more or less passive reception and verbatim repetition of facts and ideas. Not all students can bear the strain of thinking actively, of making independent judgments which may be challenged vigorously by their contemporaries. Many people will always prefer to have answers handed to them. Teachers, for their part, particularly those unused to the system, sometimes find it straining to leave the safe haven of dogmatism and meet their students on a democratic plane. The inherently dramatic and challenging character of the case system, however, although it may produce anxiety and confusion for the newcomer, also arouses his deep interest and leads him to make the effort required for adjustment.

In making the adjustment to the democratic disciplines of the case system, students typically pass through at least three objectively discernible phases. The first phase is that of discovering the inability of the individual to think of everything that his fellow students can think of. In many instances, to be sure, the challenge to original thought is pleasing from the first. Yet perhaps more often confusion and a feeling of helplessness set in: "But it's so discouraging to prepare a case as well as I can and then listen for an hour in class to other students bringing out all sorts of interpretations and arguments that I had never thought of."

The second phase is that of accepting easily and naturally the need for cooperative help. During the last half of the first year and the first half of the second year, students learn to draw more and more fully upon each other's ideas in the working out of problems. Competition for high academic standing grows more keen, to be sure, but the mutual giving and taking of assistance ceases to be a matter of secret anguish. The young men are making common cause and thereby learning the pleasure of group pooling of intellectual efforts.

The third and final phase in the march toward maturity usually comes well on in the second year with the recognition that the instructors do not always or necessarily know the "best" answers and, even when they do seem to know them, that each student is free to present and hold to his own views. When this phase is reached, the student is ready to make independent progress and to break new ground on his own account. He is operating as a responsible member of the community, taking help, to be sure, from both contemporaries and elders, but making his own decisions without fear of disapproval or search for an authoritative crutch to lean upon. An outstanding effect of the case system, in other words, is to put upon students the burden of independent thinking.

No method is foolproof. A badly handled case system cannot but be an academic horror. Improperly handled, a case is merely an elaborate means for confusing and boring students. If, moreover, the teacher insists on being a patriarch—if he is sure he has the right and only answers and visualizes his task as one of forcing the students, the case facts, and *his* answers into an affectionate rapport—it will be found that the out-and-out lecture system is infinitely less costly and less straining to everyone concerned. Such authoritarian use of cases perverts the unique characteristics of system. The opportunity which this system provides the students of reaching responsible judgments on the basis of an original analysis of the facts is sacrificed.

In addition to the possibility that the case system will be misused, and so become merely a wasteful way of telling the students what the teacher thinks, it must be recognized that the case does not provide a perfect replica of a business situation. In the properly conducted class using business cases, the students are put in the position of the executives who must arrive at definite conclusions to be followed by specific actions whose merits will be tested by resulting developments. Yet there is no escaping the fact that the students' decisions are not tested in this way. As Winston Churchill is reported to have remarked on one occasion, there is a great deal of difference between being responsible for an order which may lose several valuable ships and expressing an opinion without such responsibility. It is too much to expect that anything except experience can be exactly like experience.

Nevertheless, a training period which allows students this relative irresponsibility has great advantages. The serious student gets the essential background for responsible decisions without the risks to himself and to his firm which are inseparable from amateurish action. He is led to active consideration of a tremendous number of diverse and related real situations, which it would take him at least a lifetime of experience to encounter, and he is thus given a basis for comparison and analysis when he enters upon his career of business action.

The case system, properly used, initiates students into the ways of independent thought and responsible judgment. It confronts them with situations which are not hypothetical but real. It places them in the active role, open to criticsm from all sides. It puts the burden of understanding and judgment upon them. It provides them the occasion to deal constructively with their contemporaries and their elders. And, at least in the area of business, it gives them the stimulating opportunity to make contributions to learning. In short, the student, if he wishes, can act as an adult member of a democratic community.

As for the teacher, the case method of instruction provides him richly with the basic means of research. Not only does the existence of a stream of recorded business experiences enable him to keep in touch with business life and to make continuous necessary modifications in his inductions and general conclusions. In addition, the relations which the case system sets up between himself and his students give the teacher the continual benefit of fresh, imaginative points of view which always hold the possibility of true advance. Manifestly, it is the student after studying under the case method who is in the best position to describe the experience which he has undergone. When Professor Malcolm P. McNair of the Harvard Graduate School of Business Administration was at work on his volume, *The Case Method at the Harvard Business School*, he invited several young staff members who were recent graduates to write papers describing their own reactions to instruction by the case method. One of these papers, which the authors of this book feel will be particularly useful to the student encountering the case method for the first time, is reproduced here.

STUDENT REVIEW QUESTIONS

1. What qualities does Gragg believe are needed by effective businessmen?
2. What features of the so-called case method of instruction facilitate the development of these desirable qualities?
3. What are the major phases of student maturity under the case system?
4. Why does Gragg contend that the answers to business problems cannot be found in the "back of the book"?
5. Is the case approach useful for the development of managers of nonbusiness organizations?

chapter 2

Introduction to
Organizational Strategy

The Meaning of Organizational Strategy

Utility of Strategy

The Strategic Process

Formulation of Strategy and Major Elements within
    Strategy
    Strategic Objectives
    Product-Market Scope as a Major Element within
      Strategy
    Allocation of Resources, Risk Horizons, and Time
      Horizons

Implementation of Strategy

Evaluation of Strategy

Summary

Readings

ORGANIZATIONAL STRATEGY has become a most important management concept in both business and nonprofit institutions. The concept of strategy has long been recognized by the military and employed widely in that environment. Although the meaning of strategy in other organizations may differ in some ways from military usage, it is acknowledged that managers have borrowed from the military a most valuable approach to the study and operation of enterprise.

THE MEANING OF ORGANIZATIONAL STRATEGY

What is strategy within an organizational context? Several scholars have advanced explanations. Tilles has defined strategy as the set of goals and major policies of an organization.[1] This definition encompasses the basic objectives of the organization and the major means that will be employed

---

[1] S. Tilles, "How to Evaluate Corporate Strategy," *Harvard Business Review*, July–August 1963, p. 112.

to reach those objectives. It says in essence that strategy determines *what* the basic nature of the entity is or will be, and further it determines *how* the entity has reached or will reach that state of being.

An important study on the subject found the following definition to be extremely useful: "Strategy is defined as the basic goals and objectives of the organization, the major programs of actions chosen to reach these goals and objectives, and the major patterns of resource allocation used to relate the organization to its environment."[2] Similarly, Alfred Chandler states that strategy is ". . . the determination of the basic long term goals and objectives in an enterprise and the adoption of courses of action and the allocation of resources necessary for carrying out these goals."[3] A highly functional statement about strategy holds that it is "the pattern of objectives, purposes, or goals, and major policies and plans for achieving those goals, stated in such a way as to define what business the company is in and the kind of business it is or is to be."[4] The authors of this statement observe further that strategy denotes the personality or enduring character of the organization.[5] Another study echoes the same idea in the statement, "Thus a long range strategy is designed to provide information about a company's basic direction and purpose, information which will guide all its operational activities.[6] This comprehensive view of strategy is a very useful approach for both students studying enterprise and operating top managers who seek to view an organization with an encompassing perspective.

A somewhat different definition of strategy in a business context has been advanced by Ansoff who proposes a concept of strategy which: (1) provides a broad concept of the firm's business; (2) sets forth specific guidelines by which the firm can conduct its search; and (3) supplements the firm's objectives with decision rules which narrow the firm's selection process to the most attractive opportunities.[7] This concept of strategy seems to separate strategy from objectives. However, the employment of strategy to attain objectives is emphasized by Ansoff. While strategy and objectives are presented as separable in nature, they are recognized as necessarily complementary in operation.

This book views strategy as including both objectives and means. *An*

---

[2] Dan Schendel and Kenneth J. Hatten, "Business Policy or Strategic Management," Professional Papers, 1972 national meeting of the Academy of Management, Minneapolis, Minn., August 1972, p. 4.

[3] Alfred D. Chandler, Jr., *Strategy and Structure* (Cambridge, Mass.: The M.I.T. Press, 1962), p. 13.

[4] C. R. Christensen, K. A. Andrews, and J. L. Bower, *Business Policy: Text and Cases* (Homewood, Ill.: Richard D. Irwin, Inc., 1973), p. 107.

[5] Ibid., pp. 16–17.

[6] Brian W. Scott, *Long Range Planning in American Industry* (New York: American Management Association, 1965), p. 76.

[7] H. I. Ansoff, *Corporate Strategy* (New York: McGraw-Hill Book Co., 1965), p. 104.

organization's strategy is where it wants to go and how it intends to get there.

UTILITY OF STRATEGY

The usefulness of a concept lies in its clarity, completeness, and applicability. Whether studying or actually managing an enterprise, it is helpful to utilize the concept of strategy. In doing so, one can appreciate in a comprehensive sense the nature of the top-management job. As soon as one begins to employ analytically the strategy concept in case analysis, business games, computer simulations, or in actual operation of an organization, objectives must be considered separately from the plans, policies, or decision rules which will be employed to reach the objectives. But while setting objectives is the first step in the overall process of management, plans, policies, and decision rules follow closely behind. Thus, it is helpful to focus attention on the nature of the top manager's job as was done in the previous chapter. Strategy, if viewed in this context, will be understood by student and manager, and will be utilized properly by both.

A company's strategy provides a central direction to the activities of the organization and to the people who man it. It provides a theme and *raison d'être* to the internal organizational world and often to the world outside. In fact, it is often at least as important to inform the public or the market about the company's strategy as it is to inform the inside organization. And although the total picture is not usually discussed, a large portion of the strategy must be communicated to suppliers, dealers, wholesalers, creditors, and customers if their cooperation is to be gained.

George Romney noted this requirement when he was president of American Motors Corporation. He is reputed to have stated that it takes around seven years for a new idea of a strategic nature to be fully understood and accepted. Here he was speaking beyond the AMC internal organization, and referring to the firm's customers, dealer organization, and even its advertising agency. This difficult job, he felt, must be done by a major communications effort with all these groups to explain and "sell" the new idea or product-market strategy. In this particular case, Romney was referring to the then new concept of an economical compact car, and he personally toured the country explaining the idea to all who would listen.[8]

But just as important as communicating an established strategy, it is crucial also that an organization recognize these many "outside" groups even at the time it is establishing its major strategy and substrategies.

---

[8] "American Motors Corporation" Case, in Christensen et al., *Business Policy*, pp. 162–63.

This is particularly true of the customer or market since in the final analysis, it is usually in the market that success or failure materializes. The business and its managers must continually be apprised of market changes and developments, however slight or subtle, if they are to remain in the most advantageous competitive posture. "What is our business is not determined by the producer but by the consumer . . . by the want the consumer satisfies when he buys a product or service."[9]

Successful action by Procter & Gamble in making and selling paper produces in competition with Scott Paper Company typifies this market-oriented attitude.[10] Some airlines also recently have taken a broader view of their business than in the past, and have included in their business definitions, "servicing" the travel needs of business executives. Japan Air Lines in its 1972 advertising campaign emphasized full service for business executives encompassing air transportation, car rental, lodging, and even business cards printed in English and Japanese. In essence, what business a company or even an industry or a nonprofit organization is in, is not determined by its product (or service) alone. It is more clearly designated by its product-market scope or strategy, and even this broader idea is not necessarily a complete view of the "business" a company is in. Also included would be the direction of growth, the basic means by which it will compete, and the way in which all aspects of its strategy fit together and support one another.

Clearly then, the top manager must in his or her management job define the strategy of his organization. It is this aspect of his job that, if accomplished well, provides the purpose and focus for all other activities. It is this endeavor that starts the organization on the road to successful operation. Obviously, the formulation of strategy is only the beginning, but the beginning is a most significant point in any endeavor. The late President John Kennedy was fond of quoting a proverb which emphasized that every long journey starts with the first step. If well done, the articulation of the strategy will answer the question of what business the company is in. As Peter Drucker has pointed out, the failure to ask this question clearly is the most important single cause of business failure.[11]

THE STRATEGIC PROCESS

Having considered above what strategy means and what its value is to an organization, we can ponder profitably the various phases of the strategic process. Essentially, these include the *identification* or *formu-*

---

[9] Peter Drucker, *The Practice of Management* (New York: Harper & Row, Publishers, 1954), p. 50.

[10] "Marketing Classic: How P.&G. Put the Squeeze on Scott Paper Co.," *Wall Street Journal,* October 20, 1971.

[11] Drucker, *The Practice of Management,* p. 50.

lation of a strategy for an organization, the *implementation* of a strategy and the *evaluation* of the strategy. These activities constitute the most important elements of top management's job, and as depicted in Exhibit 2–1, they form a continuous process in organizational life.

EXHIBIT 2–1
The Strategic Process

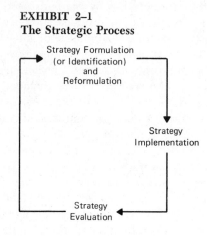

Within this framework, top managers must set objectives and establish plans and policies for their attainment. They must establish the product-market scope of their operation; that is, the total concept of their product lines, markets to be served, channels to be utilized, and all other aspects of the product and market. Further, top management must organize and staff the organization so as to best ensure its survival and further success. Through a planning and control system, they must look continually ahead and back in order to select the right opportunities, to make the right decisions, and to solve the right problems. The entire process described here requires timely and appropriate information about the internal operations of the firm and its various external environments, as well as the continuous communication from top management which the organizational membership utilizes for direction.

The remainder of this chapter will examine the strategic process including the formulation or reformulation of strategy, the implementation of strategy, and the evaluation of strategy.

FORMULATION OF STRATEGY AND MAJOR ELEMENTS WITHIN STRATEGY

The logical start of the strategic process is the development or formulation of the strategy which includes the articulation of basic organizational objectives. This activity leads to decisions regarding the product-market scope of a business. Since subsequent chapters will be devoted to the area of strategy development, only four major elements of that topic will be introduced here. They are: (1) a thorough analysis of the internal resources and strengths and weaknesses to assess capability for continued operation and success considering the external environments and changes therein; (2) a thorough search of external environments for opportunities and problems to which the organization should address itself; (3) recognition of the values and personal objectives of influential interest groups and individuals within the organization's sphere of influence; and (4) determination of the organization's view of its responsibilities to society. By reflecting upon these basic influences, the organization will establish its objectives and decide its product-market scope as well as other major policies or substrategies. The relationships among these important elements are shown in Exhibit 2–2 and are discussed in the following pages.

EXHIBIT 2–2
Major Elements of Organizational Strategy

Basic Influences determine *Strategic Objectives* which determine *Major Policies*
or
Substrategies

External environ-	Survival	Product-
ment	Growth rate and	market scope
Internal resources	diversification	Bases of com-
Personal values	Profitability	petition
(of major de-	Market share	Resource Alloca-
cision makers)	Social	tion policies
Responsibility	contribution	Risk horizons
to society		Time horizons

Strategic Objectives

How does a company happen to find itself in the business it is in? Hopefully, the answer for the well-managed company is that management chose to be there; that is, it was their objective to be in that business. Although this often is not the case (some companies seem to just stumble into a particular business), it should be. Corporate objectives, thus, should guide the company into a particular business and provide the desired direction in terms of growth and profit. Also significant is the nature of the growth; for instance, whether diversification is desirable. These aspects of corporate objectives, of course, assume that the organization is beyond the stage of struggling for survival. Sometimes survival is the all-consuming objective as has been true of countless smaller companies during the money crunch of the early 1970s and many large and small companies during the recession of 1974–75.

But after survival considerations, profit and growth in some form become almost universal basic objectives for most business organizations. Success in business is commonly measured by profits and growth, and size in itself seems to become almost an obsession to some nonprofit organizations including universities, hospitals, and government bodies. Growth is usually sought by companies because of what it ultimately will bring to the corporation in the way of profits. Nonprofit organizations ideally seek growth to serve society better. In the process, growth might also produce economies of operation, competitive advantage, prestige to management, and the like. But if growth and/or profit are to be useful objectives for organizations, each must ultimately be defined in very specific terms. How much growth and of what kind? What level of sales and profits? What share of market and amount of plant assets are questions that must be answered. To identify profit and growth as general objectives is not enough if these are to become useful elements of strategy. Many specifics are required to construct viable objectives and, because these specifics can change with time and circumstances, objectives must be monitored on a continuing basis and be changed as conditions require.

It is important also to note that in recent years growth has often taken on connotations more qualitative than quantitative. As with an individual, an organization may wish to grow in dimensions other than physical. Included in such objectives might be growth toward more responsible behavior within the society, or growth that results in individual members realizing more self-actualization as constituents of the organizational community. Or, growth might be thought of in terms of the real contributions through product or service that an organization makes to its "customers." The president of one company in the field of acoustics believed that real growth was represented only by genuine technological innovation in his industry. He thought that growth in sales and profits were not objectives really, but were more the results of successful product innovation.[12] Although most business executives might feel that this is a limited view of growth, recent definitions of growth seem to be more broadly conceived than those of the past: growth in a social sense is well understood by many today.

The need to transform a general objective into specific terms can be further illustrated by pondering diversification which is a commonly expressed objective. At various periods, diversification has become almost a fetish for some organizations. But like profit and growth, diversification in a broad sense is rather a sterile idea and becomes a useful objective only when clad in the cloth of specific terms. Will the direction of diversifica-

---

[12] "Acoustics Research, Inc. (D)" Case, in E. P. Learned, C. R. Christensen, K. R. Andrews, and W. D. Guth, *Business Policy: Text and Cases* (Homewood, Ill.: Richard D. Irwin, Inc., 1969), p. 458.

tion be horizontal, vertical, or even conglomerate in nature? More specifically, what part of organizational efforts will go toward diversification? Other questions must be answered about diversification as an objective if it is to be a useful guide to management and a legitimate element of strategy. Does the management have experience in the new field or can it obtain it, and should the company develop the business itself or acquire a company already in the area? Failure to be specific may produce only the all too common phenomenon of "the bigger can of worms"; no real change or advantage but simply a larger version of the same situation with similar problems and weaknesses.

Growth and diversification are the most common organizational objectives, and business also includes profit in its list. These three usually draw favorable responses when noted by managers, stockholders, trustees, and many student groups. But other aspects of the situation such as the organization's social contribution should be observed before an evaluation is made. Social contribution, too, must be made quite specific if this objective is truly to be a meaningful element of strategy. The objective of consciously seeking out for employment minority group members has more effect socially, for instance, than setting an objective of being an "equal opportunity" employer.

But objectives of the organization, no matter how carefully specified, may prove to be unreasonable or unreachable unless they reflect judgments regarding the external environment, the internal resources, important personal values, and a timely sense of responsibility to society. Precise objectives must be established consistent with and inclusive of these considerations. Unless such an approach is followed the most noble and most specific objectives will depend too much upon chance for their promise of success. Thus, objectives should not just "happen." They become a useful part of the organization's strategy only when they actually guide the corporation into a specific business, or aid the organization in functioning. To serve usefully, objectives must ultimately become specific in many respects, and must be formulated with due consideration for various influences within the corporation, and many external to it.

Product-Market Scope as a Major Element within Strategy

Having reviewed the role of strategic objectives, this section will consider those elements of strategy that determine how basic organizational objectives are to be accomplished. As noted in Exhibit 2–2, the major policies so important to the achievement of objectives are:

1. Product-market scope.
2. Bases of competition.
3. Resource allocation policies.

4. Risk horizons.
5. Time horizons.

Key among these elements is the "product-market scope"[13] which relates a firm's products to its markets and customers. To clearly define what business it is in, an organization must articulate something about its products and its markets. To discuss only one or the other is often not sufficiently descriptive or particularly useful. In the past, it was common to define a business by its product, such as petroleum, steel, or education. Some companies have described their business by the market or customer served, such as selling to doctors in New England or selling to the youth market. This could seldom be accurate because the firm was supplying only a small part of the market's or customer's needs, or it might be that the markets or customers had to be reached by many different channels and required diverse forms of promotion, both beyond the competence and resources of the companies involved. More useful then, is a more precise definition of the products, markets, and other elements of the marketing approach including channels, promotion, pricing, quality, and the like.

If these product and market factors are defined, the firm's "business" can be readily understood and a reasonable beginning made toward outlining a particular strategy for advancing that business. To define itself as a steel company is not useful for a small specialized maker of tubular steel. But to say that it is a firm producing high-quality, cold-drawn tubular steel for special purpose applications is a more helpful definition. Moreover, including other factors which may further distinguish the firm can be even more helpful. For example, this firm produces high-quality, cold-drawn tubular steel in a wide range of sizes distributed through its own sales force to small customer order manufacturers and to customers with special application problems. Thus, incorporating both the products and markets and even marketing mix elements in a precise definition of a firm's business furthers the development of a useful and workable strategy. Thus, it is necessary to define a product-market scope and related policies since the organization will work through these toward the achievement of its broader objectives.

In fulfilling its product-market policies, the organization may find that its product development serves well its growth, profit, and other aims and objectives. If so, continued internal product development may be built into the overall strategy to support the product-market substrategy. But yet, as has been the case with so many technically oriented companies in recent years, particular aspects of the product or market may change. For instance, Honeywell Corporation, W. R. Grace Company, USM

---

[13] Ansoff, *Corporate Strategy*, p. 108.

Corporation, and many others have modified and even changed drastically their product-market strategies. Honeywell Corporation, in the early 1970s, became "Number Two" in the computer industry through acquisitions and product development far beyond its earlier basic product line of industrial and home control devices and systems. In the process, its entire product-market scope has been changed dramatically. So it is, too, with many universities whose response to social change have strikingly altered their curriculum offerings in search of relevant education for the 1970s. And "open campus" policies have changed greatly the "markets" served by some educational institutions. Product research, market changes, and changes in objectives are among the reasons which cause shifts in the product-market element of the overall strategy.

As the framework of strategy which is presented in this book implies, the changes or modifications in product-market strategy might be triggered by changes in the various external environments in which the organization operates, changes in the internal profile or resources of the organization, changes in the values or personal objectives of major decision makers in the organization, or changes in the way the organization sees its role in society. Or, change might come about simply because the present product-market strategy has not produced the results required by the overall objectives. Usually, thorough inspection will indicate that the basic impetus is one or a combination of the various forces mentioned above.

Frequently, a change in the external environment necessitates the change in product-market strategy, or in the type of competitive actions being utilized by a company as part of its strategy. Growing strength of a competitor, deterioration of a market for present products, major product innovations in an industry, and more recently, increased emphasis in some area of social concern are basic causes for an organization to review its product-market strategy, or to otherwise change or consider changing its major basis of competition.

The recent history of the Boise-Cascade Corporation provides an interesting illustration of the impact of social change on an organization. In the 1960s, while searching for new avenues of growth, the company decided to enter the expanding leisure field by starting major developments of vacation home communities. But the increasing concern about ecology and the environment in the late 1960s and early 1970s has made it far more difficult to achieve growth in this fashion. Legal suits as well as zoning and building restrictions in localities have added a new element of time and money costs, in addition to the possible loss of reputation that may result from being suspected of not thinking about the environment at a time when social climate places a high priority on this dimension. Thus, such shifts in the social, technological, or competitive environments will most often be the causes of shifts in major product-market policies, which in turn are aimed at furthering progress toward broader objectives of the organization.

The product-market scope changes, then, in anticipation of, or in response to, various environmental changes. Strategic policies must be incorporated which enhance a viable product—market approach for an organization. While internal product development may prove to be a sufficient vehicle for success in product-market strategy for some companies, for others, a policy of acquiring companies may be the means of working toward predefined objectives. Because of: (a) a desire to change the nature of the product-market mix; or (b) a weak research and development department; or (c) a need for faster entry into an area; or (d) a more rapid rate of growth, the route of acquisition may offer the most effective support of product-market policies within a corporate strategy. Of course, managers may often work toward organizational objectives via the two routes of product research and acquisition.

The most important conclusion here is that a viable strategy calls for a product-market "scope" in determining how major objectives will be attained. Beyond this, the product-market mix will usually change over time, and as long as changes are intentional and reasoned, a viable strategy will exist. Whether product development is relied upon solely, whether the acquisitions road is utilized, or whether both are employed, the decisions should support the product-market scope which the organization has defined as part of its overall strategy.

Allocation of Resources, Risk Horizons, Time Horizons

In the strategy of any organization, the policies evidenced in the allocation of resources will be of prime importance. Areas which gain particularly large resources will be strengthened and relied upon as crucial to the strategy while the opposite is also true. If research and development, for example, is emphasized by the allocation of major financial and work force resources, a firm will undoubtedly depend upon successful new products from its R.&D. to utilize as a major basis for competition in its strategy. Or the firm may "invest" heavily in advertising as Procter & Gamble, Heublein, Inc., and other marketing oriented organizations do. Many universities specialize in graduate work and some hospitals are noted for particular areas of expertise, and it is such noted areas which draw major resources. Thus, the key competitive strengths of an organization can usually be identified and insight into competitive strengths can be gained by assessing the resource allocation policies of the particular organization.

Intertwined with this vital area of resource allocation and also related to the sources of funds, is the attitude toward risk evidenced in major policies. American Motors Corporation in the late 1950s and early 1960s showed a propensity toward relatively low risk in their policies regarding both the sources and allocation of funds. Management repaid debt and lessened the debt-equity ratio, did not invest in fixed assets except as vitally necessary, and remained as liquid and flexible as possible. These policies exemplified a low-risk horizon which could be considered a reasonable strategic element at the time since this company was still in the process of "surviving."

Similarly, time horizons are important aspects of any strategy because entire strategies seldom remain completely unchanged for long periods of time. Organizations go through various stages with varying time dimensions, and at least some aspects of strategy change in each period. As was noted earlier the change may come about from any number of internal or external factors such as the emergence of a new competitor, the achievement of a new stage of the product life cycle, unfavorable sales and profit results, or a change in leadership of the organization. The organization sometimes simply "outgrows" its present strategy such as occurs when a "niche hunting" company becomes so large that it no longer can follow that strategy and becomes instead a major member of the basic industry. Recognizing the inevitability of change, all major policies should include a reasonable time horizon over which they may be expected to be useful. Review of such policies should be accomplished long in advance of the necessity for such change, since the time of "necessity" may well be too late for change.

In the formulation of strategy then, a product-market scope is required which is vital to the direction of the organization. The key bases for competing will be evidenced in policies and supported by appropriate resource allocation. Risk and time horizons will influence these and all other major policies and substrategies of the organization.

IMPLEMENTATION OF STRATEGY

Having introduced the nature and elements of strategy as well as the formulation of strategy, we can reflect now upon the important area of strategy implementation. This is an aspect of top management's job that is shared more widely with middle management and even lower echelons than is the development phase.

The first requirement in the implementation of a formulated strategy is to organize for that accomplishment; required is the organization of the entire operation, not simply organizing for strategic planning. Within this broad view, the aspects of organization range from the type of organization to be utilized (such as functional or product orientation), to the degree of centralization or decentralization to be employed, to the assignment of individual authority and responsibilities to managers. Every organizational aspect from the broadest to the narrowest must be included in this important management task. As Chandler has so force-fully written, the organizational job or structuring of the firm follows from the strategy which is employed.[14] Although separable from the formulation of strategy, the organizational function should be looked upon as part of the strategic process because of its vital role in achieving the objectives of the organization.

Much has been written in the literature of management about the organizational functions of the manager, but the key idea presented here is the crucial relationship that this task has to the basic strategy. It is the prime vehicle of implementation, and it should be clearly recognized that once strategy has been developed, structure must quickly follow if the strategy is to become operational. This structure must be designed by or with the approval of top management to insure that the structure follows logically from the strategy, and will serve to best implement the strategy.

The organizational function, however, is only the first of many important management tasks which are essential to the effective implementation of strategy. Others are planning, the establishment of control and motivation systems, the manning of the organization, and the establishment of information flows which will allow for the timely carrying out of the other functions. The planning and control systems should transmit throughout the organization the articulation of the strategy, objectives, plans, and policies of top management. The systems further should ideally provide a mechanism of control to inform management how well objectives are being met, and how well plans are being followed. In short, these systems allow management to know how people are performing and should further contain the elements of motivation which encourage the organizational members to strive for the successful implementation of the strategy.

Obviously, information is the key element in this process of implementing strategy. It is the "stuff" of which implementation is made and without which no strategy could achieve lasting success. Thus, establishment of the overall information system is another essential step in the implementation of strategy. Through the information system should flow the plans, controls, inducements, and communications so vital to the very existence of the organization. A combination of formal and informal information systems allows the work of the organization and its members to be carried out. If it follows that this work is directed toward the achievement of the formulated strategy, then this strategy can exist and prosper only in the presence of an effective information system. Within such a system, the other mentioned elements of the implementation phase can be woven, but the central thread is a line of communication.

---

[14] Chandler, *Strategy and Structure*, p. 16.

Although the objective in this chapter is to only introduce the topic of implementation and some of the major aspects of this phase of strategy, one additional topic should be mentioned; that is control. The control function of the manager's job ideally (a) informs him of what is going on and how well objectives and plans are being met, and (b) provides a vehicle to motivate organizational members to effectively carry out their own tasks. Thus, it is both the end of the implementing process and the beginning. Through the control process management reviews results and gains the information to replan, to begin again the implementation of the strategy or some part of it. Or it also might be the point at which management decides to change its strategy in some way. Because of its key role in the complex management function, the control task which is the subject of a future chapter warranted some introductory attention here to illustrate its importance in the implementation phase of corporate strategy.

EVALUATION OF STRATEGY

In its broadest sense, the control function is one part of top management's essential function of evaluation within the managerial process. A somewhat distinct though related function of top management is the evaluation of the overall strategy. This, of course, assumes that a strategy has previously been formulated, developed, and implemented, or at least that an implicit strategy, has been followed. It assumes that the organization has established basic objectives and other long and shorter range objectives for accomplishment, as well as the major relevant policies. It may assume also that the strategic process which determined the present strategy included an assessment of the organization's resources, a search of the various environments for opportunity, and a consideration of the personal values and objectives of the major decision makers and of other interest groups within the influence of the organization. If inspection reveals that the management did not weigh these important basic influences, this may help to explain some problems.

The evaluation phase, like the planning-control process, is both an end and a beginning of a continuous management process. This concept, pictured in Exhibit 2–1, will be more fully developed in Chapter 6 which presents in depth the evaluation and development of organizational strategy. At this stage it is sufficient to point out that the evaluation of strategy includes a thorough review of the results of the present strategy in various dimensions such as financial, operational, personal satisfaction for individuals and groups, social contribution, and other dimensions in which results can be viewed. But looking at results is not a sufficient basis on which to evaluate corporate strategy since this is only a look backward. More valuable and realistic in the evaluation of strategy is reflecting upon the future and the present and judging strategy in light of these more important time periods. In this sense, the evaluation phase of strategy starts again the development phase. The evaluation process, it should be emphasized, reviews the same aspects of strategy that are considered in the development stage. These strategic topics, discussed briefly in this chapter, are the content of the next four chapters.

SUMMARY

This chapter has introduced the subject of organizational strategy. It has further looked at strategy in the context of the top manager's job. The nature of strategy has been considered as well as the functions and elements of this concept. Beyond the identification or development of strategy, the second major aspect, implementation, was introduced, as was the evaluation phase of the strategic process.

The objective of this chapter was to develop some awareness of the breadth of strategy, its complexity, and its relationship to all aspects of the manager's job.

The reader should have an understanding of what strategy is and what it does, and be familiar with the elements of the strategic process and the basic influences upon which a strategy is built. Further, the view of strategy as a combination of objectives and major policies or substrategies should be clear, along with some of the specific objectives and policy components. Finally, the reader should recognize the relationship among the influences, the objectives, and the major policies which serve to achieve the objectives.

4. The Critical Role of Top Management in Long-Range Planning[*]

GEORGE A. STEINER

THERE IS no substitute for long-range planning in the development of profitable and healthy organizations. It is not, of course, the only requirement, but it is a major one. Too few companies, particularly the smaller and medium-sized ones, and too few government organizations try or do effective long-range planning.

In examining many long-range planning programs, I have come to two major conclusions. First, the fundamental concept of an effective long-range planning program is deceptively simple. Second, creating and maintaining a first-rate long-range program is deceptively difficult and demands, for its success, devoted attention by chief executives. I should like to discuss these two points, but first I should like to say a few words about the importance of effective long-range planning.

IMPORTANCE OF LONG-RANGE PLANNING

There exists in some business and government quarters surprising resistance to developing systematic and comprehensive planning. Naturally there are a great many reasons for such resistance, but failure to grasp the significance of effective planning is more important than it should be.

Several years ago, Mr. S. C. Beise, then President of the Bank of America, observed that for many years before World War II commercial banks did not aggressively seek savings deposits. As a result, the industry did not involve itself importantly in the related field of real estate financ-

---

[*] George A. Steiner, "The Critical Role of Management in Long-Range Planning," *Arizona Review*, April 1966. Reprinted by special permission of the *Arizona Review*.

ing. After World War II building boomed and little financial firms grew dramatically to fill the home financing need. Mr. Beise commented:

> Today these once-small savings and loan companies constitute a big industry in the United States and have given banks stiff competition for savings funds. The commercial banking industry today has made a strong comeback in the fields of savings and real estate lending, but due to its lack of foresight some twenty years ago, the banking industry gave birth to one of its own biggest competitors. I believe the industry has learned its lesson well, and it is one every industry and company should note.[1]

A recent study of the thirteen fastest growing companies in the United States revealed that all give high priority to long-range planning and manage to inspire most levels of managers to think about the future.[2]

Not only are more companies discovering the advantages of comprehensive and effective planning programs, but governments are developing organized long-range planning programs. This movement is particularly rapid among Western European governments and some developing nations. Last August President Johnson dramatically announced that the planning-programming-budgeting system introduced into the Pentagon by Secretary McNamara must be applied throughout the government.

There are many reasons why systematic and structured long-range planning is considered so important by progressive business and non-business organizations. Effective planning prevents ad hoc decisions, random decisions, decisions that unnecessarily and expensively narrow choices for tomorrow. Effective planning gives an organization a structural frame-work of objectives and strategies, a basis for all decision making. Lower-level managers know what top management wants and can make decisions accordingly. But there are also ancillary benefits. An effective planning organization, for example, provides a powerful channel of communications for the people in an organization to deal with problems of importance to themselves as well as to their organization.

It is difficult to exaggerate the importance of effective comprehensive planning to an organization. It has, for many companies, provided that margin needed for outstanding growth and profitability.

A CONCEPTUAL MODEL OF LONG-RANGE PLANNING

A conceptual model of planning at a sufficently low level of abstraction is a guide in establishing a complete system. The words *long-range plan-*

---

[1] S. C. Beise, "Planning for Industrial Growth: An Executive View," remarks before the Milan Conference on Planning for Industrial Growth, sponsored by Stanford Research Institute, 1963, mimeographed.

[2] Jack B. Weiner, "What Makes a Growth Company?," *Dun's Review and Modern Industry*, November 1964.

ning are useful in emphasizing a time dimension to planning. In describing an effective planning program, however, I prefer to speak of comprehensive, corporate or total planning.

Planning in this sense may be described from four points of view. First, a basic generic view of planning as dealing with the futurity of present decisions. This means that current decisions are made in light of their long-range consequences. It means also that future alternatives open to an organization are examined and decisions made about preferred alternatives. On this basis, guidance is provided for making current operating decisions. There are also many other conceptual views of planning; one concept, for example, recognizes planning as reasoning about how you get from here to there.

Planning is also a process. It is a process which establishes objectives; defines strategies, policies and sequences of events to achieve objectives; defines the organization for implementing the planning process; and assures a review and evaluation of performance as feedback in recycling the process.

Planning may be considered from a third point of view—namely, as a philosophy. Planning has been described as projective thought, or "looking ahead." Planning in this sense is an attitude, a state of mind, a way of thinking.

Finally, planning may be viewed in terms of structure. Long-range planning, as the term is typically used in the business world, refers to the development of a comprehensive and reasonably uniform program of plans for the entire company or agency, reaching out over a long period of time. It is an integrating framework within which each of the functional plans may be tied together and an overall plan developed for the entire organization.

Broadly, this structure includes four major elements (Figure 1). The first consists of strategic plans. These are a loose, written and unwritten set of major objectives, strategies and policies. The second is a detailed, uniform and a rather complete medium-range set of plans (two to seven, but generally five, years) covering major areas of organizational activity. The third part is short-term plans and budgets. The fourth structural part consists of planning studies which frequently are projections of things to come. A government agency, for example, may make a study of future revenues and demands for funds. A public utility may make population projections for its area. An automobile company may study changing consumer tastes, likely competitor moves and developing automotive technology. Such forecasts are not plans. The results of such studies, however, are important in actually making plans.

Long-range planning as the term is typically used in the business world does not refer so much to the future span of time covered as to the idea of management grappling systematically with future opportunities, problems

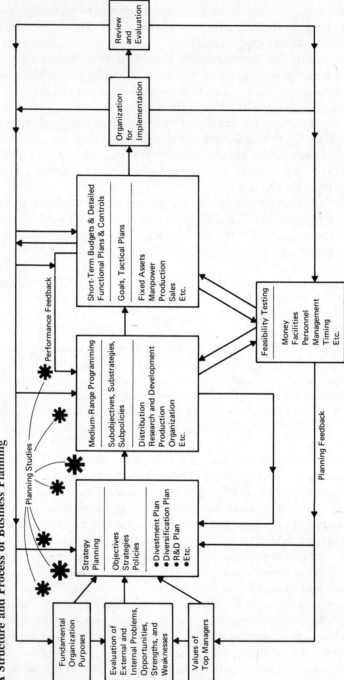

FIGURE 1
A Structure and Process of Business Planning

and alternative courses of action. Many companies typically have the pattern of plans and the concepts of planning already defined. This can be and often is called long-range planning. But I prefer other words to describe this structure.

LONG-RANGE PLANNING IN LARGE
AND SMALL BUSINESSES

All companies plan ahead in some degree. But not all have the sort of concept and structure noted here. While statistics on this subject are rather poor, I think it is probably true that close to a majority of the largest companies throughout the world have some sort of overall business planning program and a staff assigned to help executives do the work. Two years ago I held a research seminar at the Palais de Fontainebleau, France to discuss strategic business planning. About one hundred directors of corporate planning or top line managers of the largest multinational corporations of the world were present. One of the surprising conclusions reached at the seminar was that, despite the great surface diversities of planning among these companies, there was a large degree of comparability among basic planning definitions, principles, procedures and structures.[3]

There are relatively fewer numbers of medium and small-sized companies with comprehensive planning programs, but their numbers are growing. They are beginning to realize that, despite their limited resources, they have about the same fundamental planning requirements as the larger companies. Their salvation is not to ignore the problem but to develop short-cuts and rough-cut techniques for dealing with it.[4] There are many ways for a small company to get outside help at a reasonable price. Local banks can give advice. Many consulting agencies are available. Even professors are sometimes handy as consultants. Placing on his board of directors some persons who can contribute to long-range planning may also be attractive to a small businessman.

Systematic and reasonably well-structured planning programs are required by all organizations to survive and progress in the most healthy and effective manner. This is not something that only large companies need and are able to do. The requirement for effective planning exists for

---

[3] See George A. Steiner and Warren M. Cannon, eds., *Multinational Corporate Planning* (New York: The Free Press, Spring 1966).

[4] For suggestions about how to do this, see Roger A. Golde, "Practical Planning for Small Business," *Harvard Business Review*, September–October 1964; Myles L. Mace, "The President and Corporate Planning," *Harvard Business Review*, January–February 1965; and Raymond M. Haas, Richard I. Hartman, John H. James and Robert R. Milroy, *Long-Range Planning for Small Business* (Bloomington, Ind.: Bureau of Business Research, Graduate School of Business, Indiana University, 1964.

small companies, trade associations, industrial development agencies and for governments.

Professor Frank Gilmore of Cornell University presents the necessity for better planning in small business with this warning:

> The swing to strategic planning in large organizations constitutes a serious threat to small business management. It challenges one of the important competitive advantages which the small company has enjoyed— being faster on its feet than the larger company in adapting to changing conditions. It is perfectly clear that mere adaptation in the short run will no longer suffice. Trends must henceforth be made, not simply coped with.[5]

His point, of course, is that strategic planning among small businesses and smaller nonprofit organizations must accompany the better planning of the larger organizations. Smaller organizations can plan ahead systematically and continuously. First, however, there must be a recognition by the chief executive that this is possible. Then the smaller organization must devise ways and means to perform planning at a cost under benefit.

Naturally, different organizations go about meeting their planning responsibilities in different ways. Many big corporations have a large central planning staff reporting to the chief executive through a senior vice president. Each of the divisions of such a company may also have a planning staff. At the other extreme are the very small firms where the chief executive does almost all the planning. As firms increase in size, the chief executive may get help by hiring a special assistant, by using his vice presidents in ad hoc advisory planning committees or by using his vice presidents and functional officers as a permanent planning staff to help him develop plans.

In a similar fashion, basic principles essential for effective planning apply to all organizations—large and small, profit and nonprofit. Precisely how the principles are applied, however, does differ among organizations and among problems and over time.

Of cardinal importance in creating and maintaining useful comprehensive planning programs is the role played by chief executives.

TOP MANAGEMENT'S KEY ROLE IN PLANNING

There can and will be no effective long-range planning in any organization where the chief executive does not give it firm support and make sure that others in the organization understand his depth of commitment. Yet one competent observer finds:

---

[5] Frank F. Gilmore, "Strategic Planning's Threat to Small Business," mimeographed, 1966.

Probably the single most important problem in corporate planning derives from the belief of some chief operating executives that corporate planning is not a function with which they should be directly concerned. They regard planning as something to be delegated, which subordinates can do without responsible participation by chief executives. They think the end result of effective planning is the compilation of a "Plans" book. Such volumes get distributed to key executives, who scan the contents briefly, file them away, breathe a sigh of relief, and observe, "Thank goodness that is done—now let's get back to work."[6]

This, of course, shows a lack of understanding of the planning task and the responsibility of the top executive. Another competent observer says the matter is not so much a lack of understanding but abdication of responsibility. Professor O'Donnell has said:

I think one of the outstanding facts about corporate planning at the present is that the presidents of corporations have been ducking their jobs. . . . They seem to be following the practice of setting in a fuzzy way some objectives to be accomplished in the future and establishing a committee, with the staff help of a planning group, to come up with a plan for achieving the objectives. From this point until the plan is presented to him, the president almost abdicates his responsibilities. When the plan is placed on his desk it is often too late for him to exert much influence on it.[7]

It is essential that the chief executive assume primary responsibility for his organization's long-range planning. When he hires an assistant to help him, or establishes a planning staff, he is merely extending his reach. These people are helping him to do *his* job. This is a recognition that the world is too large for one man to grasp completely, and that to the extent he can get others to help him he will be more able to examine a wider range of threats and opportunities for his organization.

Issues concerning the role of the chief executive in the development of plans are subtle and complex. I participated in one conference with chief executives where the major focus was on the relationship of the president with his staff in the development of corporate plans. These executives were dedicated to the idea of comprehensive planning but were uncertain about many matters relating to their participation. The range of alternatives is very wide. Effective planning, for example, requires that the top executive "buy it." He must believe in planning as being important to the success of his enterprise. He must give more than "lip service" to the effort. He must feel committed, and his support must be visible to others in the corporation. By his actions the chief executive will set the psychological climate in which planning is done.

---

[6] Mace, "The President and Corporate Planning," p. 50.

[7] George A. Steiner, ed., *Managerial Long-Range Planning* (New York: McGraw-Hill Book Co., 1963), p. 17.

How an executive does these things will depend upon his style of management, the way his company is organized, the personalities involved and his own sense of commitment. For example, if the chief executive devotes most of his attention to short-range problems, this emphasis will not be lost on his subordinates. Even if he is interested in long-range planning, can he find the time to do it properly? I agree partly with Senator Jackson for example, when, speaking about the federal government, he observed:

> . . . I am convinced that we never will get the kind of policy planning we need if we expect the top-level officers to participate actively in the planning process. They simply do not have the time, and in any event they rarely have the outlook or the talents of the good planner. They cannot explore issues deeply and systematically. They cannot argue the advantages and disadvantages at length in the kind of give-and-take essential if one is to reach a solid understanding with others on points of agreement and disagreement.[8]

While this observation does have an important element of truth in it for a large government department or a large multinational business, it has much less for a small enterprise where the chief executive must plan if any planning is to be done. But even in the largest companies and government agencies the chief executives must get involved in the substance of planning. If they do not they will clearly be abdicating one of their major responsibilities. At the very least they will be captives of their planning staffs and thereby lose some element of control of their enterprises.

But the question still exists: how shall the chief executive participate in the substance of planning? There is no simple answer. For the first planning effort, the chief executive of any organization—large or small, profit or non-profit—ought to be deeply involved. Once the planning program has gotten on a solid footing, with periodic cycling, general understanding and acceptance, the chief executive will know more clearly at what points and how much his participation is required. If a company, for example, has just begun the planning process and is pounding out long-range objectives, the chief executive should be intimately involved. Once those objectives are established, he must help make and approve strategies to reach them. When this work is done, he may get involved in subsequent cycles of planning only with selected changes in specific objectives and strategies. Both he and his staff will know better with experience what these points are. There is no ready answer for any chief executive, however, to the question of when and how much he can delegate to and rely

---

[8] Henry M. Jackson, "To Forge a Strategy for Survival," *Public Administration Review,* vol. 19 (Summer 1959), p. 159.

upon his staff—both line and functional—what are, in the end, his planning responsibilities.

It is not enough that the chief executive participate in the planning exercise. His relationship to it must be visible to others in the organization. By various methods open to him, the chief executive must have others know about and understand his interest in the process.

DEVELOPING THE PLAN

It is a major responsibility of the chief executive to see that the proper planning system is developed and maintained. In this effort, of course, he will have help from subordinates—both line managers and their staffs. But it is his responsibility to make sure that the system is appropriate to his enterprise, and that it is done at cost (using this word broadly) under benefit which produces optimum values.

Many years ago I had the job of helping an organization develop its first comprehensive planning program. In preparing procedures and suggesting roles of people in the organization I ran into grave difficulties. People were not sure of their responsibilities, or did not want to assume the responsibility I suggested. Different people wanted to do different things which did not necessarily mesh. There were also other points of dispute. To solve the entire problem I prepared a letter for the signature of the chief executive which set forth the essential elements of the planning program, how it should be developed and who was responsible for what. This worked like a charm. From that day to this the top executives of that company have watched over the planning process. It is an outstanding system.

I am not saying, of course, that chief executives must get enmeshed in all the grubby details of a total planning program. What I do say is they must see that the job of planning the plan is done, that it is appropriate and put into operation.

Clarification of roles of participants in the planning process is important and raises complex issues. For example, since corporate planning staffs are direct aids to the chief executive he must see that their roles are clear and generally understood.

A staff, for example, which fails to distinguish between strategic planning and tactical planning may lose top management if it gets too deeply involved in the details of tactical planning. Top management is interested in both strategic and tactical planning, but principally strategic planning. I once knew a staff that simply could not get itself out of the morass of details involved in short-range tactical planning. It was not long before the top management and its planning staff stopped talking to one another. There have been managers who simply could not differentiate between their responsibilities for strategic as distinguished from short-range tactical planning. Their concentration on the latter got them involved in a sort of Gresham's law of planning: short-range planning tends to drive out long-range planning.

Subtle problems of staff role arise in the development of strategic plans by central planning staffs and plans and operations of divisions. Long-range plans made in one area of a company often make sense only when considered in light of other areas and of the company as a whole. In this light, corporate planning staffs inevitably get involved in this interrelationship. Their role in modification of plans to relate better to the company as a whole may result in bitter conflict with line officers if large issues are involved. No matter how clear staff roles may be this sort of conflict will arise. It is less likely to arise and less likely to be serious if roles are clearly specified and understood.

There is no question about the fact that planning should not be separated from doing. Upon examination, however, this is not as simple as it sounds. In the strategic planning area, for example, plans may be developed for divisional execution, and the divisions may not have much if any participation in their preparation. Even with close line and staff interrelations at central office headquarters, staff inevitably will make decisions. The mere choice of alternatives to present to line managers, for example, may implicitly be decision-making by staff. Problems of drawing a line of demarcation between staff and line decision-making, and planning and operations, vary from case to case in the development of plans, and from time to time. Their can be no simple formula. But efforts to clarify staff role can prevent unnecessary conflict.

Even when the staff role is clear, however, difficult problems of relationships may arise. In larger companies with comprehensive planning programs, corporate functional staffs, including long-range planning staffs, review divisional plans at the request of top management. Plans are submitted up the line, but staffs help line managers review them. In one instance a president asked his director of long-range planning to review the plans of a powerful division manager. The president insisted upon a rigorous examination of the plans because of the substantial capital outlays sought by the divisional manager. The planner did so and provided the rationale for rejecting the plans. He was not very happy about his role. He had been cultivating this divisional manager for a long time in order to develop a better planning program in his division and to arrange better communications to help them both do a better planning job. Now the divisional manager felt he had been double-crossed. The corporate planner will have problems in rebuilding his lines of communication with this division.

The planning process is complex. There must be understanding of authority, responsibility, procedures and timing. The chief executive is responsible for seeing that this need is met.

BASE DECISIONS ON PLANS

Comprehensive planning done with and on behalf of top management should result in operating decisions. Without decisions the planning process is incomplete. Failure to take action on prepared plans, or continuous vacillation, will weaken staff efforts. People simply will not be motivated to exert the energy, develop the creativity and use the imagination needed to make quality plans if top management ignores them or cannot seem to act upon them.

In one company I know, one month after a five-year long-range plan had been developed for the first time and approved by top management, the president announced a flat seven percent budget cut for all division budgets. This was his method to reduce costs. The announced reason was the need to bring costs within the year's anticipated revenues. With this announcement, the longer-range projects naturally were abandoned and the benefits of long-range planning cast in grave doubt.

The extent to which divisional line managers make decisions in light of strategic corporate plans raises a different type of problem. In some companies the connection between the corporate strategic plan and the divisional intermediate-range plans is very close. The two may, in effect, be prepared together. In one small company of about five hundred people making a variety of electronics equipment, there was a planning program where strategic plans were developed for the company as a whole and the divisions tied their sub-strategies and detailed long-range plans clearly and closely into the corporate plan. These were intermeshed because the two were done by about the same people and at about the same time. In other instances, the corporate strategic plan constitutes an umbrella under which the divisional plans are made but the interrelationship between the two is rather loose.

A somewhat different type of problem arises very subtly if divisional managers think that corporate planning staffs are making plans for them to execute. It can arise if chief executives do not get involved in the planning and accept staff recommendations without much or any reservation. In such cases divisional managers are likely to take this position to the corporate staff: "You made the plans, now execute them. Don't ask me to."

One of the major attributes of comprehensive corporate planning is that the structure, especially when written, permits managers down the organizational chain to make decisions with a reasonable degree of certainty they are in line with the objectives sought by higher level management. Naturally, if decisions made throughout an organization do not relate to the planning program, it will not be long before the planning program disappears.

This, of course, does not mean blind devotion to plan. Depending upon circumstances, it may be wise for a manager to make decisions which are very different than those planned. Flexibility must be injected into planning. There are a number of techniques to do this. One major method is for the chief executive to inject a philosophy and understanding of flexibility into the planning and operational decision-making process.

In sum, chief executives have an important role in assuring that decisions throughout the organization are made in light of plans and evolving circumstances—not blindly, not without reference to plans, but related meaningfully within a planning framework.

PLANNING TAKES TIME

While conceptually simple, a comprehensive long-range planning program for a large organization cannot be introduced overnight and expected to produce miraculous results immediately. Several years ago I calculated that about five years were required for a medium-sized or large company to develop an effective comprehensive planning system.[9] This was confirmed by another study.[10] Since there is so much more known today about how to develop effective comprehensive planning programs, it is possible to reduce this time span. Much depends upon the organization and what is going on inside it.

Among most initial efforts to develop comprehensive long-range planning programs with which I have been familiar, the first effort did not produce much of immediate substantive value. Yet, all those involved felt the effort worthwhile. This was so, I found, because the effort introduced a new point of view into the company which appeared to have important possibilities in future planning. It also was seen as a focal point for communicating in a common language about major problems. There are many other reasons why managements have been pleased with the first attempt at long-range planning even though it did not provide immediate substantive values. But first efforts do not always provide important bases for immediate decision.

An effective planning program of one company cannot be lifted intact and applied to another. While the fundamental process and structure may be removed from one company to another, the details of operation will vary. Furthermore, since an organization is a living, dynamic institution in a rapidly changing environment, the procedures for planning change.

---

[9] Steiner, *Managerial Long-Range Planning*, pp. 19–21.

[10] R. Hal Mason, "Organizing for Corporate Planning," Proceedings of the Long Range Planning Service Client Conference, February 7–9, 1962, Menlo Park, Calif., Stanford Research Institute.

RÉSUMÉ

Two major underlying considerations in the development of effective long-range planning are, first, understanding of an operational conceptual model of plans, and second, understanding and acceptance by the chief executive of his role in creating and maintaining quality planning.

George Humphrey used to say that the best fertilizer ever invented was the footsteps of the farmer. Similarly, the best assurance of effective planning in an organization is the active participation of the chief executive in doing it.

STUDENT REVIEW QUESTIONS

1. Discuss in detail what Steiner means by long-range planning.
2. What does the author see as advantages of long-range planning?
3. Do you agree that top management should play a key role in planning? Discuss reasons in detail.
4. In what ways should the chief executive officer participate in the substance of planning?
5. What is the role for staff personnel in an organization's planning effort?
6. What differences if any, do you see in the roles for various organizational members in the long-range planning process in business organizations, universities, and health care organizations?

5. Shaping the Master Strategy of Your Firm*

WILLIAM H. NEWMAN

EVERY ENTERPRISE NEEDS a central purpose expressed in terms of the services it will render to society. And it needs a basic concept of how it will create these services. Since it will be competing with other enterprises for resources, it must have some distinctive advantages—in its services or in its methods of creating them. Moreover, since it will inevitably cooperate with other firms, it must have the means for maintaining viable coalitions with them. In addition, there are the elements of change, growth, and adaptation. Master strategy is a company's basic plan for dealing with these factors.

One familiar way of delving into company strategy is to ask, "What business are we in or do we want to be in? Why should society tolerate our existence?" Answers are often difficult. A company producing only grass seed had very modest growth until it shifted its focus to "lawn care" and provided the suburban homeowner with a full line of fertilizers, pesticides, and related products. Less fortunate was a cooperage firm that defined its business in terms of wooden boxes and barrels and went bankrupt when paperboard containers took over the field.

Product line is only part of the picture, however. An ability to supply services economically is also crucial. For example, most local bakeries have shut down, not for lack of demand for bread, but because they became technologically inefficient. Many a paper mill has exhausted its sources of pulpwood. The independent motel operator is having difficulty meeting competition from franchised chains. Yet in all these industries some firms have prospered—the ones that have had the foresight and

---

* William H. Newman, "Shaping the Master Strategy of Your Firm," *California Management Review*, vol. 9, no. 3 (Spring 1967). © 1967 by the Regents of the University of California. Reprinted from *California Management Review*, Vol. 9, No. 3, by permission of the Regents.

adaptability (and probably some luck, too) to take advantage of their changing environment. These firms pursued a master strategy which enabled them to increase the services rendered and attract greater resources.

Most central managers recognize that master strategy is of cardinal importance. But they are less certain about how to formulate a strategy for their particular firm. This article seeks to help in the shaping of master strategies. It outlines key elements and an approach to defining these. Most of our illustrations will be business enterprises; nevertheless, the central concept is just as crucial for hospitals, universities, and other non-profit ventures.

A practical way to develop a master strategy is to:

Pick particular roles or niches that are appropriate in view of competition and the company's resources.

Combine various facets of the company's efforts to obtain synergistic effects.

Set up sequences and timing of changes that reflect company capabilities and external conditions.

Provide for frequent reappraisal and adaptation to evolving opportunities.

NEW MARKETS OR SERVICES

Picking Propitious Niches. Most companies fill more than one niche. Often they sell several lines of products: even when a single line is produced an enterprise may sell it to several distinct types of customers. Especially as a firm grows, it seeks expansion by tapping new markets or selling different services to its existing customers. In designing a company strategy we can avoid pitfalls by first examining each of these markets separately.

Basically, we are searching for customer needs—preferably growing ones—where adroit use of our unique resources will make our services distinctive and in that sense give us a competitive advantage. In these particular spots, we hope to give the customer an irresistible value and to do so at relatively low expense. A bank, for example, may devise a way of financing the purchase of an automobile that is particularly well-suited to farmers; it must then consider whether it is in a good position to serve such a market.

Identifying such propitious niches is not easy. Here is one approach that works well in various situations: Focus first on the industry—growth prospects, competition, key factors required for success—then on the strengths and weaknesses of the specific company as matched against these key success factors. As we describe this approach more fully, keep in mind that we are interested in segments of markets as well as entire markets.

The sales volume and profits of an industry or one of its segments depend on the demand for its services, the supply of these services, and the competitive conditions. (We use "service" here to include both physical products and intangible values provided by an enterprise.) Predicting future demand, supply, and competition is an exciting endeavor. In the following paragraphs, we suggest a few of the important considerations that may vitally affect the strategy of a company.

ELEMENTS OF DEMAND

Demand for Industry Services. The strength of the *desire* for a service affects its demand. For instance, we keenly want a small amount of salt, but care little for additional quantities. Our desire for more and better automobiles does not have this same sort of cut-off level, and our desires for pay-television (no commercials, select programs) or supersonic air travel are highly uncertain, falling in quite a different category from that of salt.

Possible *substitutes* to satisfy a given desire must be weighed—beef for lamb, motorboats for baseball, gas for coal, aureomycin for sulfa, weldments for castings, and so forth. The frequency of such substitution is affected, of course, by the relative prices.

Desire has to be backed up by *ability to pay,* and here business cycles enter in. Also, in some industries large amounts of capital are necessarily tied up in equipment. The relative efficiency, quality of work, and nature of machinery already in place influence the money that will be available for new equipment. Another consideration: If we hope to sell in foreign markets, foreign-exchange issues arise.

The *structure of markets* also requires analysis. Where, on what terms, and in response to what appeals do people buy jet planes, sulphuric acid, or dental floss? Does a manufacturer deal directly with consumers or are intermediaries such as retailers or brokers a more effective means of distribution?

Although an entire industry is often affected by such factors—desire, substitutes, ability to pay, structure of markets—a local variation in demand sometimes provides a unique opportunity for a particular firm. Thus, most drugstores carry cosmetics, candy, and a wide variety of items besides drugs, but a store located in a medical center might develop a highly profitable business by dealing exclusively with prescriptions and other medical supplies.

All these elements of demand are subject to change—some quite rapidly. Since the kind of strategic plans we are considering here usually extends over several years, we need both an identification of the key factors that will affect industry demand and an estimate of how they will change over a span of time.

SUPPLY SITUATION

Supply Related to Demand. The attractiveness of any industry depends on more than potential growth arising from strong demand. In designing a company strategy we also must consider the probable supply of services and the conditions under which they will be offered.

The *capacity* of an industry to fill demand for its services clearly affects profit margins. The importance of over- or undercapacity, however, depends on the ease of entry and withdrawal from the industry. When capital costs are high, as in the hotel or cement business, adjustments to demand tend to lag. Thus, overcapacity may depress profits for a long period; even bankruptcies do not remove the capacity if plants are bought up—at bargain prices—and operated by new owners. On the other hand, low capital requirements—as in electronic assembly work—permit new firms to enter quickly, and shortages of supply tend to be short-lived. Of course, more than the physical plant is involved; an effective organization of competent people is also necessary. Here again, the case of expansion or contraction should be appraised.

Costs also need to be predicted—labor costs, material costs, and for some industries, transportation costs or excise taxes. If increases in operating costs affect all members of an industry alike and can be passed on to the consumer in the form of higher prices, this factor becomes less significant in company strategy. However, rarely do both conditions prevail. Sharp rises in labor costs in Hawaii, for example, place its sugar industry at a disadvantage on the world market.

A highly dynamic aspect of supply is *technology.* New methods for producing established products—for example, basic oxygen conversion of steel displacing open-hearth furnaces and mechanical cotton pickers displacing century-old hand-picking techniques—are part of the picture. Technology may change the availability and price of raw materials; witness the growth of synthetic rubber and industrial diamonds. Similarly, air cargo planes and other new forms of transportation are expanding the sources of supply that may serve a given market.

For an individual producer, anticipating these shifts in the industry supply situation may be a matter of prosperity or death.

CLIMATE OF INDUSTRY

Competitive Conditions in the Industry. The way the interplay between demand and supply works out depends partly on the nature of competition in the industry. *Size, strength, and attitude of companies* in one industry—the dress industry where entrance is easy and style is critical —may lead to very sharp competition. On the other hand, oligopolistic competition among the giants of the aluminum industry produces a more stable situation, at least in the short run. The resources and managerial talent needed to enter one industry differ greatly from what it takes to get ahead in the other.

A strong *trade association* often helps to create a favorable climate in its industry. The Independent Oil Producers' Association, to cite one case, has been unusually effective in restricting imports of crude oil into the United States. Other associations compile valuable industry statistics, help reduce unnecessary variations in size of products, run training conferences, hold trade shows, and aid members in a variety of other ways.

Government regulation also modifies competion. A few industries like banking and insurance are supervised by national or state bodies that place limits on prices, sales promotion, and the variety of services rendered. Airlines are both regulated as a utility and subsidized as an infant industry. Farm subsidies affect large segments of agriculture, and tariffs have long protected selected manufacturers. Our patent laws also bear directly on the nature of competition, as is evident in the heated discussion of how pharmaceutical patents may be used. Clearly, future government action is a significant factor in the outlook of many industries.

CRUCIAL FACTORS

Key Factors for Success in the Industry. This brief review suggests the dynamic nature of business and uncertainties in the outlook for virtually all industries. A crucial task of every top management is to assess the forces at play in its industry and to identify those factors that will be crucial for future success. These we call "key success factors." Leadership in research and development may be very important in one industry, low costs in another, and adaptability to local need in a third; large financial resources may be a *sine qua non* for mining whereas creative imagination is the touchstone in advertising.

We stressed earlier the desirability of making such analyses for narrow segments as well as broad industry categories. The success factors for each segment are likely to differ in at least one or two respects from those for other segments. For example, General Foods Corporation discovered to its sorrow that the key success factors in gourmet foods differ significantly from those for coffee and Jello.

Moreover, the analysis of industry outlook should provide a forecast of the *growth potentials* and the *profit prospects* for the various industry segments. These conclusions, along with key success factors, are vital guideposts in setting up a company's master strategy.

The range of opportunities for distinctive service is wide. Naturally, in picking its particular niche out of this array a company favors those opportunities which will utilize its strength and bypass its limitations. This calls for a candid appraisal of the company itself.

POSITION IN MARKET

Market Strengths of Company. A direct measure of *market position* is the percentage that company sales are of industry sales and of major competitors' sales. Such figures quickly indicate whether our company is so big that its activities are likely to bring prompt responses from other leading companies. Or our company may be small enough to enjoy independent maneuverability. Of course, to be most meaningful, these percentages should be computed separately for geographical areas, product lines, and types of customer—if suitable industry data are available.

More intangible but no less significant are the relative standing of *company products* and their *reputation* in major markets. Kodak products, for instance, are widely and favorably known; they enjoy a reputation for both high quality and dependability. Clearly, this reputation will be a factor in Eastman Kodak Company strategy. And any new, unknown firm must overcome this prestige if it seeks even a small share in one segment of the film market. Market reputation is tenacious. Especially when we try to "trade up," our previous low quality, service, and sharp dealing will be an obstacle. Any strategy we adopt must have enough persistence and consistency so that our firm is assigned a "role" in the minds of the customers we wish to reach.

The relationship between a company and the *distribution system* is another vital aspect of market position. The big United States automobile companies, for example, are strong partly because each has a set of dealers throughout the country. In contrast, foreign car manufacturers have difficulty selling here until they can arrange with dealers to provide dependable service. A similar problem confronted Whirlpool Corporation when it wanted to sell its trademarked appliances publicly. (For years its only customer had been Sears, Roebuck and Company.) Whirlpool made an unusual arrangement with Radio Corporation of America which led to the establishment of RCA-Whirlpool distributors and dealers. Considering the strong competition, Whirlpool could not have entered this new market without using marketing channels such as RCA's.

All these aspects of market position—a relative share of the market, comparative quality of product, reputation with consumers, and ties with a distributive system—help define the strengths and limitations of a company.

SERVICE ABILITIES

Supply Strengths of a Company. To pick propitious niches we also should appraise our company's relative strength in creating goods and services. Such ability to supply services fitted to consumer needs will be built largely on the firm's resources of labor and material, effective productive facilities, and perhaps pioneering research and development.

Labor in the United States is fairly mobile. Men tend to gravitate to good jobs. But the process takes time—a southern shoe plant needed ten years to build up an adequate number of skilled workers—and it may be expensive. Consequently, immediate availability of competent men at normal industry wages is a source of strength. In addition, the relationships between the company and its work force are important. All too often both custom and formal agreements freeze inefficient practices. The classic example is New England textiles; here, union-supported work habits give such mills high labor costs. Only recently have a few companies been able to match their more flourishing competitors in the South.

Access to *low-cost materials* is often a significant factor in a company's supply position. The development of the southern paper industry, for example, is keyed to the use of fast-growing forests which can be cut on a rotational basis to provide a continuing supply of pulpwood. Of course, if raw materials can be easily transported, such as iron ore and crude oil by enormous ships, plants need not be located at the original source.

Availability of materials involves more than physical handling. Ownership, or long-term contracts with those who do own, may assure a continuing source at low cost. Much of the strategy of companies producing basic metals—iron, copper, aluminum, or nickel—includes huge investments in ore properties. But all sorts of companies are concerned with the availability of materials. So whenever supplies are scarce a potential opportunity exists. Even in retailing, Sears, Roebuck and Company discovered in its Latin American expansion that a continuing flow of merchandise of standard quality was difficult to assure, but once established, such sources became a great advantage.

Physical facilities—office buildings, plants, mines—often tie up a large portion of a company's assets. In the short run, at least, these facilities may be an advantage or a disadvantage. The character of many colleges, for instance, has been shaped by their location, whether in a plush suburb or in a degenerating urban area, and the cost of moving facilities is so great that adaptation to the existing neighborhood becomes necessary. A steel company, to cite another case, delayed modernizing its plant so long that it had to abandon its share of the basic steel market and seek volume in specialty products.

Established organizations of highly talented people to perform particular tasks also gives a company a distinctive capability. Thus, a good research and development department may enable a company to expand in pharmaceuticals, whereas a processing firm without such a technical staff is barred from this profitable field.

Perhaps the company we are analyzing will enjoy other distinctive abilities to produce services. Our central concern at this point is to identify strengths and see how these compare with strengths of other firms.

FINANCES AND MANAGEMENT

Other Company Resources. The propitious niche for a company also depends on its financial strength and the character of its management.

Some strategies will require large quantities of capital. Any oil company that seeks foreign sources of crude oil, for instance, must be prepared to invest millions of dollars. Few firms maintain cash reserves of this size, so *financial capacity* to enter this kind of business depends on: an ability to attract new capital—through borrowing or sale of stock—or a flow of profits (and depreciation allowances) from existing operations that can be allocated to the new venture. On the other hand, perhaps a strategy can be devised that calls for relatively small cash advances, and in these fields a company that has low financial strength will still be able to compete with the affluent firms.

A more subtle factor in company capacity is its *management.* The age and vitality of key executives, their willingness to risk profit and capital, their urge to gain personal prestige through company growth, their desire to insure stable employment for present workers—all affect the suitability of any proposed strategy. For example, the expansion of Hilton Hotels Corporation into a world-wide chain certainly reflects the personality of Conrad Hilton; with a different management at the helm, a modification in strategy is most appropriate because Conrad Hilton's successors do not have his particular set of drives and values.

Related to the capabilities of key executives is the organization structure of the company. A decentralized structure, for instance, facilitates movement into new fields of business, whereas a functional structure with fine specialization is better suited to expansion in closely related lines.

PICKING A NICHE

Matching Company Strengths with Key Success Factors. Armed with a careful analysis of the strengths and limitations of our company, we are prepared to pick desirable niches for company concentration. Naturally, we will look for fields where company strengths correspond with the key factors for success that have been developed in our industry analyses described in the preceding section. And in the process we will set aside possibilities in which company limitations create serious handicaps.

Potential growth and profits in each niche must, of course, be added to the synthesis. Clearly, a low potential will make a niche unattractive even though the company strengths and success factors fit neatly. And we may become keenly interested in a niche where the fit is only fair if the potential is great.

Typically, several intriguing possibilities emerge. These are all the niches—in terms of market lines, market segments, or combinations of production functions—that the company might pursue. Also typically, a series of positive actions is necessary in order for the company to move into each area. So we need to list not only each niche and its potential, but the limitations that will have to be overcome and other steps necessary for the company to succeed in each area. These are our propitious niches—nestled in anticipated business conditions and tailored to the strengths and limitations of our particular company.

An enterprise always pursues a variety of efforts to serve even a single niche, and, typically, it tries to fill several related niches. Considerable choice is possible, at least in the degree to which these many efforts are pushed. In other words, management decides how many markets to cover, to what degree to automate production, what stress to place on consumer engineering, and a host of other actions. One vital aspect of master strategy is fitting these numerous efforts together. In fact, our choice of niches will depend in part, on how well we can combine the total effort they require.

Synergy is a powerful ally for this purpose. Basically, synergy means that the combined effect of two or more cooperative acts is greater than the sum which would result if the actions were taken independently. A simple example in marketing is that widespread dealer stocks *combined with* advertising will produce much greater sales volume than widespread dealer stocks in, say, Virginia and advertising in Minnesota. Often the possibility of obtaining synergistic effects will shape the master strategy of the company—as the following examples will suggest.

COMBINATION OF SERVICES

Total Service to Customer.   A customer rarely buys merely a physical product. Other attributes of the transaction often include delivery, credit terms, return privileges, repair service, operating instructions, conspicuous consumption, psychological experience of purchasing, and the like. Many services involve no physical product at all. The crucial question is what combination of attributes will have high synergistic value for the customers we serve.

International Business Machines, for instance, has found a winning combination. Its products are well designed and of high quality. But so are the products of several of its competitors. In addition, IBM provides salesmen who understand the customer's problems and how IBM equipment can help solve them, and fast, dependable repair service. The synergistic effect of these three services is of high value to many customers.

Each niche calls for its own combination of services. For example, Chock Full o' Nuts expanded its restaurant chain on the basis of three attributes: good quality food, cleanliness, and fast service. This combination appealed to a particular group of customers. A very limited selection, crowded space, and lack of frills did not matter. However, if any one of the three characteristics slips at an outlet, the synergistic effect is lost.

ADDING TO CAPABILITIES

Fuller Use of Existing Resources. Synergistic effects are possible in any phase of company operations. One possibility is that present activities include a "capability" that can be applied to additional uses. Thus, American watch companies have undertaken the manufacture of tiny gyroscopes and electronic components for spacecraft because they already possessed technical skill in the production of miniature precision products. They adopted this strategy on the premise that they could make both watches and components for spacecraft with less effort than could separate firms devoted to only one line of products.

The original concept of General Foods Corporation sought a similar synergistic effect in marketing. Here, the basic capability was marketing prepared foods. By having the same sales organization handle several product lines, a larger and more effective sales effort could be provided and/or the selling cost per product line could be reduced. Clearly, the combined sales activity was more powerful than separate sales efforts for each product line would have been.

VERTICAL INTEGRATION

Expansion to Obtain a Resource. Vertical integration may have synergistic effects. This occurred when the Apollo Printing Machine Company bought a foundry. Apollo was unsatisfied with the quality and tardy delivery of its castings and was looking for a new supplier. In its search, it learned that a nearby foundry could be purchased. The foundry was just breaking even, primarily because the volume of its work fluctuated widely. Following the purchase, Apollo gave the foundry a more steady backlog of work, and through close technical cooperation the quality of castings received by them was improved. The consolidated set-up was better for both enterprises than the previous independent operations.

The results of vertical integration are not always so good, however; problems of balance, flexibility, and managerial capacity must be carefully weighed. Nevertheless, control of a critical resource is often a significant part of company strategy.

UNIQUE SERVICES

Expansion to Enhance Market Position. Efforts to improve market position provide many examples of "the whole being better than the sum of its parts." The leading can companies, for example, moved from exclusive concentration on metal containers into glass, plastic, and paper containers. They expected their new divisions to be profitable by themselves, but an additional reason for the expansion lay in anticipated synergistic effects of being able to supply a customer's total container requirements. With the entire packaging field changing so rapidly, a company that can quickly shift from one type of container to another offers a distinctive service to its customers.

International Harvester, to cite another case, added a very large tractor to its line a few years ago. The prospects for profit on this line alone were far from certain. However, the new tractor was important to give dealers "a full line"; its availablity removed the temptation for dealers to carry some products of competing manufacturers. So, when viewed in combination with other International Harvester products, the new tractor looked much more significant than it did as an isolated project.

NEGATIVE SYNERGY

Compatibility of Efforts. In considering additional niches for a company, we may be confronted with negative synergy—that is, the combined effort is worse than the sum of independent efforts. This occurred when a producer of high quality television and hi-fi sets introduced a small color television receiver. When first offered, the small unit was as good as most competing sets and probably had an attractive potential market. However, it was definitely inferior in performance to other products of the company and, consequently, undermined public confidence in the quality of the entire line. Moreover, customers had high expectations for the small set because of the general reputation of the company, and they became very critical when the new product did not live up to their expectations. Both the former products and the new product suffered.

Compatibility of operations within the company should also be considered. A large department store, for instance, ran into serious trouble when it tried to add a high-quality dress shop to its mass merchandising activities. The ordering and physical handling of merchandise, the approach to sales promotion, the sales compensation plan, and many other procedures which worked well for the established type of business were unsuited to the new shop. And friction arose each time the shop received special treatment. Clearly, the new shop created an excessive number of problems because it was incompatible with existing customs and attitudes.

BROAD COMPANY GOALS

Summarizing briefly: We have seen that some combinations of efforts are strongly reinforcing. The combination accelerates the total effect or reduces the cost for the same effect or solidifies our supply or market position. On the other hand, we must watch for incompatible efforts which may have a disruptive effect in the same cumulative manner. So, when we select niches—as a part of our master strategy—one vital aspect is the possibility of such synergistic effects.

Master strategy sets broad company goals. One firm may decide to seek pre-eminence in a narrow specialty while another undertakes to be a leader in several niches or perhaps in all phases of its industry. We have recommended that this definition of "scope" be clear in terms of:

Services offered to customers.

Operations performed by the company.

Relationships with suppliers of necessary resources.

The desirability of defining this mission so as to obtain synergistic effects.

But master strategy involves more than defining our desired role in society. Many activities will be necessary to achieve this desired spot, and senior executives must decide what to do first, how many activities can be done concurrently, how fast to move, what risks to run, and what to postpone. These questions of sequence and timing must be resolved to make the strategy operational.

STRATEGY OF SEQUENCE

Choice of Sequence. Especially in technical areas, sequence of actions may be dictated by technology. Thus, process research must precede equipment designs, product specifications must precede cost estimation, and so forth. Other actions, such as the steps necessary to form a new corporation, likewise give management little choice in sequence. When this occurs, normal programming or possibly PERT analysis may be employed. Little room—or need—exists for strategy.

Preordained sequences, however, are exceptional in the master strategy area. A perennial issue when entering a new niche, for instance, is whether to develop markets before working on production economies, or vice versa. The production executive will probably say, "Let's be sure we can produce the product at a low cost before committing ourselves to customers," whereas the typical marketing man will advise, "Better be sure it will sell before tooling up for a big output."

A striking example of strategy involving sequence confronted the Boeing company when it first conceived of a large four-engine jet plane suitable for handling cargo or large passenger loads. Hindsight makes the issue appear simple, but at the time, Air Force officers saw little need for such a plane. The belief was that propeller-driven planes provided the most desirable means for carrying cargo. In other words, the company got no support for its prediction of future market requirements. Most companies would have stopped at this point. However, Boeing executives decided to invest several million dollars to develop the new plane. A significant portion of the company's liquid assets went into the project. Over two years later, Boeing was able to present evidence that caused the Air Force officials to change their minds—and the KC 135 was born. Only Boeing was prepared to produce the new type of craft which proved to be both faster and more economical than propeller-driven planes. Moreover, the company was able to convert the design into the Boeing 707 passenger plane which, within a few years, dominated the airline passenger business. Competing firms were left far behind, and Convair almost went bankrupt in its attempt to catch up. In this instance, a decision to let engineering and production run far ahead of marketing paid off handsomely.

No simple guide exists for selecting a strategic sequence. Nevertheless, the following comments do sharpen the issue:

Resist the temptation to do first what is easiest simply because it requires the least initiative. Each of us typically has a bias for what he does well. A good sequence of activities, however, is more likely to emerge from an objective analysis.

If a head start is especially valuable on one front, start early there. Sometimes, being the first in the market is particularly desirable (there may be room for only one company). In other cases, the strategic place to begin is the acquiring of key resources; at a later date limited raw materials may already be bought up or the best sites occupied by competitors. The importance of a head start is usually hard to estimate, but probably more money is lost in trying to be first than in catching up with someone else.

Move into uncertain areas promptly, preferably before making any major commitments. For instance, companies have been so entranced with a desired expansion that they committed substantial funds to new plants before uncertainties regarding the production processes were removed.

If a particular uncertainty can be investigated quickly and inexpensively, get it out of the way promptly.

Start early with processes involving long lead-times. For example, if a new synthetic food product must have government approval, the tedious process of testing and reviewing evidence may take a year or two longer than preparation for manufacturing and marketing.

Delay revealing plans publicly if other companies can easily copy a novel idea. If substantial social readjustment is necessary, however, an early public announcement is often helpful.

In a particular case, these guides may actually conflict with each other, or other considerations may be dominant. And, as the Boeing 707 example suggests, the possible gains may be large enough to justify following a very risky sequence. Probably the greatest value of the above list is to stimulate careful thought about the sequence that is incorporated into a company's master strategy.

RESOURCE LIMITATIONS

Straining Scarce Resources.   A hard-driving executive does not like to admit that an objective cannot be achieved. He prefers to believe, "Where there's a will there's a way." Yet, an essential aspect of master strategy is deciding what can be done and how fast.

Every enterprise has limits—perhaps severe limits—on its resources. The amount of capital, the number and quality of key personnel, the physical production capacity, or the adaptability of its social structure—none of these is boundless. The tricky issue is how to use these limited resources to the best advantage. We must devise a strategy which is feasible within the inherent restraints.

A household-appliance manufacturer went bankrupt because he failed to adapt his rate of growth to his financial resources. This man had a first-rate product and a wise plan for moving with an "economy model" into an expanding market (following rural electrification). But, to achieve low production costs, he built an oversized plant and launched sales efforts in ten states. His contention was that the kind of company he conceived could not start out on a small scale. Possibly all of these judgments were correct, but they resulted in cash requirements that drained all of his resources before any momentum was achieved. Cost of the partially used plant and of widely scattered sales efforts was so high that no one was willing to bail out the financially strapped venture. His master strategy simply did not fit his resources.

The scarce resource affecting master strategy may be managerial personnel. A management consulting firm, for instance, reluctantly postponed entry into the international arena because only two of its partners had the combination of interest, capacity, and vitality to spend a large amount of time abroad, and these men were also needed to assure continuity of the United States practice. The firm felt that a later start would be better than weak action immediately—even though this probably meant the loss of several desirable clients.

The weight we should attach to scarce resources in the timing of master strategy often requires delicate judgment. Some strain may be endured.

But, how much, how long? For example, in its switch from purchased to company-produced tires, a European rubber company fell behind on deliveries for six months, but, through heroic efforts and pleading with customers, the company weathered the squeeze. Now, company executives believe the timing was wise! If the delay had lasted a full year—and this was a real possibility—the consequence would have approached a catastrophe.

Forming Coalitions. A cooperative agreement with firms in related fields occasionally provides a way to overcome scarce resources. We have already referred to the RCA-Whirlpool arrangement for distributing Whirlpool products. Clearly, in this instance, the timing of Whirlpool's entrance into the market with its own brand depended on forming a coalition with RCA.

EXAMPLES OF COALITIONS

The early development of frozen foods provides us with two other examples of fruitful coalitions. A key element in Birdseye master strategy was to obtain the help of cold-storage warehouses; grocery wholesalers were not equipped to handle frozen foods, and before the demand was clearly established they were slow to move into the new activity. And the Birdseye division of General Foods lacked both managerial and financial resources to venture into national wholesaling.

Similarly, Birdseye had to get freezer cabinets into retail stores, but it lacked the capability to produce them. So, it entered into a coalition with a refrigerator manufacturer to make and sell (or lease) the cabinets to retail stores. This mutual agreement enabled Birdseye to move ahead with its marketing program much faster. With the tremendous growth of frozen foods, neither the cold storage warehouse nor the cabinet manufacturer continued to be necessary, but without them in the early days widespread use of frozen foods would have been delayed three to five years.

Coalitions may be formed for reasons other than "buying time." Nevertheless, when we are trying to round out a workable master strategy, coalitions—or even mergers—may provide the quickest way to overcome a serious deficiency in vital resources.

THE RIGHT TIME TO ACT

Receptive Environment. Conditions in a firm's environment affect the "right time" to make a change. Mr. Ralph Cordiner, for example, testifies that he launched his basic reorganization of General Electric Company only when he felt confident of three years of high business activity because, in his opinion, the company could not have absorbed all the internal readjustments during a period of declining volume and profits.

Judging the right time to act is difficult. Thus, one of the contributing factors to the multimillion-dollar Edsel car fiasco was poor timing. The same automobile launched a year or two earlier might have been favorably received. But buyer tastes changed between the time elaborate market research studies were made and the time when the new car finally appeared in dealer showrooms. By then, preference was swinging away from a big car that "had everything" toward compacts. This mistake in timing and associated errors in strategy cost the Ford Motor Company over a hundred million dollars.

A major move can be too early, as well as too late. We know, for instance, that a forerunner of the modern, self-service supermarket—the Piggly Wiggly—was born too soon. In its day, only a few housewives drove automobiles to shopping centers; and those that could afford cars usually shunned the do-it-yourself mode so prevalent today. In other words, the environment at that time simply was not receptive to what now performs so effectively. Other "pioneers" have also received cool receptions—prefabricated housing and local medical clinics are two.

NO SIMPLE RULES

The preceding discussions of sequence and timing provide no simple rules for these critical aspects of basic strategy. The factors we have mentioned for deciding which front(s) to push first (where is a head start valuable, early attention to major uncertainties, lead-times, significance of secrecy) and for deciding how fast to move (strain on scarce resources, possible coalition to provide resources, and receptivity of the environment) bear directly on many strategy decisions. They also highlight the fundamental nature of sequence and timing in the master strategy for a firm.

Master strategy involves deliberately relating a company's efforts to its particular future environment. We recognize, of course, that both the company's capabilities and its environment continually evolve; consequently, strategy should always be based, not on existing conditions, but on forecasts. Such forecasts, however, are never 100 per cent correct; instead, strategy often seeks to take advantage of uncertainty about future conditions.

This dynamic aspect of strategy should be underscored. The industry outlook will shift for any of numerous reasons. These forces may accelerate growth in some sectors and spell decline in others, may squeeze material supply, may make old sources obsolete, may open new possibilities and snuff out others. Meanwhile, the company itself is also changing—due to the success or failure of its own efforts and to actions of competitors and cooperating firms. And with all of these internal and external changes the combination of thrusts that will provide optimum-synergistic effects undoubtedly will be altered. Timing of actions is the most volatile element of all. It should be adjusted to both the new external situation and the degrees of internal progress on various fronts.

Consequently, frequent reappraisal of master strategy is essential. We must build into the planning mechanisms sources of fresh data that will tell us how well we are doing and what new opportunities and obstacles are appearing on the horizon. The feedback features of control will provide some of these data. In addition, senior managers and others who have contact with various parts of the environment must be ever-sensitive to new developments that established screening devices might not detect.

Hopefully, such reappraisal will not call for sharp reversals in strategy. Typically, a master strategy requires several years to execute and some features may endure much longer. The kind of plan I am discussing here sets the direction for a whole host of company actions, and external reputations and relations often persist for many years. Quick reversals break momentum, require repeated relearning, and dissipate favorable cumulative effects. To be sure, occasionally a sharp break may be necessary. But, if my forecasts are reasonably sound, the adaptations to new opportunities will be more evolution than revolution. Once embarked on a course, we make our reappraisal from our new position—and this introduces an advantage in continuing in at least the same general direction. So, normally, the adaptation is more an unfolding than a completely new start.

Even though drastic modification of our master strategy may be unnecessary, frequent incremental changes will certainly be required to keep abreast of the times. Especially desirable are shifts that anticipate change before the pressures build up. And such farsighted adjustments are possible only if we periodically reappraise and adapt present strategy to new opportunities.

Master strategy is the pivotal planning instrument for large and small enterprises alike. The giant corporations provide us with examples on a grand scale, but the same kind of thinking is just as vital for small firms.

AN EXAMPLE

A terse sketch of the central strategy of one small firm will illustrate this point. The partners of an accounting firm in a city with a quarter-million population predicted faster growth in data processing than in their normal auditing and tax work, yet they knew that most of their clients were too small to use an electronic computer individually. So they foresaw the need for a single, cooperative computer center serving several companies. And they believed that their intimate knowledge of the procedures and the needs of several of these companies, plus the specialized ability of one partner in data processing put them in a unique position to operate such a center. Competition was anticipated from two directions: New models of computers much smaller in size would eventually come on the market—but even if the clients could rent such equipment they would still need programmers and other specialized skills. Also, telephonic hook-ups with International Business Machines service centers appeared likely—but the accounting firm felt its local and more intimate knowledge of each company would give it an advantage over such competition. So, the cooperative computer center looked like a propitious niche.

The chief obstacle was developing a relatively stable volume of work that would carry the monthly rental on the proposed computer. A local insurance company was by far the best prospect for this purpose; it might use half the computer capacity, and then the work for other, smaller companies could be fitted into the remaining time. Consequently, the first major move was to make a deal—a coalition—with the insurance company. One partner was to devote almost his entire time working on details for such an arrangement; meanwhile, the other two partners supported him through their established accounting practice.

We see in this brief example:

The picking of a propitious niche for expansion.

The anticipated synergistic effect of combining auditing services with computing service.

The sequence and timing of efforts to overcome the major limiting factor.

The project had not advanced far enough for much reappraisal, but the fact that two partners were supporting the third provided a built-in check on the question of "how are we doing."

REFERENCE

This article is adapted from a new chapter in *The Process of Management*, second edition, published by Prentice-Hall, Inc., in 1967. Executives who wish to explore the meaning and method of shaping master strategies still further can consult the following materials: E. W. Reilly, "Planning the Strategy of the Business," *Advanced Management*, vol. 20 (December 1955), pp. 8–12; T. Levitt, "Marketing Myopia," *Harvard Business Review*, vol. 38, no. 4 (July–August 1960), pp. 45–66; F. F. Gilmore and R. G. Brandenburg, "Anatomy of Corporate Planning," *Harvard Business Review*, vol. 41, no. 6 (November–December 1962), pp. 61–69; and H. W. Newman and T. L. Berg, "Managing External Relations," *California Management Review*, vol. 5, no. 3 (Spring 1963), pp. 81–86.

STUDENT REVIEW QUESTIONS

1. What ideas does the author offer as aids in developing a master strategy for a firm?
2. What is a "niche" strategy? Provide one example of such a strategy.
3. Discuss Newman's ideas on what he terms, "strategy of sequence."
4. Why does the author conclude that there are "no simple rules for these critical aspects of basic strategy"?
5. The author states that the "central concept [of his article] is just as crucial for hospitals, universities, and other nonprofit ventures" as it is for business firms. Do you agree?

6. Corporate Strategy: Design and Implementation*
(A Slide Presentation)

ROBERT H. CAPLAN III

SLIDE 1

CORPORATE STRATEGY

Basic Concept

> The pattern of objectives, purposes or goals and major policies
> Stated in such a way as to define:
> — What business the company is in,
>   or is to be in.
> — The kind of company it is, or is to be.

SLIDE 2

STRATEGY AS AN ORGANIZATIONAL FUNCTION

Key Premise

> That strategy can and should be:
> — Deliberately determined.
> — Specifically articulated.

Central Objective

> Formulation and execution of a strategy uniquely adapted to:
> — External opportunity.
> — Internal strengths.

SLIDE 3

PRINCIPAL ARGUMENTS FOR A CONSCIOUSLY CONSIDERED STRATEGY

- Inadequacy of stating corporate objectives solely in terms of maximization of profits.
- Necessity of planning ahead for undertakings with long lead times.
- Need for—and advantages from influencing change in the environment, rather than merely responding to such change.
- Utility of making corporate purpose visible as an inspiration to organizational effort.

SLIDE 4

CORPORATE STRATEGY

Two Major Domains

- Formulation.
- Implementation.

> — Real success can be achieved only if both domains are properly integrated and executed with skill and determination.

SLIDE 5

STRATEGY FORMULATION

Formulation of a suitable strategy begins with the identification of opportunities and risks/threats in the environment:

- Technological.
- Economic.
- Social.
- Political.

SLIDE 6

Corporate Strategy: A Framework for Analysis

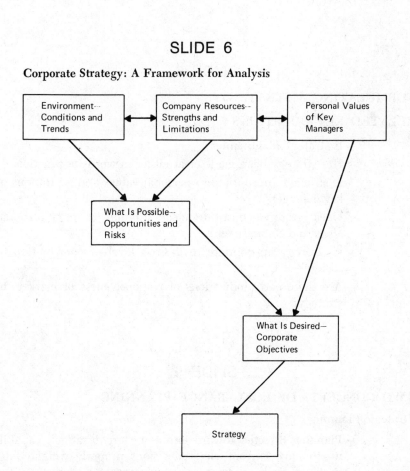

SLIDE 7

FORMULATING A STRATEGY:

CRITERIA FOR EVALUATION

- Internal consistency
- Consistency with environment
- Appropriateness in light of available resources and corporate competences
- Satisfactory degree of risk
- Appropriate time horizon
- Workability

SLIDE 8

FORMULATING A STRATEGY:

RELATED KEY QUESTIONS

- Is strategy identifiable?
- Has strategy been made clear either in words or practice?
- Is strategy appropriate to personal values and aspirations of key managers?
- Does strategy constitute clear stimulus to organizational effort and commitment?
- Is strategy appropriate to desired level of contribution to society?
- Are there early indications of responsiveness of markets to strategy?

SLIDE 9

TWO CONCEPTS OF LONG-RANGE PLANNING

Strategic Planning

- Planning directed toward improving organization's capability to have current major decisions properly weighted by in-depth study of long-term environmental change.

— Focus on adaptation to external change, particularly that which creates opportunities and threats.

Action Planning

— Procedure for describing in detail the organization's future results and supporting actions—with present strategy as a given.
— Extension of conventional planning—budgeting process to a longer time frame—frequently five years.

SLIDE 10

MAJOR DISTINCTIONS—TWO FORMS OF LRP

Action Planning

- Heavy involvement of operating managers.
- Based on strategy *already* formulated and adopted.
- *Comprehensive* treatment of *whole* business, with projected results and plans for their accomplishment.
- Highly *structured,* with systematic procedures.

Strategic Planning

- Limited to *top* management with staff assistance.
- Involves consideration of *changes* in strategy.
- Focus primarily on major strategic *issues* and alternatives for their resolutions.
- In general, fairly unstructured.

SLIDE 11

MAJOR PROPOSITIONS:

IMPLEMENTATION OF STRATEGY

- The chief determinant of organizational structure and the processes by which tasks are assigned and performances motivated, rewarded and controlled should be the strategy of the organization.

- Organizational performance is effective to the extent that individual energy is successfully directed toward organizational goals.
- An organization's management control system should be built around performance dimensions critical to success, as determined by corporate strategy.

SLIDE 12

IMPLEMENTATION OF STRATEGY—PRINCIPAL ELEMENTS

- Organizational design
- Information systems
- Management control system
- Reward system
- Staffing and management development
- Leadership

SLIDE 13

IMPLEMENTATION OF STRATEGY

Organizational Design

- Select the basic structure best suited for executing the chosen strategy.
- Identify key tasks to be performed and kinds of decisions required.
- Assign responsibility for the foregoing, together with appropriate allocation of authority.
- Provide for coordination of activities thus separated:

  —Hierarchy of supervision.

  —System of committees.

  —Project teams, task forces, etc.

SLIDE 14

IMPLEMENTATION OF STRATEGY

Information Systems

- Design and install information systems adequate for:
    - —Coordinating divided functions.
    - —Supervisory tasks.
    - —Feedback loop on adequacy of strategy.

- Augment formal systems with informal processes so as to avoid:
    - —Unbalanced perceptions.
    - —Blind spots.

SLIDE 15

IMPLEMENTATION OF STRATEGY

Management Control System

- Design system to facilitate the management control tasks— assuring the effective accomplishment of strategy in an efficient manner:
    - —Goal setting.
    - —Planning and budgeting.
    - —Performance measurement and comparison with predetermined goals and standards.

- Augment formal system based on quantitative dimensions of performance with processes for assessing the qualitative elements of performance.
- Integrate formal system with the social controls arising out of the informal organization.
- Provide for effective coupling with:
    - —Reward system.
    - —Management development.
    - —Strategic planning.

- Establish audit programs adequate for insuring:
    - —Creditability of performance information.

—Compliance with corporate policies.

—Visibility of dysfunctional activity.

SLIDE 16

IMPLEMENTATION OF STRATEGY

Reward System

- Adopt a comprehensive plan for compensation, consistent with corporate strategy and needs of personnel:

    —Base salary.

    —Incentive compensation.

    —Equity participation.

- Provide specialized forms of recognition designed to:

    —Reward unusual accomplishments.

    —Fit individual needs.

- Incorporate system of constraints and penalties, as needed to constrain dysfunctional behavior.

SLIDE 17

IMPLEMENTATION OF STRATEGY

Staffing & Management Development

- Establish a selective system of executive recruiting based on the needs of corporate strategy, the philsophy of management, and the organizational climate.
- Assign individuals to essential tasks in accordance with the knowledge and skills they possess or can develop.

    —Adjust assignments to the nature of available skills, where necessary.

- Provide for the continuing development of requisite technical and managerial skills by means of a soundly conceived and effectively administered program:

—On the job.

—Formal instruction and study.

SLIDE 18

IMPLEMENTATION OF STRATEGY

Leadership

- Provide the leadership necessary for the successful formulation and implementation of strategy, integrating the following roles into a harmonious unity:

    —Architect of strategy.

    —Organization leader.

    —Personal leader.

- Lead in building and maintaining an organizational climate conducive to successful accomplishment of strategic purposes:

    —Commitment to chosen strategy.

    —Motivation for accomplishment.

    —Encouragement of cooperation.

    —Development of individual competence.

SLIDE 19

PRINCIPAL BENEFITS

- Facilitate adaption to environmental change in an optimal manner.
- Provide framework for internal consistency of policies and practices.
- Facilitate the exercise of influence over the direction of change in the environment.
- Permit greater delegation of responsibility and authority, and greater reliance on "self control."

SLIDE 20

Strategy: Design and Implementation Interrelationship of Elements

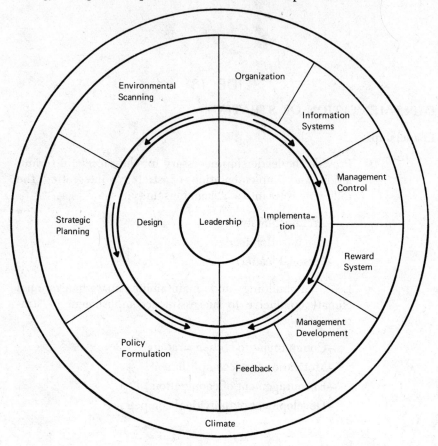

- Contribute to a sense of mission and commitment to corporate objectives.

SLIDE 21

UNIQUE RESPONSIBILITIES OF TOP MANAGEMENT

- Monitoring the environment.
- Strategic planning.
- Securing required resources.

- Appraising managerial performance.
- Developing successors.
- Providing leadership.
- Monitoring effectiveness of chosen strategy.

STUDENT REVIEW QUESTIONS

1. What are the advantages for an organization of a consciously developed strategy?
2. Discuss the interrelationships among environmental factors, organizational resources, personal values of key managers, and the organization's strategy.
3. What distinctions does Caplan make between "strategic" planning and "action" planning?
4. Discuss the relationships among the organization's management control system and its reward in the implementation of strategy.
5. Do you think the implementation of strategy is easier in business organizations than in nonprofit organizations? Why or why not?

chapter 3

Resource Profile: Assessment of Internal Strengths and Weaknesses

Objectives and Results of Comprehensive Analysis
The Role of Internal Analysis in Evaluating and
Formulating Strategy
The Process of Analysis
Internal Areas for Analysis
Analyzing Management, Departments, and Functions
    Management
    Finance and Accounting
    Marketing
    Production, Manufacturing, and Engineering
    Research and Development
    Other Areas
The Human Side of the Enterprise
Top Management Viewed in Perspective
Summary
Readings

OBJECTIVES AND RESULTS OF COMPREHENSIVE ANALYSIS

THE INTERNAL ANALYSIS of an organization is a basic requirement in the study of business policy and in the development of strategy. To be effective in evaluating and formulating strategy, both student and operating manager must understand the analytical process and be able to analyze a corporation or other organization in breadth and depth. For the active manager, internal analysis is an assessment of a live functioning company

106

and its operations; for the student, it is an appraisal of a simulated situation such as in a case or business game. In each circumstance, the ability to analyze well and to make sound decisions based on clear analysis is the hallmark of effectiveness. The analysis of internal resources will tell the analyst what the organization is capable of doing in view of its resource profile.

Procedurally, in performing the internal analysis, the analyst assembles and analyzes available information such as facts, opinions, statements, and observations, and also notes what is not known. Such analysis facilitates the preparation of a profile of resources, strengths and weaknesses about the organization as a whole and also its various parts. From this profile, judgments are made about the organization and its parts, about the people in the organization, and about the way in which the organization has been managed. If in fact a strategy is in effect, judgments may be made about the strategy itself or various facets of it. *Primarily, however, the internal analysis of resources should tell the analyst what the company is capable of doing; what it has the resources to do. This might well be different from what it is doing or what it wishes to do.*

The internal analysis by itself reveals much about where the company has been (or what it has been doing) and where it is now (or what it now is doing). It also should reveal something about the ways in which the future is being approached or not approached. However, to have a complete analysis of an organization's situation, factors external to it must be weighed heavily. Combining the internal and external analysis will produce the complete assessment which will allow the analyst ". . . to be able to see what the business is, what it does, and what it can do."[1] *It will allow him to see not only what the organization is capable of doing in light of its resources, but often what it ought to be doing considering the external environment in which it operates.*

Thus, in the process of evaluating and/or formulating strategy, the ultimate objective of the internal analysis is to draw a profile of the entity and its resources and capabilities that provides both a segmented and integrated internal picture of the strengths and weaknesses of the entire organization. The internal analysis is the subject of this chapter. Chapter 4 discusses the external analysis. The two chapters combined provide a thorough consideration of organizational analysis.

THE ROLE OF INTERNAL ANALYSIS IN EVALUATING AND FORMULATING STRATEGY

In developing a strategy (or evaluating one), a logical starting point is the organization's present strategy and the resources it has or may be

---

[1] P. Drucker, *Managing for Results* (New York: Harper & Row, Publishers, 1964), p. 127.

able to acquire or develop. Most managers and all students typically deal with "going concerns" in their contacts with policy and strategy and, therefore, this exposition assumes as a subject the "going concern"; that is, the organization that has been functioning for some time.

To determine "where we are now," the internal analysis must consider what the firm's resources are; what business the firm is in; what its objectives, plans, and policies are; and how well it is achieving them. For example, the appraisal of a firm's present strategy must answer the major question: Is this strategy consistent with the various resources of the enterprise? But an even more important query is whether the available resources are appropriate to any changes in strategy or new strategies which may be under consideration. The results and conclusions of the analysis, although important in judging how well the company has done and where it is now, are crucial ingredients in determining what the future strategy might be, can be, and in ultimately deciding what it *should* be. Later chapters will indicate that the "should" aspect of strategy is often more heavily influenced by factors such as the external environment of the organization. But it must always be recognized that any action initiated after viewing the environment must be undertaken with full understanding of the internal capabilities and resources of the organization.

While indicating what the firm's resources are, the internal analysis also judges how well these assets have been utilized by management. It also suggests how resources might be utilized in the future by the same management. Thus, such analysis requires the analyst to appraise the management's utilization of resources; its formulation and implementation of strategy; and its performance in the various functions required by the strategy. The internal analysis, then, is a very important element of the process of strategy formulation and evaluation. But it is only one element of the complex process of strategy formulation, and as noted earlier, it is only part of the overall analysis of a total organization.

To illustrate this point, the internal analysis of a defense-oriented company in the early 1970s would have considered much about how the company was allocating its resources of people, inventories, plant, equipment, and so forth. It would also have observed sources of funds, organizational structure, motivation systems and more such internal aspects of the organization. Results of past operations would have been analyzed as well as the present position. But without including the external environment, the analysis would have been incomplete. It would not have considered changes in public opinion toward defense spending, not have anticipated government cutting defense contracts, or even technological changes occurring in the industry. However, the internal analysis is a start toward the total analysis of this type of organization, or any other, since it clarifies what the organization is capable of in light of its resource profile.

THE PROCESS OF ANALYSIS

Although the major topic of this chapter is the "what" aspect of internal analysis, the analyst must know "how to" analyze, as well as "what to" analyze. The mastery of data, information, facts, and opinions is the beginning of this process. Because in action situations so great a premium is placed upon decisions, many students and managers will move directly to decisions and action after mastering and perhaps marshaling information. Yet, proper analysis requires the reaching of conclusions or judgments based upon the facts, opinions, observations, and other evidence available.

Conclusions may be of various kinds but a common one is that a problem or problems exist, or an opportunity is present. The precise articulation of specific problem or opporunity is for most of us a decidedly difficult task. One wag has said that, "Washington is a land of solutions looking for problems." Solving the wrong problem, dealing only with symptoms, or making decisions in the wrong areas, is a common criticism made of administrators and managers. Yet, all are under great pressure to solve problems and to make decisions.

If the analytical process is understood and undertaken in a fashion appropriate to the magnitude and time dimensions of the situation, then the probability of an appropriate decision is increased markedly. An appropriate decision addresses the right problem or opportunity considering the time, financial, political, human, and other constraints of the situation. The major steps useful in an organizational decision-making situation are noted below.

EXHIBIT 3–1
Steps in an Analytical Decision-Making Process

Gather and analyze data about the organization, its environment, operations, and people.

Based on these data, formulate conclusions about the organization and its environments, operations, people and other resources.

Determine and appraise feasible alternatives to improve particular conditions in light of established criteria.

Select an alternative which is most "appropriate" in view of previously established criteria.

Implement the selected alternative, and initiate an appropriate feedback system to monitor results if one is not presently in use.

Once information has been analyzed and conclusions have been reached, it is necessary to consider alternative solutions and actions. At this point in the decision-making process, decisions will not be far behind. In evaluating and formulating strategy where the decisions made are so crucial to the existence of the company as well as basic to its successful operation, thorough analysis is a mandatory prerequisite to decision making. The stakes are high for success is always uncertain, and various types of costs must be incurred. The time and/or financial costs of analysis must be met. Yet the probability of effective decision making increases when the decisions are based upon sound (albeit expensive and time-consuming) analysis. Because basic policy and strategy are so crucial to an organization's health, constant review and necessary change are important. The basis for this constant review is, of course, a continuing analysis.

INTERNAL AREAS FOR ANALYSIS

What must be analyzed by the student or practitioner of a business or organizational policy? The total entity and everything in and around it. Of course, all subjects are not considered with the same degree of thoroughness, and some may be neglected because of time and other costs. But, the desired analysis is most demanding. One approach considers the company as a composite of numerous parts and requires an analysis of each functional activity (marketing, finance, production, and so forth). Another method attempts to describe the essential nature of the company, for example, by considering it as a company in the automobile industry which will rely primarily on the highest quality of workmanship and advanced engineering to achieve its success in selling to those customers who appreciate this aspect in automotive products. The most common method employed in corporations is a combination of these two approaches.[2] Thus, in performing this combination analysis, one must first examine separately all parts of the company, then observe the interrelationships between the parts, and synthesize the parts into a view of the whole company. Then the basic nature or fundamental key of the company's existence or success must be sought and articulated as accurately as possible. This combined approach for analyzing the relevant internal aspects of an organization will be the subject of the remainder of this chapter.

In examining the parts of a business organization for purposes of internal analysis, it is necessary to consider the departments or functional areas of accounting and control, marketing, finance, production, engineering, research and development, personnel and industrial relations, logistics, and also lesser areas of activity such as legal and others that may be appropriate for a particular firm. For an agency such as the

---

[2] Brian W. Scott, *Long Range Planning in American Industry* (New York: American Management Association, 1965), p. 79.

Peace Corps, some areas for inspection are educational endeavors, community projects, human resources, and financial sources and needs. Other nonprofit organizations must also be segmented in an orderly manner before analysis. Information will be gathered and digested, problems and symptoms will be exposed, and conclusions will be reached. The result shall be a profile of strengths and weaknesses within, between, and among various departments and functional areas of organization.

This profile will cover one important dimension of the internal analysis, that of the functions which must be analyzed in the particular firm. The second dimension is the management of the organization. The analysis of management requires a study of how the managerial functions have been and are being performed. To be considered are the functions of planning, controlling, organizing, directing, staffing, motivating, delegating, and communicating. The same functions are also applicable to nonprofit organizations. But as functions do not occur in a vacuum, the analysis of these must be cross-referenced to the departments and/or functional areas of the organization to gain a thorough picture of management performance. Analyzing the organization structure, staffing, control, and motivation of the accounting-control area in a decentralized company and of the nursing staff in a hospital, are two examples of "cross-referencing" departments and functions in analysis.

Finally, in achieving an internal view of the organization, the human side of the enterprise, its individuals, their personalities, ambitions, values, motivations, and so forth must be reviewed carefully. This human component that permeates the functional and managerial areas is often the most important aspect of the entire analysis.[3]

The major areas to be considered in the internal analysis of an organization will now be more fully discussed, but for a summary view, Exhibit 3–2 should be useful to the student by clarifying the areas discussed thus

EXHIBIT 3–2
Internal Areas of Analysis

(1)	+	(2)	+	(3)	+	(4)	=	(5)
Analysis of functional areas		Analysis of management areas		Analysis of human side of the enterprise		Analysis of interrelationship among 1, 2, and 3		Comprehensive analysis of internal organization

far as necessary areas for analysis. An exhaustive dissection of each would be of limited value here since various checklists and matrices for

---

[3] For a thorough exposition of this point of view, the reader is referred to James G. Cyert and Richard M. March, *The Behavioral Theory of the Firm* (Englewood Cliffs, N.J.: Prentice-Hall, Inc., 1963).

analysis do exist.[4] A short introduction to each of the particular areas will reveal the scope of the task of analyzing a firm from an internal point of view.

ANALYZING MANAGEMENT, DEPARTMENTS, AND FUNCTIONS

Management

The internal analysis of an organization, with the objective of developing a profile of strengths and weaknesses, begins and ends with the management of the organization. Actually, management is considered throughout the analysis for everything else is (or should be) dependent upon the leadership or actions of the firm's management group. The profile of strengths and weaknesses is an evaluation of management in the light of what it has done and not done, and what it has achieved and not achieved. Furthermore, management should also be evaluated within the perspective of the job that it faced, its present job, and the job to be faced in the future. If more than one group of managers is involved, the respective time periods should be separated in order that each group may be evaluated in view of the job at a particular time. And beyond that, various individuals and groups within the overall management may also be evaluated separately if additional understanding or value is gained by the analyst in so doing.

To assess the management of an organization, it is necessary to consider how well the management functions were performed and with what results. This distinction is made because results alone do not always tell the entire story. Sometimes firms show short-run successes in their financial reports during times when mismanagement is setting in. As the management functions take place largely within the departments and functional areas of the firm, an analysis of those areas, which also considers the performance of the management functions, will provide considerable insight to the analyst. Furthermore, in appraising management it is necessary to examine the overall direction of the firm in the broad area of strategy formulation and implementation. An analysis limited to functional areas alone will not cover well this aspect of overall organizational management.

Thus, management is actually being appraised as the individual functional areas and departments are being reviewed. In addition, management is further scrutinized in a summary evaluation that reflects the overall company as a functioning entity. For example, a review of all

---

[4] For two books which offer helpful checklists for analyzing areas of a firm, see W. T. Greenwood's *Business Policy: A Management Audit Approach* (New York: Macmillan Company, 1967). Also R. B. Buchele, *Business Policy in Growing Firms* (San Francisco: Chandler Publishing Company, 1967).

functions may reveal that the company is strong in research and engineering but less so in marketing, particularly within advertising. Its accounting may be excellent as far as reporting past results is concerned, but of little help to management in its planning and control of operations. Finally, a summary view is required which assesses the company as a totality (from an internal view). It is in view of all such considerations that management is ultimately judged. Exhibit 3–3 is helpful in appraising either functional or "corporate" management.

EXHIBIT 3–3
Some "Key Questions" to Be Asked When Appraising a "Corporate" Management or Functional Management (based on internal analysis)

What situation did the management face initially?

What results have been achieved?

What is the present status of the organization or particular department?

Where is the organization or particular department heading at this time?

What kind of people are involved and how do they behave and perform?

How long have the managers been involved in their present job situations, and what have been their previous experiences?

What is being done at present?

What should management be doing that it is neglecting or not doing enough of?

What is revealed in the situation based on opinions of those involved in the organization or department?

How important is the particular department or function to the overall operation of the organization?

Finance and Accounting

The securing and utilization of funds, together with planning for both, controlling expenditures, and reporting all important transactions and results to appropriate parties is of crucial importance to both profit-oriented and nonprofit institutions. Thus, this area is a likely place to begin an analysis of any organization. Gaining insight into the financial situation may place the entity's condition into perspective relatively quickly. Many hard facts can be gathered in the initial perusal of operations, and tentative conclusions can be readily drawn. Then further probing, figuring, and analyzing can provide information and an understanding in considerable depth.

Financial statements offer an abundance of information about the present position of an organization as well as showing the results of operations over time. The current portion of the balance sheet tells of cash, receivables, and inventories, and corresponding liabilities. The job of the analyst is to "make the figures talk." Ratios may be calculated and various formulas may be employed to learn more. But what about the nature of the inventory? An inventory of small cars in early 1974, for example, was about as liquid as cash. But a perishable commodity or high-style product may quickly become almost worthless even though it appears on the balance sheet at considerable value. Looking behind figures, then, to see what is actually represented is a mark of solid analysis.

A common tendency of students is to state conclusions rather than the facts when analyzing financial statements. Rather than reporting, for example, that receivables turn over every 45 days, some will assert that the company is too slow in collecting its bills. But the competitive situation or the company's stage of development might mitigate against speeding up collections. Thus, the first response to information from the financial statements should be factual and substantially quantitative. Inferences and conclusions can be drawn later. A similar caution could be offered to the analyst who, after quickly calculating a ratio, concludes that the company has too much debt and is too heavily leveraged. But a study of the company's return on investment and the nature of its business might indicate that excellent financial management was being employed. The balance sheet and income statements, then, provide factual information within the limitations of accounting principles. Inferences and conclusions, however, are better made after considering other information as well, rather than relying solely upon the statements.

As valuable as is the information provided by financial statements, the analyst should realize that it is historical when it becomes available, and often from a relatively distant past. The balance sheet position is of a specific past date, and the operating results from a period gone by. These data can show much of what has happened and much of what the situation was, but factually that is all they can show. Trends can be drawn and extended into the future and it is wise to draw them. Yet, the basic assumption is usually that conditions will remain similar enough to extrapolate data; this important limitation must be recognized, and all relevant data utilized to test this assumption.

Some analysts might argue that the only real problems are financial problems contending that the organization which is financially sound usually can survive. Although this is a gross oversimplification, it does indicate the crucial role of the finance function. Even the most noble of nonprofit institutions must pay its bills to continue its operations. Likewise, even though profit as such is not an objective to such organizations, an excess of income over expenses allows churches and universities to grow larger and stronger, and to accomplish better those objectives which truly make them "nonprofit" institutions. Thus, regardless of the type of institution, the finance function must be examined in order to gain some insights into its "health." Has a university, for example, balanced its income against its expenditures over a particular period? Failure to do so caused the demise of many during the early 1970s. Has the corporation being analyzed lost money over the past year? Or is a new and growing company in a cash bind because of notable success in marketing its product? Finally, in a relatively mature company, are prices declining in the face of rising costs to bring about the seemingly ubiquitous "profit squeeze"? These are some of the questions which can be asked when studying financial statements. While some answers can be obtained directly from an analysis of the statements, it is often necessary to combine the financial data with information from other areas of the organization to achieve the insights necessary to draw sound conclusions.

Results, then, are important even though they may be somewhat outdated when received by the analyst. They indicate the financial consequences of earlier decisions and conditions. But significantly, study of the finance and accounting areas teaches much about management that goes beyond this area, and provides insight to management's way of running its business. The management functions of planning, controlling, and communicating vitally involve financial information. Thus, the thorough analysis of the financial area will go far beyond operating results to explore whether management is performing well some of its important functions. The analysis will include such questions as those given in Exhibit 3–4.

EXHIBIT 3–4
Some "Key Questions" in Finance and Accounting Areas to Be Utilized in Evaluating Management of the Functions and of the Organization

What are financial results and the financial status of the organization? (Use appropriate ratios, percentage analysis, and other techniques.)

Is a financial plan tied into the overall strategic and operating plans for the organization?

Who is involved in putting together the plan or budget? Is it only the controller or is operating management playing an active role?

Are cash flow projections and pro forma statements prepared, and are they utilized in planning?

What reports are prepared and which managers receive them? Are the reports appropriate, timely, and utilized by managers to plan and control operations, or by top management to evaluate and reformulate strategy?

Do reports compare results against plans or standards and is corrective action taken where warranted?

EXHIBIT 3–4   (continued)

What is the attitude of people toward planning and controlling documents like the budget? Are these ignored, subverted, or utilized as a proper motivational element in the organization?

If a computer is utilized, does it provide meaningful information in timely fashion, or does it produce paper by the ton which is of no particular value to management?

Having reviewed the financial area, one has learned much about any organization and its management. Particularly, financial results indicate whether revenues have been increasing in a profitable manner, or whether the opposite is true. And the financial status of the firm reveals much about its relative strength or weakness. Together the financial results and present financial status (including financial planning and control systems) tell much about company management. A broad perspective is drawn within which to proceed to other areas for analysis. Much of what is learned is about the past, however, and only predictions can be made of the future. But predictions may at least be based on sound information and observations of management, its activities, and its results. To conclude at this stage, however, that one knows enough would be shortsighted. Other areas of operation and management also warrant attention, and should be analyzed with the background information about finance available. Interrelating, subsequently, what is seen in other areas with what has been learned in the financial and accounting analysis, will bring to light new information and allow new conclusions to be drawn. This is a major advantage of thorough analysis, and drawing insights from the interrelationships between and among areas is actually creating new insights and carrying analysis to a deeper and more valuable dimension.

As should be recognized at this stage, the analysis described thus far is important to strategy. It shows much about the financial resources of the firm and how well they have been and are being utilized. It reveals further much about management and the systems utilized in the process of managing. All of this is important in considering the appropriateness of present and future strategies, as well as the implementation of strategies, past, present, and future. Upon this foundation an examination of the marketing area is an appropriate subsequent building block.

Marketing

Analysis of the marketing area from the overall perspective so necessary to students of business policy requires inclusion of the product-market strategy and much that is *external* to the firm. Although this vital aspect will be covered primarily in the next chapter, it must be mentioned at times here because of its importance in the overall mosaic of the marketing function. Marketing is the area which brings together the organization and many external parties and environments so crucial to the very existence of the organization. It is an absolutely vital requirement that profit-oriented and nonprofit organizations alike look outside to customers, competitors, and various changes in the technological, social, and other environments. To have this external outlook is a necessary charge to the marketing members of an organization. It is they who usually bridge the gap between the entity and those people and events outside the entity which so vitally affect its future. In market research, market analysis, market forecasting, sales forecasting, advertising, applications engineering, and direct selling, the marketing organization carries out the mission of bringing information back to the organization and forward to its customers. The marketing area is a vital communications link between the organization and the outside world. It is by acting effectively in this capacity that the marketing group makes its greatest contributions. If this job is done well, sales at an appropriate price should follow, or in nonprofit terms, revenue at appropriate cost levels should result. The failure to heed these marketing-oriented issues has spelled trouble during the 1970s for some hospitals, universities, and public agencies as well as for numerous companies.

Since attention will be devoted to this area in the following chapter, this chapter will raise only some of the major questions, issues and relationships to be considered when analyzing the marketing function within the perspective of overall policy. Particularly important are some interrelationships with other areas within the organization. Some of the major internal relationships of the marketing group are with the research and development, product engineering, and manufacturing personnel, and with the long-range planning area if this is a separate activity. A major question concerns how and in what ways marketing communicates with these groups, and vice versa. Is there an organizational arrangement to ensure that such groups communicate with marketing and marketing with them? Product managers, project managers, and information coordinators of various kinds have been employed by various organizations striving to accomplish, among other things, effective communication between marketing and other departments, and hence between the outside world and the internal organization. If other areas are to perform as they should, they must have information to utilize in decision making, and some of the crucial information must come from marketing members of the organization. The sales forecast as a basis for the budget and financial plan is an obvious illustration, as is market research information for guiding product development. Likewise, the price at which a product might be sold will often determine how finely it should be engineered. Thus, the analyst must determine the effectiveness of the company's marketing communication and information? He must note the part marketing plays in the organization and whether there is a "marketing perspective" existent in the organization. What relationships do the people in marketing have with others in the firm and do they play as significant a role as their function usually warrants? The answers to these and similar questions will place the marketing function into perspective in the overall analysis of the organization.

Beyond the broader aspects of the marketing analysis of an entity, however, is a demand for more detailed analysis. As in other areas, a list of "key questions" such as those given in Exhibit 3–5 will be helpful to the analyst in meeting this demand.

EXHIBIT 3–5
Some "Key Questions" to Be Asked When Appraising the Marketing Area and Marketing Management

With regard to an overall perspective, what areas of the total marketing job are being performed by the firm, and should these be dropped, or others undertaken or emphasized?

Is market research being utilized and has it been a factor in the past in determining what products should be offered and to whom?

Regarding the product line, how does it sell overall, and what is the relative success of each product in terms of sales and profit contribution?

How is the product sold, through which channels, and is there reason to consider changing or shifting emphasis due to new developments in distribution?

In the area of pricing, has any study been made of sales volume and price relationships? Has a pricing policy been established, for example, to "skim the cream" or "penetrate the market" to maximize share?

How is the product or service promoted; what means are utilized and are they coordinated with one another?

What is or are the key elements of competitive strategy for the firm in the marketing area such as quality, speed of delivery, low price, or service by a broad and deep sales force and support personnel? Are the firm's policies in these areas appropriate to industry structure and conditions? Or should changes be considered because the industry has changed?

Is marketing policy attuned to competition, technological change, and other environmental aspects which could bear importantly on the firm?

Initially, when studying the marketing function, as was true in the area of finance, the job of the analyst is to observe carefully and to obtain information consisting of facts, opinions, recommendations, and other sorts of data. Armed with information, he can evaluate and draw conclusions about the adequacies and inadequacies, strengths and weaknesses of the marketing area of the firm. As marketing has many interrelationships both inside and outside of the firm, these must be observed and evaluated as to their effectiveness. Then within the overview drawn up after a thorough analysis of the marketing area, the product-market strategy of the organization can be determined and articulated. Is there a stated product-market strategy and has it been followed? Or is a "sort of" strategy in effect, one not really clarified for members of the organization? The analysis of the marketing function answers these questions and thus reveals much about the firm's overall strategy or the absence thereof.

The analysis suggested thus far leads to conclusions about the management of the marketing area which may be supplemented by considering other specific questions. What kinds of people are involved, with what backgrounds, outlooks, and of what ages? Are they truly marketing-oriented individuals or nonmarketers filling marketing jobs? In view of other parts of the organizational analysis (especially finance and accounting), how have these individuals performed, as a group and as individuals? What quantitative results have been achieved and what else (qualitatively) has been done? What management functions have been performed and how well? Is the area well organized and staffed with a good marketing control system in effect, and does marketing management plan well? Finally, does the marketing group bring appropriate and timely information into the company to be utilized in decisions of a strategic nature? The answers to these and other questions will aid greatly in evaluating the marketing function in a firm as well as the management of that function. Analyzing the marketing function will eventually lead to recommendations of what to do about marketing and marketing management in the organization, and ultimately to strategy considerations of an overall corporate nature.

Production, Manufacturing, and Engineering

In analyzing the areas of production, manufacturing, engineering, and related functions, the student should be familiar with the relationships of these areas to the marketing area. After a brief discussion of key relationships with marketing, these areas will be considered in relation to other areas within a firm. Finally, the areas themselves will be analyzed in some detail.

As advocated above in the analysis of the marketing function, production should rely heavily upon information from sales and marketing. Production schedules usually are based upon sales orders and forecasts if the firm is making "what it can sell." As a first question the analysts might ask: are production or manufacturing and engineering communicating with and listening to the representatives of marketing? Is the firm in fact "engineering and producing" what it can sell? Further, are products engineered with the selling price in mind, and are products manufactured in the volume and on a schedule which causes the market to be satisfied? While these questions imply a "marketing concept" oriented company, one must recognize that production and manufacturing management are expected to meet budgets and to perform within cost limits. Are they doing so and is marketing and/or sales management cooperating in this endeavor? Or are production schedules disrupted constantly to satisfy pressure from marketing, such as excessive special orders, immediate deliveries and other such impositions? Insights into the relationships between the marketing and production areas provide a logical transition from the marketing analysis into the analysis of production, manufacturing and engineering.

The manufacturing and engineering groups in a firm also have communications with and interactions with areas other than marketing. They also must work effectively with research and development in order that the items developed may be manufactured and engineered in a manner which considers the cost involved and the effectiveness of the finished product. These demands spotlight the constant dilemma and task of manufacturing: to maintain quality and reliability, but at as low a cost as possible. Again, a review of some "key questions" will aid the analyst in determining how well this dilemma is being solved. (See Exhibit 3–6.)

EXHIBIT 3–6

Some "Key Questions" to Be Asked When Appraising the Areas of Production, Manufacturing, and Engineering

What do the financial statements indicate about costs? What are the present levels of costs in the production or manufacturing area, and the cost trends both as absolutes and as percentages? Are these rising in relation to sales dollar volume, and is this due to cost increases or a "cost-price squeeze" which might even see unit prices declining as costs increase?

What about inventory levels and composition of the inventory by types such as "in-process" and finished goods? Is inventory rising beyond what might be expected? What is the "key" cost element such as labor or material, and is attention being directed to control of this element? Does a cost control program exist, are there standards, and are these action-oriented, current, and useful?

Does the firm have effective production control and scheduling and is communications effective in these functions?

Do production and manufacturing personnel receive accurate, timely, and helpful information from quality control, cost control, sales, and other groups whose information is vital to functioning of the production area?

EXHIBIT 3–6   (continued)

Are facilities and physical resources adequate, and in good repair, and how do these compare with competition?

Are new developments in machinery and procedures appraised on a regular basis?

What are replacement policies for machinery and equipment, and are replacements in kind or is the latest and most efficient purchased, or at least considered as an alternative?

What is the level of fixed assets and how does it compare to the industry? What is the nature of these assets—are they multipurpose and flexible or narrow, single-purpose elements? Is the plant and equipment highly automated or is labor a very important aspect?

What is the place of and relationship to production of the various engineering groups in the firm?

How important is engineering to the particular organization and what kind of engineering is "key"?

What is spent in this area and is the company getting full value for its dollar?

Is engineering oriented to the market and customers, to the product aspects only, or to both of these?

What is the reputation of the firm in this area and what is called for by industry and environmental conditions?

With regard to the logistics area including purchasing and materials management, how are these functions organized and operating?

What relationships and communications do these areas have with production or manufacturing and marketing?

What is the situation regarding cost and effectiveness in these areas?

Have management science, generally, and the computer, specifically, been utilized effectively?

Although these lists are not purported to be exhaustive, they do channel the analyst into the key areas to be considered. As in other areas already discussed, the production, manufacturing, and engineering departments must be analyzed thoroughly to gain information not only about the areas themselves, but also about interrelationships of these with other areas. Also important is the effect that production and its related areas have had on the financial statements. Much information can be gathered, then evaluated. Judgments and conclusions will follow which will weigh relative strengths and weaknesses. Managers will be evaluated in light of what they have done or have not done, what they have accomplished and not accomplished. Management should be viewed both as a group and as individuals as to background, age, experience, and other factors. Not only top production management but backup management must be considered and evaluated in the context of the production, manufacturing, and engineering functions.

Having reached this point in his or her analysis, the student or manager has completed much of the internal analysis. The financial, physical, and personnel resources have been considered in several key functional areas of the organization. But other areas in any organization are also important, and a major area is often that of research and development.

Research and Development

The importance of the research and development function varies, of course, with the nature of the organization in question. In some cases it is of minor importance such as in retailing operations and others which do not directly produce a product. The R.&D. of concern to the analyst is normally a product-oriented effort. A broader interpretation of research and development, however, would recognize this area to be important to even a wider spectrum of firms than those with a product orientation. If the concept of research and development is extended to markets, organizational research, applications engineering, and human development, almost every organization becomes involved. But the current usage of the term "research and development" is oriented toward products and it is in this sense that the topic will be discussed.

Although many firms develop new products for purchasers and ultimate consumers, those with technically oriented products are most involved in research and development. Numerous dramatic examples are available to illustrate the effect that the technological revolution has had on industrial companies. Many today are making only a few of the products that made up their lines only eight or ten years ago. The remarkable advances in solid state electronics and miniaturization, electrical-mechanical technology, and other fields have received much attention. Companies in these industries, or in industries related in any way to these basic industries, *must* engage in research and development. For many social organizations R.&D. is accomplished at great expense, but it is recognized as a vital necessity if the firm is to prosper, or perhaps even survive. Between 1953 and 1960 alone, Xerox Corporation is reputed to have "invested" nearly $70 million in the development of xerographic products, but the result was the establishment of one of the world's most successful companies. Many nonprofit entities such as hospitals and universities also engage heavily in research and development in health and education. They expend large sums in support of medical and educational staffs and equipment to improve their products, services, and contributions to society. For all organizations, insights can be gained to the R.&D. area by asking "key questions" such as those in Exhibit 3–7.

EXHIBIT 3–7

Some "Key Questions" to Be Asked When Appraising the Area of Research and Development

What is the organization's commitment to R.&D.? Does the industry spend heavily on R.&D.? Does the nature of the product call for continual development, or does the nature of the consumer or competition demand continual advancement in products?

What would be the "payoff" for a breakthrough in the product area? Does the opportunity appear to be realistic in terms of risk and return? Would a major social good be accomplished by success in R.&D. (such as polio vaccine)?

How much can the organization afford to devote to the R.&D. effort? How much can or should be devoted to any one product or project? What risks can the organization take in view of its resources?

What technical expertise does the organization possess? Given the organization's skill profile, what areas of endeavor in R.&D. would most likely produce success? What does the organization's charter call for regarding R.&D.? (For example, should a municipal hospital spend large sums of taxpayer money on medical research?)

Is the R.&D. resource being utilized well? What have been the results in terms of new products or improvements in old products? Has the organization had a satisfactory stream of new products, or improvements? From which products do sales materialize, old ones or the new?

How is the R.&D. effort organized? How are communications achieved with marketing and production, and are relations with these functional groups satisfactory and productive?

How is creativity encouraged? Has the development aspect of R.&D. been overstressed with adverse effects on creative personnel? Is the management of R.&D. viewed as a specialized task? Is enough attention paid to this vital area and to the individuals who work in it?

The questions asked here and in other functional areas are, of course, of more importance to some organizations than to others. The analyst must, from a view of both the organization's business and from a view of its external environments, decide which questions are appropriate. How important has research and development been to the organization? But more to the point, how important should it be in the future? If the organization has particular strengths in R.&D., or if the external environment demands it, the organization should likely be committed to a research and development effort.

In this area as in others, analysts must again gather their facts, draw conclusions, and make recommendations for change. In the process, a vital aspect of the organization's strategy becomes apparent and it must be integrated fully into the overall analysis and resulting profile of strengths and weaknesses. The research and development area may be a major resource to be utilized in an organization's strategy, or a staggering weakness to be corrected or overcome by a change in strategy.

Other Areas

The thorough analysis of a particular organization may require consideration of other areas which, like research and development, vary in importance with the nature of the organization. The legal area, for example, is of great importance to insurance companies, utilities, and others such as proved to be the case for companies engaged in franchising. The nature of the organization's business and its relationships will generally determine the importance attached to the legal function. Public relations or government relations will be particularly important to some companies and nonprofit institutions, but of far less concern to others. Here again, in all "minor" departmental or functional areas, the analyst must observe, digest, and decide. The absence of a function may well indicate a problem for the organization rather than being a reason for the analyst to ignore that function. What has been the situation and what should it be? These are the two basic questions to be answered, and the answers will depend largely upon the nature of the organization and of the business in which the organization is engaged.

THE HUMAN SIDE OF THE ENTERPRISE

Because the human element permeates all other segments and divisions within an organization, it should be considered independently, in addition to being a subject for analysis within each of the individual areas. So although analytical attention has been given in the separate functional areas to the human element, an overall profile of the organization should view the human resource of the firm as an area in itself. The analyst, then, must judge whether the human element is actually a resource and strength for the organization, or whether it is a weakness that may well nullify efforts of management to employ other resources successfully. It should go without saying that the human resources analysis of an organization may begin with, but must go far beyond, a look at the personnel or industrial relations department! As in other areas discussed earlier, some "key questions" will guide the analyst in his evaluative tasks. (See Exhibit 3–8.)

The subject of organizational behavior and human relations so permeates the nature of a company or any other type of organization that it must be considered as a major element of the internal analysis. Many

EXHIBIT 3–8
Some "Key Questions" to Be Asked When Appraising the Area of
Human Resources in an Organization

Is attention devoted to the human side of the enterprise in formal departments (like personnel and industrial relations) and more importantly, in the overall managerial philosophies of the organization?

Are there clear and equitable policies covering people associated with the organization?

Is there effective communication, action, and results in the areas of hiring, training, and placement of individuals within the firm?

Is the firm "competitive" with others in its policies of wages, promotion, education, benefits, and the like?

How are policies communicated throughout the organization?

If unionized, how does the company deal with the unions and have relations been at least adequate and perhaps even beneficial?

In all areas, does the organization have adequate and well-qualified personnel backed up by others being trained for further responsibility?

Are there "holes" in the organization at any level and if so, how crucial are the spots at which these "holes" exist?

Is there a morale problem at any or all levels, and how does the problem manifest itself? Does management strive to achieve harmony within the organization?

Has management given a purpose for commitment to members of the organization, and has it been accepted?

What is the prevailing "climate" of the organization? Does it indicate health and vitality, or a malaise which is counter-productive to organizational and even individual goals?

What is the overall relationship between individuals and the organization? Is there a balance and do individuals appear to fulfill personal and/or organizational goals?

Is management viewed with suspicion, or with a spirit of admiration leading to corporate effort by organizational members?

Is there a policy of "management by objectives," and if so is it actually implemented or only a slogan?

Is an "informal" organization apparent and if so does it support or counter efforts of the formal groups?

Is management sensitive to the entire spectrum of human behavior in the organization, and has it shown wisdom in dealing with these aspects of organizational life? Or has management relied upon a mechanistic view of the organization with an ultimate neglect of important human considerations?

areas must be considered and many questions must be asked. If an organization can be judged "healthy," however, management has done much of its job and the crucial human resources of the firm are probably a major asset to the organization. At a minimum level of "health," the employees are satisfied generally and do not resist the organization in attempts to achieve objectives. At a higher state of "health," individuals subscribe to organizational goals and actively work toward the achievement of these goals, while simultaneously achieving personal goals. The human element is vital at all echelons in the organization. Trouble at any level can well disrupt other levels and quickly turn the human resources into liabilities rather than assets. If this occurs, it is unlikely that financial or physical resources will long remain strong. They are too closely interrelated to and dependent upon success in the area of human resources.

Management, then, can accomplish a great deal by properly managing human resources. In the entity being analyzed, is management doing so? Is the staffing function, the supervision and the direction at all levels being performed well? Do people know what is going on when they should; in other words, does management's communication system work? And probably most important of all, has management succeeded in giving purpose to the organization? In the view of one outstanding writer on the subject, this is a major job not only of top management but also of the entire executive organization.[5] If management has succeeded here, high morale is likely to follow. Purpose followed by proper supervision and direction will go far toward developing the positive climate so desired in all organizations. When it is present, its effects are unmistakable. Does the organization being analyzed have this basic strength so vital to effective utilization of its human resources? Strength in the human side of the organization is crucial during the implementation of strategy as will be indicated in later chapters dealing with this subject.

TOP MANAGEMENT VIEWED IN PERSPECTIVE

One of the major reasons for making an internal analysis of an organization and developing a profile of strengths and weaknesses is to obtain an assessment of the top management of the organization. Even if this were not a reason for making the analysis, it is unavoidably one result of such an endeavor. By "top management" here is meant primarily the major managers who guide the overall destiny and operations of the organization; that is, those primarily responsible for organizational strategy. The individual managers and their performances are also of

---

[5] Chester I. Barnard, *The Functions of the Executive* (Cambridge, Mass.: Harvard University Press, 1938), p. 233.

interest, but the important questions to be asked are: How has the organization been managed? How is it being managed now? The second question, particularly, has many implications about how well the company is prepared to face the future.

In analyzing the various individual areas, much is learned about management and the managers of the particular areas. Much can also be inferred about the overall management under whose aegis the individual events have occurred. But it is only by pulling together the separate areas in the overall profile or analysis of the entire organization that the top management can be analyzed and evaluated in depth. With all available information integrated and conclusions reached, it is feasible to make statements about the firm as a whole, its top management, and the strategies of the past, present, and future (or lack thereof). General statements made and conclusions drawn before this time will of necessity be based on incomplete information. In business policy, conclusions and decisions should be based upon as comprehensive information as is obtainable in a time and at a cost which can be considered reasonable, given the importance of this comprehensive subject.

Results are always a most valuable input to the analysis of management, and included here are results of all types (such as production, marketing, cost, and the human dimension) covered thus far in this chapter, and not just financial results. For instance, when considering nonprofit institutions it must be realized that financial results are only one set of measures and likely not the most important in those situations. But even here financial results or cost data are important in determining the cost effectiveness of operations. In many nonprofit organizations, cost effectiveness is of utmost importance and its influence is spreading among such organizations including government, hospitals, and universities. Of course, in profit-oriented businesses, financial results are of undeniable importance to the institution. The issue being raised here is not that profits and other financial results are not important, but rather that other results of an organization's activities are also important. These include results within the accounting, marketing, production, engineeering, "R.&D.", and all other areas including the human element of these activities. Failing to keep up in research and development may show "better" financial results in the short run, but beyond that period, serious problems may arise. Or a serious morale problem which developed during a cost-cutting drive might produce poor quality results which will not appear until some later date. Finally, with respect to results, perhaps the most important question of all is, "were objectives established and measures developed against which to compare the results which were achieved?" Then, "were such planned results accomplished in all important areas within the organization"? Although it is an incomplete view of the operations of a company, and of its management, an analysis of overall results is an excellent place to begin. A thorough look at results in profits, sales, cost reduction, research and development, buildup of plant, increase in morale, social contribution, and other result areas will show much about the condition of the organization as well as the quality of its management.

Beyond the results achieved, however, which too often are measured only in quantitative terms, an analysis should also have considered the operations of the various departments, the projects underway, the type of leadership being exhibited in the departments, the response of the work force to supervisors, and of junior levels of management to their seniors, and other areas as appropriate to the firm being studied. Many of these areas are, of course, explored when analyzing the managerial functions mentioned earlier. Generally, it can be expected that good performance in the functional areas will lead to good overall results, financial and otherwise. This is not necessarily the case in the short run, however. As in the examples of research and development and cost-cutting cited above, better planning may actually cause lower profits in shorter term periods because of investment spending or additional research. Similarly, the installation of a control system or a program of management education may slow down purely financial results in the short run but have beneficial long-run effects. Thus, the analysis must consider an appropriate time frame in which to view results which have occurred. Results must also be viewed in the perspective of the other events, operations, decisions, and management practices which are taking place in the firm. Only in this broader light do results have a useful meaning to the analyst.

In interpreting results, a relative view is needed to gain perspective, and some appreciation must be shown for the job which was faced by the management. In what condition was the organization when the present management took over? What was the state of the economy in general, and of the industry in particular? How did the company do relative to comparable institutions? What was the size of the company relative to competition? In light of the job to be done, was the company big enough to compete effectively, or if not, has it become more able to accomplish the job at hand? At what stage of development was the institution and its major products—just beginning, mature, on the decline? How well did management do in assessing its position, planning for change, and carrying out change?

Was a strategy developed, utilized, and implemented? On the human side, was a purpose provided which was meaningful to the members of the organization? Was morale raised and in other ways was true leadership exhibited? Were objectives articulated, communicated, and understood by those responsible for implementing the objectives? Of extreme importance, was there an atmosphere conducive to development and education to provide for growth of individuals within the organization? Related to this question, has management succession been provided for?

Have decisions been made by one man or by a group? Do lesser managers have a real voice in directing operations and in making decisions?

Unless management overlaps heavily with ownership, the stockholders of the business organization have the basic rights of ownership, and a voice ostensibly stronger than that of management. Has management considered the stockholders, acted in their best interests, and made decisions which over the long run would most benefit the stockholders? If they have not, they have failed in one of the basic charges to all managements; that is, to protect and enhance the investment of the firm's owners. Here, too, immediate profit is not the sole criterion for evaluation.

Regarding stockholders, the analyst should also explore the following questions. How do stockholders collectively make themselves heard? What is their representation on the board of directors? Is the board active or inactive, an inside board or outside, or does it have mixed representation? Is the composition of the board varied and logical considering the nature of the organization and its business? And perhaps the most significant question, has the board of directors exercised its prerogative of participating in setting the basic objectives of the organization and has it had a voice in the determination of basic strategy?

Referring directly to top management, have these executives shown an open-minded approach to running the business? Have they been self-analytical?[6] Have they been open to and have they initiated change readily? Have they shown qualities of responsiveness and decisiveness? Finally, does the top management appear to have people for the times, people who seem fit for the job to be done, and has the president complemented his strengths by picking other managers with different strengths and attributes?[7] Or has he brought around him only those who fit his image? The answers to such questions tell much of the future possibilities of the organization, as well as about the present.

SUMMARY

In evaluating the corporation's functional and managerial resources from the profile of internal strengths and weaknesses, numerous key questions must be asked. This chapter has presented many of these ques-

---

[6] See Alfred P. Sloan, Jr., *My Years with General Motors* (Garden City, N.Y.: Doubleday & Company, Inc., 1964), for numerous illustrations of self-analytical reflection.

[7] The board room of a major railroad has presidential portraits on the wall. An early president was a railroad builder and a railroad man completely in the days when the roads were just beginning. Financial men followed who were in command during periods of expansion and merger. A legal man ascended to the top during a period of particularly involved negotiations with government, labor, and other companies which were subject to acquisition and merger.

tions. Answers will reveal how the organization looks as a totality and in its various parts, how the management has solved problems, and how it selected the problems for solution. Further, analysis and conclusions will reveal whether management has seen the real job to be done at various times, and whether it has set objectives, planned for their accomplishment, and "done the job." Insights will be gained which will show whether management has been oriented toward change and the future, has recognized the job that lies ahead, and whether management has been able to accomplish its job. In summary, answers to "key questions" will reveal whether the management established a strategy for the institution, with objectives, policies, and plans, whether it organized to accomplish the strategy, and whether it set into motion the administrative apparatus needed to implement the strategy. The detailed analysis and answers gained will also show how the functional areas and the management of these fit into overall internal resource profile of the organization.

Obvious at this stage should be the necessity to go beyond the internal aspects of analysis and to consider the external environment. A thorough evaluation of management cannot be made without doing so. The internal analysis and resulting profile is valuable for showing what the organization has been good at in the past, and what it is good at presently. It also reveals the things the institution has not been good at doing. It should clarify, too, why the present situation has been as it has, and directions for change should become apparent. Key issues should arise which will again have implications for future action, and the part of the job to be done which reflects itself *within* the organization should also come to light. Since so much will be learned about the organization and its operation, many conclusions will be drawn about the management and a preliminary evaluation may be made of top management and individual managers.

But although a partial evaluation of management can be made from an analysis of the internal situation, future actions depend heavily upon an appraisal of the external environment. The analysis of external aspects will be presented in the next chapter and coupled with the exposition of this chapter will provide the insights for a thorough evaluation of an organization and its management.

Having evaluated thoroughly the internal resources of an organization, the analysts can move ahead to the complete evaluation of an organization and its strategy. Because they understand the internal profile of the entity's resources, they know what the entity is capable of doing. It remains for them to match this knowledge with an analysis of the external environment to find out what the organization might be doing considering that environment. In fact, analysis of the internal aspects of an organization will dictate or recommend the areas of the environment which deserve closest scrutiny. The strengths and weaknesses noted in the organization's resource profile will bring to light "opportunities" or potential opportunities provided the environment is supportive of these. The facets of the environment which will determine whether these apparent "opportunities" are in fact real opportunities for the organization will, thus, be given the deepest and most critical analysis. Similarly, whether certain conditions in an organization are assessed as strengths or weaknesses depends largely upon the kinds of environmental "opportunities" that the management (or analyst) has in mind. Thus, the interrelationships that exist between the "assessment of internal strengths and weaknesses" and the "environmental analysis or search for opportunity" becomes readily apparent. The two are interwoven in actuality and in the framework of strategy. Each may be analyzed separately for convenience, but in actuality the analyses are in parallel and are interactive; both the internal and environmental aspects are pulled together in a final combined analysis.

After completing a combined analysis, the analyst can recommend changes and thus move closer to strategy formulation. A complete analysis, however, must also include the topics of objectives, personal values, and strategy implementation which will be the subjects of later chapters.

7. How to Evaluate a Firm[*]

ROBERT B. BUCHELE

Gone are the days when a security could be analyzed by tearing down the company's balance sheet and asking a few pointed questions. Shrewd analysts today must not only X-ray its management and marketing potential, but also its vulnerability to future shifts in technology. Here is an in-depth approach to determine what a firm is really worth.

THE SHARP DROPS in earnings and even losses recently suffered by many so-called "growth" companies, whose stocks had been bid so high, have cast doubts upon the adequacy of the established methods which are used by investment specialists to evaluate companies.

Equally dramatic but less evident have been the serious declines of numerous companies shortly after having been rated as "excellently managed" by the best known of the evaluation systems using a list of factors covering numerous aspects of corporate management.

What has happened to render these evaluation systems so inadequate? What lessons can be learned by persons whose work requires them to do overall evaluations of companies—investors, acquisition specialists, consultants, long-range planners, and chief executives? Finally, what are the requirements for a system for evaluating firms that will function reliably under today's conditions?

After all, the decline of even blue chip companies is not a new phenomenon. To quote from an unpublished paper recently presented by Ora C. Roehl before a management conference at UCLA:

> The Brookings Institution sometime ago made a study of the 100 top businesses in the USA in the early 1900s, and they found that after 40 years only 36 were still among the leaders.

[*] Robert B. Buchele, "How to Evaluate a Firm," *California Management Review,* Fall 1962, pp. 5–16. © 1962 by the Regents of the University of California. Reprinted from *California Management Review,* Fall 1962, pp. 5–16, by permission of the Regents. The author, while retaining full responsibility for the content of this article, wishes to express thanks to Drs. Harold D. Koontz, William B. Wolf, J. F. Weston, and Mr. Ora B. Roehl for suggestions that have been most helpful.

We all look at the Dow-Jones Industrial Average practically every day and we know the companies that are a part of the Average today—from Allied Chemical, Aluminum Company of America, and American Can to U.S. Steel, Westinghouse, and Woolworth. But, as we go back in time a bit, we find names that once were important enough to be a part of the Average and which we have heard of, such as Hudson Motors, Famous Players-Lasky, and Baldwin Locomotive. It is not long, however, before we run into one-time business leaders whose names are strange to us, such as Central Leather, U.S. Cordage Company, Pacific Mail, American Cotton Oil Company, and one with a nostalgic sort of name, The Distilling and Cattle Feeding Company.[1]

What is new, however, is the current pace of such events. Stemming in part from the rise of industrial research expenditures from less than $200 million in 1930 to an estimated $12.4 billion in 1960,[2] the pace of industrial change has been accelerating for many years. It is now so rapid that firms can rise or fall more quickly than ever before.

Sophisticated technologies are spreading to many industries; in addition, as we shall see in this article, various management techniques contribute to the quickening pace of change. In consequence, the rapid rate of change now affects a great many American firms rather than just that minority known as "growth" companies.

PRESENT EVALUATION METHODS

Financial Analysis. This method typically consists of studying a "spread" of profit and loss figures, operating statements and balance sheet ratios for the past five or ten years. The underlying assumption is that the future performance of a company can be reliably projected from trends in these data. The reasoning is that these data represent the "proof of the pudding." If they're sound, the company as a whole, particularly its top management, must be sound, for a competent top management will keep a firm healthy.

Through the years this method has worked well because the basic assumption has been reasonably valid. Despite the fact that some blue chip companies have failed, it is still reasonably valid for the large firms who are thoroughly entrenched in their markets and who make substantial investments in executive development, in market development, and in any technology that promises to threaten one of their market positions.

---

[1] "Evaluating Your Company's Future," an unpublished paper presented at the Fourth Annual Management Conference, UCLA Executive Program Association, Los Angeles, October 20, 1960, p. 2.

[2] Data from the National Science Foundation, cited in *Research Management*, vol. 3, no. 3 (Autumn, 1960), p. 129.

However, the assumption is becoming less safe, especially in connection with medium-sized and small firms, as the pace of industrial change steadily accelerates. Thus, a firm whose financial record is unimpressive may be on the verge of a technological breakthrough that will send its profits rocketing ahead; conversely, a company that looks good in financial analyses may be doomed because it is being bypassed technologically or marketing-wise or because rigor mortis has taken over the executive offices.

In practice the financial analysis method is often supplemented by market research in the form of interviews with leading customers, by interviews with the firm's top executives, and by consultation with scientists capable of evaluating technological capabilities and trends. While these supplementary activities help, financial analysis still is neither adequately comprehensive nor adequately oriented to the future.

Thus, this type of market research can yield some insights into the effectiveness of past and present performance but is too superficial to tell much about the future. The interviews with top executives can be more misleading than informative simply because they are conducted by financial people inexperienced in management, marketing, or technology.[3] The use of scientists is a commendable step forward. However, it provides help in only one and possibly two of the many areas essential to a thorough evaluation.

Key Factor Ratings.   Systems more comprehensive than the financial analysis method have been developed, mainly by consultants seeking to understand firms' overall strengths and weaknesses in order to be able to prescribe for them. Such systems typically involve ratings based on a series of key factors underlying the financial factors themselves. Little has been published about these systems because the consulting firms regard them as proprietary secrets. One system that has been published and, therefore, is well known is that developed by the American Institute of Management.[4] That this system is not adequately future-oriented is clearly proved by the fact that numerous companies have encountered

[3] Lee Dake explains in detail a case in which a financial analyst and a management consultant arrived at opposite conclusions about a firm's prospects in "Are Analysts' Techniques Adequate for Growth Stocks?" *The Financial Analysts Journal*, vol. 16, no. 6 (Nov.–Dec., 1960), pp. 45–49. Dake's thesis can be confirmed many times over in the present author's experience. Particularly distressing was the case where a persuasive but incompetent chief executive persuaded three investment firms to recommend his stock less than six months before declaration of losses exceeding the firm's tangible net worth!

[4] The factors are: (*a*) Economic Function; (*b*) Corporate Structure; (*c*) Health of Earnings; (*d*) Services to Stockholders; (*e*) Research and Development; (*f*) Directorate Analysis; (*g*) Fiscal Policies; (*h*) Production Efficiency; (*i*) Sales Vigor; (*j*) Executive Evaluation. The factors and their use are explained in detail in a series of ten reports: *The Management Audit Series* (New York: The American Institute of Management, starting in 1953).

Outline for Evaluation of a Firm

I. PRODUCT LINES AND BASIC COMPETITIVE POSITION

A. Past

What strengths and weakness in products (or services) have been dominant in this firm's history—design features, quality-reliability, prices, patents, proprietary position?

B. Present

What share of its market(s) does the firm now hold, and how firmly? Is this share diversified or concentrated as to number of customers? In what phases of their life cycles are the present chief products and what is happening to prices and margins? How do customers and potential customers regard this firm's products? Are the various product lines compatible marketing-wise, engineering-wise, manufacturing-wise? If not, is each product line substantial enough to stand on its own feet?

C. Future

Is the market(s) as a whole expanding or contracting and at what rate? What is the trend in this firm's share of the market(s)? What competitive trends are developing in numbers of competitors, technology, marketing, pricing? What is its vulnerability to business cycle (or defense spending) changes? Is management capable of effectively integrating market research, R&D, and market development into a development program for a new product or products?

II. R&D AND OPERATING DEPARTMENTS

A. R&D and Engineering

What is the nature and the depth of its R&D capability? Of engineering capability? What are engineering's main strengths and weaknesses re creativity, quality-reliability, simplicity? Is the R&D effort based on needs defined by market research, and is it an integral part of an effective new product development program? Are R&D efforts well planned, directed, and controlled? What return have R&D dollars paid in profitable new products? Have enough new products been produced? Have schedules been met?

B. Marketing

Nature of the Marketing Capability—What channels of distribution are used? How much of the total marketing job (research, sales, service, advertising and promotion) is covered? Is this capability correctly tailored to match the nature and diversity of the firm's product lines? Is there a capability for exploiting new products and developing new markets? Quality of the marketing capability —Is market research capable of providing the factual basis that will keep the firm, especially its new product development and R&D programs, truly customer-oriented? Is there a capability for doing broad economic studies and studies of particular industries that will help management set sound growth and/or diversification strategies?

C. **Manufacturing**

What is the nature of the manufacturing processes, the facilities and the skills—are they appropriate to today's competition? How flexible are they—will they be, or can they be made, appropriate to tomorrow's competition? What is the quality of the manufacturing management in terms of planning and controlling work schedule-wise, cost-wise, and quality-wise? Is there evidence of an industrial engineering capability that steadily improves products and methods? Does manufacturing management effectively perform its part of the process of achieving new products?

D. **Summary on R&D and Operating Departments**

Is this a complete, integrated, balanced operation; or have certain strong personalities emphasized some functions and neglected others? What is the quality of performance of key R&D and operating executives; do they understand the fundamental processes of management, namely planning, controlling organizing, staffing and directing? Are plans and controls in each department inadequate, adequate or overdeveloped into a "paperwork mill?" Is there throughout the departments a habit of steady progress in reducing overhead, lowering breakeven points and improving quality? Are all departments future-minded? Do they cooperate effectively in developing worthy new products geared to meet the customer's future needs?

III. **FINANCIAL ANALYSIS AND FINANCIAL MANAGEMENT**

A. **Financial Analysis**

What main strengths and weaknesses of the firm emerge from analysis of the trends in the traditional financial data: earnings ratios (to sales, to tangible net worth, to working capital) and earnings-per-share; debt ratios (current and acid tests, to tangible net worth, to working capital, to inventory); inventory turnover; cash flow; and the capitalization structure? What do the trends in the basic financial facts indicate as to the firm's prospects for growth in sales volume and rate of earnings? Does "quality of earnings" warrant compounding of the earnings rate?

B. **Financial Management**

What is the quality of financial management? Is there a sound program for steadily increasing return on investment? Do the long-range financial plans indicate that management understands the cost of capital and how to make money work hard? Have balance sheets and operating statements been realistically projected for a number of years into the future? Is there careful cash planning and strong controls that help the operating departments lower break-even points? Are capital expenditures inadequate or excessive with respect to insuring future operating efficiently? Are capital investment decisions based on thorough calculations? Does management have the respect of the financial community? Is the firm knowledgeable and aggressive in tax administration?

IV. **TOP MANAGEMENT**

A. **Identification of Top Management and Its Record**

What person or group constitutes top management? Has present top management been responsible for profit-and-loss results of the past few years?

B. **Top Management and the Future**

What are top management's chief characteristics? How adequate or inadequate is this type of management for coping with the challenges of the future? Will the present type and quality of top management continue? Will it deteriorate, will it improve, or will it change its basic character?

C. **Board of Directors**

What influence and/or control does the Board of Directors exercise? What are the capabilities of its members? What are their motivations?

V. **SUMMARY AND EVALUATION STRATEGY**

What other factors can assume major importance in this particular situation? (Use a check list.) Of all the factors studied, which if any, is overriding in this particular situation? Which factors are of major importance by virtue of the fact that they govern other factors? What are the basic facts-of-life about the economics and competition of this industry now and over the next decade? In view of this firm's particular strengths and weaknesses, what are the odds that it will succeed, and at what level of success, in this industry? What are the prospects of its succeeding by diversifying out of its industry?

deep trouble shortly after being rated "excellently managed" by the AIM.[5]

---

[5] Most dramatic was the case of the Douglas Aircraft Company whose "excellently managed" rating for 1957–8–9 was followed by staggering losses in late 59 and 60. Among numerous other examples that can be cited are the 1957 ratings of Olin Mathiesen Chemical Co. and Allis-Chalmers Manufacturing Company, both of whom, soon after receiving "excellently managed" ratings, suffered serious declines that have been openly discussed in business magazines. For the ratings, see *Manual of Excellent Managements* (New York: The American Institute of Management, 1957). For accounts of the travails of these firms see *Business Week*, April 15, 1961, pp. 147–149 and April 9, 1960, p. 79.

Professor Erwin Schell a decade ago set forth a comprehensive system with some future-oriented elements; however, he recently stated that his system should be revised to give greater emphasis to the future via more attention to the R&D function.[6]

As indicated in the Outline for evaluation which accompanies this article, the evaluation of a firm, as it is at present and as it will be in the future, can be organized around a series of penetrating questions. Thorough study of the areas covered by these questions will yield a picture, oriented to the future, of the strengths and weaknesses of the firm under consideration and a reliable indication of its chances for success in the future.

There are, as the outline shows, four vital areas in a firm about which you should ask questions. They are: its product lines and basic competitive position; its R&D and operating departments; its financial position as revealed by analysis of the traditional financial data plus an estimate of the quality of its financial management; its top management with emphasis not only upon its past record, but also on its adequacy to cope with the future.

When these data have been assembled and summarized, you are in a position to evaluate both the present situation and potential of the firm under study as an investment possibility or as a management problem.

The rest of this article will be devoted to a discussion of these factors one by one. First we shall pose the questions contained in the outline; then we shall discuss the techniques professional analysts use for obtaining such data and determining what it means.

PRODUCT LINES AND COMPETITION

The first things to investigate are a firm's product lines and its basic competitive position. This involves a study of its past, present, and future. Here are the lines your inquiry should take:

> **Past** . . . What strengths and weaknesses in products (or services) have been dominant in this firm's history—design features, quality-reliability, prices, patents, proprietary position?

---

[6] "Industrial Administration Through the Eyes of an Investment Company," *Appraising Managerial Assets—Policies, Practices and Organization,*" General Management Series no. 151 (New York: American Management Association, 1950). The new emphasis is suggested in a postscript to a reprint published in 1960 by the Keystone Custodian Funds, Inc. (Boston, Mass.: 1960), p. 13). Professor Schell suggested increased emphasis on tax administration, too. The original factors were: (*a*) Breadth and variety of viewpoint in administration; (*b*) Vigor and versatility in operating management; (*c*) Clarity and definiteness of long-term objectives; (*d*) Vigilance in matters of organization; (*e*) Dependence upon far-reaching plans; (*f*) Maintenance of integrated controls; (*g*) Upkeep in harmony with an advancing art; (*h*) Improvement as a normal expectancy; (*i*) Creativeness through high morale; (*j*) Effectiveness of managerial attitudes; (*k*) Resources for consistently distinguished leadership in a specific industry.

Present . . . What share of its market(s) does the firm now hold, and how firmly? Is this share diversified or concentrated as to number of customers? In what phases of their life cycles are the present chief products and what is happening to prices and margins? How do customers and potential customers regard this firm's products? Are the various product lines compatible marketing-wise, engineering-wise, manufacturing-wise? If not, is each product line substantial enough to stand on its own feet?

Future . . . Is the market(s) as a whole expanding or contracting, and at what rate? What is the trend in this firm's share of the market(s)? What competitive trends are developing in numbers of competitors, technology, marketing, pricing?

What is the vulnerability to business cycle (or defense spending) changes?

Is there the capability effectively to integrate market research, R&D and market development into a new products development program?

The past-present-future structure furnishes the material needed to determine whether the firm has presently or in-the-pipeline the type of products needed for success in the future.

A key technique here is to determine how much quantitative information the company executives have and, then, to spot-check the quality of that information by the evaluator's own research. The firm that has sound, pertinent market data usually has achieved the first step to success —a clear definition of the job to be done. Conversely, the firm that has only sparse, out-of-date, out-of-focus data and relies heavily on executives' opinions is usually a poor bet for the future. Unsupported opinions, no matter how strongly held or ably stated, can be misleading. Although top management often must rely on such opinions, failure to secure the data that are available is a serious weakness.

LIFE CYCLE CURVES FOR PRODUCTS MADE

Another device for focusing on the basic facts of life about a product line is the building of S, or life cycle curves. Those curves plot sales and/or margins for a product against time. For a given firm such plots picture clearly the life expectancy of products. Composite plots can show the trends in life expectancies. Also, they can indicate developing gaps. When past data are joined to carefully projected estimates of the future, dangerous situations can be revealed. Thus, the firm that is currently highly profitable but has not provided for the future will show virtually all of its products at or near the period of peak profitability.[7]

The question of compatibility of product lines may seem too elementary for mention; however, major mistakes are made in this area,

---

[7] For an illustration and discussion of use of life-cycle curves, see C. Wilson Randle, "Selecting the Research Program. A Top Management Function," *California Management Review*, volume 2, no. 2 (Winter 1960), pp. 10–11.

especially by firms headed by scientists. Seeing their own skill as the key one in business, scientists tend to underestimate the importance and difficulty of other management activities. In consequence, they often develop or acquire products that present marketing problems far beyond the financial or managerial capability of the firm.

One science-based and scientist-led company, after an acquisition binge, was attempting to market ten distinct product lines through one centralized marketing organization, all with a total of less than $18 million annual volume. None of the products could individually support a top-flight marketing organization; yet no two of them could be effectively marketed through the same people. The result was disaster.

Integration of market research, R&D and market development into an effective new product development program is one of the newer and more difficult arts of management. Such integration, which is the heart of profit planning, apparently accounted for much of the success of the Bell and Howell Company during the decade of the 50s.[8]

In vivid contrast to the coordinated profit planning of Bell and Howell, is the case of the small glamor firm that "went public" in early 1961 for $1,000,000 and has since seen the price of its stock triple. The scientist-president and his associates have developed a dazzling array of technically ingenious new products; however, they have little data on the market for the products and have not yet started to build an organization for distributing and selling them.

R&D AND OPERATING DEPARTMENTS

Having probed a firm's product lines and competitive position, the second vital area for investigation is its R&D, marketing, and operating divisions. Good questions to guide your analysis are:

> **R&D and Engineering** . . . What is the nature and the depth of the R&D capability? Of the engineering capability? What are the main strengths and weaknesses re creativity, quality-reliability, simplicity?
>
> Is the R&D effort based on needs defined by market research, and is it an integral part of an effective new product development program? Are R&D efforts well planned, directed and controlled? What return have R&D dollars paid in profitable new products? Have enough new products been produced, and have schedules been met?

A truly basic change in American industry since the start of World War II has been that thousands of companies have R&D programs whereas earlier only a handful of firms did so. The figures cited earlier concern-

---

[8] The Bell and Howell methods are described in two articles: "How to Coordinate Executives," *Business Week*, September 12, 1953, p. 130 ff., and "How to Plan Profits Five Years Ahead," *Nation's Business*, October 1955, p. 38.

ing the growth of R&D expenditures indicate that sophisticated technologies and rapidly changing products and markets characterize not only electronics and defense industries but also such diverse fields as food processing, photography, communications, pharmaceuticals, metallurgy, plastics, and equipments used in industrial automation processes. The consequence is that most firms beyond the "small business" category must have R&D programs; increasingly a firm must take on the characteristics of a "growth" firm in order to survive.

HOW TO EVALUATE A FIRM'S R&D

One of the newest of management activities, R&D management, is one of the hardest to evaluate. For lack of better technique, the vogue has been to assume that the volume of dollars spent on R&D is commensurate with results achieved. However, we now know that there has been great waste; also, there has been deception by firms "padding" their reported R&D expenditures to give the impression of being more R&D oriented than they really are.

A growing literature reports useful techniques for conceiving, planning, controlling and directing R&D programs and for evaluating R&D output.[9] The truth is being established that R&D management is a capability different from and much rarer than the capability of performing straight engineering or scientific work.

The first task of the evaluator is to determine whether the selection of R&D programs is integrated with a sound overall long-range plan and is based on market research findings. The next task is to compare the nature and depth of the R&D capability with the job to be done. Can it cope with the firm's future needs in regard to maintaining and improving market position by an integrated new products program? The third job is to compare cost and output. Techniques for evaluating output include assessing the quantity and quality of patents produced, measurement of the contribution of R&D to increased (or maintained) sales volume and

---

[9] An invaluable review of this literature up to early 1957 is given in: Albert H. Rubenstein, "Looking Around: Guide to R&D," *Harvard Business Review*, vol. 35, no. 3 (May–June, 1957), p. 133 ff. Among the most pertinent articles since Rubenstein's review are: Ora C. Roehl, "The Investment Analyst's Evaluation of Industrial Research Capabilities," *Research Management*, vol. 3, no. 3 (Autumn 1960), p. 127 ff.; Maurice Nelles, "Changing the World Changers" (Paper presented at the Ninth Annual Management Conference, The Graduate School of Business Administration, University of Chicago, March 1, 1961); C. Wilson Randle, "Problems of R&D Management," *Harvard Business Review*, vol. 37, no. 1 (January–February 1959), p. 128 ff.; James B. Quinn, "How to Evaluate Research Output," *Harvard Business Review*, vol. 38, no. 2 (March–April 1960), pp. 69 ff.; and "Long-Range Planning of Industrial Research," *Harvard Business Review*, vol. 39, no. 4 (July–August 1961), pp. 88 ff.

profit margins, and measurement of the contribution to lowered break-even points via improved materials and methods.

ARE ITS INNOVATIONS WELL-TIMED?

An evaluator needs to understand the time cycle required for research, development and introduction to application; also, he must be able to relate this understanding to the basic facts about the market being served. Such an evaluator can tell when a firm is proceeding in the vanguard of the competition or when it is jumping on a bandwagon too late—as so many electronics firms did with respect to the transistor bandwagon.

MARKETING

Closely allied with R&D and product innovation are the marketing skills of the firm under analysis. Strengths and weaknesses in this area can be uncovered by digging into the following topics.

> **Nature of the Marketing Capability** . . . What channels of distribution are used? How much of the total marketing job (research, sales, service, advertising, and promotion) is covered? Is this capability correctly tailored to match the nature and diversity of the firm's product lines?
>
> Is there a capability for exploiting new products and for developing new markets?
>
> **Quality of the Marketing Capability** . . . Is market research capable of providing the factual basis that will keep the firm, especially its new product development and R&D programs, truly customer-oriented? Is there a capability for doing broad economic studies and studies of particular industries that will help management set sound growth and/or diversification strategies?

The evaluator will already have learned much about market research capability in answering the product line questions posed earlier in this article. There it was indicated that the firm that knows the facts about trends in its market and technologies is well on the way to success in the future. This clearly places great responsibility on market research, a field still neglected or abused by many science-based firms, especially those in defense work.

To cope adequately with the challenges of the future requires more than market research in the old narrow concept; rather, it requires an ability at economic analysis of entire industries. Survival and growth in a rapidly changing economy sometimes demands more than a stream of new products; often it requires diversification into substantially different fields that offer greater growth and better profits for a given time period.

Diversification strategy is another subject that is currently being developed.[10] The aircraft industry today presents a case study in which certain firms are prospering because ten years ago they started to diversify while other firms are suffering badly because they failed to do so.

The accelerating rate of change in industry is a process that feeds on itself. Thus, sophisticated methods of market research and planning not only help a firm cope with rapid change but also foster more rapid change.

The evaluator must know enough about quantitative methods of research to be able to distinguish between valid use and abuse of market research. If not so equipped, he is at the mercy of the super-salesman with a smattering of scientific lore who can spin great tales about how a given firm has made a technological breakthrough that soon will have tremendous impact upon the market.

The evaluator must also be able to distinguish between creative market research and pedestrian fact-gathering that plods along a year too late to help management conquer the future. Only when market research secures fresh quantitative data on future markets can management integrate market development with product development.

MANUFACTURING

Next area to be studied is production. Questions to be asked include:

> **Manufacturing** . . . What is the nature of the manufacturing processes the facilities and the skills—are they appropriate to today's competition? How flexible are they—will they be or can they be made appropriate to tomorrow's competition?
>
> What is the quality of the manufacturing management in terms of planning and controlling work schedule-wise, cost-wise, and quality-wise? Is there evidence of an industrial engineering capability that steadily improves products and methods? Does manufacturing management effectively perform its part of the process of achieving new products?

The answers to these questions call mainly for conventional type analysis which need not be commented upon here. This is not to say that there are not now, as always, new and better techniques being developed in the manufacturing field. Certainly an alert manufacturing management will use such progressive techniques as "value engineering" to simplify product designs and, thus, reduce costs; and it will use electronic data processing and other modern industrial engineering methods of controlling the work pace and other cost elements.

But, basically, manufacturing management still is, and long has been, evaluated on the basis of performance schedule-wise, cost- and quality-

---

[10] H. Igor Ansoff, "Strategies for Diversification," *Harvard Business Review,* September–October, 1957.

wise, and techniques for such evaluations are among the oldest and best-developed tools of management consultants and others concerned with industrial engineering.

The quickening pace of technological change does, however, require special attention to the ability of the engineering and manufacturing departments to cooperate effectively in bringing new products into production and in utilizing new processes. Also, it requires special caution with respect to firms with heavy investments in inflexible capital equipment because such investments might be susceptible to almost sudden obsolescence.

SUMMARY ON R&D AND OPERATIONS

To make the most of information acquired about a firm's operating departments and R&D, it is well at this point to pull all this sometimes diffuse information together into a sight summary that pulls the whole picture of operations into focus. Questions running along lines such as these help clarify it.

The Overall Picture . . . Is this a complete, integrated, balanced operation; or have certain strong personalities emphasized some functions and neglected others?

What is the quality of performance of key R&D and operating executives; do they understand the fundamental processes of management, namely planning, controlling, organizing, staffing, and directing? Are plans and controls in each department inadequate, adequate, or over-developed into a "paperwork mill"?

Is there throughout the departments a habit of steady progress in reducing overhead, lowering breakeven points and improving quality?

Are all departments future-minded; do they cooperate effectively in developing worthy new products geared to meet the customer's future needs?

Finance is the third area of a corporation which should be analyzed carefully in appraising its present and future development. In this connection, both the men handling a company's finances and the figures on the balance sheet should be studied. Beginning inquiries could be:

Financial Analysis . . . What main strength and weaknesses of the firm emerge from analysis of the trends in the traditional financial data: earnings ratios (to sales, to tangible net worth, to working capital) and earnings-per-share; debt ratios (current and acid tests, to tangible net worth, to working capital, to inventory); inventory turnover; cash flow; and the capitalization structure?

What do the trends in the basic financial facts indicate as to the firm's prospects for growth in sales volume and rate of earnings? Does "quality of earnings" warrant compounding of the earnings rate?

Although this article has already pointed out limitations of financial analysis standing alone as a method of evaluating firms, its importance as one of the key elements of an evaluation should never be overlooked. Because financial analysis has been so important for so long, its techniques have been well developed. Therefore, it is not necessary to discuss them here.

One concept concerning "growth" companies, however, does require comment. The technique of evaluating a growth firm on the basis of an assumption that it will "plow back" its earnings and thereby achieve a compounded rate of increase in earnings per share is of questionable validity. By compounding earnings on a straight-line (or uninterrupted) basis, financial analysts arrive at estimates of future earnings that justify stock prices from 40 to 100 times present earnings per share.

NO FIRM PROGRESSES EVENLY

The concept of straight-line progress just doesn't square with the facts of life as observed by students of management. Especially in small and medium-sized companies, progress typically occurs in a saw-tooth, rather than a straight-line pattern. This phenomenon is based partly on the existence of business cycles and partly on the fact the firms are affected by the strengths and limitations of humans in key positions. There are stages in which the typical growing firm requires managerial talents greater than—or, possibly, only different from—those talents essential to its start.

At these critical periods the earnings per share may slow down or even turn into losses. Such events devastate the compounding process; if one compounds a more realistic 5–10 percent rate of growth per year, the result is far less sensational than is secured by compounding a 20–25 percent rate. It is exceedingly rare that a firm achieves the higher percentages for any sustained period. Litton Industries and IBM appear to be the exceptions that prove the rule. The reference to quality of earnings is meant to shed light on the sustainability of the rate of improvements in earnings. Here the evaluator must distinguish between continuous, sustainable improvement and isolated events (such as a single acquisition or securing an especially favorable contract) or cyclical events (a period of high profitability certain to be followed by a corresponding low).

THE MONEY MEN

Figures alone don't tell the complete financial story of a firm. Its money management must be rated and this involves an evaluation of both policies and men, not only those in the financial division but also the men in charge of planning and top management. You need to know their attitudes about . . .

>   **Financial Management** . . . Is there a sound program for steadily increasing return on investment? Do the long-range financial plans indicate that management understands the costs of capital and how to make money work hard? Have balance sheets and operating statements been realistically projected for a number of years into the future?
>   Is there careful cash planning and strong controls that help the operating departments lower breakeven points? Are capital expenditures inadequate, adequate, or excessive with respect to insuring future operating efficiency? Are capital investment decisions based on thorough calculations?
>   Does management have the respect of the financial community?
>   Is the firm knowledgeable and aggressive in tax administration?

While many financial departments function only as record-keepers and rules-enforcers, some play a truly creative role. Financial management can today contribute as much or more to improvement in earnings per share as can any other part of management.[11] In fact, in recent years bold use of the newer forms of financing have in many cases contributed as much to the rapid rise of companies as have technological innovations. And, alas, bold but unwise financing has ruined many a promising young company.

The questions here are designed to help the evaluator discover whether or not the financial people are vigorously contributing in a number of ways to the steady improvement of earnings currently and in the long run.

RATING TOP MANAGEMENT

All study of management invariably and understandably leads to a searching examination of the top management men. Here there are pitfalls for the unwary. The analyst must first identify the true top management before he can examine their performance record. Things, in terms of who actually runs the show, are not always what they seem on the organization chart. So key topics are:

>   **Top Management and Its Record** . . . What person or group constitutes top management? Has present top management been responsible for profit-and-loss results of the past few years?

The problem is to determine the individual or group of individuals who contribute directly and regularly to those decisions that shape the basic nature of this business and significantly affect profit and loss results.

---

[11] For an exposition of this thought as applied to large firms, see: "The New Power of the Financial Executive," *Fortune*, vol. 65, no. 1 (January 1962), p. 81 ff. See also the new text by J. Fred Weston, *Managerial Finance* (New York: Holt, Rinehart & Winston, 1962).

This usually cannot be determined reliably by direct questions to persons in key positions; few men are objective about themselves on these matters.

WATCH THEM WORK

Rare is the top executive who will admit that he is a one-man rule type; rare is the vice-president or department head who will admit that he is a highly-paid errand boy. Accordingly, direct observation of management at work is needed. Some additional information can also be gained through examination of minutes of meetings and files of memos.

After top management has been identified, the evaluator must ask whether this management has had time to prove itself one way or the other. The criterion is whether or not major decisions and programs put forth by this top management have come to fruition. It is not simply a matter of looking at profit and loss figures for a few years. We all know that in certain situations factors other than top management capability (for example, an inherited product line that is unusually strong) can produce good profits for a number of years.

Next comes consideration of:

> **Top Management and the Future** . . . What are top management's chief characteristics? How adequate or inadequate is this type of management for coping with the challenges of the future?
>
> Will the present type and quality of top management continue, or will it deteriorate, will it improve, or will it change its basic character?

We must ask how and why top management has achieved the results that it has achieved so that we can judge how adequate it will be for meeting tomorrow's challenges. Exploring the how and why gets the evaluator into the subject of types of management and their effects on profitability—the thorniest area of contemporary management theory. Over the past twenty years a tremendous literature has accumulated on such subjects as participative leadership, autocratic vs. bureaucratic vs. democratic types of management, and related subjects.

Some writers have claimed or implied great virtues for participative-democratic methods; others have attacked such methods as wasteful and ineffective, wholly inappropriate in industrial life and have advocated "benevolent autocracy." The confusion recently reached a zenith with the almost simultaneous publication of conflicting views by eminent professors from the same university.[12]

---

[12] Rensis Likert, reporting on a decade of social science research into patterns of management makes a case for participative management in *New Patterns of Management* (New York: McGraw-Hill Publishing Co., 1961). George Odiorne, reporting on studies of successful managements, warns strongly against the views of social scientists and makes a case for the more traditional, somewhat autocratic, business leader in *How Managers Make Things Happen* (New York: Prentice-Hall, Inc., 1961). Both authors are professors at the University of Michigan.

Industrial psychologists and sociologists have provided valuable insights into management practices and their effects upon profitability. While a skilled social scientist could contribute importantly to the evaluation of a firm's top management, there is a more direct way of evaluating top management's capability for coping with future challenges.

The direct method is to determine how top management has in the past coped with the future. This technique is based on the idea that management is essentially the process of planning to achieve certain goals and, then, controlling activities so that the goals are actually attained. It is in the processes of planning and controlling that top management does its major decision-making. Since planning and controlling are the heart of the managerial process, it is in these activities that top management most fully reveals its vital characteristics.

The evaluator can probe deeply into the content of the firm's past and current long-range and short-range plans, into the methods by which the plans are formulated, and into the controls used to bring those plans to fruition. This technique gets away, to a considerable extent, from subjective judgments; it deals with such facts as what was planned, how it was planned and what actually happened.

Fortunately these activities can be studied without great difficulty and by persons who do not have formal training in the behavioral sciences. A simple yet highly informative procedure is to compare succeeding sets of old long-range plans with one another, with present plans and with actual events.

DO THEIR PLANS WORK?

First, a firm that is effectively tomorrow-minded will have long-range plans. These may not be neatly bound in a cover labeled "long-range plans"; however, they will exist either in minutes of meetings, in memos, in reports to stockholders or in other places. Second, the old plans will contain evidence as to whether top management truly has studied the future to determine and anticipate the nature of the opportunities and threats that will inevitably arise.

Third, the old plans will contain evidence of the nature and quality of the solutions developed for meeting the challenges of the future—how creative, agressive and realistic management has been in initiative matters such as selecting R&D programs, establishing diversification strategy and program, developing new markets, planning the organizational changes needed to keep fit for new tasks, and effectively utilizing advanced techniques (e.g., operations research, automation, etc.) when feasible.

Special attention to initiative matters will indicate whether or not top management is creative and aggressive enough to keep up with an accelerating rate of change.

Fourth, comparison of succeeding sets of plans will indicate whether consistent progress has been made or top management is recklessly aggressive in that it undertakes unrealistic, ill-conceived, unachievable plans.

The same technique can be applied to short-range plans such as annual budgets, sales forecasts and special developmental programs of many types. This study will indicate whether or not forecasts are typically accurate, whether or not plans typically are successfully completed, whether or not new products are developed on schedule, and whether or not they are supported by marketing, finance, and management programs ready to go at the right time. Again, as in the case of long-range plans, the inquiry will reveal whether decision-making is mature or immature. Has management made profitability a habit, or just a subject of wishful thinking?

A management that knows how to bring plans to fruition builds into every plan a set of controls designed to give early warning of problems and an indication that corrective action is needed. Examination of the controls and the ways in which they are used will indicate whether or not top management is on top of its problems.

WHO MAKES THE PLANS?

Investigation of the methods by which plans are formulated and control is exercised will reveal a great deal about whether top management is autocratic, bureaucratic or democratic. This inquiry holds more than academic interest; the extent to which lower levels of management contribute to the formulation of plans and the extent to which they are held accountable for results will tell much about the firm's down-the-line strength.

EXECUTIVE TURNOVER

Also, these factors are particularly important indicators of whether top management will retain its vigor, will improve or will deteriorate. Thus, they indicate whether or not top management is making sincere efforts to recruit and develop middle management that will become a new and better generation of top management. Other insights into whether management is bringing in too little or too much new blood can be gained by examining age patterns and statistics on turnover in executive ranks, by reviewing formal executive development efforts and by interviews with some of the men.

YARDSTICK TO GAUGE GROWTH FACTORS

In summary, the technique of probing deeply into the firm's actual plans and controls and methods of planning and control can yield abundant evidence to indicate whether or not top management has the characteristics of a growth firm. These characteristics have been set forth in a major study by Stanford Research Institute of the factors that usually distinguish growth from nongrowth firms. They are:

Affinity for growth fields.

Organized programs to seek and promote new opportunities.

Proven competitive abilities in present lines of business.

Courageous and energetic managements, willing to make carefully calculated risks.

Luck.

Incidentally, this study found that high growth companies had twice the earning power of low growth companies, while maintaining four times the growth rate.[13]

THE BOARD OF DIRECTORS

Rounding out the top management of every corporation is an enigmatic, unpublicized group of men about whom a competent analyst should be most curious. They are the Board of Directors. Questions such as these should be asked about them: What influence and/or control does the Board of Directors exercise? What are the capabilities of its members? What are their motivations?

In the author's experience one of the most frequent and serious errors of small and medium-sized firms is failure to have and use effectively a strong Board of Directors. Too often the entrepreneurial types who start firms disdain help until they are in deep trouble.

Especially in firms headed by a scientist or a super-salesman, a strong and active Board can be invaluable in helping make up for the top executives' lack of rounded managerial training and experience. Except

---

[13] *Environmental Change and Corporate Strategy.* (Menlo Park, Calif. Stanford Research Institute, 1960), p. 8. A more recent report on this continuing research project is given by Robert B. Young, "Keys to Corporate Growth," *Harvard Business Review,* vol. 39, no. 6 (November–December 1961), pp. 51–62. Young concludes: "In short, the odds for corporate growth are highest when the top executives of a firm treat their future planning as a practical decision making challenge requiring personal participation, and direct their planning efforts toward the origins of opportunity itself. Such an approach can make the difference between having constantly to adapt to day to day crises and enjoying profitable future growth."

in a few unusual situations, a Board must be an "outside," or non-employee, Board to be strong.

DUMMIES OR POLICY MAKERS

To be active and helpful, an "outside" Board must have some motivation, either financial or the psychic motivation involved in being confronted with real problems and being able to contribute to their solution. Examination of files and minutes of Board meetings will reveal whether or not there is a good flow of information to the outside directors and a contribution by them to the solution of significant problems.

ADDING UP THE FACTS

With all the data in about the four vital areas of a firm, products and competition, operations and R&D, finance, and top management, the analyst ends his task by posing one more set of questions which might be called Summary and Evaluation Strategy. They should run something like this:

What other factors (use a checklist)[14] can assume major importance in this particular situation?

Of all the factors studied, which, if any, is overriding in this particular situation? Which factors are of major importance by virtue of the fact that they govern other factors?

What are the basic facts of life about the economics and competition of this industry now and over the next decade? In view of this firm's particular strengths and weaknesses, what are the odds that it will succeed and at what level of success, in this industry? What are the prospects of its succeeding by diversifying out of its industry?

DETERMINING OTHER VITAL FACTORS

There is a purpose behind every evaluation study. That purpose or the particular nature of the firm and its industry might place importance upon any of an almost infinite number of factors. Accordingly, the evaluator must thoughtfully run through a checklist containing such considerations as: personnel management practices (e.g., labor relations, profit-sharing, compensation levels), valuation questions (e.g., valuation of fixed or real assets or inventory or unique assets), geographical locations as related to labor markets, taxes, cost of distribution, seasonality factors, in-process or impending litigation or any matter foot-

---

[14] For one such checklist, see Robert G. Sproul, Jr. "Sizing up New Acquisitions," *Management Review*, vol. 49, no. 1 (February 1960), pp. 80–82.

noted in the financial reports so that the auditing firm is, in effect, warning of an unusual circumstance.

The purpose of a particular evaluation study often will determine which factor, if any, is overriding. Logically, the quality of top management should usually be the overriding factor. By definition a highly competent top management group can solve the other problems such as securing competent scientists and other personnel, developing new products, getting financing, etc. However, there may be an investment or acquisition situation in which the product line, for example, is the overriding factor because it is so obsolete that even the finest management could not effect a recovery within existing time and financial parameters.

MATCHING BUYER AND ACQUISITION

If the evaluation is being done to help decide the advisability of an acquisition, many additional considerations come into play. The problem is one of matching the acquiring and acquired firms; many firms have acquired grief rather than growth because they have neglected this point. At one extreme, acquisition of one healthy company by another may be unwise because the two are so different that the acquirer may mismanage the acquired company. At the other extreme, it may be wise for one unhealthy company to acquire another unhealthy one if the strengths of one remedy the weaknesses of the other, and vice versa.

THE CHARACTER OF THE COMPANY

The acquirer must precisely define his objectives in acquiring. Also, he must carefully consider the "character," or "climate," of the other firm in relation to his own. The subject of "company character" has not been well developed in management practice or literature.[15] Nevertheless, a consideration of the "character" of the two companies is highly relevant, and the outline presented in this article will help the evaluator consider some of the more obvious elements of "company character" such as the nature of its engineering and manufacturing skills, the type of distribution channels and marketing skills required, the type of managerial leadership practiced and top management's aggressiveness and the quality of its decisions in initiative matters.

In sum, the evaluation of a firm requires a clinical judgment of the highest order. The purposes of the evaluation study set the criteria for the judgment. Except in a few instances in which conditions are highly

---

[15] A new textbook brings together for the first time the few and scattered writings on the subject of "company character." See William B. Wolf's *The Management of Personnel* (San Francisco: Wadsworth Publishing Company, Inc., 1961), pp. 8–43.

stable, the day is rapidly passing when simple financial analyses, or even financial analyses supplemented by a few interviews and judgments of scientists will suffice for evaluation of a firm.

STUDENT REVIEW QUESTIONS

1. Is a strong financial condition in terms of the balance sheet and income statement, a reasonable guarantee that a company has a good future?
2. Of what value is an analysis of the "product life cycle" in evaluating either a profit oriented or nonprofit organization?
3. What does Buchele mean when he says that "no firm progresses evenly"?
4. What criteria can be utilized in rating the top management of an organization? Would the criteria be the same for major managers in both profit oriented and nonprofit organizations?
5. In evaluating an organization today, what would you want to analyze that Buchele does not cover in his article?

8. The Capability Inventory: Its Role in Long-Range Planning *

E. KIRBY WARREN

SEVERAL YEARS ago a bombshell burst on the management scene in the form of an article by Theodore Levitt entitled, "Marketing Myopia."[1] Few articles have had the impact this one had on top management. More reprints were sold and more speeches on the theme given than either Mr. Levitt or the publisher could have imagined.

The article's thesis was disarmingly simple, and once postulated left the reader feeling, "This is so obvious, why didn't I think of it?" Levitt pointed out that in a world experiencing an unprecedented rate and magnitude of change in virtually every aspect of human and industrial activity, the surest way to corporate collapse was to follow a "myopic" view of the reason for a business's success. He used the railroads as a classic example.

> Less than 75 years ago American railroads enjoyed a fierce loyalty among astute Wall Streeters. European monarchs invested in them heavily. Eternal wealth was thought to be the benediction for anybody who could scrape a few thousand dollars together to put into rail stocks. No other form of transportation could compete with railroads in speed, flexibility, durability, economy and growth potentials.
>
> . . . If you had told . . . (the railroad tycoons) . . . 60 years ago that in 30 years they would be flat on their backs, broke, and pleading for government subsidies, they would have thought you totally demented. Such a future was simply not considered possible.[2]

* E. Kirby Warren, "The Capability Inventory: Its Role in Long-Range Planning," *Management of Personnel Quarterly*, vol. 3, no. 4 (Winter 1965), pp. 31–39. Reprinted by special permission of the publisher.

[1] Theodore Levitt, "Marketing Myopia," *Harvard Business Review*, July–August 1960.

[2] Ibid., p. 56.

To Levitt, the impossible took place largely because the railroads failed to recognize that while their economic relevance, the basis for their profit, stemmed from their ability to meet certain basic needs for moving people and products from one point to another quickly and economically, two very important types of changes would take place.

First, new ways of meeting their transportation needs would be developed, and second, the needs themselves would change as the people and products changed. The railroads' failure to anticipate and capitalize on these changes, as Levitt saw it, stemmed from their myopic definition of their business. They thought of themselves as being in the "railroad business," not the "transportation business."

MYOPIA AND LONG-RANGE PLANNING

Coupled with the increased attention being given to more formal long-range planning at the time of this article, the concept of redefining the nature of one's business caught on like wildfire. Within a year or two, few successful companies were willing to run the risk of not having a "Director of Long-Range Planning," if for no other reason than leaving the right impression at Security Analysts' luncheons on Wall Street. Of equal importance was having a modern definition of the business—one which showed respect for the past, but none the less reflected an awareness of the broader future recognized by the farsighted president.

In the course of a survey I was doing on long-range planning practices in fifteen large corporations,[3] I raised the question of broader definitions of a business with the president of a large industrial company serving the railroad industry. Paraphrasing Levitt, I asked the president whether he felt one of the major reasons for the decline of railroads was the tendency by leaders of that industry to view themselves as being in the railroad business rather than the transportation business.

His reply was quite candid. "Probably, the most fortunate thing that has happened in the transportation industry is the fact that most railroads are not in it. The simple fact is that with the exception of a few of the Western railroads, not many have what it takes to be successful in the transportation business."

He went on to explain the basis for this statement by observing that most of the older railroads not only lack the funds to succeed in other areas of transportation, but far more important, lack a sufficient number of men with the talent, training and temperament to be successful managers of a more fully integrated transportation business.

On the surface, this may appear to be an unlikely criticism. Certainly

---

[3] For a full description of this study, See E. Kirby Warren, Long-Range Planning: The Executive Viewpoint (Englewood Cliffs, New Jersey, 1966).

success in the railroad business should demand that the railroads have men with the very same talents, training and temperaments needed in other phases of transportation. For example, trucking and shipping require skills in setting rates, devising schedules, working under state and federal regulation and a host of activities carried out by railroads. Yet, it was this president's contention that the general lack of challenge and growth in many railroads and their excessive reliance on seniority had made it extremely difficult for them to attract top notch talent in these or more general management areas. Moreover, the environment in these companies often is not conducive to attracting men with the kind of temperament to succeed in the more creative and aggressive fields of transportation.

In short, while the railroads should have *an inventory of capabilities* just right for the transportation business, only the more dynamic ones have succeeded in providing the growth opportunities and challenge necessary to attract the kinds of people needed. The railroads which fail to attract this talent must carry out these same functions (for example, rate setting and scheduling) but with second or third rate talent. As a result, they are not very successful in the railroad business and probably would be even less successful in the transportation business.

Perhaps all of these limitations might have been overcome with an earlier awareness of the need and potential for such a business, but it seemed clear to this president that for the leaders of most of today's railroads to think of themselves as being in the transportation business would be worse than myopia. It would be folly firmly based on a foundation of fantasy.

Several months later, following a talk to a group of senior executives participating in a management training program, the president of a large company, which has gained most of its success in the computer industry, was asked how he defined his business. He replied, "Most people think of us as being in the computer business, while actually we are in the information processing business."

His questioner then asked, "Oh, where are your paper mills?"

"Paper mills? We don't own any paper mills," was the quick reply.

"Do you have a pencil factory?" he was asked.

"No," answered the puzzled president.

"Then how can you say you are in the information processing business? Certainly pencil and paper are still two of the most important ingredients in information processing."

As the discussion progressed, it became apparent that these questions had not been raised lightly or simply to embarrass the president. Both he and his company are too highly regarded for that to be the case. His interrogator, it developed, had also read "Marketing Myopia" and was in full agreement with the thesis that too narrow a definition of a business can be disastrous. He was concerned, however, with *how* top management went about broadening their definition and did it in a meaningful way. In effect, he was asking how does a president or chairman go about defining what business he is in and do it in a way which has operational meaning to him and the rest of his management team?

Where Are We? Where Can We Be?

In seeking to develop a more formalized approach to long-range planning, consultants, academicians and practitioners agree that after giving some attention to selection of key people to work on the "plan for planning" and considering the best way of integrating this activity into the political framework of the company, the first key step is to develop objectives.[4] As a backdrop for developing more detailed goals and strategies, some hold that management must first ask and answer several broader questions. You have, quite likely, seen one or more such listings, and while there are numerous variations, the most common will include:

1. Where are we right now? What are our present strengths and weaknesses?
2. Where are we headed if we continue along present lines?
3. Where do we want to be in the next 3–5 years?
4. Where *can* we be? What capabilities and constraints must be recognized?

Having seen such lists, perhaps ad nauseum, the operating executive may be heard to cry (if he has not himself published one) "O.k., I'll buy the questions. Now how do I get the answers?"

A fair amount has been written seeking to provide answers or at least an approach to getting answers to the second and third questions. Much less is to be found aimed toward answering the first and fourth; namely, where are we now and where can we be?

One of the few penetrating attempts to get at these issues is an article by Gordon Conrad, entitled "Unexplored Assets for Diversification."[5] In this thoughtful article Mr. Conrad points out that many attempts at diversification fail because the management of the companies involved had failed to analyze the more subtle core skills and talents possessed by their firms. While they may have analyzed their present products and

---

[4] A good example of such efforts is consolidated in Stewart Thompson's, "Management Creeds and Philosophies," New York, American Management Association, Research Study No. 32.

[5] Gordon R. Conrad, "Unexplored Assets for Diversification," *Harvard Business Review*, September–October 1963.

markets, perhaps even their facilities and financial resources, few companies have really analyzed the types of human talents and temperaments which play a key role in permitting them to profitably sell present products. In short, this vital element in defining what the company now is and can become is not given the consideration it deserves.

Effective Use of Human Resources

The problem facing most successful corporations today, despite the present profit squeeze they face, is not so much limited profit as limited opportunities for profitably utilizing the income and talents now at their disposal. It is not at all uncommon for such corporations to extrapolate growth curves in their existing markets which will fail to fully utilize the resources the company has and will continue to generate if it is to remain successful.

The most obvious but probably less serious problem is with cash flows. An executive vice president of a very successful grain company stated, "We anticipate roughly a two percent gain per year in our present business, but our cash flow generated through past and present sales is and will continue to be far in excess of our needs to meet this demand."

One might suggest that a simple solution would be to simply pay higher dividends or invest these funds in securities. Aside from tax and leverage considerations, these may be feasible solutions, but in few cases does it satisfy the capable executive's desire to see his organization grow and grow at a profit rate consistent with past success. The effective utilization of continued cash flow from existing markets is indeed a difficult problem but by no means *the* most serious problem faced by such a corporation. *More serious* is utilizing the human talents needed in existing markets in the past and perhaps to a lesser degree in the future.

Any large corporation, whether in the grain business or the computer business, to continue to be successful in its existing markets, must develop and maintain certain key talents or capabilities. Whether these be the talents of experienced grain buyers or the types of engineering and production competences needed to design and build good computers, the successful company distinguishes itself by its ability to attract men who possess the talent and temperament necessary to carry out the key functions of the business. In a company growing at a relatively slow rate, it becomes extremely difficult to attract the kinds of core competences required. Men whose talent and temperament could make them outstanding grain buyers find greater outlets and opportunities for growth in other industries, and men with potential engineering and production competences needed in computer companies may find greater challenge and growth in the more exotic electronic applications areas.

This does not come about solely because the work they do is more challenging as much as the fact that they sense the greater challenges and opportunities to be found in the so called "growth industries" or "growth companies."

The opportunity to attract the very kind of technical and managerial talents and temperaments which led to the success of a "maturing" company may diminish not so much because the work has changed, but because opportunities for advancement and innovation diminish as the company sinks into the rut of seeking greater efficiency in relatively slow growth areas.

Thus, the company which seeks growth through diversification, unless it is willing to see its present business atrophy, should seek areas which will challenge and utilize to the fullest possible degree its human resources rather than merely its physical and financial resources.

The large and successful consumer finance company facing increased competition from new as well as old sources may forecast a declining growth rate. To maintain its share of this business, it will have to attract first rate minds with talents and attitudes which will lead to keen judgments on, say, decisions involving actuarial probability. Where will it find opportunities for promotion and growth for these kinds of people in a relatively static growth environment? Some companies in this industry have recognized that the same kind of talent and temperament needed to evaluate these factors is required in successful insurance companies. For this and other reasons, several finance companies now find themselves in the "insurance business." With this new avenue for growth and advancement for certain key people, these companies are finding it much easier to attract the kinds of talents they seek not only for continued success in the finance business but for new profits in insurance.

Conrad[6] cites a number of examples of how such diversification may be planned by seeking to list and analyze the key kinds of competences required for success in one's present business. In conducting this kind of "internal audit," one goes a long way to answering that first question, "Where am I now?" not in terms of products or markets but on a deeper level. It unearths the underlying competences which (1) have led to the successful exploitation of present products and markets, (2) may be required to serve profitably these markets in the future and (3) can be used to expand profitably into new areas. An example of what can happen when such an inventory is not carefully conducted may be helpful in gaining a fuller understanding of not only the need but the techniques for carrying it out.

---

[6] Ibid.

A CASE HISTORY

In order to protect the guilty, we will call this company Whitman Thermostats, Inc.[7] (It is in fact a large and successful company, and the description which follows reflects what actually took place.) Founded during World War II, Whitman produced thermostats exclusively for the United States Government primarily for use in military aircraft. Great stress was placed on high quality and precision (sensitivity), for the failure of such temperature control devices would not only be disastrous to the aircraft using them, but, as a result, disastrous to Whitman's future sales.

At the end of the war, with the cancellation of most government contracts, Whitman found that its stress on quality and precision had enhanced its reputation to the point where the company made a relatively easy transition into serving the commercial aircraft companies and manufacturers whose processing work required such temperature control devices. By 1953, Whitman had more than 1,500 products in its line and was introducing new ones about once a month.

The company's return on assets was better than 40 percent before taxes, and its before tax return on sales approximately 18 percent. However, the president and several board members became concerned about the company's heavy dependence on one or two key industries and, moreover, one or two key companies in these industries. They felt that their profit was much too vulnerable and that diversification into the appliance thermostat market (e.g., toasters and irons) would provide a mass market with relatively stable sales volume and thereby offset any short term losses in the less stable aircraft and process manufacturing industries.

Their sales manager spoke with several appliance manufacturers who exhibited much interest in a higher quality, more sensitive thermostat. Buoyed by this enthusiastic response, he forecast their potential in this market at one million appliance thermostats per month of a total market of eight million a month. Manufacturing facilities, limited by demand for Whitman's other products, were set for initial production of 100,000 units a month.

After seven years of frustration, the records show that Whitman had averaged only 10,000 units a month in sales and had taken a book loss before taxes of close to $100,000 per year. Two questions demand answers. First, why had this happened, and second, why did it take seven

---

[7] A full analysis of this company's activities in the area discussed may be obtained from the Harvard Business School Case Clearing House, *Whitman Thermostats*, EA-G 127R.

years to do something about it? The second question, unfortunately cannot be answered in the scope of this article, if at all. At the very least, the company's continued success in other areas of its business and the board's enthusiastic recommendation of the venture may provide clues. The first question, why the product was such a failure, can be answered and serves as an excellent illustration of the need for answering the "where are we now?" and "where can we be?" questions *before* trying to determine "where we want to be?" in the future.

A way of doing this is to consider each of the key functional areas of Whitman and seek to identify the types of human knowledge, skills and attitudes required for success in the industrial thermostat market and then compare these to the requirements for success in the appliance thermostat market. This should prove helpful, not only in seeking to identify the source of Whitman's difficulties, but more important in providing insight into how any business may actually go about answering the "where are we?" and "where can we be?" questions as a first step in a meaningful definition of what business they *are* in and *should be* in.

Engineering Function

To design thermostats for use in aircraft and processing industries, Whitman had to attract a cadre of engineers with strong background and interest in a combination of electrical and mechanical engineering and physics and sophistication in the field of instrumentation and control. To assure high quality and precision where cost is a less important variable in sales, these men must continually search for new and better ways of designing temperature control devices.[8]

Moving beyond the design state, these engineers must be capable of developing production techniques which assure quality and precision and have built in quality control devices which provide for detection of flaws or deviations during production so that it is not necessary to wait for final testing of a costly and complicated mechanism.

Designing a competitive appliance thermostat requires none of this sophisticated training and skill development on the part of the engineers and moreover would leave Whitman's engineering staff feeling unchallenged and bored. On the other hand, it would require engineering skills in the design of a mass produced product using simple stamping, sampling techniques for quality control and a greater need for miniaturization.

The kind of engineers working for Whitman had many skills which were wasted on the appliance thermostat, lacked several skills which

---

[8] An indication of the engineering orientation in Whitman is illustrated by the fact that they had 100 engineers of a total personnel of 530.

were vital to its success and, most important were temperamentally un-suited to working on this product.

Manufacturing Function

As might be inferred from the description of the engineering compe-tence required for industrial thermostats, manufacturing required equip-ment and facilities for essentially a job-shop operation. With more than 1,500 variations of industrial temperature control devices, no single product was likely to require a long production run. Machinery had to be selected with versatility in mind and arranged in such a way as to facil-itate shifting production schedules.

The men and women workers in production, while primarily in low or semi-skilled job categories, had to be selected and trained to work in a job-shop environment where quality and precision were uppermost in their minds.

If the company ever approached its million units a month volume for appliance thermostats, new machinery and layout would have been essen-tial. Of at least equal importance is the recognition of the fact that the workforce would have to possess not only less technical training but would have to develop skills and attitudes required for an assembly line form of production. It was not surprising to find that the workforce as-signed to the appliance thermostat found it an unrewarding experience which they saw as a drop in status. The factory manager complained of a morale problem with foreman and workers assigned to the appliance thermostat.

A final note on differences in desired attitudes toward production of industrial versus appliance thermostats relates to make or buy decisions on parts. To assure quality and precisions of the industrial thermostats, few parts were bought. The production manager felt that to assure high standards Whitman must make almost all parts. This same philosophy, however unnecessary with respect to the appliance thermostat, prevailed on this product as well. A study of the assembly parts list revealed that in a company making a 40 percent return on assets, and operating at close to full capacity, Whitman was making their own standard hexagonal nuts and washers for the appliance thermostat.

Marketing Function

The marketing function in Whitman involved essentially four types of activities. Namely:

1. Market forecasting and analysis of customer needs.
2. Pricing.

3. Promotion.
4. Supervision of sales force.

Each of these activities could be analyzed in detail with respect to the types of knowledge, skills and attitudes required to market industrial versus appliance thermostats, but a more summary analysis should suffice.

Forecasting and pricing of industrial thermostats required primarily engineering skills in designing the right control device to meet a relatively few customers' needs and then estimating cost at the anticipated volume. Price was secondary to design, precision and quality usually was determined on a cost-plus or bid basis.

For the appliance thermostat, forecasting involved analyzing the needs of a mass market which wanted quality and precision, but only if the price was right. An ability to estimate demand sensitivity and translate customer attitudes into a demand schedule and price structure is vital to the successful marketing of appliance thermostats. Whitman's sales people had virtually *no* experience or *skill* in these areas. They made initial forecasts on some rough data found in trade journals and interviews with "several sales and engineering executives in the electrical appliance industry."[9]

They interpreted interest in a more precise, higher quality appliance thermostat[10] as a blank check. Whitman's average unit price, based initially on cost plus estimates, was 81 cents. The nearest competitor's was 73 cents. Customers wanted a better product but not for eight cents more per unit. Even at the 81 cent level Whitman was losing 86 cents per unit on a full cost basis and estimated incremental costs were at least 78 cents per unit.

Evidence of the inability of Whitman's marketing people to deal with this forecasting and pricing problem is indicated by the fact that after seven years of failure, they are still talking about anywhere from 10 to 25 million unit sales a year if we could "cut our prices and do some minor redesigning of our product."[11]

In the area of promotion, Whitman's marketing departments had no experience in selling this kind of product to this type of market. Their advertising budget was only $190,000, and they placed most of this in aircraft and chemical industry trade journals plus four advertisements in *Fortune*.

Whitman's sales force consisted of eight salesmen who did missionary selling in aircraft and industrial processing industries. In addition, they sold through 30 manufacturing agents who handled products going to

---

[9] Harvard Business School Case Clearing House, *Whitman Thermostats*, p. 4.

[10] Whitman's appliance thermostat was sensitive to $\pm$ 0.10 degrees, while most competing models were sensitive at best to $\pm$ 5.00 degrees.

[11] Harvard Business School Case Clearing House, *Whitman Thermostats*, p. 12.

aircraft and processing industries. Nearly all of the salesmen and agents were graduate engineers with training in heating engineering.

Again, as in the engineering function, the sales force had many skills and contacts which were wasted on the appliance thermostat, lacked skills and contacts which were vital to its success and were temperamentally unsuited to "degrade" themselves by selling the kind of appliance thermostat which the market would buy.

Finally, consider the kinds of skills and attitudes required to plan for, supervise and motivate the company's present sales team, and contrast this to what would be needed to supervise a sales force slugging it out in the price competitive, volume based appliance thermostat market.

Whitman Summary

It is possible to continue this analysis out of the functional areas up to top management to show the different types of managerial skills and attitudes which would be required in organizing and administering a company pursuing both successful industrial and successful appliance thermostat operations. However, this should not be necessary. The basic point should be clear; for Whitman to succeed in the highly competitive appliance thermostat business they would require not only different facilities and techniques but quite a different assortment of *knowledge, skills* and *attitudes* in each of the key functional areas of their business.

Can they not acquire such people? Of course! The question of designing an organization structure and work arrangements which will allow them to work effectively under the same corporate roof with the types of people needed in Whitman's industrial business is another matter, however. That they can attract such talents seems obvious, but the key question is, *should they?*

If they succeed, they will be in what amounts to virtually a new business. A rose may be a rose, but an industrial thermostat market is not an appliance thermostat market. They may either recruit individually the several talents they need or obtain them at auction through an acquisition. But what reason do they have for believing that they are going to be successful in this new business? What do they contribute, besides cash, which would lead you as an investor to believe they were going to make money in this area? Check your response by considering the preceding analysis of their functional departments (engineering, production and marketing).

Even if they should succeed in acquiring the knowledge, skills and attitudes essential to success in this market, what has happened to their initial objective of protecting themselves from the vulnerability of their present markets? If they should lose a large segment of their industrial market, how many of the people and facilities no longer needed there could be easily shifted to a hopefully expanding appliance thermostat division? Not many! Even if they maintain a steady share of a slowly growing industrial market, how much opportunity for growth and challenge is provided by the possibility of horizontal movement of key personnel between the new and old business? Again, not much.

Success in the appliance thermostat industry may allow Whitman to "hedge their bets," but the only hedge they have is on profits. If they lose income in one market, there may be enough coming in from the other to keep the wolf from the door. But if this is the sole reason for diversification, why not simply invest in a good portfolio of common stock in companies which at present seem to have more of what is required for success in their business than Whitman has at present in the appliance thermostat business?

The ideal solution to Whitman's problems is to find new markets and products which not only hedge against losses in their present business but which will utilize the kinds of capabilities Whitman now has and will continue to need to remain successful in its present business. As you consider these capabilities, analyzed earlier, what kinds of ventures would you recommend to Whitman?

SETTLING FOR SECOND BEST

Assuming you can find no new fields which promise the same growth and profit potential as the appliance thermostat market, you may wish to settle for second best. Many companies move into new fields which utilize few of the competences they now have or will require for their existing business. A few even do this consciously. It should be recognized, however, that they are settling for second best. They cannot hope to get the same flexible use of their internal capabilities, and they must deal with the complex problems noted earlier of trying to design and manage an organization made up of groups of people with very different talents and temperaments. This is no mean task but can be accomplished. The difficulties experienced by such companies as General Dynamics or Curtiss Wright provide good case histories of the problems involved.

Some companies have met these challenges quite successfully. Textron is a good case in point. On the surface, one might analyze Textron's success by saying that the only ground rule followed there was shrewd judgment on whether a given new venture promised to be profitable. Though the company began by supposedly building an integrated textile empire it soon became apparent, with its entrance into electronics and other fields unrelated to textiles, that Royal Little was not to be constrained by his ability to build on the internal competences found within his existing business. It is probably equally true that failure of any one division of the Textron company would produce little shifting of talents from it to one of the more successful divisions.

However, a more careful analysis of the Textron story tends to support rather than reject the hypothesis of this article. What has been the single greatest reason for Textron's success up to now? What combination of talents and temperaments gave it its eminence? Was it not the incredible financial genius and risk taking temperament of Royal Little and a rotating cadre of financial wizards with which he had surrounded himself? This was the real key to Textron's success. He had an uncanny ability to identify companies which could be acquired at the right price. These same companies were then financed and controlled by the techniques Mr. Little had at his disposal and more often than not became more profitable as a result. If the new addition appeared headed for serious trouble, these same financial skills enabled him to spot this sooner than potential buyers and the potential trouble was usually spun off at a profit.

Thus, Textron, in the early years of its growth, tends to support rather than negate the wisdom of setting long-range goals with an understanding of the company's capabilities in mind. While Textron offered little in the way of production, engineering or marketing competence to its newly acquired company, these were not areas which required an infusion of new talent.

In Royal Little and his close associates lay the key financial talents and risk taking temperament to identify companies which could be acquired at an attractive price and/or made more profitable with Textron's funds, financial skills and market image behind them. He built his empire with what appears to be a clear concept in mind as to what Textron was and what it could become. Whether these financial talents and temperaments were sufficient to hold the empire together on a profitable basis now appears doubtful, and recent changes in Textron seem designed to give it a broader yet integrated base at the top management level.

CONCLUSIONS: THE NEED FOR BIFOCALS

Peter Drucker, generally regarded as the master of management maxims, in his landmark book, the *Practice of Management*[12] asks two of the key questions we have been considering. He asks, "What is our business?" and "What should it be?" But, like Levitt, he seems to place an undue amount of emphasis on looking ahead to the ever changing nature of the market to find the answers. Drucker suggests that in defining a business in its present state and understanding the nature of its desired future state, the thoughtful executive first must focus his attention on the nature of the consumer needs his company now satisfies. By seeking to understand these needs and the ways his products satisfy them, the imaginative executive may anticipate new and better ways of satisfying *not*

---

[12] Peter F. Drucker, *The Practice of Management* (New York: Harper & Brothers, 1954), see chapters 4 and 5 in particular.

his customer's *present needs,* for these will change, *but* the *future forms of* these *present needs.*[13]

To do this kind of forecasting requires not only looking ahead to technological and competitive changes in the product, but social and cultural changes in the customer. No one suffering from myopia will ever make such vital forecasts or act on them even if they are made for him. The management literature in recent years has picked up this theme and offered numerous prescriptions for the kind of "eyeglasses" necessary for these kinds of long-range looks into the future.

However, what the executive needs is not merely distance lenses but bifocals. To successfully remold, redesign and administer his business in the least disruptive manner, as he seeks to anticipate and prepare for the vistas which lie ahead, the executive must also clearly see what lies *immediately* around him. He must be capable of clearly identifying those talents and temperaments which make his business and seek to select from among alternative avenues of long-run growth those which best balance market potential with the internal competences which will influence profit potential.

Of at least equal importance to understanding the nature of customer needs is understanding the nature of those types of knowledge, skills and attitudes which your business possesses which have enabled or may enable you to meet these needs. Such a capability inventory is a *first step* in answering such questions as "Where should my business be in 3–5 years?" and "Where can it be?" It paves the way for identifying those kinds of future activities which can be profitably exploited by the company in a manner which utilizes, to at least some degree, the competences which exist and will remain vital to continued profit in existing products and markets.

Such a capability inventory, taken through the lower lenses of the bifocals, will indicate ways of profitably utilizing the scarest of all corporate assets—not money but human capabilities. It will point toward greater profit in new ventures, but of equal importance, it will point to ways of offering growth and challenge to the people responsible for the past and future success of the present business.

STEPS IN DEVELOPING AND USING A CAPABILITY INVENTORY

1. Analysis of Key Tasks

   a. What are the pivotal tasks which spell the difference between profit and loss?

   Consider each key product and market and ask what is it that

---

[13] Ibid., pp. 52–56.

you do in design, production and marketing, which allows you to bring the right product or service to the right market, at the right time and at the right price. If they are likely to change, seek to identify the nature of the changes.

b. Who performs these key tasks?

Identify those individuals or work groups who carry out these tasks. If you can find examples of a key task which is carried out well by one individual and poorly by another, be certain to identify both, and seek to pinpoint the reasons for the differences in the next phase of the analysis.

2. Analysis of Key People

a. What kinds of knowledge are required to carry out key tasks?

Knowledge is often used to describe both awareness and understanding of information, facts and theories, and skill in applying these cognitive bits to real world situations.[14] Both types of knowledge are usually necessary to carry out key tasks, but it is worth distinguishing between them. Consider first the kind of formal training (e.g., book work and academic activities) needed to gain a theoretical understanding of the things required to carry out key tasks. For example, in Whitman Thermostat a key task is the design of precise, high quality temperature control devices for use in aircraft. Key people would include design engineers who have knowledge *about* physics, electrical and mechanical engineering and the fields of instrumentation and control.

b. What kinds of skills are required to carry out key tasks?

Here, seek to identify the most capable individuals, and the kinds of skills or abilities needed to apply the more theoretical forms of knowledge considered above to real world situations. Whitman's design engineers must be able to translate the knowledge of physics to specific applications needed to design a temperature control device which will meet the needs of aircraft companies and still be produced and sold at a profit. What are these skills, and how are they acquired?

c. What kinds of attitudes or temperaments are required to carry out key tasks?

The individuals who carry out the key tasks quite often share certain common attitudes or perspectives about their work or the

---

[14] Charles E. Summer, Jr., in *Factors in Effective Administration* (New York: Graduate School of Business, Columbia University, 1956), deals in considerable depth with the nature of knowledge or skills and attitudes in administration.

company. Identify these attitudes. What motivates them? What makes them angry or frustrated?

Again, using Whitman as an example, the semi-skilled production workers who are key people in the successful manufacture of industrial thermostats developed certain attitudes toward job-shop production of high quality, precision products. Though they had more than enough knowledge and skill to work on mass produced, low quality, less precise products, they would be temperamentally unsuited to do such work. If Whitman sought to use them in this way, morale and production efficiency would be likely to suffer as a result.

3. Conducting the Capability Inventory

   a. The need for a multi-level approach.

To answer the several types of questions raised by such an inventory will require work done at virtually all levels of the company. It is essential to get both the broad views held by top management and the identification of more specific capabilities which must be carried out by key line and staff managers at all levels of the company.

   b. The coordinating function.

If your company has a director of long-range planning or some individual responsible for coordinating future planning or diversification, he may be the ideal man to oversee this activity. He should design the forms used and see to their consolidation and summary. In addition, he may profitably undertake an independent inventory of his own, hopefully reflecting the objective and relatively broad perspective he should have.

   c. The role of the personnel department.

Particularly in companies which conduct formal appraisal programs, the personnel department should be a source of key data and should be deeply involved in this activity. You must be careful, however, to get from personnel answers to the kinds of questions raised above and not just answers to questions on which they have data available. Quite often, as in the accounting area, data which must be collected to meet recurring operating needs may need revision and change in focus to highlight the factors vital to specific surveys such as this. Typically the personnel department has the kind of data needed or is in an ideal position in terms of its talents and temperaments to collect and analyze them.

   d. The role of outsiders.

In some cases, it may be desirable to utilize the services of management consultants, and perhaps even industrial psychologists, to add further objectivity and expertise in analyzing the types of knowledge, skills and temperaments found within the company.

4. Using the Capability Inventory

   a. What other types of work will require similar knowledge, skills and attitudes?

Seek to identify other bundles of work which require people who possess combinations of knowledge, skills and attitudes which characterize your key people. The key production people in Whitman may be much closer to having what is required to produce quality gauges and complex servo-mechanisms, or even hi-fi speakers, than appliance thermostats. Just as care should be taken to analyze whether changes in technology are likely to alter the kinds of capabilities you will require for continual success in your present business, the analysis of other types of work which might utilize these capabilities must be future-oriented as well.

   b. Combining capability considerations with non-human resource considerations.

Not to be overlooked is the degree to which new ventures will utilize existing facilities, funds or such intangibles as market image. Little attention has been given to these considerations in this article, not because they are unimportant, but rather because they are seldom overlooked in defining the present nature of the business or identifying opportunities for diversification. In fact their more tangible nature often leads to their overshadowing human considerations. The capability inventory when considered in conjunction with these factors *measures feasibility.*

   c. Combining capability considerations with market potential.

A thorough analysis of those types of work which require capabilities similar to those your key people possess should assist in uncovering opportunities for growth and diversification which can be most easily integrated with your existing business. Two questions remain to be answered. First, does the work which will utilize these capabilities represent *key* elements in the success of the other businesses? Second, do these other businesses offer sufficient growth and profit potential to justify the investment of capital and human resources?

STUDENT REVIEW QUESTIONS

1. How does the author link myopia and long-range planning? Give one example of myopia in business.
2. Do you think that human resources constitute a more valuable capability for an organization than financial resources?
3. What was the problem in Whitman Thermostats, Inc. which was described in Warren's article?
4. What does Warren think was the key capability of Textron which led to that company's success?
5. What steps must be taken in an organization to develop and use a capability inventory?
6. Does the capability inventory process apply to a university as well as to a business organization?

chapter 4

The Search for Opportunity: Assessment of the External Environment

Introduction

The Need for Appraisal of the Environment

The Major Environmental Forces

Technological Forces

Sociocultural and Psychological Forces

Legal-Governmental Factors

Economic Factors

Industry Structure and Practices—Competition

On Appraising the Environment

Summary

Readings

INTRODUCTION

THE SEARCH for opportunity can be viewed as the external analysis of the organization. As noted in the previous chapter, it is a crucial aspect of the overall or combined analysis of the organization as a totality. In evaluating the organization and its strategy, and in looking to the future with regard to potential strategies and opportunities, it is vital to consider the environment of the organization: those influences which though beyond the entity's control affect it in as great a magnitude as any internal force or influence, and even more dramatically in many cases.

To perform a total analysis of an organization, the analyst (manager, or student) must consider the pervasive influence of the external environment and view how well management has dealt with or is dealing with this set of forces. The analysis should consider these factors in a comprehensive interrelated fashion after considering individually the various elements of the environment to be discussed in this chapter. Thus, thorough external analysis identifies and analyzes environmental influences individually and collectively to determine the effects and potential effects on an organization and the consequent problems or opportunities. It considers management's skill or lack of success in its previous interaction with the environment, and it assists in determining what will be required in the future if the organization is to have a strategy that will be successful in the environment as it appears to be changing.

The institution that intends to develop a viable strategy with which to pursue its future, then, must engage in this continuing task of evaluating its environment in search of opportunity. This chapter discusses in detail the nature of the environment, or more precisely, the various environments that are critical to the life and vitality of a business firm or any other type of organization.

Just as a human being is a product of heredity and environment, so, too, is an organization. Its heredity corresponds to its history and often this is the primary behavioral determinant. But like a man's heredity, an organization can do virtually nothing about its past history. Also like a human, however, an organization can do much about its environment: analyze it; predict it; attempt to change it in various ways; adapt to it; or leave it (or some major part of it). But before a management can make a prudent decision to change, to adapt, or to leave its organization's environment, management must first analyze that environment and predict its future. Analyzing and predicting the environment includes not only the situation as it is, but more importantly, how it appears it will be.

As suggested above, it may be clearer and more accurate to consider environments in the plural sense, for the environment of an institution is composed of numerous elements and forces which act and react to the benefit or detriment of the organization. The overall effect of these forces on the organization will depend to a great degree upon its preparation for benefiting from or countering such forces. Thus a dynamic strategy must incorporate as a major element a procedure for the continuous appraisal of the organization's environment. Risk always remains in the possibility of a major environmental force erupting without prior knowledge or warning to the organization. The less immediate threat of missing an opportunity by being unaware of developing environmental change is not so dramatic but can be often as significant to the life of an organization.

Thus, a management has as major functions seeking opportunity and limiting risk, both in degrees acceptable to the constituencies of the organization. This is most successfully accomplished by developing a workable corporate strategy which in turn requires effective interaction with the environment, based upon accurate environmental appraisal and assessment. Without this basic element of the strategy formulation process, an organization's management cannot properly control its destiny, plan for the future, limit risk, or select from among major alternative opportunities in an informed and intelligent manner.

As difficult as it may be to foresee the future or to recognize the harbingers of change, it must be the continuing job of top management to attempt to do just that. The skill and ingenuity which bring success to this task will often be the scarcest of corporate resources. As such, they must be cultivated and developed in a planned fashion and implemented in a coordinated way into the strategic planning process of an organization. Of the various facets of the managerial job, the task of environmental appraisal seems to have received too little attention over the years considering the vital and far-reaching impact it has on an organization's success, and even survival.

The ability to deal well with the environment has enabled organizations to survive and even prosper despite other weaknesses. Correspondingly the "best managed companies" whose managements may be currently devoting their efforts and energies in a direction not in tune with a changing environment may be headed for serious difficulties and possible disaster. This threat exists because of the enormous influence and impact which environmental change may have on a business firm or other type of institution. Thus the importance of environment appraisal to any organization's success cannot be overemphasized.

This chapter and other parts of the book will examine the vital elements of the environment and indicate their influences in the strategy formulation process. While the particular focus of this book is business policy, the concept of organizational strategy and the role of top management in strategy formulation and implementation has value for nonbusiness organizations. A key element in the strategic process is the continuous appraisal of the present environment, the prediction of future states of the environment, and the subsequent formulation of appropriate action by all types of organizations.

THE NEED FOR APPRAISAL OF THE ENVIRONMENT

The organization of the 1970s is part of a complex world; it does not exist in isolation. If the "build a better mousetrap and the world will beat a path to your door" philosophy of business practice ever made good management sense, and one may doubt that it ever really did, it is not a useful guideline for management practice today. Yet this is a lesson that even two mousetrap manufacturers have had to learn the hard way![1]

An alert management must be continually tuned in to the forces present in the environment that influence the demand for existing products and services, and that create opportunities for new products and services. This is so whether the organization is profit oriented or nonprofit. Management must continually be asking: What changes are occurring that will affect our position in our market(s) five, ten, or more years hence? Fifty-seven of the 100 corporations which dominated U.S. industry in 1918 had within the succeeding 50 years either gone out of business or suffered a drastic reduction in importance. "In most of these 57 cases, the deterioration of these organizations has been traced to their inability to organize for and adapt to a changing business environment."[2]

The impact of environmental change extends beyond the product or service offered by an institution. External, uncontrollable factors and conditions can influence the ability to obtain capital or other funds; can affect the supply and the attitudes of labor; can diminish the utility of plant and equipment or render technology obsolete; can impair raw material sources; can limit or otherwise influence the planning and decision making of management.

Although change is ever present in the environment, most institutions are not organized to carefully appraise what is happening outside. Often, there is an elaborate data gathering system for measuring and reporting internal operations and changes. Daily, weekly, monthly, quarterly, and yearly reports measure and interpret what is happening within the organization, and "report" various internal information to inside and even to the outside world. But the significant events taking place outside the organization must also be continuously monitored. The entity's future will be greatly influenced by what is occurring in the environment. "In order to grow, to innovate, to manage change, a business must convert its unknown environment to a known and, it is hoped, friendly one. If it is friendly, it presents an opportunity for innovation. If it is hostile, it presents a threat to the continued success of the enterprise, and some form of innovation is required to respond to the challenge."[3]

The involvement between an enterprise and its environment is, of course, not just one way; that is, the enterprise reacting to the environment. The environment also reacts to the enterprise, and this reaction is

---

[1] See Matthews, John B. et al., *Marketing: An Introductory Analysis* (New York: McGraw-Hill Book Co., 1964), pp. 3–6, for the story of the better 7 cent mousetrap that flopped, and the *Wall Street Journal*, March 7, 1967, p. 1, for the story of the better $29.95 mousetrap that also was unsuccessful commercially.

[2] *On Target*, vol.1, no. 4 (October 1968), p. 1.

[3] Robert D. Bruce, "The Role of Technoeconomics in Managing Innovation," *Michigan Business Paper*, no. 41 (1964), p. 51.

especially apparent when an enterprise's technological innovation causes major changes in the environment. The impact of the development of the automobile, the radio, the television, the airplane, and vaccines, on the environment of the pioneering organizations has become so profound as to appear with hindsight to be self-evident.

But the effects of change are most easily seen and documented after change has taken place. For a business firm this recognition may be too late, for its world (the needs and wants in the marketplace that is satisfied) may now be the province of a competitor. There are many historical examples of the failure of companies to recognize and react to changing conditions. Levitt in his classic "Marketing Myopia" cites the railroad, movie, and oil industries.[4] It is interesting to look back at the automobile companies and the models that existed a few decades ago. Many of the names (Marmon, Franklin, Reo, Cord, Auburn, Teraplane, Essex) are unknown to today's auto shoppers.[5] All firms cannot expect to be skillful and lucky enough to correctly identify and anticipate all the developments that will influence the future and be ready for the resulting opportunities. Some may interpret the forces of change incorrectly or be unwilling to acknowledge that significant change is taking place, or that the change will affect them greatly. As in all managerial decision areas, the firm's management must be right often enough on balance, especially in those critical cases that could eventually spell ultimate failure or success.

The reaction of elements of the environment to the organization also cause undesirable events. The increased awareness and concern about the possible effects on the environment of various forms of alleged industrial pollution has led to the boycott of products (detergent companies) thought by some to be responsible for environmental pollution. For one company, Dow Chemical Company, unfavorable reaction to its production of napalm led to threats of personal harm to company executives; in some cases they were virtually held prisoner in recruiting rooms on college campuses during the late 1960s.

The state of the environment may be such that it is not ready to receive an organization's offered innovation. The innovation that appears ahead of its time (made available before the environment is ready to react favorably to it) is usually not successful. An organization several years ago test-marketed a new aspirin tablet which could be chewed and swallowed without the usual drink of water. It was unsuccessful.[6] Universities sometimes offer new courses and programs that find few interested students and thus are canceled. This situation can be characterized

[4] Theodore Levitt, "Marketing Myopia," *Harvard Business Review*, July–August 1960, pp. 45–56.

[5] Robert J. Holloway and Robert S. Hancock, *Marketing in a Changing Environment* (New York: John Wiley & Sons, Inc., 1968), p. 311.

[6] Ibid., p. 58.

as being the earliest pioneer and getting the sharpest arrows. Pioneering is not all glamour and reward; risk is always prevalent in such situations.

Usually there is some remaining opportunity to act before it becomes too late for an institution that is slow to change, but often at a significant loss in market position. Recent retailing history provides two major examples of industry leaders not responding to environmental changes which created opportunities for innovators who became well established before the leaders followed. In the 1930s, the supermarket concept (a result of the interaction of a number of environmental forces) was spurned by a major food retailer, popularized by independents, and only belatedly adopted by the dominant food retailing companies. Likewise in the general merchandise area, it was the independents who in the 1950s undertook to popularize so-called discounting; in recent years established mercantile giants have begun to operate general merchandise "discount outlets." McNair has aptly observed: "At the outset he [editor's note; a retailing innovator] is a bad odor, ridiculed, scorned, condemned, or 'illegitimate.' Bankers and investors are leery of him. But he attracts the public on the basis of the price appeal made possible by the low operating costs inherent in his innovation."[7]

A failure to respond in some way to the changes taking place in the environment can and typically does result in the eventual failure of the institution no matter how well it might have been operated internally. Even the most efficient buggy whip manufacturer would no longer be in business.[8] Likewise hospitals that have not kept up with medical technology and advances cannot attract patients today. But if management recognizes that products and services have life cycles and that today's winners will decline tomorrow, it is planning their successors—"tomorrow's breadwinners."[9] And it is planning to have the resources needed to produce and market these successors to a receptive environment. This process of planning must focus on the external environment.

THE MAJOR ENVIRONMENTAL FORCES

The major forces which influence organizations and which are essentially uncontrollable by the individual company are: technological, sociocultural, psychological, legal-governmental, economic, and also facets of the "industry" structure. Taken as a whole, this complex of interrelated

---

[7] Ronald E. Gist, *Retailing: Concepts and Decisions* (New York: John Wiley & Sons, Inc., 1968), p. 89.

[8] Harvey M. Bonini, Robert K. Jaedicke, and Charles P. Wagner, *Management Controls* (New York: McGraw-Hill Book Co., 1964), p. 291.

[9] Peter F. Drucker, *Managing for Results* (New York: Harper & Row, Publishers, 1964), p. 144.

factors external to the entity and uncontrollable by it, is generally considered to be its environment.

TECHNOLOGICAL FORCES

The most apparent and dramatic environmental force is often technology. It usually becomes known in the form of a breakthrough that receives widespread publicity. (Often, however, the inventor, discoverer, or other researchers have been conducting relevant research for many years in companies, hospitals, or universities.) When the technological breakthrough has obvious implication for the general public its impact is widely ballyhooed. Organizations likely to be affected cannot help but be apprised of it. However, when the ramifications are not immediately apparent, potentially significant technological breakthroughs may be unheralded or overlooked by those likely to be influenced. The failure of IBM to assess the impact of Chester Carlson's first pattern on xerography despite the efforts of a young IBM marketing man for a year and a half to interest his company in the invention is an example.[10]

While 20th-century industrial development provides numerous examples of the effects of technological innovation. It also reveals that the time gap between a scientific discovery and its commercial application has been greatly reduced in recent years. For example, it took 112 years for photography to become a commercial product, and 56 years for the telephone. But television took just 12 years and transistors only 5.[11]

But the alert management must not only be aware of developments of technological import; it must attempt to accurately assess their impact. Considerable publicity was given to the Curtiss-Wright Aero-car, the Wankel engine, RCA's ultrafax transmission reproduction facsimile demonstration, and the Allis Chalmers fuel cell powered tractor. "All were impressive demonstrations of new technology in use, but they have not yet become operational."[12] Likewise research continues on a cure for cancer with apparent breakthroughs periodically, but an actual cure has thus far eluded the researchers.

As guidelines for the effective appraisal of significant technological advances, Bright has suggested:

1. Searching the environment for signals that may be forerunners of significant technological change.
2. Identifying the possible consequences (assuming that these signals are not false and the trends that they suggest persist).

---

[10] James R. Bright, "Evaluating Signals of Technical Change," *Harvard Business Review*, January–February 1970, p. 66.

[11] *On Target*, p. 1.

[12] Bright, "Evaluating Signals of Technological Change," p. 66.

3. Choosing the parameters, policies, events, and decisions that should be observed and followed to verify the true speed and direction of technology and the effects of employing it.
4. Presenting the data from the foregoing steps in a timely and appropriate manner for management's use in decisions about the organization's reaction.[13]

But managements must recognize that the impact of technological developments and breakthroughs is experienced in other important areas besides the product line. The technological innovation that becomes a major product feature for the organization producing a kind of processing equipment presents a decision to those institutions that might be prospective customers for the equipment. For example, the management of an airline considering the purchase of jumbo jets in the early 1970s may have decided that the innovation had such promise that such planes had to be incorporated as soon as possible into the company's service. In other cases (such as the use of industrial robots), the opportunity may have to be weighed against such considerations as the costs involved, the disruption of ongoing processing, and concern about the speed of obsolescence. In these instances, the effect of a new development can influence not only the production line, but also the financial function (how to finance the new process) and the personnel function (obtaining and/or training personnel to operate the new equipment).

The impact of technological change and developments can even reach the executive suite. Certainly the computer has had a major influence on the kinds of information reaching management. New computer-related approaches to decision making may eventually alter dramatically the executive's performance of his task.

SOCIOCULTURAL AND PSYCHOLOGICAL FORCES

While technology may tend to be the most visible force, the most important forces from the organization's point of view are sometimes those affecting the behavior of people. If one understands that the ultimate requirement for the firm's existence is the sale of its products (the major source of revenue for the firm), then one recognizes the importance of consumer behavior. And for a nonprofit organization, also, the product or service must be wanted if the organization is to survive. While from an analytical point of view consumer behavior may be considered as a separate environmental factor, it needs to be understood that just as the effects on the organization are a result of the interrelationship of the various environmental forces, consumer behavior (the decisioning process of the consumer) reflects the interaction upon the prospective buyer of

---

[13] Ibid., p. 64.

the various forces in the consumer's environment. Likewise it needs to be recognized that consumer behavior reflects not only the total sales achieved by the organization but also the negative purchase decisions, resulting either from conscious decisions by the consumer, or lack of knowledge about or interest in the firm's product(s). Consumer behavior in the aggregate is a resultant of individual decisions each of which may be differently affected by the considerations discussed below.

Behavioral forces have other significant effects besides their influence on consumer behavior. The organization itself, that is, its employees and management, is influenced by behavioral forces. Likewise are suppliers affected including the suppliers of funds. Knowledge developed in the fields of anthropology, sociology, and psychology is especially important for the environmental analyst. Of widespread effect is what might be broadly labeled "group behavior." Groups can be defined in a variety of different ways and sizes, perhaps from societies, or races as an entity to social classes, religions, down to families, even subgroups within families, or small work or social groups. Members of groups share certain characteristics, or beliefs, or attitudes, standards of behavior, or likes, dislikes, and so on. The individual's need to conform to group norms or to seek approval of other group members can influence his behavior. The effect can be felt by the business firm in the purchase of its products, in the behavior of its employees, or the actions of its management. For example, consider the impact of the attitudes developed by groups toward personal appearance. In the clothing industry, manufacturers of garments must constantly try to predict whether a particular style may become fashionable and have a major effect on demand for its products. Managements of other firms in other industries may find themselves trying to decide whether various garments are acceptable on-the-job clothing for employees.[14] The attitudes of nurses, teachers, professors, and other professionals toward unionization is a behavioral factor vital to numerous nonprofit organizations.

Another useful sociological concept that provides some insights to people's behavior is the life cycle. Exhibit 4–1 presents the life cycle as formulated by Wells and Gubar.[15] This approach has obvious implications for attempting to analyze the demand for one's products, as well as for governments in determining what services must be offered. It also can be useful, however, in attempting to appraise the motivations and behavior of one's employees. One obviously would not expect the "solitary

---

[14] The controversies over slack suits, "hot pants," and "no bras" are examples, and IBM dress policies have made news. See *Wall Street Journal*, May 6, 1971, p. 1; also Ibid., February 23, 1971, p. 1, and March 25, 1971, p. 17.

[15] From *Journal of Marketing Research*, November 1966, p. 362, reproduced in William Lazer, *Marketing Management: A Systems Perspective* (New York: John Wiley & Sons, Inc., 1971), pp. 444–45.

survivor in labor force" and the "young single not living at home" to have very much in common. Yet these individuals may be co-workers, may need to interact regularly on the job, may be members of the same union, but may need to be managed very differently.

Similarly, Warner's well-known social class concept may provide useful insights into one's customers and one's employees.

While associative or belonging groups have an important influence on individual behavior, a subtle influence is caused by people's tendencies to associate with reference groups, groups to which the individual does not actually belong but to which he aspires. As one anthropologist has written:

> Each consumer has some group deep in mind that he would like to be like, some group in mind that he unconsciously copies; so when you are aiming something at the consumer, you've got to know not only the group he belongs to but what is his reference group—what has he in mind that he would like to be like.[16]

Hugh Hefner is thought by many to have had this concept in mind when aiming his "Playboy" concept at many who would only aspire to that status.[17]

Just as individuals belong to any number of different groups, many probably aspire to membership in various reference groups, depending on the subject or activity involved. The perceptive manager, then, as he or she appraises the environment of his or her organization must be cognizant of the relevant groups that influence the behavior of his customers, employees, fellow managers, competitors, and suppliers, and continually seek to uncover signs of changes and attempt to determine the effect of these changes on his operation.

The behavior of people is also influenced by broad social forces that are present in our society. These forces reflect a multiplicity of interacting developments, changes, trends, subtle and bold, gradual and sudden, that seem to come together in the form of a major influence. Leisure is one such influence that vividly illustrates profound change over a wide time span. Veblen wrote *The Theory of the Leisure Class* to describe leisure as an upper class privilege. Today, it is a mass phenomenon that affects the values of our society and marketplace opportunities.[18] It has

---

[16] Margaret C. Piery, "Anthropologist Classifies Buyers by Social Class and Finds 'Upper Middle Is the Lush Key Target,'" *Advertising Age*, April 12, 1958, pp. 87–88, reproduced in William Lazer, *Marketing Management: A Systems Perspective* (New York: John Wiley & Sons, Inc., 1971), p. 485.

[17] See "H.M.H. Publishing Company" Case, in E. P. Learned, C. R. Christensen, K. R. Andrews, and W. D. Guth, *Business Policy: Text and Cases* (Homewood, Ill.: Richard D. Irwin, Inc., 1965), p. 406.

[18] Lazer, *Marketing Management,* pp. 506–10.

EXHIBIT 4-1
An Overview of the Life Cycle

Bachelor Stage: Young Single People not Living at Home	Newly Married Couples: Young—No Children	Full Nest I: Youngest Child under Six	Full Nest II: Youngest Child Six or over Six	Full Nest III: Older Married Couples with Dependent Children
Few financial burdens.	Better off financially than they will be in near future.	Home purchasing at peak.	Financial position better.	Financial position still better.
Fashion opinion leaders.	Highest purchase rate and highest average purchase of durables.	Liquid assets low, dissatisfied with financial position and amount of money saved.	Some wives work.	More wives work.
Recreation oriented.		Interested in new products like advertised products.	Less influenced by advertising.	Some children get jobs.
Buy: Basic kitchen equipment, basic furniture, cars, equipment for the mating game, vacations.	Buy: Cars, refrigerators, stoves, sensible and durable furniture, vacations.	Buy: Washers, dryers, baby food, chest rubs and cough medicines, vitamins, dolls, wagons, sleds, skates, T.V.	Buy: Larger sized packages, multiple unit deals.	Hard to influence with advertising.
			Buy: Many foods, cleaning materials, bicycles, music lessons, pianos.	High average purchase of durables.
				Buy: New, more tasteful furniture, auto travel, nonnecessary appliances, boats, dental services, magazines.

EXHIBIT 4-1 (continued)

Empty Nest I: Older Married Couples, No Children Living with Them, Head in Labor Force	Empty Nest II: Older Married Couples, No Children at Home, Head is Retired	Solitary Survivor in Labor Force	Solitary Survivor Retired
Home ownership at peak.	Drastic cut in income.	Income still good but likely to sell home.	Same medical and product needs as other retired group; drastic cut in income.
Most satisfied with financial position and money saved.	Keep home.		Special need for attention, affection and security.
Interested in travel, recreation, self-education.	Buy: Medical appliances, medical care products which aid health, sleep, and digestion.		
Make gifts and contributions.			
Not interested in new products.			
Buy: Vacations, luxuries, home improvements.			

Source: William D. Wells and George Gubar, *Journal of Marketing Research*, November 1966, p. 362. Reproduced in William Lazer, *Marketing Management and Systems Perspective* (New York: John Wiley & Sons, Inc., 1971), pp. 444–45.

spawned innumerable new products and services and has had a significant effect on people's life-styles. It affects not only the product-planning activities of business firms, but also the attitudes and behavior of employees. For example, it provides as desirable alternatives to a pay raise, shorter working hours, or longer vacations.[19] Other effects can readily be developed and the manager must grasp the significance of all to his or her particular situation.

Other forces that have widespread impact and therefore need to be recognized by managements appraising the environment are the increased mobility of people brought about principally by the widespread possession of the automobile and the construction of far-flung highway networks, the suburban migration of large numbers, and the attractiveness found in simplicity and convenience. The former chairman of General Foods Corporation, Charles S. Mortimer, cited the following elements as part of the "craving for convenience . . . the success factor of just about every type of product and service that is showing steady growth."[20]

1. Convenience of form (fresh, frozen, canned, powdered, flaked, solid, cake, jar, paste, cream, liquid, etc.).
2. Convenience of quantity or unit.
3. Convenience of time.
4. Convenience of place.
5. Convenience of packaging.
6. Convenience of combination.
7. Convenience of automation.
8. Convenience of consumer credit.
9. Convenience of selection.
10. Convenience of readiness.[21]

The early 1970s have begun to witness the effect of a force that has always been present to some degree in the environment, but which is increasing in power; that is, what has been labeled "consumerism." Clearly identified with the activities of Ralph Nader, this force has the promise of major impact on the design and performance of products and on the ways companies interact with the environment. It also creates opportunities for companies.[22]

What will be major social forces that may significantly affect the success of an organization next year or three, five, ten years from now?

---

[19] Philip Kotler, *Marketing Management, Analysis, Planning and Control* (Englewood Cliffs, N.J.: Prentice-Hall, Inc., 1967), p. 38.

[20] *The Tobe Lectures in Retail Distribution at the Harvard Business School,* Harvard University Graduate School of Business Administration, Boston, Mass., 1961, p. 111.

[21] Ibid., pp. 112–115.

[22] See Philip Kotler, "What Consumerism Means for Marketers," *Harvard Business Review,* May–June 1972.

Will, for example, there be a migration trend back to the core of cities? Will the wave of "consumerism" or "Naderism" die out, or continue to grow as a potent and perhaps eventually the dominant force influencing management action? What will be the future impact of other present social forces? The successful organization will be the one able to antici- pate the dominant influencing forces of future years and to take advantage of them for the betterment of its particular situation.

Also important is an understanding of other more personal or individual factors that influence people's behavior. Knowledge being uncovered in the field of psychology is particularly relevant. People's needs, attitudes, perceptions, and motivations affect their behavior. But exactly how is seldom known. There are varying theories and interpretations, but some useful concepts have developed.

Maslow's hierarchy of motives provides a useful and widely cited approach to understanding basic human motivation.[23] Maslow classifies people's needs as:

Physiological—food, water.
Safety—security, protection.
Love—affection, belonging.
Esteem—self-respect, prestige, success.
Self-actualization—self-fulfillment.

He postulates that people act so as to satisfy these needs in the definite order in which they are listed; that is physiological first, and self-actualization last. It seems reasonable to believe that the basic physiological need for food would be the most compelling drive of one who has nothing else and was hungry; and that having achieved physiological satisfaction, one would then strive to satisfy needs for security and protection; and that one would not strive to satisfy self-actualization needs until the other lower order needs had been achieved.

However, in our advanced, affluent society the step-by-step process may not take hold as postulated for all. For some, satisfaction of varying degrees may be sought simultaneously at different levels in the hierarchy; and for others (as Maslow suggests) higher order motives, perhaps prestige and success may be more potent than affection or protection needs.[24] Nevertheless, Maslow's concept provides a useful basis for a manager's efforts to try to understand the motivation of his customers and employees.

Psychological research has indicated that an individual's behavior can also be influenced by his or her perception, aspiration, images, self-image and other concepts. A complete discussion of such concepts is beyond the

---

[23] A. H. Maslow, *Motivation and Personality* (New York: Harper and Brothers, 1954), especially pp. 80–106.

[24] Ibid., pp. 98–101.

purpose of this chapter and would not provide clear-cut guidance to the manager. There is no body of knowledge that definitely indicates how people behave as consumers, employees, or even as competitors. But as difficult as it may be for trained psychologists to understand and predict behavior, managers are constantly making decisions that imply such understanding and ability to predict. As they appraise their environments they should be seeking whatever knowledge can assist them and then should be alert to future contributions of behavioral science research.

LEGAL-GOVERNMENTAL FACTORS

Management's ability to act on the basis of changes in environmental factors is not limited just by the resources available to it and its perceptions of the need for change. There are various legal and governmental restrictions on what management might do. The impact can be far-reaching: some industries are under very extensive governmental regulation such as utilities and transportation companies. For other firms there is moderate governmental regulation. Some firms may have little specific governmental intervention (in terms of what they must do or cannot do), but may still be influenced by existing laws or the threat of regulation. Nonprofit institutions, also, must be aware of laws as well as of attitudes of government bodies if they are to avoid conflicts and to prosper in their privileged status.

In general the impact of government is far-reaching and increasing. For example, consider that for some firms government influences the design or composition of the product (drugs); the processing of the product (meat-packing); the distribution of the product (liquor); the labeling of the product (furs); the pricing of the product (minimum markup laws in various states); the advertising of the product (cigarettes); the wages paid the employees (minimum wage law); the accounting practices used (income tax regulations); the amount of net profit earned (various taxes on income, inventory, and so on); the issuance of stock and reporting to stockholders (Securities and Exchange Commission regulation), and so forth.

There is a wide body of federal legislation which has developed major acts including the Sherman Antitrust Act, the Pure Food and Drug Act, the Meat Inspection Act, the Federal Trade Commission Act, the Clayton Act, the Robinson-Patman Act, the Miller-Tydings Act, the Wheeler-Lea Act, and various state acts. The details of the implications of these laws are beyond the intent of this chapter, and beyond the understanding of most executives. Obviously, considerable responsibility is placed upon an organization's legal staff or legal consultants for guidance and interpretation. However, responsible managers must know there are actual and potential legal constraints upon the action of their organization, must seek out interpretations of the relative degree of restriction, and be attuned for changes in interpretation of existing statutes resulting from new cases that may affect their organization. For while the legal-governmental facet of the environment may seem easy to describe because statutes do exist, laws are being constantly modified, superseded and reinterpreted.

Furthermore, there is continually new governmental action. Recent years have seen the impact of "consumerism" resulting in laws, for example, governing credit practices (so-called truth in lending); government efforts to set standards for performance of various parts of an automobile; governmental efforts to restrict and standardize the sizes and labeling of packages; and efforts to outlaw "nonreturnable" bottles; efforts to control door-to-door salesmen; and control of prices and wages. Systematic appraisal of the legal-governmental facet of the environment must be an integral part of the appraiser's task. Current forces indicate that it will become increasingly more important.

ECONOMIC FACTORS

Economic forces are important environmental concerns of top management. On the one hand they have a significant effect on the demand for the organization's products or services. Particularly relevant is the overall economic condition. An expanding economy provides opportunity for many operating firms and for the establishment of new firms. A major recession or depression can bring about failure as was common in the late 1960s. Yet, for some it may bring about opportunity. For example, "During the U.S. recession of 1969–70 some firms were burnt badly while those offering lower-priced goods did very well. Retailers such as Kresge, J. C. Penny, and Woolworth had sales gains, as did sellers of used cars, copying equipment, wedding gown rental services and fabrics for making one's own clothes."[25]

Demand for products at a particular time will be partly determined by the number of people with a need for the product, their income, the existing price levels, and their expectations about future income and future prices.[26]

Influencing these factors will be some of the following considerations:

Total population.

The population of various segments of the total (age groups, sex, race, religion, nationality, and so on as relevant to the particular organization).

---

[25] E. Jerome McCarthy, *Basic Marketing: A Managerial Approach,* 4th ed. (Homewood, Ill.: Richard D. Irwin, Inc., 1971), pp. 76–77.

[26] Holloway and Hancock, *Marketing in a Changing Environment,* p. 163.

Number of households.

Births and death rates.

The geographic distribution of population.

Level of income.

Distribution of income.

Proportion of disposable and/or discretionary income.

Availability of consumer credit.

Level of education.

Trends and changes in the above singularly or in combination.

These elements interact and their eventual effect usually results from some combination of them. Certainly as examples from some of the developing countries suggest, population alone without purchasing power cannot produce demand. But Levitt has pointed out that population and purchasing power cannot be relied upon to guarantee success. He cites as one of the conditions present with every dead or dying "growth" industry to be "the belief that growth is assured by an expanding and more affluent population."[27]

It also should be recognized that economic factors interact with behavioral forces in influencing demand and consequently the state of the economy. Katona has reported:

> Psychological factors such as motives, attitudes, expectations and group belonging are intervening variables operating between the stimuli of marketing conditions and the responses to them in the form of economic decisions. The psychological factors do not alone determine the final decisions but under certain conditions they are powerful enough to alter individual as well as mass reactions and thereby influence the entire economy.[28]

The negative effects of poor general economic conditions may influence not only the demand for products; for example, automobiles, major appliances, furniture, but also other major business activities. A planned stock issue may have to be curtailed because of adverse economic conditions negatively influencing the level of stock prices. An increase in the prime rate may cause a planned borrowing, perhaps for an expansion program, to become too expensive. Or severe inflationary spirals in the construction industry can alter plans for a new plant or office. All of these conditions existed simultaneously in the U.S. economy during 1974.

The effects of an economic slump that do not seem to be currently influencing a particular firm may be felt further in the future and should

---

[27] Levitt, "Marketing Myopia," p. 47.

[28] George Katona, *The Powerful Consumer* (New York: McGraw-Hill Book Co., 1960), p. 5–6.

be anticipated and planned for before they materialize. What steps have to be taken now? Curtail production? Cut back on inventories? Cut research and development? These steps can have major implications if unwisely taken, or similarly if they are not taken.

Obviously shorter run difficulties in the availability of resources brought about by economic factors can have longer run impact on the organization's product output. Thus in assessing economic factors, management must be careful not only to consider those that affect demand for a product in the short run, but also those that influence the firm's longer run ability to satisfy that demand. For example, increases in the costs of a firm's capital resulting from a change in general economic conditions such as occurred in 1974 can interfere with plans to construct a new plant, thus limiting the firm's ability to satisfy expected future demand. Increases in financial costs might also cause a cutback in expenditures for research and development, the consequences of which might take several years to become significant.

Thus the surveillance of general economic conditions is a necessary part of the environmental appraiser's task and he must constantly keep himself appraised of the latest actual situation and the forecast for future periods of such indices as the gross national product, corporate profits, consumer expenditures, disposable income, business investment level, stock prices, interest rates, unemployment, price indexes and so forth. At the same time, however, he must assess their implication for the particular industry of which he is a part, and then most importantly for his own particular organization. For nonprofit organizations such as universities and medical institutions, the level of government spending in areas which support their particular activities is of prime importance.

While from an analytical point of view it seems useful to examine general economic conditions, then specific "industry" conditions, and then to consider the particular organization's situation, the practitioner is usually doing these three tasks simultaneously. The major pitfall, of course, and one that afflicts many institutions is the pace of day-to-day operations. It is the tendency to attempt only to consider the direct effect of "current events" on the organization without making a careful and detailed assessment of general economic and more specific "industry" conditions. With such a myopic view important changes or developments are often neglected and faulty assumptions usually of a "status quo" nature are made about others. Such an approach can be fatal at worst and cause severe problems at the least.

INDUSTRY STRUCTURE AND PRACTICES—COMPETITION

Each entity while striving to succeed because of or at least in spite of the external environment is also part of a subenvironment which comprises the industry of which it is a member, and which to some extent determines the organizations with which it is in competition. The word "industry" is defined loosely in the framework of strategy. Teaching hospitals or universities in the Chicago area are two examples of such loose "industry" definitions. For some organizations, defining industry membership or ascertaining competition appears to be relatively easy. Firms producing coal were considered members of the coal industry. As such they were influenced by various customs and practices of the industry and affected by the attitudes and actions of the United Mine Workers Union as well as by the customers for their products. However, as the demand for coal decreased during the 1950s and 1960s, coal-producing firms were not only competing with other coal-producing firms but also with other energy-producing firms. As obvious as such situations appear in hindsight, many institutions of various types have failed to recognize the true nature of their "industry" and competition. Often this problem resulted from a preoccupation with the product or services being offered, rather than also considering the needs of the consuming group being served.

Thus, scanning this facet of the environment has two major tasks: (1) appraising changes within the collection of firms producing like products and the related and associated middlemen, generally considered the "industry"; and (2) appraising "competition" broadly which includes not only those companies making like products but also substitute products. And one needs to recognize that the degree of relative substitution may not be apparent on the surface and may only be best identified by the consumer who not only substitutes oil or gas or electricity for coal to heat his home, but also substitutes a vacation for a new car, or a savings account for a new wardrobe.

In appraising its industry, management must be aware of basic economic factors that influence successful operation such as the availability of labor, raw materials, supplies, and capital; the cost characteristics of the industry, such as the ratio of fixed to variable costs and the behavior of incremental costs; the technological state of the industry, including the level and pace of research and development, as well as marketing and advertising practices, pricing, and the like.

An additional factor, sometimes overlooked, is the appraisal of changing conditions in more limited areas such as the channels of distribution. Obviously, for those business firms engaged in direct sales of the product to the consumer, this factor does not appear to be important. However, there are times when a firm might consider the substitution of indirect for direct distribution. In such a case it becomes vital for the firm to understand the attitudes and operations of the middlemen involved, who after all are members of the "industry."

It is essential that management acquire as much information as possible about various facets of competitors' operations, not only as they are, but as they appear to be changing. For each competitor, as far as possible, detailed analyses should be made of the product line, product design, and performance. Packaging, customers or markets served, channels of distribution used, and which are most effective, prices not only to end use customers but also to various buyers in the channels of distribution, advertising and promotional tactics, receiving arrangements and policies, major investments or financing decisions, often can be uncovered. Comparisons should be made with the firm's products, policies, and tactics to uncover relative advantages and disadvantages and changes by competitors must be carefully scrutinized.

In addition to the essential marketing analysis of competition discussed above there are many other facets of competitor's operations that require study or surveillance. The relative overall profitability of competition is important to know as are any advantages in raw material supplies, labor conditions, manufacturing processes, cost structure, financial condition, technological competence, amount and nature of research and development expenditures, relative degree of integration, image with the consumer and within the industry. The profile could be as extensive as the internal and external analysis of one's own firm. Judgment and priorities will temper the scope of the task.

As difficult as it may be to gather all the information about existing competition as might be desired, it is obviously much more difficult to appraise potential competitors. But this vital activity must be constantly carried out and management must assess competitors seeking to uncover relative advantages. In addition, management must react to create relative advantages of its own, and prepare to counter new challenges. In the view of one knowledgeable source, it is this differentiation or advantage over competition that is the fundamental basis of a business firm's strategy.[29]

ON APPRAISING THE ENVIRONMENT

While it is possible to suggest in a general way the areas that one must consider in appraising the environment, it is difficult to suggest specifically how it should be done. But it should be apparent that the task has to be done as part of the top-management function. It is easy with the press of day-to-day internal problems for the external appraisal to be put aside. It must be a constant concern. It must become a sensitivity that causes the manager to constantly ask of all that he sees, hears, reads, "what is happening," "what is the implication for my organization"?

---

[29] Bruce D. Henderson, *Construction of a Business Strategy* (Boston: The Boston Consulting Group, 1970), p. 2–3.

Obvious contributory steps are the daily reading of the press (national and local), the reading of general business, or professional periodicals, the reading of special reports, the attendance and participation in special "industry" events, and intraorganization communication. Aguilar on the basis of field research has reported the commonest sources of data to top business management about the external environment to be: personal experiences, journals, reports, books, professional meetings, industrial conferences, colleagues, board members, friends, and employees.[30]

The task is a formidable one, the multiplicity of forces interact. This chapter does not purport to be all-inclusive, it is only suggestive of the areas in need of appraisal. There is a premium on perceptive selectivity by the management seeking to gather, filter, assess and act on what is important for its organization.

SUMMARY

Although the external analysis is recognized as a vital and often the most important element of the strategy formulation process, it must be considered together with the other necessary elements. Only when combined with the internal analysis and personal values and objectives of various individuals and groups does the external analysis fully serve the organization in the development of strategy. These aspects, considered separately in Chapters 3, 4 and 5, will be combined in Chapter 6 when strategy identification and the strategy formulation process is discussed.

---

[30] Francis Joseph Aguilar, *Scanning the Business Environment* (New York: Macmillan Co., 1967), p. 11, Exhibit 1–2.

9. If You're a Businessman, This Chart May Be the Shape of Your Future*

It shows how the birthrate in the U.S. has been declining until it's now below the rate of replacement. This will have tremendous economic, social and political repercussions.

A DECADE AGO Gerber Products sold as high as 32 times earnings, and even last year was at 22 times earnings. It was a growth stock. Today in a rising market it sells for barely 14 times probable 1972 earnings. It has fallen from grace.

Why? The chart gives the answer. Gerber has chiefly to do with babies, and things to do with babies no longer titillate The Street. The Baby Boom has turned into a Baby Bust.

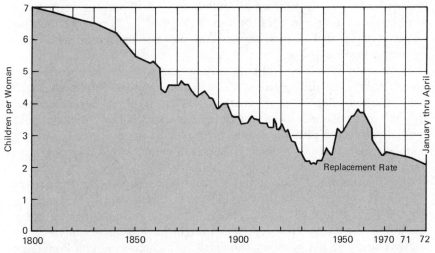

Note: Prior to 1917 data available only for white population; after 1917, for total population.

---

* "If You're a Businessman, This Chart May Be the Shape of Your Future," *Forbes* Magazine, September 1, 1972. Reprinted by permission.

It all happened so suddenly. The alarmists were still crying about the population explosion when it was already turning into an echo. In the early sixties, there were around 116 births per year for every 1,000 American women of childbearing age. At that time, in her lifetime, the average woman would have 3.6 children, enough to replace her and her husband and enough left over to put a big bang into the population explosion. By the first four months of 1972, the birthrate had dropped to the point where the average woman would have only 2.1 children in her child-bearing span. At the new figure, she and her husband would not quite be reproducing themselves, for a certain number of children will die before maturity or will never marry.

No, zero population growth isn't here yet. It won't be for a long time. The U.S. is still a young nation, and while the birthrate is low, so is the death rate. But as the proportion of children declines and today's young become tomorrow's old, the death rate will rise. It will take roughly 70 years at current rates for the two lines to cross and for the population to level off. In the meantime, the important thing is this: The rate of population growth will get smaller and smaller.

There are those who think the birthrate will rise again, but the trend of history is against them. Ironing out temporary squiggles like that after World War II, the U.S. birthrate has trended down since around 1800.

CHANGING ATTITUDE

Along with changes in life styles, there have been changes in attitudes toward family size. In 1967 a Gallup Poll showed 40 percent wanted four or more children and in 1971 this figure dropped to 23 percent. Another survey revealed that 80 percent felt there was nothing wrong with childless marriages.

What are the business and political implications? Are they worrisome? Alfred Sauvy, the distinguished French demographer, thinks so. In his book, *General Theory of Population,* he argues that France's social, cultural and economic ills are the direct result of the fact that its population has remained virtually stable for more than a century. A growing population is a stimulus to society, he says; a nation with a stagnant population eventually will stagnate.

On the other hand, look at Japan. "The Japanese miracle" in part is a result of the government's drive to cut the birthrate sharply by encouraging abortions. Had it not done so, the result might have been catastrophic. Already suffocatingly crowded, Japan might have become unlivable.

After studying the problem, the President's Commission on Population Growth and the American Future concluded: "We have looked for, and have not found, any convincing economic argument for continuing national population growth. The health of the economy does not depend on it. The vitality of business does not depend on it. The welfare of the average person certainly does not depend on it.

"In fact, the average person will be markedly better off in terms of traditional economic values if population growth follows the two-child projection rather than the three-child one. Slower growth will give us an older population and this trend will require adjustments. . . ." However, these adjustments are "well within the ability of the nation to provide."

Perhaps that last sentence is the key; perhaps whether a nation profits from slow population growth or gets into trouble depends on whether the people can make the necessary adjustments. In this connection, one has to consider the differences in the French and the Japanese characters. The French are a highly individualistic people, almost an anarchistic one; they are constantly in conflict with each other and have been for hundreds of years. In contrast, the Japanese are a well-disciplined people with an extremely strong social sense. In Japan, capital, labor, the banks and the government all work together as one.

What about the American character? One can only speculate about it. In explaining the sharp decline in the birthrate, some experts point out that women coming of childbearing age today were born in "the era of Spock." They were reared "permissively." Their parents indulged their every wish and they grew up not with the Puritan ethic but as hedonists. They don't want the expense and trouble of bringing up a large family if that means sacrificing anything for themselves, whether a swimming pool or a holiday in Europe.

ON THE OTHER HAND

A people who have rejected the Puritan ethic for hedonism don't seem like the stuff on which a nation can thrive economically. However, other experts point out that another reason for the decline in the birthrate is that more and more women are entering the labor force, staying longer and marrying later. It's a truism among demographers that "the later the less." In addition, more and more women are career-minded; they go back into the labor force as soon as their children are ready for school. That hardly makes them seem like hedonists. Or does it?

All that is a matter for speculation. Meanwhile, this much is certain: A nation in which the average family has two children will have a higher per-capita income than one in which the average family has three. It's a matter of simple arithmetic: If the family has an income of $10,000 a year, three children will mean a per-capita income of $2,000; two children, $2,500.

This means that in the years to come an increasing number of Americans will have more *disposable* income, for travel, for entertainment, for a house at the beach, for a motorboat. People won't eat more, but they will eat more convenience foods, more gourmet foods, on which the profit margins are higher.

In a study entitled *The Demography of the 1970s: The Birth Dearth and What It Means*, Ben J. Wattenberg, a leading writer on population trends, cites figures to show that in 1985 Americans will be spending 79 percent more on food, drink and tobacco than in 1968 in terms of 1968 dollars; 95 percent more on clothing and clothing materials; 107 percent more on transportation; 110 percent more on household operation and furnishings; 149 percent more on recreation, education and the like; 172 percent more on housing; 185 percent more on personal and medical care.

Meanwhile, certain developments already are taking place: The work force is growing larger, both in numbers and in percentage of the population. This is one reason (though not the only reason) for the persistence of unemployment despite the upturn in business. The problem will get increasingly acute. The economy will have to run faster and faster just to stand still.

At any rate, the economic consequences are already visible. According to Susanne Stoiber, assistant to the executive director of the Committee for National Health Insurance, the nation's maternity wards are running at only 40 percent of capacity, even though other hospital wards are overcrowded. This obviously is a terrible waste of money and space. The committee's solution: for the hospitals in each community or region to get together and work out a rational plan, under which some will take on the maternity load of the others, while the others use the wards thus emptied to relieve the overcrowding.

WHAT CLASSROOM SHORTAGE?

There has been a sharp drop also in the school population. Only a few years ago, as recently as the middle Sixties, there was a severe shortage of classrooms in the U.S. and a severe shortage of teachers. Every suburb was under pressure to build more schools and hire more teachers. In almost every suburb, the most bitterly fought political issue was whether to raise school taxes, whether to float another series of bonds to build another school. Except in a few communities, this issue has disappeared.

The school population, says Dr. Sidney P. Marland Jr., U.S. Commissioner of Education, "peaked somewhere in 1970 at 51.4 million, and in the ensuing two years we have begun to drop in total elementary and secondary education to a number now about 50.4 million, or down about 1 million children from the peak of 1970. Most of the reduction occurred in the elementary schools. At the moment, the secondary schools—we'll call them for the purposes of statistics grades 9 through 12—are stable. Somewhere between 1972 and 1975 we'll begin to see a decline in the secondary schools, reflecting the present decline in elementary schools. By 1980 we'll be down a million and a half."

In the Sixties there was a shortage of teachers: salaries, obeying the law of supply and demand, soared. At the same time, students poured into the schools of education. This was partly because teachers' salaries had become attractive and partly because the shortage caused many draft boards to exempt teachers. Now there is a teacher glut. The National Education Association estimates that more than 130,000 of the nation's over 3 million teachers are unemployed. "This will be a continuing situation," Dr. Marland says. "Thousands of teachers in the U.S. will just have to go into other professions."

Thousands have already been forced into driving cabs, waiting on tables, working behind store counters, becoming an intellectual proletariat, with what social and political consequences one can only guess at.

The drop in the birthrate has already created what Dr. Michael Sumichrast, chief economist of the National Association of Homebuilders, calls a revolution in homebuilding—a switch from detached houses to condominiums. Dr. Sumichrast says: "It started overnight—two years ago, a year and a half ago. Take Washington. A year and a half ago there was just one project in Washington. Today there are nearly 50. It's that kind of fantastic change. And it's happening not only in Washington, but in just about every other city.

"These are people who have no kids. My wife is doing a study of one project. I looked at it. In this project, about 70 percent have no children. And only 5 percent have more than three."

According to Dr. Sumichrast, the average condominium apartment has roughly half the floor space of the average house. In Washington, he says, "a typical house has 2,500 square feet. These condominium apartments start from 900 and go to 1,200."

Naturally, he says, they sell for about half the price. This gives the condominium owners more expendable income for things like travel, boating, skiing. And second homes. "It's amazing, the growth of the second-home market," Dr. Sumichrast says.

The growth of the condominiums also is bound to have an effect on the home furnishings industry and the household equipment industry: smaller and fewer units, but probably of better and better quality and higher price. For example, Dr. Sumichrast says that couples who buy apartments in condomiums usually insist on a king-size bedroom because they want to furnish it with a king-size bed.

WHO'S HELPED? WHO'S HURT?

ZERO population growth isn't here yet, but the baby boom is definitely over. Who will be helped? Who hurt? Below *Forbes* makes some general judgments on the probable long-range effects of the Baby Bust.

Probably Helped

Industries Benefiting from Disposable Income. For example: travel; autos; jewelry; watches; photogaphy; restaurants; vacation homes.

Service Industries. Those replacing things the housewife used to do herself, especially. For example: convenience foods, childcare, specialized housework chores.

Advertising. Big shifts in packaging and marketing. Less sharp distinction between women's products and men's appeal as men do more housework and as women work more outside of home.

Sports. Manufacturers of athletic equipment and boatbuilders should prosper. Professional sports should continue to boom.

Health Care. Anything to do with relieving the aches and pains and infirmities of middle and old age, as the average age of the population inexorably rises.

Probably Hurt

Commodity Industries. For example, steel, aluminum, stone, lumber, glass, many types of food and clothing, tobacco, liquor.

Children- and Youth-Oriented Operations. Toys, records and summer camps.

Broadcasting. More demand for maturity in programming, less for children's and for all-ages-type programming. Fragmentation, as via CATV or pay TV.

Movie Theaters. It's the youth who fill them now, while the middle-aged stay home and watch their favorite flicks on TV.

Life Insurance. Less concern and less need for it because more wives will be working and there will be fewer kids to raise.

REPAIRLESS EQUIPMENT

One company that appears to have done more than thought about the implications of the declining birthrate is Whirlpool Corp., which hired a group of five prominent university professors to study it. John Smallwood, director of economic and marketing research of Whirlpool, was in charge. He says people are bound to demand smaller appliances, appliances "capable of storage somewhere where they will still be visible but blend into the surrounding better, appliances which do a number of things in order to save space." He also believes it will be necessary for companies like his to make appliances that never need repairs. A wife with a job can't sit around the house all day waiting for a repairman, he points out.

Another company that has given a good deal of thought to the decline in the birthrate is, understandably enough, Gerber Products, the nation's leading manufacturer of baby foods. Says William Francis, sales forecasting supervisor: "We've gone into a line of nonfoods—clothing, knitwear pants and shirts and socks for children, distributed through grocery outlets, a line of sleepwear for children, distributed through department stores. If we can keep mothers our customers for another six months, it's like another 2 million births. We have a certain amount of sales at the old end of the market right now; for many years now, old people have been using our baby foods for their soft diets. That market should grow."

As smart a marketing company as Johnson & Johnson has started to roll with the punches. It is now running television commercials that show hard-hatted workers using Johnson's Baby Powder.

Says Dr. Patrick Lynch, director of corporate development at Westinghouse Electric Corp.: "The most immediate concern to us is the changing life style, the changing social values, which are really at the heart, we think, of the change in population growth. Population growth changes are really symptomatic of something much deeper, and it is those things we must be concerned about in running our business—the changing attitudes toward life, how people want to run their lives, their concern with the environment and with the good life; these are having a much more immediate effect on us than the change in numbers. Two-thirds of what we do is involved in power systems. The concern with the environment has encouraged the development of nuclear power."

Dr. Lynch believes that as the population grows older, "what we are going to see are subsidies by the Government to increase health-care delivery, to try to upgrade preventive health care, and these are areas in which we think we can provide some service."

At Melville Shoe, President Francis Rooney Jr. is sure the drop in the birthrate will lead shoe buyers to "upgrade." He says: "I think the trend of women working and, therefore, adding to the family income, plus the new life style—not just staying at home barefoot and pregnant—makes women more viable customers. They won't have a guilt complex about spending the income of their husbands to buy a new dress or shoes."

Dr. Seymour Marshak, manager of market research at Ford, says of the decline in the birthrate and the consequent rise in per-capita income: "It could mean that cars will become more luxurious, since people will have more in the way of discretionary funds. More luxurious but smaller."

Borden Inc's vice president in charge of marketing, Clayton Rohrback, anticipates a change in the mix of Borden's sales and in the packaging. In addition, he believes that small, smart food companies may prove able to react more swiftly to the changes in life style that appear to have brought about the drop in the birthrate than some larger companies.

He says: "In a large company, you have products that sell through all age groups, with specific emphasis of some products on specific ages. For example, Cracker Jack is eaten mainly by small children; so, if there are fewer of them, the task for Cracker Jack is to get more people to eat it, by means of conventional marketing methods. While smaller kids are decreasing in number, the 13- to 18-year-olds are growing in number, and they happen to be a big potato chip group, so what we may be losing on Cracker Jack we may be picking up on potato chips. In the long run, I think you will see more and more foods that are packaged for the smaller family—like frozen peas packaged for two. We're already getting letters from people saying why don't we put out something or other in a small package. We've already done that with our instant potatoes."

HOW GE SEES IT

General Electric's chief economist, Dr. R. S. Villanueve, makes economic forecasts four times a year and a long-range forecast every three years. Like many other economists, he considers the decline in the birthrate inseparable from the change in living style. The services he sees as the businesses of the future are entertainment, learning, medical facilities and mass transportation.

Not every U.S. corporation has considered what the decline in the birthrate will mean to its business. Several of those queried by *Forbes* insisted that it probably was just temporary; there would be another upsurge soon, they said, just like the upsurge in the Fifties. Others shrugged their shoulders and said there was nothing they could do. A spokesman at Colgate-Palmolive said, "We're in consumer goods," and conceded, "the thought is there, but nothing in general has been done; probably we should be doing something."

That's one way of looking at things, but it's a shortsighted way. The change has already dropped Gerber from the growth-stock category to the lowly cyclical. It may well do the same with other companies. There are companies now selling at ten times earnings that will be growth stocks because of the empty hospital cribs. The change in the birthrate will cause some companies to fade and others to flourish. It is probably the most momentous thing that has happened to U.S. business in a couple of decades.

STUDENT REVIEW QUESTIONS

1. What is the overall significance for business executives of zero population growth?

2. Why is it difficult to formulate strategy under a long-range forecast of zero population growth?
3. Discuss the significance of this population trend for various "nonprofit" organizations.
4. Discuss in depth how one selected industry may be hurt by this trend, and how one may be helped by the trend.
5. What implications does this population trend have for your personal career strategy?

10. Evaluating Signals of Technological Change*

JAMES R. BRIGHT

To anticipate innovation, the political, social, and other factors influencing its progress must be systematically monitored

FOREWORD

In this fast-paced era, corporations are finding that it is not enough to be technically competent; they must be able to anticipate technological change in order to take advantage of it. The author shows how the process of evolution from a scientific concept to a marketable product or technique is affected not only by technological advances, but also by developments in the political, economic, and social environments. He describes a methodology for monitoring these environments for signs of change.

Mr. Bright is Professor of Technology Management and Associate Dean—responsible for long-range planning—of the Graduate School of Business, University of Texas at Austin, and is also President of Industrial Management Center, Inc., a firm consulting on and instructing in technological matters.

THE FOLLY of ignoring technological advances is readily apparent. For their well-being, all institutions in our society, particularly industry and government, must anticipate radical technological changes that sweep aside existing practices and open new opportunities—or create new problems. The company that neglects this task runs a serious risk.

To the thoughtful and imaginative manager the need is obvious. The question is: How can he meet it?

A common assumption is: "Our research and development department is automatically doing this job by serving as the technological lookout agency for the company." Discussions with several hundred

* James R. Bright, "Evaluating Signals of Technological Change," *Harvard Business Review*, January–February 1970. © 1970 by the President and Fellows of Harvard College; All Rights Reserved. Reprinted by permission.

research and engineering managers during the last eight years have convinced me, however, that this role is played neither widely nor well in many R&D departments. The reasons are:

Most R&D departments are expected to concentrate on product development and refinement and new applications. They tend to keep their eyes on the technological workbench immediately before them— on the technology of today, on the one- to five-year time horizon, and on the company's immediate concerns. Management's expectations, corporate custom, and conditioning by traditional practices do not often encourage them to study the technological environment outside their immediate areas of activity.

While many alert R&D managers (and some marketing managers) are extremely concerned about the need for long-range, broad-band technological surveying and are eager to assume the responsibility for undertaking it, they lack support from higher levels.

They try their best to keep up to date by reading the professional literature, attending association meetings, and making personal contacts. Unhappily, their managements have not recognized the necessity for such work, and they usually lack the funds and the manpower to conduct systematic surveys outside their companies' product areas.

When, by energy or chance, a company's R&D manager does identify matters of great but not imminent concern, who will listen? How can he bring his information or suspicions to top management's attention so that the company's collective wisdom can be applied to further assessment?

Of course, if he walks in with a new product in hand, he has little trouble getting a hearing. But persuading top management to explore a totally new technology, to undertake systematic investigation of an alien concept that *might* cause a current product to be superseded, is something else.

The R&D director usually lacks a systematic methodology for assessing the innovative process. I am speaking not of technological capabilities, in which he clearly is well qualified, but of application of technology and its diffusion. The process of turning a scientific concept into economic reality involves far more than just capabilities. Economics, sociology, politics, and sometimes ecology affect the rate and significance of technological progress, as I shall demonstrate later.

ASSAYING THE FUTURE

There has been some progress lately in putting technological forecasting on a more systematic basis. In the last three years I have conducted seven seminars on the subject that were attended by more than 600 persons from industrial, academic, and governmental organizations in 10 countries. I estimate that about one in four participating organizations has started a forecasting program.

There has also been a great deal of work in developing tools for better forecasting.[1] One very promising new concept is the cross impact matrices developed by the staff of the Institute for the Future.

But technological forecasting is still an infant science and art. It remains inadequate for some of management's needs because: (a) any forecast is certain to embody some degree of imperfection as conditions change; (b) forecasts of technical capabilities do not necessarily deal with their *diffusion,* input requirements, and impact.

So I suggest that another concept can be useful to management in anticipating and responding to technological progress. I call it monitoring the environment for impending technological change. I have been using it since 1961 in teaching at the Harvard Business School and the University of Texas and in consulting work with industry. Since use of the approach depends on an understanding of the process of technological innovation, let us first establish some findings from research in this field. Studies of several dozen post-World War II innovations by a number of researchers, including myself, show that certain factors are present:

A radical new technological advance is made visible to society first in written words, then in increasingly refined, enlarged, and more effective material forms, long before it achieves widespread usage.

The potential impact of the innovation is usually evident years before the new technology is in use on a scale great enough to affect existing societal conditions appreciably.

Social, political, and, now to an increasing degree, ecological changes may alter the speed and direction of the innovation's progress, as I indicated previously.

Innovation may be abruptly influenced by decisions of key individuals who control supporting resources or determine policies that affect their application.

Technological capabilities—e.g., parameters such as speed, power, miniaturization, strength, and capacity—increase exponentially over time, once bottlenecks are broken . . . but will begin to level off if they encounter scientific, economic, or social barriers. (Failure to accept or accurately gauge this characteristic of acceleration happens to be a principal reason why "expert opinion" from very competent technologists, economists, and study groups so often proves to be fantastically conservative, if not totally wrong.)

There are, of course, occasional exceptions to these points. The atomic bomb project, for example, was kept a close secret from 1942 to

---

[1] For recent *Harvard Business Review* articles on industrial use of technological forecasts, see James Brian Quinn, "Technological Forecasting," *Harvard Business Review,* March–April 1967, p. 89; Harper Q. North and Donald L. Pyke, " 'Probes' of the Technological Future," *Harvard Business Review,* May–June 1969, p. 68; and Maxwell W. Hunter, II, "Are Technological Upheavals Inevitable?" *Harvard Business Review,* September–October 1969, p. 71.

1945. When it did become "visible" to society, of course, its capability was so obvious that it immediately altered military technology, strategy, and tactics, as well as international politics. Most technological innovations, however, are visible in theories, laboratories, and field trials long before they are operationally applied; and their effects are apparent before use becomes widespread.

To the extent that this is true, it should be possible to monitor the environment to detect the coming, the progress, and the consequences of significant technological advances. Monitoring, by my definition, includes four activities:

1. Searching the environment for signals that may be forerunners of significant technological change.
2. Identifying the possible consequences (assuming that these signals are not false and the trends that they suggest persist).
3. Choosing the parameters, policies, events, and decisions that should be observed and followed to verify the true speed and direction of technology and the effects of employing it.
4. Presenting the data from the foregoing steps in a timely and appropriate manner for management's use in decisions about the organization's reaction.

Note that monitoring includes much more than simply "scanning." It includes search, consideration of alternative possibilities and their effects, selection of critical parameters for observation, and a conclusion based on evaluation of progress and its implications. The feasibility of monitoring rests on the fact that it takes a long time for a technology to emerge from the minds of men into economic reality, with its resulting societal impacts.

There are always some identifiable points, events, relationships, and other types of "signals" along the way that can be used in an analytical framework. If a manager can detect these signals, he should be able to follow the progress of the innovation relative to time, cost, performance, obstacles, possible impacts, and other considerations. Then he will have two more important inputs to his decisions: (a) awareness of the new technology and its progress; and (b) some thoughtful speculation about its possible impact.

The traditional analytical procedures used by business and government evaluate only factors in the technical and economic environments. But often the key events—changing values and relationships that determine the ultimate significance of the technology and its timing—lie in social and political spheres. The transportation companies and public utilities, for instance, long have had to consider the political sphere. And it deserves reemphasis that today ecological factors are becoming a stronger source of pressure for change.

Furthermore, the interaction of events between these environments can prove to be the significant force. The closing of the Suez Canal—a *political* move—affected the *economics* of supertankers, for instance. It follows that monitoring requires us to look for signals in all these environments.

Whither ICE?

The importance of multienvironment considerations is evident in current demands for new kinds of automobile engine power.

The auto producer in the past has responded—and still responds—to demands for economy and power, which are both economic and social factors. He conscientiously studies the technical and economic facts of the internal combustion engine (ICE) and its competitors. He takes comfort from evidence that no other vehicle power plant can provide the performance and economy required of the U.S. family car. He knows, furthermore, that recent engineering refinement of the ICE has eliminated 70 percent to 80 percent of exhaust emissions.

But such an analysis neglects at least two potentially significant signals:

1. The Congressional hearings on the electric car in March 1967 indicated powerful potential economic support for other kinds of auto power plants—regardless of economics. This support could arise from the political environment in the form of arbitrary and mandatory government purchases of electric and steam cars, plus possible legislation restricting use of ICE cars.

2. The trend toward multicar family ownership clearly makes special-purpose vehicles feasible. In one study, a student of mine observed that the second and third cars in two out of three families which he studied each traveled on average less than 9 miles per day, and in traffic that prohibited speeds of more than 25 miles an hour. Such power demand is well within the capability of today's electric vehicle power plant—provided that the user accepts the costs and other complications.

Another student found that at least 4 couples (out of about 120) living in a Texas retirement-vacation resort had sold their second cars and were using their electric golf carts for local transportation! He later learned that this practice is widespread in some similar communities, such as Palm Springs, California.

The transportation requirements of persons in retirement communities and of many families in large urban areas are such that they do not necessarily need a second vehicle with the same power capability as the first.

When the industrialist begins to consider all possible influences, a plethora of questions can come up. For instance: What is the likelihood that utilities will offer special rates and locations for battery recharging? Is there any significant technical development under way in foreign countries? Are any government agencies supporting research in steam cars? What are the latest findings on air pollution?

The conclusion for the industrialist is obvious but still needs emphasis: conventional business wisdom—meaning economic and technical analysis only—can mislead you about the forces affecting technological progress.

TYPES OF SIGNALS

Within each environment many types of parameters and events serve as indicators of potential change.

In the Technological Environment

Time series of technical parameters and figures of merit (combinations of technical and economic parameters) are very suggestive when projected into the future. For example, the increase in the number of electrical circuits per unit of space or area in solid-state electronic systems points to a coming compression of system size at least 1/100th of the size of the 1960 circuitry. Meanwhile, circuit cost also is declining exponentially. Devices employing electronics—radio, radar, TV, the computer, and military equipment—will become much smaller, more portable, cheaper, and more reliable, and hence will gain more widespread use. These devices will be available for use in many new situations.

Look at the curves in Exhibit 1, showing a forecast by the U.S. Air Force Avionics Laboratory, which underwrote the development and first application of integrated circuits. The forecast of technical capabilities, made several years ago, has proved to be reasonably accurate. These curves tell the electronics equipment manufacturer that:

Large-scale cost and size reductions in the equipment still lie head.

Electronic products in almost any present configuration will be rapidly and continuously made obsolete over the next five to ten years.

A new product in this field must be exploited very quickly, since its market life probably will be short.

The wisdom of Solomon or the gambling instincts of an oil-well wild-catter will be needed, at times, to set production and marketing policy and tactics in this environment of rapid product change.

Reflections of interest in certain areas, problems, or phenomena also provide signals. A company may announce that it is establishing a laboratory to develop holography. An executive may state in a speech that his company sees opportunity in home entertainment centers.

Or a professional society (such as the American Society of Mechanical Engineers) may expect 100 engineers at a conference on underwater

EXHIBIT 1
Projection of Cost Reduction in Electronic Circuitry to 1970, as Forecast in 1962

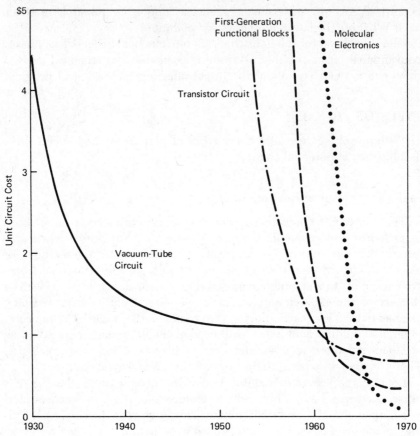

technology, but 500 attend. Is this unusual response a signal of major progress and coming effort, or does it merely reflect wishful thinking or a "bandwagon" effect? We must monitor this technical activity to determine its true significance.

Information about Products. Demonstrations of new products, announcements of research progress, patent awards, and trade paper and professional society reports of materialization of new technology deserve scrutiny.

An important example is Chester Carlson's first patent on xerography. The report of the patent award in *The New York Times* in 1940 was spotted by a young International Business Machines Corporation marketing man. During the next year and a half he tried to interest IBM in Carlson's invention. He failed, and so his company failed to capitalize on the potential in the new technology that public disclosure had placed in its hands. The signal was there, but the assessment of Carlson's first crude demonstration was inadequate.

In 1943 Eastman Kodak Company's technical publication, *Patent Abstracts,* published an abstract of Carlson's first patent. Kodak picked up the signal, but apparently no one monitored the progress of the technology, or management was not persuaded that it was significant.

In October 1948, the little Haloid Company held a major demonstration for the press in New York City. Company representatives not only showed, with laboratory-scale equipment, how xerography could be used to copy letters and other office paper work, but they demonstrated a camera that took and developed pictures in two minutes and showed a model printing press running 1,200 feet per minute. These and other potential applications were thoroughly discussed in the press, ranging from *Business Week* and *The New York Times* to dozens of trade journals. Industry had its signal.

It is most important to note that two of these applications have not yet materialized for Xerox Corporation, Haloid's descendant, after 20 years(!), while copying, of course, has exploded in use. An appraisal of potentials made at that time could easily have been wrong. Progress should have been monitored to detect the ultimate true course.

In 1965 Xerox demonstrated its high-speed Model 2400 copier. Company announcements, speeches, and other reports, plus the growing speed of copying in previous model refinements, were evidence of accomplishment and an impending invasion of the duplicating field—of which no doubt the duplicating industry was well aware. In October 1969, Xerox advertisements described a new and higher speed copier.

Now, what does xerography's growing capability imply for printing, either as a technical competitor of printing presses or as a device which reduces the need for printing? Those concerned should be monitoring this possible development.

Monitors should, however, be wary of overoptimistic statements—no matter how sincere—about forthcoming technology. Recall the publicity about the Curtiss-Wright Aero-car and the Wankel engine in the mid-1950's, RCA's Ultrafax transmission-reproduction facsimile demonstration (almost simultaneous with Haloid's 1948 demonstration of xerography), and the Allis Chalmers fuel cell-powered tractor. All were impressive demonstrations of new technology in use, but they have not yet become operational.

I do not mean to disparage these and other demonstrations. Some of these products fail for good technical or economic reasons. Others are displaced by superior technology. Still others, such as the Wankel engine (apparently), are merely delayed much longer than anyone had imagined.

My point is that demonstrations should be studied as signals. The Wright brothers' first flight was 110 feet—a joke in performance. Now we know that the distance was irrelevant; the significance of the event lay in the nature of the accomplishment itself.

Other Indicators. Performance data on technological improvements also must be scrutinized. These data are often mentioned in trade journals, professional society papers, technical reports of government agencies, and advertising literature. When related to earlier achievements in a time series, they reveal (possibly!) the state of the art, and they may suggest rates of technical progress.

One of the benefits of such reports is identification of problem areas and limitations, which helps to show what critical technical-economic factors must be monitored and where bottlenecks lie. A recent article in *Fortune* suggests that electronic typesetting and printing may become a threat to phototypesetting and conventional printing.[2] The speed capability gain is enormous, but graphic arts' quality is still low. What technological improvements have to be made to close this gap? This is a question of utmost importance to equipment manufacturers and users.

Usage and applications data, of course, provide information on value and extent of adoption of a device with which to build estimates of technological needs and opportunities.

The nature of usage can sometimes point the way to other technologies that must be created. Consider the growing use of plastics to replace metal. If plastics are to compete with cold-rolled steel sheet, vacuum-molding equipment must be developed to produce shapes of appropriate size and form for end-product applications.

Have the plastic press manufacturers identified this signal and considered their alternative courses of action? Has anyone made exploratory designs of molding equipment large enough to handle auto parts? The signal is there, and the industrialists concerned should be monitoring further progress.

In the Economic Environment

Time series of costs point to relationships that are promising—or are intolerable. Time series of production, consumption, and sales activity point to volumes of production and services which create new levels of facility and material needs that cannot be satisfied without major changes.

Industrial and governmental financial commitments, budgets, and allocations indicate the support that will be given to a technology. Pre-

---

[2] Lawrence Lessing, "The Printed Word Goes Electronic," *Fortune,* September 1969, p. 116.

sumably this foreshadows its progress. Compare, for example, the federal commitment of millions of dollars for oceanography versus billions for the space effort.

There are, of course, many powerful signals emerging from economic trends. Since thousands of economists labor in this field, I will not presume to survey the possibilities. Suffice it to say that signals can be found in time series of costs, capacities, demand, available resources, rates of production, and consumption, among other data.

In the Social Environment

Population trends are a prime source of signals relevant to the 10- to 30-year horizon. Hindsight reviews of technological forecasts suggest that population figures are very neglected and unappreciated as criteria for assessing the economic significance of technical changes.

For instance, the Paley report (*Resources for Freedom*) on our needs for materials in 1975, published in 1952, was largely based on 1950 statistics. Because of erroneous population forecasts, the report greatly underestimated consumption of and demand for many materials (and, therefore, production facilities). Business and government should give much more consideration to the use of the most complete and recent demographic data in assessing the significance of new technology and in corporate planning.

Measures of activities, such as leisure time usage, education, occupational interests; measures of social conditions, such as the incidence of disease, poverty, crime, and air pollution; and measures of values, such as consumer attitudes, preferences, and interests, and political opinions—all these can provide useful parameters of social change. For instance, changing attitudes on overpopulation may give new impetus to birth-control measures.

We must also recognize the formation of special interest groups, the delivery of speeches, the appearance of personalities capturing public attention, and the publication of books such as Ralph Nader's *Unsafe at Any Speed* and Rachel Carson's *Silent Spring*.

When assessing social attitudes, the manager or analyst must not apply his own value system. Though he may believe that Nader grossly misrepresents the facts of auto safety, that Rachel Carson exaggerates the effect of insecticides, or that antifluoridation groups are scientifically in error, he must keep in mind that their influence on technological progress stems from the attitudes that they create, and *not* from the accuracy or completeness of their statements. The industrialist, secure in his technical-economic logic, can easily underestimate the force of public opinion when it differs from his perception of what is true.

In the Political Environment

Today it is the political environment in which many technological directions are initiated, resources are committed, and use is determined. So governmental actions that support technological development, underwrite development or finance utilization, or prohibit or limit applications must be watched very closely.

Early signals may be available, since formal government actions almost invariably are preceded by major committee reviews and recommendations, and by reports of debates about alternatives. Ronald Smelt, a vice president of Lockheed Aircraft Corporation, has pointed out the importance of the government committee review as a signal of impending technological progress in his industry:

> [A] current example is . . . the growth of the surface effect ship. Work on support by an air bubble has been going on for many years, all over the world; a few years ago it grew into a specific program in England. In the United States the breakthrough occurred about three years ago when the Maritime Administration and the Navy together formed a special committee which recognized that the state of technology would now permit the development of a new class of vehicles, satisfying special needs for high-speed water transportation.
>   . . . [The] growth of science and technology is a relatively continuous process, with most technological advances casting shadows well ahead. (This is probably why the breakthrough seems to come in several countries at roughly the same time, even without conscious communication between the workers.) A definite stimulus is provided, in the majority of examples, by the formation of a government committee— probably the most effective method of bringing the technology face to face with the need.[3]

Occasionally one can look beyond these public modes of decision making to their instigators. There may be a strong signal in the appointment of a certain person to a department or bureau, from which he can influence the activity of a major agency. Identifying the interests, opinions, aims, and even obsessions of such individuals can help determine what technology is likely to be explored and supported.

MISSILES AND AIRCRAFT

To understand the monitoring concept and to clarify the analytical approach needed, let us look at a hindsight example. For a dramatic and

---

[3] Quoted from a letter to me.

quickly grasped case, consider the coming of the missile and its impact on the airplane manufacturing industry.

If somebody in that industry had been tracking events from the first extensive use of missiles in World War II, trying to determine their significance, and thinking about what further consequences to look for, his "journal" might have looked like Exhibit 2.

His hypothetical analysis of the implications at each event would have been done, of course, at the time it was observed.

He would have tried to establish those factors—figures of merit, effects, decisions, and so on—that were pertinent in the context of possible implications (the last column in Exhibit 2). No matter how our mythical observer might have interpreted these signals, with hindsight we know that the large manufacturers who long had controlled aircraft production and design failed to recognize the technological revolution that was occurring and did not capitalize on the advent of the missile era.

The "journal" takes us up to the power struggle between the Army and Air Force for control of long-range missiles. Other straws in the wind in the 1950s included frequent discussion in print and speeches of "limited war" concepts, DOD and Air Force budget allocations for R&D, and Sputnik.

That the industry had missed the signals was evident from a speech made in 1955 by Robert Gross, then president of Lockheed. As a trade magazine reported it:

> Of 22 major weapons systems now under development, only nine are controlled by airframe companies, Gross pointed out. . . . "Shall we bend with the storm and see our industry splintered or face the wind and build more of the weapons systems ourselves?" he asked.
>
> He cited the growth of the guided missile field and technical advances such as new types of powerplants and automatic flight as reasons for the situation now facing the industry.[4]

As if to underscore what he said, in that year the Air Force first awarded a major missile development system contract to an unknown little newcomer, Ramo-Wooldridge Corporation. By 1960 the six largest aircraft manufacturers were suffering from reduced profitability, and the Department of Defense had formally recognized that the missile had replaced the manned bomber as the primary deterrent weapon.

A tremendous industrial upheaval and technological shakeout took place from 1957 (the year of the Sputnik) through the early 1960s. Signals of what was to come, however, had been evident in the decade following World War II.

---

[4] *Aviation Week,* March 28, 1955, p. 14.

EXHIBIT 2
Sample Journal of Technical Progress in Missile Development, from Aircraft Manufacturer's Point of View

Date	Event and Technical-Economic Data	Possible Significance	Things to Consider
1944	V-1 used. 400 mph; 150-mile range. Can be deflected or shot down by interceptors and AA guns. Pilotless. Poor accuracy, small payload (2,200 pounds). Different power plant (ram jet). Simple launch facilities. Cannot be recalled or redirected. Weather no limitation on use.	New method for delivering a warhead. Expendable and cheap; thousands might be used. Does not use conventional plane manufacturing skills or technology. Low-skill operating work force. No present threat to bomber. Probably very low cost.	Accuracy, payload, range, and speed are poor. If each capability were improved, an alternative to the bomber? Counterweapon available?
1945	V-2 used. 3,600 mph; 200-mile range. Pilotless. Rocket motor. Cannot be stopped by planes or guns. Poor accuracy, small payload. No sound. No warning. Germany launches about 1,300.	Conventional bomber defenses unable to stop this weapon. Uses chemical motor for propulsion; this technology not in airplane manufacturer's skills. V-1 speed limitation surmounted.	Launching facilities? Material? If accuracy, range, and payload improve, this is real threat. What are U.S. Army, Navy, Air Corps attitudes re future adoption?
1945	A-bomb. Explosive force is thousands of times greater than anything previously known. Can be delivered only by manned bomber because of weight and size. Expensive, scarce raw materials. Terrible effects and aftereffects.	Only a few bombers needed to deliver a given explosive force. Too heavy for use in a missile, but radius of damage makes need for accuracy less significant. Horror weapon, probably will have limited use. But what if explosive force were diminished or the device miniaturized?	What happens if size of bomb reduced to missile capacity? Availability of fission materials? Cost? Clean-up of aftereffects? Reduction in power? National policy? International reaction to atomic warfare?

Date	Event	Implication	Question
War ends, 1945	Russians and U.S. Army race to grab German rocket scientists. U.S. Army ships back 200 German missiles and establishes White Sands Missile Range.	Military badly wants this technical knowledge. Army Air Corps apparently not interested. Army Ordnance deeply interested. Potential enemy deeply interested.	Air Corps still favors our products. But might the missile, in hands of Army Artillery, reduce Air Corps mission, hence plane needs? Advances in missile accuracy, range, and payload?
1946	Regulus and Navajo missile contracts let by DOD. Range 5,000 miles. Nuclear warhead.	Real threat to bomber and SAC mission. Navy to obtain strategic defense role?	Technical success. Future funding. Response of Air Force to prototype performance.
1946	Electronic computer developed.	Computation speeded exponentially. Hence missiles can be guided and redirected to different targets more rapidly.	Effect on missile and guidance systems. Computation speed. On-target assignments.
1947–1948	Greek and Berlin crises, crystallization of communist policy.	Russians intend to advance communism. Arms race to continue. Technical progress of all weapons systems will have priority.	Limitations in missile (and aircraft) performance will be gradually removed. Planes needed for what missions?
1948	Convair proposes ICBM.	Would turn into a major program affecting traditional bomber missions. Plane makers getting into missile business in big way?	Air Force response? What skills needed to make missiles? What mix of planes and missiles will be used?
1948	Development of transistor is announced.	Miniaturization of control. Reliability improvement. Both lead to missile guidance improvement.	What technical effect on missiles, planes, computers, and control systems?
1950	Korean War. Nuclear weapons not used. Missile-carrying planes, ground-to-air missiles appear.	Confirms that airplanes still are essential. Bombers remain necessary for tactical support.	Trends in plane and missile usage. Role of each? Further technical progress.
1950	Electronic content of plane now up to 46 percent of cost.	Plane manufacturers' need for electronic skills and for facilities probable, or else dependence on subcontracting.	R&D budget of Air Force. Cost of missiles and bombers? Skills and facilities needed.

CONCLUSION

Although precise technological forecasts obviously are desirable aids to management, inevitably they are only partially correct and cannot possibly be all-inclusive. Therefore we must monitor the environment to determine the ultimate course of technology, and its importance. The corporate management that ignores the warnings and opportunities in signals of impending technological change is trusting to luck, intuition, and the assumption that it will still have adequate freedom of action.

I suggest that a monitoring assignment be established in the corporate planning office and manned by the functional specialists—those in marketing, production, finance, and R&D, and even corporate planners themselves. An alternative is to establish this function under the vice president for research and engineering, provided he is given a strong marketing, economics, and sociology resource. In either case, the monitoring manager must train each of his specialists to take into account the political influences that might affect their respective areas.

A monitoring report should be presented to top management prior to the annual planning-budgeting meeting, with recommendations for further steps. Of course, conditions should be brought to top management's attention whenever there is a strong signal that implies a need for quick action.

Here are some thoughts to keep in mind when monitoring activity is going on:

Technology rarely achieves major economic impact until it is adopted on a significant scale, so there is ample warning. Production problems and the time needed for diffusion of radical new ideas delay the major economic impact for at least 5 and maybe even 20 years.

A signal usually has a number of possible implications, so all of them must be followed until it becomes clear which are the correct ones.

But we tend to be too limited in our assessment of implications in that we consider only the state of technology at the moment of review. We should mentally extend the nature and degree of technical progress to be observed and then consider the implications.

There are many false and misleading signals in the environment, and it is hard to isolate the valid signals from the "noise." Since we lack the wisdom to be certain in our selection of relevant items, we must follow many possibilities with care. This is difficult, and the results will be imperfect, but it is not impossible to gain *some* guidance. After all, when Sputnik I was launched, it was rather late to conclude that rockets were here to stay.

At times the role of an individual is decisive; an able and determined man in a key position can dominate the direction or the timing of technology. President Kennedy's appointment of General Maxwell D. Taylor as Chairman of the Joint Chiefs of Staff in 1962 was a strong signal that the emphasis in military development might shift from the old posture of massive retaliation to a more flexible response—that is, emphasis on technology other than bombers and missiles.

Another signal, in turn, could be found in Taylor's 1960 book, *The Uncertain Trumpet*, which described the point of view that he was likely to bring to this position.[5] It follows that if the Army was to have "nap of the earth" capability, the helicopter—representing the only available technology—was likely to receive greater government funding.

Many technological refinements are offered to solve some problems, and most never materialize in economic form. There are more contenders than winners. Therefore we must monitor many developments, realizing that only time will tell which is the truly significant technology.

STUDENT REVIEW QUESTIONS

1. What are the shortcomings of reliance upon R&D departments for technological forecasting efforts?
2. What activities does Bright include in monitoring the technological environment?
3. What signals of change exist for assessing the technological and economic environments?
4. What signals of change exist for assessing the social and political environments?
5. Is technological forecasting needed by nonbusiness organizations?

---

[5] Maxwell D. Taylor, *The Uncertain Trumpet* (New York: Harper & Row, Publishers, 1960).

chapter 5

Objectives—
Organizational and
Personal

Introduction

The Need for Objectives
   Essential to Strategic Planning
   Defines the "Reason for Being" of an Organization

The Nature of Objectives
   Achieving—Becoming—Attaining
   The Personal Dimension
   Levels of Objectives: Strategic to Operating
   Hierarchy of Objectives
   An Illustration of the Hierarchy

The Personal Dimension of Objectives
   Influence of Personal Values and Needs on Organizational
      Objectives
   Management by Objectives

Social Responsibility as an Objective

Balancing Objectives
   Needed in Strategy Formulation and Implementation
   A Basis for Evaluating Management and Strategy

Summary

Readings

INTRODUCTION

EARLIER IT was observed that some writers consider objectives to be part of the organizational strategy while others view objectives and strategy as closely related but separate. The most important point noted, however, was that objectives are essential to strategy and are a vital prerequisite to successful operation of an organization. Analysts of busi-

218

ness, management, and administration agree that objectives must be established if an institution is to function well relative to its opportunities; if it is to be well managed.

When the concept of strategy is employed whether in case analyses, business games, computer simulations, or in the actual operation of an organization, objectives are paramount. Further, objectives may be viewed separately from plans, policies, and decision rules employed to reach the objectives. This chapter discusses objectives as an integral part of the strategic process in an organizational setting, and emphasizes the vital role of objectives in the managerial process, regardless of the nature of the institution.

THE NEED FOR OBJECTIVES

Essential to Strategic Planning

Peter Drucker, in discussing the folly of attempting to manage without objectives, states: "This is simply another way of saying that a business *must* be managed by setting objectives for it. These objectives must be set by what is right and desirable for the enterprise."[1] The aspects of "right and desirable" will be discussed subsequently, but this section explores why objectives are so unanimously proclaimed as indispensable to good management.

Several analysts have recognized that setting objectives is the first step in the strategic planning process, and is necessary to the proper operation of the entire strategic process. "As discussed, development of clear goals and objectives is crucial to the effective development of the rest of the business policy process: evaluation of a firm, development of a corporate strategy, and implementation of the strategy—for all of these are intended to help the firm reach these goals."[2] A Research Report of the National Association of Accountants states: "As a rational process, planning presupposes objectives. Therefore the long range profit plan cannot be made without first specifying the objectives toward which the future operations should be directed."[3] Scott, whose research was referred to earlier, writes: "Objectives are always present in a planning process even though they are sometimes unconsciously established."[4] Since the planning process has been so broadly recognized as one of management's

---

[1] Peter Drucker, *The Practice of Management* (New York: Harper & Row, Publishers, 1954), p. 60.

[2] William F. Glueck, *Business Policy: Strategy Formulation and Management Action* (New York: McGraw-Hill Book Co., 1972), p. 23.

[3] National Association of Accountants Report Number 42, *Long-Range Profit Planning*, 1964, p. 47.

[4] Brian W. Scott, *Long Range Planning in American Industry* (New York: American Management Association, 1965), p. 94.

prime functions, the inseparability of objectives and planning has brought much attention to the setting of objectives as a major managerial task. As noted above, if management is to do planning, it must first deal with objectives—perhaps unconsciously—as essential inputs to the management process.

There are additional reasons why organizations require objectives. In noting what objectives together with strategy contributes to a firm, Ansoff has written, "Thus strategy and objectives together describe the concept of the firm's business. They specify the amount of growth, the area of growth, the directions for growth, the leading strengths, and the profitability targets."[5] He also concludes that "when made explicit within the firm, objectives become multi-use tools in appraisal of performance, control, and coordination, as well as all phases of the decision process."[6] Objectives in this case are recognized as being valuable during the control phase of the planning-control system. For besides being required in planning, objectives facilitate and actually permit a control process to be effective in an organization. This is understandable since objectives specify the desired end results, in addition to providing the original impetus and direction for coordinated action. Two sources well versed in the management of government agencies conclude that objectives are vital in the resource allocation process. "Top management's primary job in any enterprise is the allocation of limited resources—for selected mission purposes, in proper dimensions of time, for the furtherance of specified objectives."[7]

In summary, the various sources referred to here examine the job of top management and conclude that the establishment of objectives is necessary in the management of any enterprise whether that enterprise is a profit-making business, a major agency of government, or any other nonprofit organization. With such a pervasive presence in the management process, it should be clear why objectives have gained so must attention from analysts of policy, management, and strategy.

Defines the "Reason for Being" of an Organization

It is apparent that organizations come into being to serve some purpose or purposes. It is the function of management to clarify, articulate, implement, and in large measure to define the purpose or purposes for an organization's existence. This is done through the establishment of

---

[5] H. I. Ansoff, *Corporate Strategy* (New York: McGraw-Hill Book Co., 1965), p. 112.

[6] Ibid., p. 29.

[7] Donald J. Smalter and Rudy L. Ruggles, Jr., "Six Business Lessons from the Pentagon," *Harvard Business Review*, March–April 1966, p. 65.

objectives which has been observed to pervade the managerial process, and is recognized as a basic function for managers and administrators. An organization not guided by objectives is an organization not being managed. As a noted writer of management theory has concluded: "Unless we have a purpose there is no reason why individuals should try to cooperate together at all or why anyone should try to organize them. This, however, is very easily forgotten. Once an organization is set up, a human group is in being, all the individual and personal motives which induced persons to join the group, which keep them in the game and playing the game, assume great importance in their minds."[8]

How many times in your own experience have you seen the situation which Urwick is describing? No purpose, no direction, empire building, suboptimization, or by any other means, poor management due to a lack of organizational objectives. Without objectives, an organization may continue to exist, but it cannot be considered to be under the control of a management—it is drifting. In such circumstances, one can rightly question whether the organization should exist at all. At a minimum, such enterprises have increased their risk of not surviving.

The relationship between objectives and strategy should now be clear. Objectives as an element of strategy show what the enterprise wishes to achieve and to become. As such, they provide the rationale for the planning and policies which will guide the firm in specific ways during defined time periods, toward the achievements of the objectives. Together the objectives and major plans and policies constitute the strategy of an organization.

THE NATURE OF OBJECTIVES

Having discussed the importance of having objectives to guide an organization, it is appropriate to clarify the meaning of objectives. Although most could give a reasonable definition of an objective, it is far more difficult to discuss this term and its significance in depth. This section describes some basic characteristics which are helpful in defining objectives and in clarifying the nature of this vital element of the strategic process.

Achieving—Becoming—Attaining

"Corporate goals are an indication of what the company as a whole is trying to achieve and to become. Both parts—the achieving and the becoming—are important for a full understanding of what a company hopes

---

[8] L. F. Urwick, *Notes on the Theory of Organization* (New York: American Management Association, 1952), pp. 18–19.

to attain."[9] Apparent in this definition are several aspects of the nature of objectives, achieving something, becoming something, attaining something. This statement notes the necessity of including the dual ideas of achieving as well as becoming if objectives are to be valuable and meaningful guides to organizations.

The Personal Dimension

It is helpful to recognize that goals or objectives must be viewed as multidimensional. Tilles brings out a most important dimension when he delineates the relation of organizational goals to personal needs and goals. "Both money and product policy are part of a statement of objectives; but it is essential that these be viewed as the concrete expressions of a more abstract set of goals—the satisfaction of the needs of significant groups which cooperate to ensure the company's continued existence."[10] The human wellspring upon which organizational objectives depend for their existence has not always been recognized in management theory as uniformly as it is today. This topic will be developed in depth later in the chapter.

Levels of Objectives: Strategic to Operating

Another insight into the nature of objectives has been provided in an analysis that differentiates between objectives in the "framework of the planning process," and "company objectives." The former objectives are "statements of planning purpose developed within any kind of a business plan," while "company objectives . . . are statements of those primary purposes toward which a company (or sometimes a given unit of a company) is directing its activities."[11] The conceptual distinction drawn here is based on the level of abstraction in which objectives are visualized. Companies have specific or "planning" goals in various areas such as production, marketing, and finance, but these derive from broader and more abstract "company" objectives which in turn are based upon personal needs, values, and goals of individuals and groups within the organization. The same basic point is developed in more detail below. "Long range objectives are usually formulated within a framework of basic company philosophy or broad strategic goals. The goals are general and enduring statements of purpose that express management's fundamental intentions, and provide guidelines for the further development of

---

[9] S. Tilles, "How to Evaluate Corporate Strategy," *Harvard Business Review*, July–August 1963, p. 112.

[10] Ibid., p. 113.

[11] Scott, *Long Range Planning in American Industry*, p. 95.

the enterprise."[12] "Stemming from management's broad goals for the company, and intended to translate them into accomplishments, long range planning objectives are established to specify the results desired during the planning period."[13] Again, the degree of abstraction is the key to understanding the characteristics of organizational objectives. Objectives by nature vary both in the level of precision with which they are described, and in the breadth of their coverage within an organization. Many difficulties in understanding objectives can be avoided or overcome if the nature of objectives and the distinctions that have been presented here are understood. Personal goals and values, corporate objectives, and planning objectives by whatever names they may be called are various levels to be clarified when discussing objectives.

Finally, objectives deal with specific decisions, performance, and expected results. "Objectives are needed in every area where performance and results directly and vitally affect the survival and prosperity of the business."[14] Similarly, "Objectives are decision rules which enable management to guide and measure the firm's performance toward its purpose."[15] Both statements contain ideas of action, decision, performance and results rather than *only* direction and purpose. In essence, these statements emphasize the particular characteristic of objectives that ties them closely to results or end actions.

It should be apparent here that an understanding of the concept of management control depends upon a clear understanding of the nature of objectives. There is a direct linkage between objectives and results, and very specific objectives must be set, against which results must be compared in a management control system. These more specific objectives are, of course, dependent upon the earlier establishment of broader objectives as described previously. These broader objectives were viewed as important elements in corporate strategy. Specific objectives, then, derive directly from the broader objectives and state more clearly the shorter term, more measurable goals which must be achieved if broader strategic objectives are to become reality for the organization.

Hierarchy of Objectives

A crystallization of the ideas presented above can be achieved by discussing the concept of "hierarchy of objectives." Although the term has been employed by a number of authors in the field of management, one of the most comprehensive accounts of the "hierarchy" has been pre-

---

[12] National Association of Accountants, *Long-Range Profit Planning*, p. 47.

[13] Ibid., p. 47.

[14] Drucker, *The Practice of Management*, p. 60.

[15] Ansoff, *Corporate Strategy*, p. 38.

sented by C. H. Granger. He states ". . . there is a ranking or hierarchy of objectives proceeding in concept from the very broad to the specific." (Exhibit 5–1 is an illustration of this concept taken from the Granger article.)[16]

The exhibit indicates clearly the hierarchial nature of objectives in an organization. The top of the pyramid represents the broadest and most basic objectives, and the major influences upon them. As is true throughout the exhibit, specific examples of the objectives are provided.

EXHIBIT 5–1
Hierarchy of Objectives in Terms of Level of Need or Activity

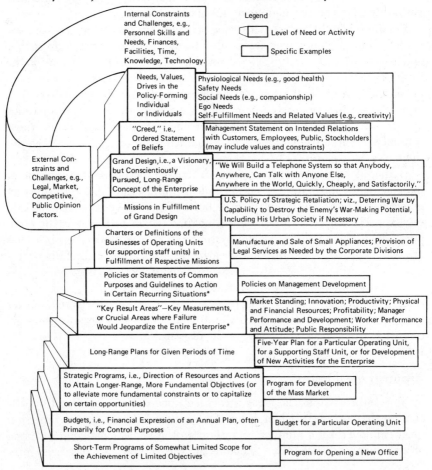

Internal Constraints and Challenges, e.g., Personnel Skills and Needs, Finances, Facilities, Time, Knowledge, Technology.

Legend

▭ Level of Need or Activity

▭ Specific Examples

Needs, Values, Drives in the Policy-Forming Individual or Individuals — Physiological Needs (e.g., good health); Safety Needs; Social Needs (e.g., companionship); Ego Needs; Self-Fulfillment Needs and Related Values (e.g., creativity)

"Creed," i.e., Ordered Statement of Beliefs — Management Statement on Intended Relations with Customers, Employees, Public, Stockholders (may include values and constraints)

External Constraints and Challenges, e.g., Legal, Market, Competitive, Public Opinion Factors.

Grand Design, i.e., a Visionary, but Conscientiously Pursued, Long-Range Concept of the Enterprise — "We Will Build a Telephone System so that Anybody, Anywhere, Can Talk with Anyone Else, Anywhere in the World, Quickly, Cheaply, and Satisfactorily."

Missions in Fulfillment of Grand Design — U.S. Policy of Strategic Retaliation; viz., Deterring War by Capability to Destroy the Enemy's War-Making Potential, Including His Urban Society if Necessary

Charters or Definitions of the Businesses of Operating Units (or supporting staff units) in Fulfillment of Respective Missions — Manufacture and Sale of Small Appliances; Provision of Legal Services as Needed by the Corporate Divisions

Policies or Statements of Common Purposes and Guidelines to Action in Certain Recurring Situations* — Policies on Management Development

"Key Result Areas"—Key Measurements, or Crucial Areas where Failure Would Jeopardize the Entire Enterprise* — Market Standing; Innovation; Productivity; Physical and Financial Resources; Profitability; Manager Performance and Development; Worker Performance and Attitude; Public Responsibility

Long-Range Plans for Given Periods of Time — Five-Year Plan for a Particular Operating Unit, for a Supporting Staff Unit, or for Development of New Activities for the Enterprise

Strategic Programs, i.e., Direction of Resources and Actions to Attain Longer-Range, More Fundamental Objectives (or to alleviate more fundamental constraints or to capitalize on certain opportunities) — Program for Development of the Mass Market

Budgets, i.e., Financial Expression of an Annual Plan, often Primarily for Control Purposes — Budget for a Particular Operating Unit

Short-Term Programs of Somewhat Limited Scope for the Achievement of Limited Objectives — Program for Opening a New Office

* May occur at various organizational levels.
Source: From C. H. Granger, "The Hierarchy of Objectives," *Harvard Business Review*, May–June 1964, pp. 65–66.

---

[16] C. H. Granger, "The Hierarchy of Objectives," *Harvard Business Review*, May–June 1964, pp. 65–66.

Although unstated in the exhibit other dimensions of the hierarchy are implicit. The broadest objectives, for instance, are formulated by the policy makers within the organization, those at the highest levels of the organization. Also, the time to fulfillment is longest for those objectives at the top of the hierarchy, and correspondingly the commitment of the organization in terms of resources and strategy involvement is greatest at the top levels. Finally, it is most difficult to measure results against objectives at the top of the hierarchy.

The concept of a hierarchy helps to clarify the nature of objectives, particularly strategic objectives. Beyond suggesting that it is not wise to consider only a single objective for any institution, the concept demonstrates that a multiplicity of objectives and goals must be clarified if an organizational situation is to be clearly understood. Moreover, the hierarchial concept provides much help in placing goals and objectives into an orderly and logical framework ranging from the broadest to the narrowest. Under this framework, the nature of objectives can be more readily analyzed, understood, and described.

An Illustration of the Hierarchy

The case of the XYZ Equipment Corporation, a relatively small manufacturer and distributor of specialized computers, is useful to illustrate the application of the hierarchy concept. What objectives are reasonable for this company operating in an industry dominated by giant firms where IBM alone captures around 70 percent of the market? XYZ and other firms in a similar position must first think of survival as a basic objective and then might look to growth and profit through technical expertise embodied in superior products. The degree to which any one of these objectives is stressed as being most important would depend upon the values and objectives of stockholders and major decision makers within management. All of these basic objectives are required in some degree. Survival is an obvious basic goal for a small company in an industry dominated by large firms. Some growth is required to even survive in such a fiercely competitive environment and satisfactory profit is required to maintain operations or to justify the infusion of new funds. Certainly some reasonable degree of technical competence is required to even survive in an industry characterized by technological change.

For such companies, then, the most basic goals may be established with some ease. It is in clearly defining the strategy of the firm that the job becomes more difficult since it is necessary then to convert these basic goals to more specific objectives within a strategic framework. The goals of XYZ Equipment Corporation might further be refined. Still assuming a survival goal, a seven-year growth objective might be specified as an average compound growth rate of 20 percent per year with a profit after-tax return on investment of 10 percent for the first two years (to allow for start-up) and 18 percent annually thereafter. The technical expertise may be defined more specifically as leadership in the technology of miniature-sized memory units to produce the most technically superior mini-computer. These goals are now specific enough to continue in the development of a strategy based upon them.

To progress as a company, even more specific levels of objectives must be established in major areas. The market sought might be limited to the segment requiring mini-computers, and an objective of capturing 30 percent of that market might be set. A product line objective might be to have a full line of at least five sizes with variations to satisfy the market. And a related objective in R.&D. might be to update the products substantially and have a major improvement every two years through emphasis on continued miniaturizing of memory units and increases in speed of processing. More specific financial objectives might include an initial debt-equity ratio target of 55 percent decreasing to 35 percent over the seven-year period, and a target return on sales of 12 percent before taxes. Sales objectives will have to be specified to reach the desired compound growth rate and might be supported by more specific objectives in terms of sales quotas for each sales representative or region. Objectives in the manufacturing areas will necessarily be specified in areas of cost levels, units of production, quality standards, and the like.

Thus, the very broad or "bedrock" objectives are refined into more useful strategic objectives to guide the XYZ Equipment Corporation. The fairly broad strategic objectives will be put forth in plans containing more specific objectives or goals. But to carry out the strategy of the enterprise and to achieve the encompassed objectives, even more specific goals will be required as operational guides in each area of the organization where results are expected. These lower levels require precise objectives that are operational in nature and not strategic. However, such objectives stem from and support the broad strategic obectives described above. It is the concept of the hierarchy of objectives which helps to pull these various types of objectives together in a coherent manner for the analyst or student.

THE PERSONAL DIMENSION OF OBJECTIVES

Influence of Personal Values and Needs on Organizational Objectives

The values and needs of those who set objectives will influence greatly the objectives that ultimately are established. As illustrated in Exhibit 5–1, this is most apparent at the higher levels of the organization and can be observed in the behavior of top managers when establishing organizational strategy. "We shall see at once that executives in charge of company destinies do not look exclusively at what a company might do and can do. Sometimes—in apparent disregard of at least the second of these considerations—they seem heavily influenced by what they personally *want* to do."[17] Because of the broad recognition that corporate objectives and the major goals of all organizations should not simply "happen," studies have been undertaken of the decision-making process analyzing the importance of personal values and needs of the decision maker. These same studies generally recommend that executives or other decision makers strive to gain a full understanding of themselves, their values and needs, and to be conscious of these influences when making decisions and when establishing objectives.

Guth and Taguiri have recognized clearly the critical role of personal values in setting corporate objectives. "For it is quite clear, on the basis of both observation and of systematic studies of top management in business organizations, that personal values are important determinants in the choice of corporate strategy."[18] These authors provide the following useful definition: "For our purposes a value can be viewed as a conception, explicit or implicit, of what an individual or group regards as desirable, and in terms of which he or they select, from among alternatives available, the means and ends of action."[19]

Many can recall observing some objective or decision in an organization that did not seem to make sense. Close scrutiny, however, might well have revealed that the situation was congruent with the values of a major decision maker in the organization. Likewise a research and development company which appears to lack direction might actually be reflecting the widely diverse value systems of the top policy makers and scientists.

A totally rational view of business might conclude that in business organizations there is less disruptive diversity because the profit motive quells the competition among value systems. This is more likely the case in larger companies where single personalities tend to be less dominant than in smaller firms. But though the degree of influence may vary, the value systems of individuals and groups do affect the objectives which are set for all institutions, including business organizations. At some point in the process of formulating objectives, the needs and values of the involved personalities will exert influence. If this were not so, it would be unlikely that managers would support the objectives once they were operating as guides for the organization. It is difficult to follow for long a course to which one has no real commitment. That commitment can

---

[17] C. R. Christensen, K. R. Andrews, and J. L. Bower, *Business Policy: Text and Cases* (Homewood, Ill.: Richard D. Irwin, Inc., 1973), p. 432.

[18] W. D. Guth and R. Taguiri, "Personal Values and Corporate Strategy," *Harvard Business Review*, September–October 1965, p. 123.

[19] Ibid., p. 124.

be assumed only if the objectives are in reasonable accord with an individual's own values.

Management by Objectives

As broad strategic objectives are influenced by the values and objectives of major decision makers, so too are more specific objectives influenced by the values and personal objectives of those who establish goals at lower levels in the enterprise. Recognizing this, many students of management have advocated involvement in the establishment of objectives of those who will be affected. At every level in the objective hierarchy, those having responsibility for results should be given some voice in the establishment of objectives. It is essential that participants in an organization see enough compatibility between their personal goals and the goals of the organization. Lack of a minimum amount of agreement will usually cause an individual or group to withhold from the organization service or cooperation. An undesirable result could be the failure to achieve broader organizational goals.

Participation of individuals in the process of setting objectives has been advocated by such authorities as Peter Drucker and Douglas McGregor, and has become embodied in the term "management by objectives." This idea states that people work best who help to set, and thus understand and accept the objectives that tell what is expected of them as a person or group. Again, the personal element in objective setting becomes a vital factor. The personal values and objectives of major decision makers are critical inputs to the major objectives and thus to the strategy of any organization. But if a strategy is to be successfully implemented and if broad goals are to be achieved, more specific objectives must be established consistent with the strategy. Those who work toward the achievement of these more specific goals should have a voice in the establishment of such goals in order to ensure their commitment to the implementation of the strategy.

SOCIAL RESPONSIBILITY AS AN OBJECTIVE

Social good is the objective of most nonprofit organizations. In recent years, business has been urged to adopt as one phase of its strategy the idea that it has an obligation and an opportunity to contribute to the society in which it operates. A strong argument can be advanced that it is the responsibility of business in general, and of individual companies in particular, to take a positive position on influencing the environment and especially social change. When a large portion of the potential work force is unemployed, and sometimes unemployable, little real progress can be made without positive action by companies to hire and train such people. When an atmosphere of idealism exists in so many of the youth of the country, business may well lose some of the talent it so vitally needs unless business executives recognize the place of idealism and social responsibility in their roles as leaders. A second negative motivation also is present. "Many of the businessmen involved now fully understand that the laws to which they object are not the result of perversity of politicians and exposé journalists but of the actions of business itself. By not heeding the changes in the social structure they have virtually asked for government regulation."[20] Social change is a major factor of the environment and a responsive government must take heed. Because of its importance and pervasiveness in the society, business must be affected. Given these circumstances, business must include social responsibility as a major objective in its strategy. Corporate strategists, state some authors, must consider the public good and rights in their corporate objectives and decisions because of their own morality first, and secondly because if they do not the government will step in.[21]

But not only academicians and theorists recommend social responsibility to business and business executives. One former business executive who is aware of the need for change is Arjay Miller, former president of the Ford Motor Company. Beginning with the belief that management cannot effectively discharge its long-run responsibility to stockholders unless it also behaves responsibly toward employees, customers, government, education, and the public at large, Mr. Miller has expressed strong opinions on the need to find out in advance what the corporation's position should be in society rather than be forced to react after events have occurred.[22] Numerous examples of companies' efforts to make socially responsible decisions have appeared. IBM has built an operation in the heart of the ghetto area of a major city. Raytheon Corporation has been involved in a campaign to hire previously "unemployable" workers, as other companies have done. Avco Corporation and IBM have run "Job Corps Centers" to train disadvantaged youths for meaningful employment.

"Nevertheless, a look back through business history reveals that people have always held some concept of the responsibility owed by business management to society. It is the contention here that concepts of social responsibility have moved through three distinct phases. . . . Phase III, which may be called the quality of life concept of social responsibility, has become popular in recent years."[23] Business executives are still deciding just how business, or their particular corporation, fits into society.

---

[20] "D.E.W. Line for Business," *Saturday Review of Literature*, September 9, 1967, p. 60.

[21] Christensen, Andrews, and Bower, *Business Policy*, p. 578.

[22] For a more complete discussion of this topic, see "D.E.W. Line for Business," p. 60.

[23] Robert Hay and Ed Gray, "Social Responsibilities of Business Managers," *Journal of the Academy of Management*, March 1974.

In making this determination, some companies' chief decision makers are altering or redirecting their objectives and strategies to reflect the view that social responsibility must be included. For an attitude to become operational in a business organization (or any other organization), the attitude must be expressed in the strategy and objectives, and subsequently in the actions which implement the strategy. "The source of the ethical element in business decisions is the objective of the enterprise. . . .Thus, there is a hierarchy of means and ends in business decision making. At the source of this hierarchy is the objective of the enterprise, the purpose for which it was founded and continues to exist."[24]

BALANCING OBJECTIVES

Needed in Strategy Formulation and Implementation

Some may contend that social responsibility is only a constraint on the legitimate objectives of the business enterprise, rather than actually an objective in itself. Yet, given the theory that objectives are influenced greatly by personal values and needs, it follows that social responsibility may indeed be an objective in itself at any level in an organization's hierarchy. Rather than discuss whether "the" objective of business is to maximize profits,[25] it is more useful to consider in totality the things which are desirable or necessary in the overall strategy of an organization. Although maximization of profit may be a logical financial guide to decision makers in a business, it is modified by so many factors in actuality that it is of limited value when considered alone. But when basic objectives such as stimulating growth, increasing profitability, surviving, and achieving greater operational stability, are considered together, a foundation is established upon which to build even more specific objectives.

A vital task of top management is to balance the multiplicity of objectives in an organization. Profitability must be a factor in the growth aspirations of any business firm, just as financial stability must be balanced with growth in nonprofit organizations. Neither growth nor profit objectives should be set which jeopardize the survival of any profit-oriented, or nonprofit organization. Social responsibility is today important to business enterprises just as it has always been to most nonprofit institutions. Management must include these various objectives, as well as many more specific objectives of the organization and its members, as

---

[24] T. A. Petit, "Making Socially Responsible Decisions," *Journal of the Academy of Management,* December 1966, p. 308.

[25] For a thorough discussion of this point of view, see Milton Friedman, "The Social Responsibility of Business Is to Increase Profits," *New York Times Magazine,* September 30, 1970.

the strategic process is accomplished in any institution. It is by the successful balancing of various and often conflicting objectives that management proves its value to an organization.

A Basis for Evaluating Management and Strategy

In appraising an organization's objectives a key question is whether management, in formulating strategy, has developed realistic objectives in light of the organization's internal and external situations. Beyond the formulation of strategic objectives, has the top-management team recognized other objectives which have been established at levels lower in the hierarchy? Likewise, has management been able to integrate into an action plan those objectives which would enhance the future of the organization? For instance, has management adopted specific financial and social objectives which are realistic considering the total situation of the organization, and dismissed other objectives (which may have been supported by some in the organization) which clearly were beyond the resources and competence of the institution? In summary, has management been able to "balance" the objectives of the organization and of all participants in the organization; owners, management, labor, customers, government, and the public? When organizational objectives are being achieved at a level satisfactory to those who established them, and when the various groups and individual organizational members see their objectives being satisfactorily attained, the top management and strategists have succeeded in balancing objectives.

In the establishment of objectives, the major strategists of the organization must be aware of various organizational groups and forces, and must in their objectives and strategy recognize the sentiments and powers of these groups. Unless this is done in the initial establishment of basic objectives, conflict and inefficiency could result. Top management must look ahead, anticipate events and reactions, and establish objectives which maintain equilibrium in the organization. Subsequently, as it implements strategy, carries out plans, and acts toward the achievement of objectives, management must continue to balance its own objectives with those of various other groups. Without having basic strategic objectives as bench marks, or lacking an understanding that objectives in an organization comprise a hierarchy or system, it would be virtually impossible for management to maintain this precious but always precarious balance.

SUMMARY

The place of objectives in corporate structure should be recognized as vital by the student of organizations. Broad, strategic objectives provide the direction for rational planning and policy making in an organization.

As more specific goals are established consonant with the broader strategic objectives, they serve as standards or bench marks against which to measure results.

A full understanding of the nature of objectives is not easy to achieve. A framework helpful to understanding is the "hierarchy of objectives" which notes the various levels of specificity among objectives set at the different levels in an organization. A particularly important influence on objectives is the personal values and needs of objective setters. Social responsibility, long the province of nonprofit institutions, has lately become an objective of many business organizations. All of these aspects covered in this discussion of objectives add insight to the strategic process in organizations. Personal values and objectives affect the strategy both in its formulation by major decision makers, and in its implementation at lower levels in the organization. Social responsibility is an input which helps to define some specific objectives that *should* be part of any organization's strategy.

Finally, this chapter has emphasized that balancing a multitude of objectives is a key job of top management in setting strategic objectives, and of managers at all levels when acting toward fulfillment of these broad objectives.

The following chapter will discuss the development of corporate strategy and will again emphasize the essential role of objectives in strategy formulation.

11. Personal Values and Corporate Strategy*

WILLIAM D. GUTH and
RENATO TAGIURI

SOME MANAGERS may feel that their choices of corporate strategy are entirely objective. This may well be so *if* they include their personal values among the elements they take into account in their analyses and decisions. For it is quite clear, on the basis both of observation and of systematic studies of top management in business organizations, that *personal values are important determinants in the choice of corporate strategy.*

NEED FOR EXAMINATION

Unfortunately, our values are so much an intrinsic part of our lives and behavior that we are often unaware of them—or, at least, we are unable to think about them clearly and articulately. Yet our values, along with other factors, clearly determine our choices, as can be proved by presenting men with equally "reasonable" alternative possibilities and comparing the choices they make. Some will choose one course, others another, and each will feel that his election is *the* rational one.

Problem in Strategy

In early 1961 the four top executives of U.S. Research, Inc. (disguised name), a large research and development company with a high proportion of its business in government work, were considering possible strategies for the future. Three major alternatives had been identified:

* William D. Guth and Renato Tagiuri, "Personal Values and Corporate Strategy," *Harvard Business Review,* vol. 43, no. 5. (1965). © 1965 by the President and Fellows of Harvard College; all rights reserved. Reprinted by permission.

1. Attempt to triple, over the next three to five years, the company's volume of busines by broadening its base of research "products" and thus capturing a larger share of the then growing government expenditures for space exploration.
2. Aim for the same growth objective, but achieve it through the development of commercially exploitable hardware products generated in the research activity.
3. Aim for a slower rate of growth, continuing the business along the lines in which it had achieved its present position.

The president, convinced that each top executive of the company needed to be personally committed to the strategy finally chosen, held a number of meetings directed at achieving consensus on one of the alternatives. The meetings proved fruitless. All three possibilities were strongly favored by one or more of the officers, each of whom justified his choice as the only "objectively" feasible alternative.

The president believed, on the basis of the evidence available, that all three alternatives were equally feasible. It occurred to him that further progress might be made in achieving a personal commitment from each manager if attention were focused on the relationship of the managers themselves to the nature of the alternatives. Using knowledge about *personal values*, he was able to identify differences between himself and the other three top officers which seemed to account for their choices among the strategic alternatives:

> The vice president who favored the first alternative—tripling the volume of business through broadening the company's base of research products—was seen by the president as having the values of a businessman-scientist whose involvement in the company was motivated by a desire to earn as much money as possible while at the same time being associated with the intellectual stimulation of a research "atmosphere." He wanted the company to grow rapidly and become more profitable, but he also wanted it to remain exclusively a research company.
>
> The vice president who favored rapid growth through the development of commercially exploitable hardware products was seen by the president as having the value orientation of a businessman whose involvement with the company was predominantly motivated by an interest in economic progress as measured by growth and profitability. Rapid growth and increased profitability for the company were his prime interests, along with efficiency and orderliness in the company's day-to-day operations. He believed that the company would, by getting into commercial production, grow rapidly and increase its profitability. Also he believed that competition in the commercial field would create additional concern for efficiency and orderliness in the company's day-to-day operations.
>
> The third vice president, favoring continuation of the present activity aimed at achieving a slower rate of growth, was seen by the president as

having the values of a scientist who joined the company with the principal objective of working on research projects with practical applicability. This vice president viewed the possibility of getting into commercial production with alarm, believing such activity would disturb the company's research climate. In addition, he believed that substantial company growth in any field might lead to bureaucratic organizational practices also potentially inimical to creative research.

The president saw *his own* values as an almost equally balanced combination of economic, scientific, and human-relations concerns. His involvement in the company reflected not only economic and scientific objectives, but also an interest in working closely and productively with a tightly knit group of men who were all personally involved in the company's efforts.

On the basis of these insights, the president switched from favoring the first alternative to favoring a modification of the third alternative, which called for attempting to double the company's growth in the next five years through continuing the business along the lines in which it had achieved its present position. He believed this new alternative matched the values of the *group* of top executives better than any of the three previously identified alternatives. Armed with this analysis, he was able to lead the group toward consensus on the modified third alternative. The strategy chosen has proved itself successful, and the top executive group of the company remains very satisfied with the choice.

Few of us make the effort of studying our own values to the point of being able to be explicit and articulate about them. The busy executive is no exception. Indeed, being primarily a man of action, he may spend less time over this matter than other people do. Thus many top-level managers do not have an explicit and useful way of thinking about personal values and about the influences these have on the strategic choice processes of the company. As a result, this important element is often left unexamined.

NATURE OF VALUES

For our purposes a value can be viewed as a conception, explicit or implicit, of what an individual or a group regards as *desirable,* and in terms of which he or they select, from among alternative available modes, the means and ends of action.

Values are such an intrinsic part of a person's life and thought that he tends to take them for granted, unless they are questioned or challenged. He acquires them very early in life. They are transmitted to him through his parents, teachers, and other significant persons in his environment who, in turn, acquired their values in similar fashion. Child-rearing practices are expressions of a family's values, and of the values of the social group to which the family belongs.

Although there are dramatic cases of deviation from values acquired early in life, an adult's values are usually the result of the interplay of (a) what he learned from those who reared him, and (b) his particular individuality and "times." Undoubtedly, this is not a simple process of faithful transmission from one generation to another. However, much of the process takes place early in life, and this portion of it affects the possibilities for later modifications and acquisitions of values.

As in the case with most important characteristics acquired in the first few years of life, we have difficulty identifying values until we come face to face with situations that force us to recognize their presence in our makeup. Parents themselves, often not being articulate about their own value systems, transmit them and teach them to their children more by means of examples, rewards, and punishments than by the use of words and labels that would make the children explicit about alternative value systems. Nevertheless, language helps and delimits the development of values. Indeed, the value system of a society and its language are often closely related, the language having developed special mechanisms useful for conveying the value alternatives chosen by that society. This sometimes makes it difficult for people to understand the values of other cultures where the language system is quite different.

Values are closely related to personality; indeed, they are part of it. If we say that a man decides among alternatives on the basis of whether the choice will maximize his usefulness to others, rather than on the basis of considerations of personal gain, we are describing his values as well as his personality. Values can be thought of as the guidance system a personality uses when faced with choices of alternatives. They are a very stable feature of his personality, especially if some values clearly dominate over others.

Values may be identified by noting differences between individuals or groups in dealing with similar problems. Naturally, not all differences can be accounted for by variations in values; for instance, some variations are produced by differences in accumulated knowledge and intellectual skills. Yet there appears to be an interdependence among knowledge, skills, and values. Sometimes, a change in the first two will lead to a change in the third.

CONTRASTING PROFILES

Individuals express their value systems in any number of ways: some very abstract, with word labels attached to them, others in unselfconscious, concrete ways, mostly in terms of specific situations and behaviors. In order to treat the subject of values in a way useful to the present task of seeing how they enter into the process of choosing between alternative strategies, we need a scheme that will help us distinguish, classify, and compare values and value systems of individuals, groups, or cultures. Let us look at one such conceptual scheme and at the differences it illuminates in different groups' values.

Classification Scheme

Much has been written on values, on classifications of values, and on the value differences among people, cultures, professions, and generations. One classification of values that should prove quite useful to us was developed by a German philosopher, Eduard Spranger, for the purpose of distinguishing among types of men.[1] He found it helpful to identify six kinds of value orientations:

1.   The *theoretical* man is primarily interested in the discovery of truth, in the systematic ordering of his knowledge. In pursuing this goal he typically takes a "cognitive" approach, looking for identities and differences, with relative disregard for the beauty or utility of objects, seeking only to observe and to reason. His interests are empirical, critical, and rational. He is an intellectual. Scientists or philosophers are often of this type (but they are not, as we shall see, the only ones).

2.   The *economic* man is primarily oriented toward what is useful. He is interested in the practical affairs of the business world; in the production, marketing, and consumption of goods; in the use of economic resources; and in the accumulation of tangible wealth. He is thoroughly "practical" and fits well the stereotype of the American businessman.

3.   The *aesthetic* man finds his chief interest in the artistic aspects of life, although he need not be a creative artist. He values form and harmony. He views experience in terms of grace, symmetry, or harmony. Each single event is savored for its own sake.

4.   The essential value for the *social* man is love of people—the altruistic or philanthropic aspect of love. The social man values people as ends, and tends to be kind, sympathetic, unselfish. He finds those who have strong theoretical, economic, and aesthetic orientations rather cold. Unlike the political type, the social man regards love as the most important component of human relationships. In its purest form the social orientation is selfless and approaches the religious attitude.

5.   The *political* man is characteristically oriented toward power, not necessarily in politics, but in whatever area he functions. Most leaders have a high power orientation. Competition plays a large role in all life, and many writers have regarded power as the most universal motive. For some men, this motive is uppermost, driving them to seek personal power, influence, and recognition.

---

[1] *Types of Men*, translated by P. Pigors (Halle, Germany, Niemeyer, 1928). For other instances of classifications and discussions of values, see C. Kluckhohn, "Values and Value-Orientations in the Theory of Action," in *Toward a General Theory of Action*, ed. Talcott Parsons and Edward A. Shils (Cambridge, Mass.: Harvard University Press, 1951); and Florence R. Kluckhohn and F. L. Strodtbeck, *Variations in Value Orientations* (Evanston, Ill.: Row, Peterson and Company, 1961).

EXHIBIT 1
Value Profiles of Four Top Executives

Mr. A		Mr. B		Mr. C		Mr. D	
Value	Score	Value	Score	Value	Score	Value	Score
Religious	57	Theoretical	65	Aesthetic	48	Economic	58
Political	41	Aesthetic	45	Social	44	Political	49
Theoretical	36	Religious	37	Economic	43	Theoretical	37
Economic	36	Political	33	Theoretical	36	Religious	37
Aesthetic	35	Economic	32	Political	35	Social	31
Social	35	Social	28	Religious	34	Aesthetic	28

6. The *religious* man is one "whose mental structure is permanently directed to the creation of the highest and absolutely satisfying value experience." The dominant value for him is unity. He seeks to relate himself to the universe in a meaningful way and has a mystical orientation.

Averages for Executives

Spranger's value classification served as the theoretical underpinning for a questionnaire designed to measure quantitatively the *relative* strength of each of the six value orientations in an individual.[2] Recently we gave the questionnaire to high-level U.S. executives attending the Advanced Management Program at the Harvard Business School.[3] The following average value profile resulted:

Value	Score
Economic	45
Theoretical	44
Political	44
Religious	39
Aesthetic	35
Social	33
	240

(The questionnaire was designed so as to yield a total of 240 points, distributed over the six value dimensions.)

Thus the major orientation of these men is a combination of economic, theoretical, and political values. The economic and political orientations are clearly in line with our stereotypes of businessmen. The theoretical value may surprise us, but for a moment only. The high-level executive

---

[2] G. W. Allport, P. E. Vernon, and G. Lindzey, *The Study of Values* (Boston: Houghton Mifflin Company, 1960).

[3] See Renato Tagiuri, "Value Orientations and the Relationships of Managers and Scientists," *Administrative Science Quarterly*, June 1965, pp. 39–51.

needs to have theories and cognitive and rational approaches to his work in order to satisfy his economic and political values. He works with and through others; he has to explain, teach, express, be explicit, be rational. And he also has to be abstract, since he is removed from direct operations and has the function of integrating human and material resources. In short, the executive shows up here as a bit of a theoretician while we suspect he likes to think of himself as a man of action.

The values just reported are averages. There are, among executives, enormous individual variations, and it is these that lead to diverse choices among alternatives. Exhibit 1 shows, in order of importance, the values of four individuals, all high-level managers, included in our sample. Each of these cases differs greatly from the average value configuration of the group; yet each man is an effective member of some top-flight team.

Such individual differences notwithstanding, our study indicates that the values of executives, *on the average,* are different from the values of men in other professions. In the field of religion, for example, a sample of ministers had values in the following order of decreasing importance: religious, social, aesthetic, political, theoretical, economic.[4] This pattern is virtually opposite to that of the executives.

EFFECT ON STRATEGY

How, exactly, do an executive's values affect his thinking about strategy? First, bear in mind that a corporate strategy is an explicit and shared set of goals and policies defining what the company is to achieve and become in the future and how it must operate in order to reach its goals.

Not all companies have corporate strategies. Most executives, however, have personal concepts of what their company's corporate strategy is or ought to be. In the absence of a viable degree of consensus on a particular set of goals and policies, each executive will tend to behave in accordance with his own concept and, in turn, his own values.

Should there be great divergence in the unstated concepts of corporate strategy among company executives, there will tend to be conflict and disorganization in the company's operations, possibly without clear recognition of the source of the difficulty.

Criteria for Strategy

The process by which an individual's concept of or feel for his company's strategy is formulated includes assessment of environmental oppor-

---

[4] Adapted from G. W. Allport, P. E. Vernon, and G. Lindzey, *Manual for the Study of Values* (Boston: Houghton Mifflin Company, 1960), p. 14.

tunities and risks and of company resources. Such an assessment results in reasoned or intuitive judgments as to what the company might achieve and become over some period of time if it operates in certain particular ways. The individual's system of values is then applied to these judgments, and a choice among the alternative corporate strategies is made.

Until this last step is taken, the man is not really engaged with strategy. He remains uncommitted, uninvolved in the key choices affecting the company's future and determining its basic character. Since his personal values are such an intrinsic part of his life and behavior, however, he will eventually have to use them as criteria in making his conscious choices. If he is not very conscious or articulate about his personal values, they will impose themselves no less forcefully on his actual choices, i.e., those evidenced by his behavior.

Thus, consciously or unconsciously, personal values are one of the determinants of a manager's concept of what his company strategy ought to be. For example:

> If economic values clearly dominate his other values, he will be more inclined to emphasize opportunities for growth and profitability and to make strategic decisions which call for stretching or adding to present resources to attain these goals.

> If, on the other hand, other values dominate his personality, he will match his company's opportunities, risks, and resources in terms of the values he does emphasize, possibly at the sacrifice of growth and profitability. Thus, an executive with strong and dominant political values may tend to choose among alternative strategies the particular one which maximizes his opportunity to gain additional power.

Values in Action

The role and influence of personal values are much in evidence in decision making. Consider these two examples:

> The president of National Duplicating Products Corporation, a small manufacturer of office duplicating equipment, ranked relatively high on the social value, giving particular attention to the security, welfare, and happiness of his employees. Second in order of relative importance in his scheme was the aesthetic value. The remaining four values were undifferentiable in importance on the basis of the available evidence.

> When faced with increasing product and sales competition from other firms in the industry and with increasing opportunity from expanding markets, the president chose to stay with the company's traditional strategy. The key elements of this strategy were:

> Slow to moderate company growth.

> Emphasis on a single product.

> An independent-agent form of sales organization.

Very high-quality products with aesthetic appeal.

Refusal to compete on a price basis.

In addition, this strategy included a policy of refraining from setting time standards or other production-scheduling constraints on the factory workers for fear of "making a slave shop out of the place." Another critical policy set by the president was to spend considerable amounts of money on the maintenance of elaborate physical facilities for both himself and the employees of the company.

The president was aware of many of the economic risks and losses of opportunity entailed by this strategy. But the dominance of his social value over his other values was so great that he chose to take the economic risks and opportunity losses in order to maximize what in his view was the stability, security, welfare, and happiness of the employees of the company, and the aesthetic appeal of his company's offices, plant, and products.

Though not a major stockholder in the company, the president had voting control over a majority of the stock outstanding. This element of the situation helped to minimize the amount of pressure on him to pay greater attention to the satisfaction of economic values.

Except for the vice president and treasurer, the top management team members of Acoustic Research, Inc., a manufacturer of high-fidelity loudspeaker systems, placed theoretical and social values over other values; the company's strategy reflected this orientation. The key elements of the company's strategy were:

Scientific truth and integrity in advertising.

Lower margins to dealers than competitors were paying.

Maintenance of "truth and honesty" in relation to suppliers, dealers, and employees.

High quality at the lowest possible price to the consumer (based on a vaguely defined concept of a minimum acceptable level of profitability).

These policies were maintained in the face of significant pressure from the optimistic claims and nonscientific appeals in the advertising of competitors; from dealers, many of whom refused actively to push the company's products; and from economically oriented outsiders, who insisted that changes in company policies should be made in order to capitalize on the substantial opportunities for growth which existed in the rapidly growing high-fidelity phonograph market.

In both of the foregoing cases it was our judgment as close observers that the top managers involved had realistically assessed opportunities, risks, and resources of their firms. Just as the president of National Duplicating Products Corporation chose to forgo the opportunities for rapid growth and increased profitability in order to minimize the pressures of change and growth on himself and on his employees, so the executives of Acoustic Research chose to forgo the opportunity of greater sales through less "scientific" advertising and more dealer "push" in order to keep the price of their products low and to retain their scientific integrity.

Consistency and Conflict

At the same time that personal values serve as the basic ends or goals toward which an executive would like to see company activity directed, they also affect his decisions concerning implementing policies. If, for example, the dominant value of an individual executive is economic and he faces two new product alternatives promising to yield equal degrees of growth, he may choose one course over the other because it is more consistent with his other values. To illustrate:

> Hugh Hefner, president and founder of HMH Publishing Company, publisher of *Playboy*, worked for several magazines prior to striking out on his own. Having dominant economic and aesthetic values, he found the jobs with other magazines wanting in opportunity to achieve personal satisfaction. Accordingly, he started his own company to publish a magazine which represented his aesthetic point of view. Fortunately for him, his particular form of aesthetic value was shared by many others, and a market existed for *Playboy*. As a result, Hefner not only works each day on something consistent with his concept of what a magazine should be, but his labors also make him increasingly wealthy, bringing economic satisfaction as well.
>
> The executives and staff of *The New York Times*, according to all published sources of information, appear to have a highly dominant theoretical and social value orientation. Their product—yesterday's news reported intelligently, accurately, and without bias or sensationalism—is apparently valued more for its own sake than as a means of economic ends. This high level of personal commitment to the product has been a defense against increasing pressures to modify *The New York Times* in the interest of economy and expanded circulation. The present product and the pattern of operations supporting it yield at best only moderate growth and return on investment.

For a great many managements, of course, economic values are in fact dominant, and these may come into conflict with other values dominating in other groups in American society. For example:

> Some of the pharmaceutical companies have found that their efforts to achieve economic growth and profits through manufacture, distribution, and sale of medicines have come into conflict with the social value of some powerful individuals to whom virtually any effort to relate economic growth and profits with sickness raises the image of unhealthy, unfortunate people being bilked for private gain.
>
> Even publications about the extensive advances in pharmacology made possible by the industry's reinvestment of earnings in research and

development have tended to be ineffective against this value perspective. The fact that many companies in this industry have experienced relatively high returns on investment in comparison with industry in general reinforces the negative judgments made of them, rather than serving as an indication of their relative competence as economic institutions.

STEPS TO UNDERSTANDING

Businessmen are seldom self-conscious and articulate about their values, although they feel uncomfortable when these values are violated and at ease when they are fulfilled. Also, they often do not clearly perceive the strategy that underlies and guides their business and corporate actions.

The manager could benefit by paying more attention to the operation of his values. He may then be able to kill two birds with one stone; for if his strategy is not explicit and if his values play a role in its formation, then by making his values more clear he may also become more aware of the actual nature of the strategy itself. In addition, he may be better able to analyze the relationship and interdependence between values and strategy.

This is *not* to say that he should try to filter out the influence of his values on his concept of corporate strategy and alter it in order to make, for example, a "hard economic choice." On the contrary, if he understands more exactly the nature of what he is doing, he may be able to attain an even more satisfying match between personal values and corporate strategy. In other words, under conditions of clarity of assumptions, personal values may be allowed to influence the manager's concept of corporate strategy more than they would otherwise, not less.

Self-Analysis

How does a manager go about making his values explicit to himself? One thing he can do is examine his behavior from time to time with the question in mind of what values he holds. Here, the approach of comparing and contrasting his behavior with the behavior of others facing similar situations and problems is very helpful. But care must be taken to distinguish variations due to the nature of the information available about the situation and problem from variations that result from different values. The latter is what we are interested in.

This approach has been very effective in helping students in management programs at the Harvard Business School to identify and clarify their personal values. The instructors separate, in the case material, the factual description of the situation from the analysis and corporate strategy choices made by the individual managers actually involved in the case. They then ask the students to make strategy recommendations based on their own analysis of the *situation,* being careful to ensure that the class has a common understanding of the facts. Then they present the students with descriptions of the strategic analyses and conclusions of the executives in the case. Through the process of comparison and contrast with their own analyses and recommendations, the students are often able to achieve some clarification of their personal values.

Another useful approach is for the manager to take time to analyze the situation when he feels that his values have been violated or when he is prompted to explain others' behavior in terms of such phrases as "They have different values." This is the time to note the nature of elusive standards and assumptions—when they are, so to speak, stirred to the surface.

A manager can also learn something about his values by taking one or more of the tests designed to identify the relative strength of an individual's values and by analyzing the results, preferably with the help of an appropriately trained person.

EXHIBIT 2
Values of Scientists, Research Managers, and Executives—
Self-Ratings versus Ratings Expected from Others

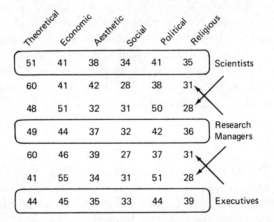

What matters most, however, is the attitude or frame of mind with which the manager approaches the problem of identifying the part his values play in his work. Two requirements are important for him to observe:

   1.   There must be personal acceptance of the fact that his personal values are related to his implicit or explicit strategy choices. This will in itself make him more sensitive to what they are and how they may operate. Yet this may be a hard first step to take. Some of us have a

difficult time accepting our personal involvement in situations, often insisting that we are being completely objective and that anyone who does not agree with us as to the validity and desirability of a particular strategic choice is simply "letting his emotions run away with him." Personal values are always involved in arriving at concepts of and "feels for" corporate strategies, and objectivity consists exactly of taking them into account, as we do with other elements in our analysis.

2.   There must be a willingness to focus on personal values as a possible explanation of differences among the concepts of corporate strategy held by various executives. Many of the same forces leading to the struggle for "objectiveness" in business pratice lead to suppression of discussion of value differences among executives. The purpose of such discussion should not be to attempt to change anyone's values, a difficult task anyway, but rather to clarify the nature and source of differences and disagreements. It is often possible, through identification of similarities and differences in personal values, to cast up new strategy alternatives that will be more satisfying to all concerned than are those choices initially contributing to the conflict.

Appraisal of Others

Understanding and taking one's own values into explicit account unfortunately is not always enough to arrive at a viable strategy. Where management operates as a team, understanding the values of the other members becomes important if a strategy is to be developed that will gain the genuine support of all concerned. (An example of the successful solution of this problem was given at the beginning of this article.) Here articulate, explicit statements of strategies and their ramifications become especially important, for without them there is no good way for a member of the group to understand what the other members' values are and what they really have in mind.

And there must be a willingness to accept the idea that while other men's values may be different from our own, they are not necessarily better or worse. Such acceptance can result in improved interpersonal relations and effectiveness in a company's executive group. There is no standard or accepted method of proving that one value is better or worse than another, and so it is foolish to view the question in these terms. One may not feel attracted to a person with very different values, but one is not intellectually justified in condemning him for holding them.

People not infrequently misjudge other persons' values. This is borne out by a study of how research managers, scientists, and executives assess each other. The study is based on the questionnaire described earlier and covers nearly 1,000 men who filled out the questionnaire anonymously:

178 research managers, in charge of research personnel, who attended the Industrial Research Institute's R&D Management seminars at the Harvard Business School in 1961, 1962, or 1963.

157 scientists who have been in industry for at least seven years with no management responsibilities except supervision of research assistants.

653 businessmen who attended the Advanced Management Program at the Harvard Business School between 1960 and 1964.[5]

The mean values of the three groups are shown in Exhibit 2 *inside* the body of each "man" representing each set of people. Also shown, on the side of each man, are the values *attributed to him by the others*, as indicated by the arrows. The "attributed" data were obtained by asking each respondent to fill out the questionnaire as if he were a typical member of one of the other two groups.

It can be seen, for example, that the research managers attribute higher economic and political value scores to the executives than the executives actually indicate for themselves. At the same time, the research managers attribute to the scientists much higher theoretical scores than the scientists give themselves. Thus while the research managers correctly identify the high values of the other two groups, they also exaggerate them, and thus perceive the two groups—scientists and excutives—as being more different than they really are.

In such cases, finding a strategy acceptable to the people involved is made more difficult by the exaggeration of value differences. The opposite difficulty—assuming similarity of values when not warranted—also is common in society. When this latter error occurs, a strategy is in danger of failing because it has less consensual support in the value systems of the members of the executive team than those concerned expect.

CONCLUSION

Personal values influence corporate strategy choices. It is useful for managers to understand this influence in the process of considering strategic alternatives. But what should be the role of values in such decisions? Should they ultimately determine the final choice? Should they be but one of the factors considered? Or should they always be disregarded in an effort to focus exclusively on maximizing the economic use of company resources?

The issues involved in these questions disappear in many situations in which the corporate managers are predominantly economically oriented. In such situations, choices dicated by personal values agree with choices dictated by the maximum economic opportunities which are identified.

In situations where the managers involved are not predominantly economically oriented, however, the issues are brought sharply into focus. We noted earlier that there were enormous variations in the relative impor-

---

[5] See Tagiuri, "Value Orientations and the Relationships of Managers and Scientists."

tance which a group of high-level executives attached to the six values in the Spranger classification. A number of these executives (a minority) ranked the economic value very low. These executives probably have faced and are likely again to face conflicts in the strategy-formulation processes of their firms when choices dictated by their personal values clash with choices dictated by identification of maximum economic opportunity.

In facing such conflicts, the executives involved might ask themselves two questions:

> 1. Are there new strategic alternatives which might effect a closer match between economic opportunity for the company and the other-than-economic values which they or their associates possess?
> 2. How much of an economic sacrifice must be made by the company to serve the other-than-economic values?

If the executive can identify no better alternative and perceives that the economic sacrifice associated with serving other-than-economic values is great, he may well choose the strategy which maximizes economic opportunity. He may continue his search for new alternatives, however, in the hope that ultimately he can identify a strategy which serves his dominant values well, while at the same time leading toward the maximization of economic return on the company's assets.

In dealing with conflicts between personal values and the maximization of economic opportunity, managers should keep in mind that corporate strategy must ultimately inspire personal commitment or else it will not be implemented. At the same time, of course, the corporation must remain viable as an economic institution.

STUDENT REVIEW QUESTIONS

1. What are the various kinds of value orientations and how might each affect the decisions of major decision makers in organizations?
2. How do a manager's values affect his thinking about strategy for his organization?
3. Discuss the "average" value profile of the business executive group mentioned in the article.
4. Discuss the differences in the value profiles of scientists, research managers, and business executives.
5. What values do you suppose are characteristic of those who become managers in health care institutions, municipal governments, and universities, and how do these values manifest themselves in the strategies of such organizations?

12. A Fresh Look at Management by Objectives[*]

ROBERT A. HOWELL

The author takes a new approach to management by objectives so that the organization, not only the workers, will benefit. The over-all goals of the organization are set by management and disseminated throughout the company. In turn, each individual formulates his objectives, which are submitted to his subunit, then communicated upward through the hierarchical structure. This vertical movement ensures that all members of the organization feel that they are participating in its operation. Lateral tradeoffs are brought about by peer groups reviewing the objectives of their fellow employees—even at the top management level. Top management must then integrate and direct the carrying out of the objectives. The entire cycle takes about four months, but the improved communications result in a better understanding of the company's purposes.

DURING THE past few years, a great deal of interest has been shown the "management by objectives" approach—in the pages of management journals, at management seminars, and in industry. Unfortunately, because of the benefits of the approach to the personnel function in the area of performance evaluation and in part because of the recent surge in interest toward the thinking of behavioral scientists, I feel that many of the companies employing management by objectives are not even beginning to utilize its potential. In this article, I will try to show that:

1. Primary emphasis for using management by objectives has stemmed from the personnel function and behavioral scientists as an aid toward improving individual motivation and for providing a sounder basis for evaluating individual job performance.

2. This emphasis leaves much to be desired in terms of the over-all usefulness of the concept to top management.

[*] Robert A. Howell, "A Fresh Look at Management by Objectives," *Business Horizons*, Fall 1967. Copyright 1971 by the Foundation for the School of Business, at Indiana University. Reprinted by permission.

3. Management by objectives should be thought of as a top management planning and control approach, rather than as an aid to the personnel function.

4. When thought of in terms of this broader point of view, the effects on the over-all organization may be very great. They would include a better integration of the objectives of the total organization, its subunits, and the individuals in it; improved communications to the individuals in the organization as to where the organization is going and how it is going to get there; emphasis on what is most important, not what is most expeditious, and thus the reduction of unnecessary work; and the elimination of overlapping responsibilities, reducing duplication of effort, interdepartmental misunderstanding, and conflict. All these would improve performance and boost morale.

In addition to these four points, I will discuss several ideas that may be included in the management by objectives system to make it even more effective. These include peer objective setting, frequent performance review, and multiple performance evaluation.

EMPHASIS ON THE INDIVIDUAL

Hardly a week goes by that I do not have at least one management article pass across my desk extolling the virtues of the management by objectives approach. After reading them I have drawn three basic conclusions.

First, articles and books are usually written by behavioral scientists interested less in the economic objectives of industry than in the health of the individual employee, or by personnel managers within industry interested in making their own jobs easier.[1] These authors emphasize the importance of having the individual participate in setting his own work objectives and the resultant favorable effect on the individual's morale and performance. Little concern is given to the question of whether the individual's objectives relate directly to those of the organization. They emphasize the performance evaluation aspects of management by objectives—that is, by having the subordinate set objectives for himself, the superior is in a sounder position to evaluate his performance.

Second, the authors describe management by objectives as a "simple" process whereby the individual in the organization plans his work in terms of the objectives he has set by himself or with his superior's help, performs in accordance with the plans, and is subsequently evaluated in terms of the previously established objectives. This description is mis-

---

[1] See, for example, Douglas McGregor, "An Uneasy Look at Performance Appraisal," *Harvard Business Review*, May–June 1957; Rensis Likert, "Motivational Approach to Management Development," *Harvard Business Review*, July–August 1959; H. H. Meyer, E. Kay, and J. R. P. French, Jr., "Split Roles in Performance Appraisal," *Harvard Business Review*, January–February, 1965.

leading and dangerous. As I will indicate later, the definition of an individual's role—that is, objectives—in the organization is not easy.

Third, the authors state that the individual and the personnel manager benefit from management by objectives. For the individual benefits include: (1) knowledge as to what his superior expects to be accomplished, which assures that he directs his efforts toward what is most important; (2) an understanding on the part of each subordinate as to where he stands with his superior in terms of relative progress; (3) a better basis for performance evaluation than is possible through evaluation based on a list of personality traits (ability, initiative, integrity, judgment, health, and appearance); and (4) ultimate higher individual performance and morale.

For the personnel manager, the advantages include: (1) a reservoir of personnel data and performance information on a periodic basis for updating personnel files; (2) the determination of personnel development needs within the organization; and (3) a sound basis for promotion decisions and compensation practices.

In addition to articles and books, a number of management seminars also emphasize the importance of management by objectives for the individual. The following quotations illustrate some of the claims made:

> . . . a workable tool for more effective planning and self appraisal.
> . . . focuses attention on individual achievement, motivates individuals to accomplishment, and measures performance in terms of results.
> . . . a managerial method whereby the superior and subordinate manager in an organization identify major areas in which the subordinate will work, set standards for performance, and measure results against these standards.
> . . . effective alternate to the largely inadequate traditional approach to measuring results is a method that establishes definite results which the individual is to achieve in a given time frame. This is called management by objectives, goals management, or management by results.

Effect on the Organization

We may question what effect the emphasis on the benefits to the individual has had upon the implementation of management by objectives within industry. I feel it has had much effect—unfortunately, not all favorable. Based on studies I have made over the past several years, I find the following to be typical of what is happening in many companies using management by objectives.

One company, a large U.S. corporation, has had a management by objectives system in operation since the early 1960s. All supervisory personnel participate in the program. Around mid- to late November, the personnel managers in the various plants issue requests to all managers in their respective location asking them to begin formulating their objectives for the following year. The objectives are then forwarded to the manager's superior for approval and submitted to the personnel department for filing. All objectives are supposed to be approved and submitted before the beginning of the new year. Thus the individual manager has from three to five weeks in which to set his objectives. During the year, little emphasis is placed on evaluating performance; in fact, I could find no evidence of formal periodic evaluations. Toward the end of the year, again around mid- to late November, another request is issued by the personnel manager asking each superior to evaluate his subordinates in terms of their established objectives and to encourage them to formulate new objectives for the ensuing period. This evaluation cycle is similarly short. The three- to five-week period is all that is provided for evaluating, counseling, and approving the new objectives of the subordinate manager.

Shortcomings

Most of the benefits to be gained from using such an approach have been mentioned. In my estimation, there are also valid criticisms. *First,* top management plays a very passive role in this approach to management by objectives, with the personnel manager serving as the active agent. *Second,* the objectives of top management are not communicated downward in the organization to the subunits and individuals who also have objectives to set. *Third,* the objectives that do get set are not interwoven or integrated, and there is little assurance that major areas requiring attention have been covered or that other areas of lesser importance are not covered several times over. *Finally,* confusion exists as to where the organization is going, how it is going to get there, and who is going to do what; misunderstanding and conflict are the outcome.

A BETTER APPROACH

Top Management Involvement

My first recommendation is to put the management by objectives concept into the hands of top management where it can do the most good for the organization as a whole. This will require considerable effort on the part of both personnel and top management. Although personnel will stand to benefit from the management by objectives system data regarding individual performance, it must look at the system primarily in terms of its usefulness to the total organization and, second, in terms of the usefulness to itself. Such restraint is always difficult.

Top management, meanwhile, must be willing to spend the time and exert the effort necessary to implement and maintain a management by objectives system aimed at improving over-all performance and morale. This task, too, will be difficult. At the start of the year, for example, top management must spend the necessary time to define these objectives and the yardsticks by which performance will be measured. In turn, these over-all objectives must find their way to the heads of the subunits and finally to the individuals. Only in this way can the objectives of subunits and individuals be integrated with the over-all objectives.

One should not get the idea that what is being proposed here is *top-down autocracy.* At the same time that the chief executive and his staff are setting objectives for the company, the individual managers in the organization should be formulating their own objectives. When the objectives of the chief executives are disseminated to the organization and interact with the individual's objectives a reaction should take place that causes the individual to modify his goals to fit the organization's, or the organization to adopt some of the individual's. This is the key aspect of the whole objective-setting process. If this reaction does not take place, the potential effectiveness of the management by objectives system is drastically reduced.

Next to the lack of top management involvement, the failure to allow sufficient time for development is the major downfall of most objective-setting systems. To provide the needed integration of objectives through-out the organization—down, up, and across functional lines—requires considerably more time than just a few weeks. In fact, a preparation cycle of three to four months might be more appropriate.

The normal budget cycle in a typical organization starts with a projection of sales at estimated prices, and on this basis distribution and advertising expenses are tentatively set. From the sales projections in total and the demand spread over time, a production budget indicating the timing and quantity of production units and indicating material, labor, and overhead expenses is tentatively developed. Finally, budgets for such discretionary areas as administrative expenses, research and development, and capital additions are prepared.

The result is a first-cut plan, which is probably not acceptable to all functional areas or levels of the organization. Top management may not accept the projected profit performance. The chief executive may have a profit objective in mind, but because the marketing and production managers consider sales volume and product quality their primary objectives, the former may cut price to achieve his volume objectives while the latter may overengineer the product, both moves adversely affecting profits. The functional areas may be in conflict over what one ought to do and what another thinks it can do. Built-in cushions may have to be eliminated and disputes over perceived inequities resolved. The reason for the differences of viewpoint reflected in the first-cut budget is that schedules developed at one stage depend not only on information from prior steps but also on the information from succeeding steps. The first-cut budget, then, is a starting point; as many as a dozen trials may be necessary before a satisfactory budget plan is put together.

Just as the approved budget is the result of revisions and tradeoffs, so the objective-setting process is the result of compromise. Top management has some definite objectives for the organization—for example, in terms of profit and return, market share or growth, new product development, product equality, productivity, personnel development, and community relations. The interpretations of the chief executive's objectives may conflict with what the subordinate thinks can be done. Thus, complete acceptance of the top executive's objectives is probably impossible, just as complete acceptance of the initial sales objectives based on estimated prices is impossible. It is clear then that the objective-setting process must be a series of vertical tradeoffs between the objectives of top management and the objectives of the individual.

Peer Goal Setting

The management by objectives process must also include lateral tradeoffs similar to those made during the budgeting cycle when marketing, for example, sets quotas that are impossible to achieve given the existing production capacity, and marketing expectations must be relaxed to meet production limitations. Such lateral tradeoffs are just as important as the vertical tradeoffs if maximum integration of objectives is to be achieved. One worthwhile approach to this lateral understanding is peer goal setting.

Peer goal setting means that individuals at a given organizational level, whether it be the staff of the chief executives or peers at a considerably lower level, develop their objectives together. Two major benefits appear to result from such an approach. The first is that peers (managers, for example) may be in a position to give a particular manager unbiased viewpoints of those things to which he should be applying a major portion of his time, and they may be able to suggest solutions to recognized problems. The second benefit is the better understanding that should result between individuals in lateral relationships with the assurance that the objectives set by various individuals do not duplicate each other. The activity managers in the total organization, by working out their objectives together, may reach a better mutual understanding of how their various activities interrelate and how their efforts should be integrated for the good of the over-all organization.

Frequent Performance Review

One of the major faults of many of the existing management by objectives systems is that the objectives set at the beginning of a given time period remain fixed without any appraisal of progress or reevaluation of objectives. Such treatments casts doubt on how seriously the system is being uitilized.

To get the most out of the objective-setting process, it is extremely important that a periodic evaluation (for example, on a quarterly basis) be made of an individual's objectives, and that the individual be informed by his superior of his progress toward the completion of the objectives. At this time new objectives should be set if the old ones are completed or otherwise need to be changed. When the individuals in the organization know that their superiors are going to be evaluating their performance formally on a frequent basis, it is highly unlikely that they will slough off the objectives by which they will be evaluated.

Multiple Evaluations

The concept of multiple performance evaluations is similar to peer objective setting. The manager's performance will be evaluated not only by his immediate superior but by his boss's boss and a third party familiar with the particulars of his work efforts. This third party could very well be a peer involved with the individual's objective setting at the outset of the period. While each evaluation is made independently, the pooling of the information obtained should provide a multidirectional picture of the individual's performance with greater validity than any of the individual evaluations.

The Superior's Role

Finally, emphasis must be placed on the individual superior and the importance of his role in assuring completion of several aspects of the program. He must be sure that:

1. Objectives developed by his subordinates contribute meaningfully to the objectives of the organizational unit and to the total organization.

2. Objectives are challenging and as specific and measurable as possible.

3. They must be reviewed periodically, and the individual must be counseled as to the progress he is making. The objectives are changed as conditions warrant.

4. Evaluations are based on the ability to meet or exceed the previously mutually-established measurable objectives. Evaluations distinguish between levels of individual performance.

5. The reward structure—promotion practices, training and development, recognition, and salary compensation—is a function of the explicit delineations of performance accomplishments.

Advantages

Some of the advantages of management by objectives in terms of its usefulness to the total organization as a planning and control concept have been mentioned. Let us now look at these advantages a little more closely.

Integration of Objectives. Under the approach to management by objectives that allows for a very short cycle of preparation there is little or no assurance that the objectives set by the individuals will be integrated and aimed toward the over-all objectives of the organization. The proposed process of establishing objectives with the emphasis on top management objectives to be felt by lower management and vice versa, and peer objective setting, should provide for a much higher degree of integration. The result is that those objectives which the individual finally sets for himself are tied closely to the objectives of his immediate activity and to the objectives of the total organization, and, in fact, contribute directly to them. This provides for more potential efficiency than under the traditional approach to using management by objectives.

Improved Communications. Top management gets involved in the objective-setting process and clearly defines and disseminates its objectives into the organization. This fact cannot help but have a favorable effect on the members of the organization in that they know the direction top management wants the organization to take. Then they are in a position to assist management in defining its goals and assuming responsibilities. Thus, the channel of communications is automatically opened by this concept of management by objectives in that downward dissemination of objectives is basic and upward suggestions are encouraged. The individual feels a part of the organization because he generates suggestions, as well as contributes to their realization.

Emphasis on Significant Areas. The primary purpose of any objective-setting system is to highlight those significant goals that must be accomplished if superior results are to be achieved. Both the objective-setting approach aimed toward the individual and the approach described in this article aimed toward the total organization emphasize the significant, but in the former case the determination of what is significant is left exclusively to the individual and his immediate superior. In the proposed approach, those objectives deemed important for the individual are also important to the total organization.

Less Duplication. Finally, the objective-setting process described here should result in the elimination of overlapping responsibilities and of the duplication of effort and misunderstanding common between groups within organizations. This change, too, leads to a potential increase in over-all internal efficiency.

Problems

It is naïve to think that the use of management by objectives, with its emphasis on direction from top management rather than from the personnel department, is a simple matter of implementation and maintenance. In fact, the approach takes a lot of work and has several associated problems that warrant attention.

Getting Started. In my estimation, it takes three years of concerted effort on the part of a management to introduce management by objectives into an organization. Many managements want a quick solution and are not willing to spend this length of time. *First,* the individuals in the organization would write objectives for themselves in collaboration with their superiors. The superiors should in turn conduct frequent evaluations of their personnel. *Second,* the individuals would establish more measurable objectives for themselves and start the integration of objectives in the organization. During both the first and second year, I see performance evaluation as a strict supervisory responsibility. *Third,* the organization can start to employ peer objective setting, thereby achieving the lateral integration of desired objectives. It can also place further emphasis on periodic review and reestablishment of objectives, finally introducing the concept of multiple performance evaluation. At the end of three years, which to some managers is a long time to wait for results, the management by objectives approach should begin to have a strong, favorable effect on the organization.

Time Involved. The objective-setting process described here is admittedly a time-consuming one; the proposed period of three to four months is as long as that allowed for an annual budget, and time is money. Yet the time involved or money spent is not wasted, for extensive planning should result in savings many times over from the de-emphasis of time-consuming, low contribution effort, and the improved communications that result in the elimination of lapping responsibility and duplication of effort.

Dynamics of the Firm. Business organizations are dynamic, and as a result the objective structure set at the beginning of an evaluation year may require frequent and significant revisions. But as the business is confronted by situations warranting a change in direction, it would seem logical that this change of direction be announced so that individuals in the organization can adjust their efforts accordingly.

Measurability. With the help of their supervisors, individuals can set measurable objectives. It is my feeling that everyone in the organization, if he is going to contribute to it, should be able to state what he is going to do, when it is going to be accomplished, and how it contributes to the over-all objectives of the organization. Each person, line or staff, should have a unique contribution that he can make to the organization.

Comparability. Finally, there will always be the problem of comparability. This involves setting objectives throughout the organization that are of equal difficulty to the individuals in it and the evaluation of performance by supervisors whereby two individuals evaluated equally really are of comparable performance. The approach of using peer goal setting during the initial phases of the process and multiple evaluations in the end is aimed specifically at this problem, providing a means for cross-checking the difficulty of objectives set by individuals and the comparability of evaluations given by supervisors.

What I have attempted to point out in this article is the difference between looking at management by objectives as a performance evaluation aid and looking at it as a planning and control concept for top management. Until top management recognizes the distinction and takes positive action, they will miss many of the advantages to be gained from using management by objectives.

Top management must get actively involved in the process of establishing objectives for the organization and disseminating them downward; the individuals' objectives must be initially developed and subsequently modified so that the objectives of the individuals and subunits of the organization contribute to rather than detract from the objectives of the over-all organization. The advantages to be gained from looking at management by objectives in this light include a commonality of purpose, an understanding as to what that purpose is, and an efficient use of the resources in the organization to achieve it.

STUDENT REVIEW QUESTIONS

1. How does an organization benefit under a "management by objectives" process?
2. Explain what Howell means by his statement, "management by objectives should be thought of as a top management planning and control approach. . . ."
3. What problems are often encountered in an organization which utilizes "management by objectives"?
4. How should the "management by objectives" process be integrated into the overall objective setting process of an organization?
5. In your own view, who should set objectives in an organization, and should participation in setting objectives differ according to the type of objective or the level of the individual in the organization?
6. Is "management by objectives" valid in nonprofit organizations? Discuss this process in one such organization.

13. The Social Responsibility of Business Is to Increase Its Profits*

MILTON FRIEDMAN

WHEN I hear businessmen speak eloquently about the "social responsibilities of business in a free-enterprise system," I am reminded of the wonderful line about the Frenchman who discovered at the age of 70 that he had been speaking prose all his life. The businessmen believe that they are defending free enterprise when they declaim that business is not concerned "merely" with profit but also with promoting desirable "social" ends; that business has a "social conscience" and takes seriously its responsibilities for providing employment, eliminating discrimination, avoiding pollution and whatever else may be the catchwords of the contemporary crop of reformers. In fact they are—or would be if they or anyone else took them seriously—preaching pure and unadulterated socialism. Businessmen who talk this way are unwitting puppets of the intellectual forces that have been undermining the basis of a free society these past decades.

The discussions of the "social responsibilities of business" are notable for their analytical looseness and lack of rigor. What does it mean to say that "business" has responsibilities? Only people can have responsibilities. A corporation is an artificial person and in this sense may have artificial responsibilities, but "business" as a whole cannot be said to have responsibilities, even in this vague sense. The first step toward clarity in examining the doctrine of the social responsibility of business is to ask precisely what it implies for whom.

Presumably, the individuals who are to be responsible are business-

---

* Milton Friedman, "The Social Responsibility of Business Is to Increase Its Profits," *The New York Times Magazine*, September 30, 1970. Reprinted by permission of the publisher.

men, which means individual proprietors or corporate executives. Most of the discussion of social responsibility is directed at corporations, so in what follows I shall mostly neglect the individual proprietor and speak of corporate executives.

In a free-enterprise, private-property system, a corporate executive is an employee of the owners of the business. He has direct responsibility to his employers. That responsibility is to conduct the business in accordance with their desires, which generally will be to make as much money as possible while conforming to the basic rules of the society, both those embodied in law and those embodied in ethical custom. Of course, in some cases his employers may have a different objective. A group of persons might establish a corporation for an eleemosynary purpose—for example, a hospital or a school. The manager of such a corporation will not have money profit as his objective but the rendering of certain services.

In either case, the key point is that, in his capacity as a corporate executive, the manager is the agent of the individuals who own the corporation or establish the eleemosynary institution, and his primary responsibility is to them.

Needless to say, this does not mean that it is easy to judge how well he is performing his task. But at least the criterion of performance is straightforward, and the persons among whom a voluntary contractual arrangement exists are clearly defined.

Of course, the corporate executive is also a person in his own right. As a person, he may have many other responsibilities that he recognizes or assumes voluntarily—to his family, his conscience, his feelings of charity, his church, his clubs, his city, his country. He may feel impelled by these responsibilities to devote part of his income to causes he regards as worthy, to refuse to work for particular corporations, even to leave his job, for example, to join his country's armed forces. If we wish, we may refer to some of these responsibilities as "social responsibilities." But in these respects he is acting as a principal, not an agent; he is spending his own money or time or energy, not the money of his employers or the time or energy he has contracted to devote to their purposes. If these are "social responsibilities," they are the social responsibilities of individuals, not of business.

What does it mean to say that the corporate executives has a "social responsibility" in his capacity as businessman? If this statement is not pure rhetoric, it must mean that he is to act in some way that is not in the interest of his employers. For example, that he is to refrain from increasing the price of the product in order to contribute to the social objective of preventing inflation, even though a price increase would be in the best interests of the corporation. Or that he is to make expenditures on reducing pollution beyond the amount that is in the best interests of the corporation or that is required by law in order to contribute to the social objective of improving the environment. Or that, at the expense of corporate profits, he is to hire "hardcore" unemployed instead of better-qualified available workmen to contribute to the social objective of reducing poverty.

In each of these cases, the corporate executive would be spending someone else's money for a general social interest. Insofar as his actions in accord with his "social responsibility" reduce returns to stockholders, he is spending their money. Insofar as his actions raise the price to customers, he is spending the customers' money. Insofar as his actions lower the wages of some employes, he is spending their money.

The stockholders or the customers or the employes could separately spend their own money on the particular action if they wished to do so. The executive is exercising a distinct "social responsibility," rather than serving as an agent of the stockholders or the customers or the employes, only if he spends the money in a different way than they would have spent it.

But if he does this, he is in effect imposing taxes, on the one hand, and deciding how the tax proceeds shall be spent on the other.

This process raises political questions on two levels: principle and consequences. On the level of political principle, the imposition of taxes and the expenditure of tax proceeds are governmental functions. We have established elaborate constitutional, parliamentary and judicial provisions to control these functions, to assure that taxes are imposed so far as possible in accordance with the preferences and desires of the public—after all, "taxation without representation" was one of the battle cries of the American Revolution. We have a system of checks and balances to separate the legislative function of imposing taxes and enacting expenditures from the executive function of collecting taxes and administering expenditure programs and from the judicial function of mediating disputes and interpreting the law.

Here the businessman—self-selected or appointed directly or indirectly by stockholders—is to be simultaneously legislator, executive and jurist. He is to decide whom to tax by how much and for what purpose, and he is to spend the proceeds—all this guided only by general exhortations from on high to restrain inflation, improve the environment, fight poverty and so on and on.

The whole justification for permitting the corporate executive to be selected by the stockholders is that the executive is an agent serving the interests of his principal. This justification disappears when the corporate executive imposes taxes and spends the proceeds for "social" purposes. He becomes in effect a public employe, a civil servant, even though he remains in name an employe of a private enterprise. On grounds of political principle, it is intolerable that such civil servants—insofar as their actions in the name of social responsibility are real and not just window-dressing—should be selected as they are now. If they are to be civil servants, then they must be selected through a political process. If they are to impose taxes and make expenditures to foster "social" objectives, then political machinery must be set up to guide the assessment of taxes and to determine through a political process the objectives to be served.

This is the basic reason why the doctrine of "social responsibility" involves the acceptance of the socialist view that political mechanisms, not market mechanisms, are the appropriate way to determine the allocation of scarce resources to alternative uses.

On the grounds of consequences, can the corporate executive in fact discharge his alleged "social responsibilities"? On the one hand, suppose he could get away with spending the stockholders' or customers' or employes' money. How is he to know how to spend it? He is told that he must contribute to fighting inflation. How is he to know what action of his will contribute to that end? He is presumably an expert in running his company—in producing a product or selling it or financing it. But nothing about his selection makes him an expert on inflation. Will his holding down the price of his product reduce inflationary pressure? Or, by leaving more spending power in the hands of his customers, simply divert it elsewhere? Or, by forcing him to produce less because of the lower price, will it simply contribute to shortages? Even if he could answer these questions, how much cost is he justified in imposing on his stockholders, customers and employes for this social purpose? What is his appropriate share and what is the appropriate share of others?

And, whether he wants to or not, can he get away with spending his stockholders', customers' or employes' money? Will not the stockholders fire him? (Either the present ones or those who take over when his actions in the name of social responsibility have reduced the corporation's profits and the price of its stock.) His customers and his employes can desert him for other producers and employers less scrupulous in exercising their social responsibilities.

This facet of "social responsibility" doctrine is brought into sharp relief when the doctrine is used to justify wage restraint by trade unions. The conflict of interest is naked and clear when union officials are asked to subordinate the interest of their members to some more general social purpose. If the union officials try to enforce wage restraint, the consequence is likely to be wildcat strikes, rank-and-file revolts and the emergence of strong competitors for their jobs. We thus have the ironic phenomenon that union leaders—at least in the U.S.—have objected to Government interference with the market far more consistently and courageously than have business leaders.

The difficulty of exercising "social responsibility" illustrates, of course, the great virtue of private competitive enterprise—it forces people to be responsible for their own actions and makes it difficult for them to "exploit" other people for either selfish or unselfish purposes. They can do good—but only at their own expense.

Many a reader who has followed the argument this far may be tempted to remonstrate that it is all well and good to speak of government's having the responsibility to impose taxes and determine expenditures for such "social" purposes as controlling pollution or training the hard-core unemployed, but that the problems are too urgent to wait on the slow course of political processes, that the exercise of social responsibility by businessmen is a quicker and surer way to solve pressing current problems.

Aside from the question of fact—I share Adam Smith's skepticism about the benefits that can be expected from "those who affected to trade for the public good"—this argument must be rejected on grounds of principle. What it amounts to is an assertion that those who favor the taxes and expenditures in question have failed to persuade a majority of their fellow citizens to be of like mind and that they are seeking to attain by undemocratic procedures what they cannot attain by democratic procedures. In a free society, it is hard for "good" people to do "good," but that is a small price to pay for making it hard for "evil" people to do "evil," especially since one man's good is another's evil.

I have, for simplicity, concentrated on the special case of the corporate executive, except only for the brief digression on trade unions. But precisely the same argument applies to the newer phenomenon of calling upon stockholders to require corporations to exercise social responsibility (the recent G.M. crusade, for example). In most of these cases, what is in effect involved is some stockholders trying to get other stockholders (or customers or employes) to contribute against their will to "social" causes favored by the activists. Insofar as they succeed, they are again imposing taxes and spending the proceeds.

The situation of the individual proprietor is somewhat different. If he acts to reduce the returns of his enterprise in order to exercise his "social responsibility," he is spending his own money, not someone else's. If he wishes to spend his money on such purposes, that is his right, and I cannot see that there is any objection to his doing so. In the process, he, too, may impose costs on employes and customers. However, because he is far less likely than a large corporation or union to have monopolistic power, any such side effects will tend to be minor.

Of course, in practice the doctrine of social responsibility is frequently a cloak for actions that are justified on other grounds rather than a reason for those actions.

To illustrate, it may well be in the long-run interest of a corporation that is a major employer in a small community to devote resources to providing amenities to that community or to improving its government. That may make it easier to attract desirable employes, it may reduce the wage bill or lessen losses from pilferage and sabotage or have other worthwhile effects. Or it may be that, given the laws about the deductibility of corporate charitable contributions, the stockholders can contribute more to charities they favor by having the corporation make the gift than by doing it themselves, since they can in that way contribute an amount that would otherwise have been paid as corporate taxes.

In each of these—and many similar—cases, there is a strong temptation to rationalize these actions as an exercise of "social responsibility." In the present climate of opinion, with its widespread aversion to "capitalism," "profits," the "soulless corporation" and so on, this is one way for a corporation to generate goodwill as a by-product of expenditures that are entirely justified in its own self-interest.

It would be inconsistent of me to call on corporate executives to refrain from this hypocritical window-dressing because it harms the foundations of a free society. That would be to call on them to exercise a "social responsibility"! If our institutions, and the attitudes of the public make it in their self-interest to cloak their actions in this way, I cannot summon much indignation to denounce them. At the same time, I can express admiration for those individual proprietors or owners of closely held corporations or stockholders of more broadly held corporations who disdain such tactics as approaching fraud.

Whether blameworthy or not, the use of the cloak of social responsibility, and the nonsense spoken in its name by influential and prestigious businessmen, does clearly harm the foundations of a free society. I have been impressed time and again by the schizophrenic character of many businessmen. They are capable of being extremely far-sighted and clear-headed in matters that are internal to their businesses. They are incredibly short-sighted and muddle-headed in matters that are outside their businesses but affect the possible survival of business in general. This short-sightedness is strikingly exemplified in the calls from many business-men for wage and price guidelines or controls or incomes policies. There is nothing that could do more in a brief period to destroy a market system and replace it by a centrally controlled system than effective govern-mental control of prices and wages.

The short-sightedness is also exemplified in speeches by businessmen on social responsibility. This may gain them kudos in the short run. But it helps to strengthen the already too prevalent view that the pursuit of profits is wicked and immoral and must be curbed and controlled by external forces. Once this view is adopted, the external forces that curb the market will not be the social consciences, however highly developed, of the pontificating executives; it will be the iron fist of Government bureaucrats. Here, as with price and wage controls, businessmen seem to me to reveal a suicidal impulse.

The political principle that underlies the market mechanism is unanimity. In an ideal free market resting on private property, no individual can coerce any other, all cooperation is voluntary, all parties to such cooperation benefit or they need not participate. There are no "social" values, no "social" responsibilities in any sense other than the shared values and responsibilities of individuals. Society is a collection of individuals and of the various groups they voluntarily form.

The political principle that underlies the political mechanism is conformity. The individual must serve a more general social interest— whether that be determined by a church or a dictator or a majority. The individual may have a vote and a say in what is to be done, but if he is overruled, he must conform. It is appropriate for some to require others to contribute to a general social purpose whether they wish to or not.

Unfortunately, unanimity is not always feasible. There are some respects in which conformity appears unavoidable so I do not see how one can avoid the use of the political mechanism altogether.

But the doctrine of "social responsibility" taken seriously would extend the scope of the political mechanism to every human activity. It does not differ in philosophy from the most explicitly collectivist doctrine. It differs only by professing to believe that collectivist ends can be attained without collectivist means. That is why, in my book "Capitalism and Freedom," I have called it a "fundamentally subversive doctrine" in a free society, and have said that in such a society, "there is one and only one social responsibility of business—to use its resources and engage in activities designed to increase its profits so long as it stays within the rules of the game, which is to say, engages in open and free competition without deception or fraud."

STUDENT REVIEW QUESTIONS

1. What is Friedman's principal argument in putting forth his idea on the social responsibility of businessmen?
2. What is the economic basis for Friedman's views on the limits of a businessman's social responsibility?
3. Do you agree with Friedman's ideas on social responsibility? Why or why not?
4. What is the role of profits in a business or profit-oriented organization?
5. Discuss the issue of social responsibility as it applies to managers in nonprofit organizations.

chapter 6

Identifying, Evaluating, and Formulating Strategy

Introduction

Organizing for Strategy Development
An Illustration of Roles in Strategy Development
Emphasis on the Present Strategy
Previous Chapters as Foundation for Strategy Development

Identifying the Present Strategy

Areas for Analysis in the Identification Process
    Objectives
    Product-Market Considerations
    Plant and Productive Facilities
    Financial Considerations
    Human Resources
Maytag Company

Evaluating the Present Strategy

Criteria for Evaluation
    Past Results
    Appropriateness for the Future

Rationale for the Existing Strategy: A Criterion for Evaluation

Values of Managers and Owners
Taking Advantage of Market Opportunities
Taking Advantage of Organizational Competence
Combination of Reasons

Considering Change in the Strategy

The Gillette Company

Changing the Strategy: Strategy Formulation

Value of Analyzing the Present Strategy
Limitations of Analyzing the Present Strategy
Importance of External Factors

The Need to Consider All Elements
The Importance of Balance

Summary

Readings

INTRODUCTION

THE PRECEDING CHAPTERS have demonstrated that a critical job of top management is the formulation of organizational strategy. In this process, the top manager must be an analyst and synthesizer of information as well as being a problem solver and decision maker. Perhaps above all else, he or she must possess an ability to balance: to balance motivations of himself and others; to balance objectives of many kinds and of many people; and to balance strengths and weaknesses of his organization as well as the benefits and risks of each key decision. This perspective and balance is required when confronting opportunities that are available to the organization and problems which threaten it. In the development of strategy, these requirements are called for as are many more. This chapter discusses the things managers must understand in evaluating and developing their organization's strategy. The same ideas must be understood by students when identifying and evaluating a strategy, and when recommending changes in it.

Organizing for Strategy Development

Strategy development must ultimately be the work and responsibility of top management in any organization because it is so vital to a healthy organizational life. As may be seen from earlier chapters, there is a vast amount of detailed information to be gathered, analyzed, summarized, synthesized into conclusions, and presented in useful form before decisions of a strategic nature can be made. The final result of these activities which must be integrated by top management is the strategy of the organization. The process of strategy formulation is often referred to as the "strategic planning process" and is differentiated from other levels and kinds of planning in an organization. These will be discussed in Chapter 8 when the planning-control process will be examined in relation to strategy and strategic planning.

The overall planning function in most organizations is a joint responsibility of line managers and staff specialists, with staff supplying and analyzing information for decisions by line managers. The planning cycle includes the strategic planning process which usually is closely interrelated with annual long-range planning activities. These latter functions are the province of the line organization, assisted by the previously mentioned staff support in larger companies. (The strategic planning process is essentially a staff activity in larger organizations up to the stage of presenting fairly complete analyses, conclusions, and recommendations to top management.) The final formulation of strategy and strategic decisions in all organizations must remain the function of the top level line management, including the board of directors. In the process of strategic planning these top managers must see to it that they receive the necessary information, in useful form, in time to act upon it.

Although many organizations synchronize their strategy development with other planning cycles in the organization, strategic decisions do not necessarily fit convenient time frames. Such decisions are by their nature rather opportunistic, often made in reaction to either a perceived opportunity or threat. In such circumstances decisions must be made as required by the necessities of the situation. However, if the organization has truly been involved in strategic planning, crises and emergency decisions in the area of strategy should be infrequent since management would have been receiving and utilizing information on a continuous basis, thereby minimizing "unforeseen" circumstances.

An Illustration of Roles in Strategy Development

As an illustration of the roles played by various organizational members in the strategy formulation and planning processes of an organization, consider the process as it exists in one large diversified company. The top-management Executive Committee and the board of directors make final decisions in all matters of strategy. They also initiate and are involved continually in issues of a strategic nature by participating in the annual capital budgeting and planning cycle during which resource allocations are made for approved projects. It is during this planning cycle that strategic considerations must be articulated and translated into capital expenditures which will commit the company to various strategies during the ensuing years. Thus, the Executive Committee and the Finance Committee work closely with the board of directors in clarifying strategic plans and in committing capital to accomplish these plans.

The top-management decision makers, however, have received throughout the year vast amounts of analyzed information from a planning department, new business department, R.&D. department, and from all operating divisions. Product information, market forecasts, competitive data, project studies, return on investment data, and much other information has been gathered, analyzed, and presented to top management by various line and staff groups. Some information relates to present lines of business and other information pertains to potential opportunities in new fields. Much is internal information and much deals with the external environment.

The board of directors during each annual cycle reviews its financial, growth, and other objectives and may change or modify these depending upon the additional information received. Strategic plans are formulated to achieve objectives in areas of products, markets, R.&D., and acquisitions, and financial targets are established for the company and all operating divisions. Funds are allocated to various investments in all areas, commensurate with opportunities, objectives, and expected results. Additionally, organizational issues such as staffing and compensation which are related to strategic decisions are discussed, and changes are made as appropriate.

In addition to this planning cycle which is oriented to strategy formulation, five-year operating plans and budgets are established and revised annually, and these depend greatly on the strategic capital investment decisions. The operating budget cycle occurs several months after the strategic planning cycle and follows the same organizational lines as the capital budget. In essence, the operating budget is the financial summary of operating plans in all divisions and areas of the company. Line managers of the various divisions, with staff support, prepare their own operating plans and budgets. These managers are responsible for reflecting in their plans the influences of the strategic decisions previously communicated through the strategic planning and capital budgeting process.

This example pictures a rather complete planning process which emphasizes strategy planning and development. Chapter 8 will discuss in detail the other levels of planning introduced here. This illustration also has attempted to clarify the roles which various organizational members fill in the overall planning process of a large diversified company. Smaller organizations will generally be less thorough and less formalized than the company described here. Yet, all organizations face strategic choices and should plan in a realistic fashion to ensure that the wisest strategic alternatives are developed.

Emphasis on the Present Strategy

Most situations which students and managers analyze are continuing ones, not new ones in which an organization is just beginning. Accordingly, the orientation of this chapter is the "going concern." Although much of what is presented here is also appropriate to a new enterprise, the focus is on the organization following for better or for worse some course of action. This is the typical field of endeavor for the manager and since it is, he must be concerned with the present corporate strategy as well as with potential changes in strategy. It is unrealistic to desire change and "progress" unless one first has a good understanding of the present situation, and of the reasons why things are as they are. It is sometimes argued that dwelling too much upon the past and present hinders decisions for the future because of the restrictions imposed on the imagination and creativity of decision makers. But in an organization of people, the present situation is a most important aspect which must be considered if subsequent change is to be understood and accepted by those people. The student can be guided in analysis by a framework developed in an excellent article on corporate planning: "You will notice on this master chart that Exhibit IV [reappraisal phase of the master plan] actually becomes the first phase of the total process as a result of the fact that most large corporations already will have some sort of master plan in action. The purpose of this reappraisal phase is to monitor the internal and external environments of the firm in search of problems and opportunities which are triggering circumstances that might demand some change in the current master plan."[1]

The process described above is the approach recommended and described in this chapter. An analysis of the present internal and external situations is the starting point. The initial objective is to identify the present corporate strategy, those major objectives, policies, and plans which are currently guiding the firm. The analyst should search also for strengths and weaknesses in the resources of the firm which, when viewed within the present strategy and environment, may indicate problems or opportunities for the organization. Finally, recommendations for change in the present strategy should be made if the analysis warrants.

Previous Chapters as Foundation for Strategy Development

The reader should recognize at this point that many ideas referred to in preceding paragraphs have been discussed in earlier chapters. This is as it should be since this chapter on strategy development has as its building blocks the more detailed material covered in previous chapters. The important topics of objectives, organizational resources, the external environment, and personal values of decision makers are all vital ingredients of the strategic process. Thus, these topics must be discussed in this chapter since they are critical to the process of identifying, evaluating, and formulating organizational strategy.

IDENTIFYING THE PRESENT STRATEGY

Identifying the present strategy in a situation is often difficult since the strategy may be only implied and not articulated. Likewise, it is not

---

[1] Gilmore and Brandenburg, "Anatomy of Corporate Planning," *Harvard Business Review*, November–December 1962, p. 68.

unusual to encounter a situation where no real strategy exists, where the company is simply "muddling through" and being tossed about by the force of events. In still other cases, there may be an articulated strategy that is not adhered to in operation. The analyst must expect to encounter any one of these situations and variations of them, but since the present strategy is a basis for future decisions, it must be identified before analysis and evaluation, and before changes can be suggested and implemented successfully.

It is not the first order to determine if the "right" strategy or an appropriate strategy is being followed, but simply "what" strategy is being followed. What course is the institution following which, for one reason or another, has been selected as its guide for operations? Because the existing strategy provides the direction for an organization, a clear understanding of that strategy is vital. Only after identifying and understanding the strategy is it feasible to proceed to an analysis and evaluation of the present strategy, and if appropriate, to recommendations for change. An analysis may reveal that it is only the implementation of the strategy that requires adjustment since an appropriate strategy is in operation, but is being implemented in such a way as to doom the organization to failure or ineffectiveness. In summary, a useful start to the study of business policy in an institution is the identification of its present strategy, essentially the business or businesses the organization is in at the present time as expressed in its objectives, major policies, and major plans.

If nothing has been stated by management to identify objectives or policies, the strategy must be assumed from actual events. More commonly, however, in cases or real-life situations, the analyst will find both statements and happenings. A serious obstacle to identifying the present strategy is inconsistency between statements, and various actions which are contradictory to these "policies." The student analyst or manager has the task of separating and evaluating both actions and statements, and using these in his or her attempt to identify the strategy. In some cases this will be difficult and confusing, but in order to identify the strategy and recommend changes, it is a vital and indispensable requirement. In summary, the identification of the present strategy is a determination of "what is," and this phase of the strategic process precedes the evaluation and further development of the strategy as it "should be."

Areas for Analysis in the Identification Process

In identifying the strategy of an ongoing institution, both internal and external areas must be analyzed. Included are the firm's objectives, policies, and plans, and these must be viewed within the context of the organization's functional areas and managerial situation, as well as with respect to the environment.

Objectives.   Few organizations operate without some objectives, either implied or explicitly stated. The analyst must identify these as a beginning to his identification of the strategy. Basic objectives should be identified if they exist, in the areas of financial targets, growth or even survival, and social contribution. More specific objectives in all areas such as marketing, production, and finance, as well as personal objectives of the management, must also be noted by analysts when identifying the objectives which actually guide the organization.

One company which produced and marketed a high-quality brand of vodka stated that a major objective was to make its Smirnoff brand the leading one in the liquor industry. Heublein, Inc. intended to accomplish this by appealing primarily to a younger market of beginning drinkers rather than attempting to convert older consumers from other brands of liquor. Smirnoff vodka was promoted through extensive advertising of a quality image which was aimed at the younger market. The advertising amounted to twice the industry average and was supported by a premium price on the product, which in turn allowed a gross margin level sufficient to maintain heavy advertising. The company also produced and marketed other liquor and food products, defining its business as the production and marketing of products for the consumer market rather than limiting its view of the business to the liquor industry. This definition of its business was of primary importance in influencing its objectives and policies. As can be observed in this example, the company established specific objectives and policies for its major product in terms of market share, quality, price, margins, advertising, and growth. Moreover, it defined its business in a way that emphasized the marketing side of the business and thereby required clear objectives in the marketing area.[2]

If objectives are stated clearly as in the case above, the identification of goals calls for recognizing such objective statements, and also viewing actual events to determine whether the stated goals coincide with actual goals. If objectives are not articulated, they must be identified from an analysis of events. Major policies and plans must also be clarified in the process of strategy identification. Of particular importance is the effect of objectives upon policies and plans in the various functional areas of an organization as is evident in the previous example where quality, price, and advertising as well as other policies stem from the basic objective of becoming the number one brand in the liquor industry. The demands and requirements of basic objectives create narrower objectives, major policies, and substrategies within an organization, and these are often explicit and identifiable in the operational areas. As a case in point, the decision by the management of the Underwood Corporation

---

[2] "Heublein, Inc. (A)" Case, Intercollegiate Case Clearinghouse, Harvard Business School, Boston, Mass.

to pursue a strategy of entry into the computer field during the 1950s had major ramifications on the operational policies of the company, especially its financing. The leasing of equipment which required large amounts of capital, was a vital aspect of doing business in the computer field. An analysis of Underwood's strategy in those years would have called for identifying not only its objectives, but also plans and policies in all areas of the company, including the financial policies required by leasing.[3]

Product-Market Considerations. Since strategy of an organization is so much involved with the product, market, and consumers, the present product-market policies must be identified. For example, strategic decisions by a manufacturer of quality candy called for opening a chain of retail stores when previously distribution had been exclusively through wholesalers. With the opening of retail stores, however, a new expertise was required, the operation and control of an entirely new channel to the ultimate consumer. Also required by such a move was a new marketing skill in dealing with and understanding the ultimate consumer rather than a wholesaler group. Another example of product-market policies is seen in the case of a small steel company which followed a policy of supplying small lot requirements of a particular steel product. This company had to consider its product line and why customers should buy these products rather than those of a competitor. Success required thoughtful policies concerning quality, delivery, channels of distribution, service, and price among other things, and all had to be consistent with the basic objectives of the company's strategy. Students must be able to identify the policies followed in product-market areas, evaluate them, and fit them into the overall strategy of the firm.

Plant and Productive Facilities. What takes place in this area of operation is also related to the corporate strategy. This includes plant and other productive facilities, and even the production process itself. The decisions to build new plants, to introduce conveyer lines, to concentrate on quality control, and other such decisions are dependent upon the product, market, financial goals, growth, and other elements contained in the major guidelines of an organization. These must be recognized and related to each other by the analyst when identifying the strategy. In the case of a biscuit company president who was concerned vitally with automation of production machinery, it was questionable whether changes in the production area were consonant with the broader best interests of the company since its financial position was weak.[4] Similarly, in a company producing soap and cosmetics,

---

[3] "Underwood-Olivetti (AR)" Case, Intercollegiate Case Clearinghouse, Harvard Business School, Boston, Mass.

[4] "Superb Biscuits, Inc." Case, Intercollegiate Case Clearinghouse, Harvard Business School, Boston, Mass.

whether the purchase of a new production line was necessary in view of market trends and financial policies was a question that seemed not to have been answered by the management before making its decision to allocate major resources to the new line.[5] In both companies the actions, and underlying plans and policies, should have been described in the process of identifying strategy, before an analyst could have begun an intelligent evaluation of the strategy.

Financial Considerations. The financial area and financial implications of strategy will in most cases be observed more readily than those in almost any other area. The policies guiding capital investments, cash levels, current ratios, debt-equity ratios, and the like will give some indication of the attitude toward risk held by the managers and directors. A desire to retain flexibility may also become apparent either from a review of financial statements or from an understanding of explicit or implied financial policies of the organization. The posture with regard to risk and flexibility, when combined with the organization's basic objectives, helps to clarify the actual strategy of the organization.

The strategic objectives of growth and its associated direction and pace must affect greatly the financial structure and condition of the enterprise. Referring again to the typewriter companies which attempted to diversify and grow in the direction of computers, all were required to make an extended debt commitment in the process. While pursuing the strategy, leasing became an important factor and the need for cash and higher levels of investment increased dramatically. Financial policies and plans, then, are vital elements of any strategy and must be identified and included in the strategy description, along with the overall financial objectives such as profit targets.

Human Resources. Another area crucial to the strategy of an organization is that of human resources. Both for the management ranks and the labor force, policies must be formulated which will integrate this important resource into the overall corporate strategy. Questions regarding the labor force should be answered. If skills of various kinds are required in the production process, has the company sought appropriate people in sufficient numbers? Is the quality of the work force consistent with other needs in the firm? Workers of high skill level, for example, may be unable or unwilling to produce lesser quality products. Thus a cost picture may develop which is unacceptable in the firm's competitive situation. In another instance, a company may wish to move from a standard line of items to a line which requires a high degree of technical competence in the sales force. Are the firm's resources in the sales area consistent with quality product requirements?

---

[5] "Potter Drug and Chemical Company" Case, Intercollegiate Case Clearinghouse, Harvard Business School, Boston, Mass.

Identifying policies in the area of human resources, then, is a requirement of strategy identification. These observations are combined with those made in identifying policies and plans in the areas of financial and productive resources. It is the totality of all these plans and policies, combined with the objectives of the organization, that constitutes the organizational strategy which must be identified, subsequently evaluated, and possibly changed.

Maytag Company

A clearly identifiable strategy which is fairly unique in its industry is that of the Maytag Company.[6] Basically, the strategy is to build the highest quality products, primarily clothes washers, clothes dryers and dishwashers, and sell them at premium prices to consumers interested in quality, performance, dependability, and service. Supporting these broad product and market objectives are major policies in the areas of product model changes, research and development, engineering and testing, distribution channels, dealers' margins, service, and other policies.

Maytag will not introduce a new or improved product unless it is far better than its present product or those of the competition. Thus, the company did not even introduce a dishwasher until 1961 when it developed a process which gave Maytag a competitive advantage in engineering. Still another four years was spent testing hundreds of different designs. Far from being only a "product-oriented" organization, Maytag has a clear marketing strategy which calls for selling at high prices through independent dealers who are offered high margins to build a mutually profitable relationship, while eliminating the middleman in the channel of distribution. Maytag's emphasis on service is illustrated by the fact that a factory team spent three years visiting all service outlets and dealers in the late 1960s to explain and to demonstrate a new portable dishwasher.

Although financial objectives and policies are not readily accessible, results are. Maytag's 1971 performance was one of the best of American industry with 9.1 percent after-tax profit on sales and 14 percent return on shareholders' equity.

Organizational considerations also are important in the overall strategy which could be categorized as conservative, cautious, and even plodding by some. Realizing that many potential employees, particularly executives, could become impatient in Maytag's conservative atmosphere, the company does nearly all its recruiting at college campuses where students are likely to be found who will be attracted to Maytag's small town Iowa location. Management, in view of its location and slow company "pace,"

---

[6] For a fuller explanation of the Maytag strategy, see "Maytag Company Prospers by Stressing Quality and Selling at High Price," *Wall Street Journal*, July 12, 1972.

believes that such staffing policies will attract those best suited to the Maytag strategy. Maytag "blue-collar" workers, also, are reputed to be the highest paid in the appliance industry, which is consistent with the requirements of high-quality production.

A review of the Maytag strategy, then, clarifies many elements of strategy which must be brought out by the analyst when identifying an organization's strategy. Only after a thorough description of strategy can evaluation and recommendations for change commence.

EVALUATING THE PRESENT STRATEGY

It is apparent from the preceding discussion that the first job of the student or business executive interested in the ongoing situation is not to evaluate the strategy being employed by the organization. It is rather to identify that set of objectives and policies, and to describe these things as fully and accurately as the situation allows. An evaluation must be highly questionable unless there is clarity concerning that which is being evaluated. However, in actual situations or in case analyses, both the identification and evaluation occur somewhat simultaneously during the process of analyzing strategy. Thus, when the identification and description of the strategy have been completed, an implicit or partial evaluation process has long since been underway. Some judgments will have been made already regarding various aspects of the strategy. This is unavoidable and even efficient in the overall analysis of strategy.

Criteria for Evaluation

Past Results. With what criteria are evaluations and judgments made concerning the strategy of an ongoing organization? If analysis indicates that the strategy is quite conscious in the minds of the managers, and is achieving desired results, the initial evaluation will be favorable. If the goals and policies have been well communicated to others in the organization, another plus is registered. The situation is further enhanced if various groups outside of the institution have been informed of sub-strategies, as appropriate. If the financial effects are of a desirable nature as evidenced by such things as healthy profits, dividends, and rising stock price, it is difficult to evaluate the strategy as anything but successful. Concurrently, if the results in the market are those usually judged positively, how does one evaluate otherwise? If analysis indicates that the "right" people are doing the "right" things at the "right" time, and if they are satisfied in so doing, what argument could prevail against the strategy in effect? If all indications are that the institution has a conscience, that it has been operating as a "good citizen," that it has dealt justly with groups and wisely with its environment, who could argue with the strategy, and on what basis? Finally, if internal "balance" has been achieved and if the organization is operating in a fashion consistent with its external environment, the strategy would appear to be successful.

The basic limitation of these criteria, so commonly used in evaluating the operations or strategy of a company, is that they are concerned primarily with results. Moreover, these are today's results, yesterday's, and last year's. Results are usually measured somewhat arbitrarily against an industry standard, or against a more abstract set of criteria. Much more than results to date must be considered in the evaluation of the strategy being employed by an institution, although whether it is "working" and producing desirable results is certainly one important criterion to be utilized.

Initially, results should be compared against the objectives of the organization; has the institution achieved or become what it has sought? Regardless of the particular achievements, have they been realized within the bounds of policies established by the management, and have they been achieved with a reasonable and acceptable degree of risk? Additionally, it is important to note whether the things which have been accomplished by the organization are the actual results of its strategy. Perhaps these occurred in spite of the strategy. Results alone, then, do not tell all. They must be viewed together with the identified strategy, continually reflecting from one to the other. Inconsistencies must be noted, the risks incurred must be evaluated for appropriateness in light of the total situation, and various aspects of both results and strategy must be pondered. At this point, some evaluations may be made of the strategy, its effectiveness, its risk profile, and its appropriateness for the future.

But even more depth is required in the analysis of past results. If they are favorable, all must be analyzed to determine whether they are, in fact, effects of the strategy being employed by the institution, thus indicating that a favorable view of the strategy is in order. On the other hand, if results or conditions are not "what they should be," is this because of the strategy, thereby precipitating an initial condemnation of the strategy? Even in such situations as this, the strategy may have been a most reasonable one at the time it was formulated, given the nature of the opportunity and the amount of risk and return involved. Because the Underwood Typewriter Company (referred to earlier) ran into problems pursuing its strategy of the early 1950s, one cannot conclude that the strategy was inappropriate. Perhaps conditions, unforeseeable and beyond the control of the company, erupted in the environment. It may have been that the basic objectives were appropriate but that all policies were not consistent with attainment of the objectives. Or the company management might have been "high rollers" who risked much to gain a high return.

In many cases, it is not a faulty strategy that produces undesired results, but rather it is the poor implementation of the strategy. All of these considerations, then, are aspects of the initial evaluation of the present organizational strategy. They must be considered individually and in relation to one another if a strong start is to be made in the evaluation of a strategy. Only if considered in this comprehensive fashion can a review of operating results be of real help in the overall process of evaluation.

Appropriateness for the Future.   Because strategy has its major use as a guide to an organization's future, the total job of evaluation cannot be accomplished simply by a review of results. Although periodic evaluations are made which view results and the present situation, the major test of a strategy's worth is its future value to the institution. Whether the present strategy was helpful and effective in the past is history. Whether it will be a useful compass in the uncharted waters of the future is the major criterion when evaluating the strategy with which the company has charted its course.

The study by Tilles provides complete and effective coverage of the various criteria for evaluation. This article emphasizes the importance of the future in evaluation, stating with regard to the criteria of "consistency with the environment" that there exists both a static and dynamic aspect. "In a static sense, it implies judging the efficacy of policies with respect to the environment as it exists *now*. In a dynamic sense, it means judging the efficacy of policies with respect to the environment *as it appears to be changing.*"[7] The changing environment and its message for strategists should be felt throughout an organization which employs a viable and responsive strategy. Because of the opportunities such environmental changes create or destroy, and the possible effect internally of such changes, a strategy must exhibit the dynamic aspect of which Tilles writes. It must continually look to the future in addition to guiding operations in the present. With this quality, a strategy is evaluated as appropriate and useful. Without this quality, regardless of the past or even the present benefits it has wrought, the strategy must be judged as lacking and must be revamped if it is to fulfill the crucial function for which it was intended.

RATIONALE FOR THE EXISTING STRATEGY: A CRITERION FOR EVALUATION

After the existing strategy has been identified, described, and partially evaluated as a guide to the future as well as to present operations, and

---

[7] S. Tilles, "How to Evaluate Corporate Strategy," *Harvard Business Review,* July–August 1963, p. 115.

after its many implications have been reviewed and analyzed in the process, it is helpful in gaining deeper insight to ask *why* this strategy has been pursued. This question will probably have been asked time and again in the identification and evaluation, and may well have been partially answered before this point. Yet, once the existing strategy and its implications have been understood fully, a determination of why the strategy has been utilized helps to establish criteria against which further evaluation is possible.

Values of Managers and Owners

Part of the identification process was a review of institutional goals which told something of the reason for the strategy. Later evaluation included a comparison of results and goals, and once again considered why this direction was pursued by the organization.

Because the question of "why this strategy is being pursued," is so fundamental to a total understanding of the strategic concept, it must be separated out and analyzed as an individual facet in the evaluation of the present strategy. A most important basis for the strategy may well lie in the backgrounds, needs, desires, and values of the owners or management, or of whomever may be formulating the strategic direction of the organization. In the case of a relatively small company producing various electromechanical components, the company existed and pursued this direction largely because of the research and technology orientation of the principal owners and managers. A second factor in the establishment and strategy of this company was a desire of the individuals involved to run their own business, getting away from the perceived rigidities of operating in a large business. Their backgrounds, desires, and values, then, clearly influenced the strategy of the company which they founded.[8] This set of personal managerial and owner characteristics and the resultant influences upon strategy is often quite obvious in smaller companies. It is, however, also an important factor in the direction of larger companies, depending often upon the amount of actual control in the hands of one or a few individuals. When relatively small blocks of stock are held by owners and none can exert a major pressure, management has more opportunity to act in accordance with their own personal needs and values. Although the amount of influence varies, these characteristics of owners and management invariably play a part in the development of strategy. In view of this, it is necessary in every analysis to consider personal values and objectives as a rationale for the existing strategy.

Depending upon the analyst's view of the legitimacy or appropriate-

---

[8] "Instruments Incorporated" Case, Intercollegiate Case Clearinghouse, Harvard Business School, Boston, Mass.

ness of the personal values and objectives he identifies, he likely will evaluate the strategy as proper and appropriate, or the opposite. If the student, for instance, agrees with the owner-president of a small company producing and marketing speakers for the acoustics field, that quality should be maximized and price minimized to best serve the consumer (and the company over the long run), he will evaluate this product-market strategy as being appropriate based upon its consistency with the values of the chief decision maker. The student may evaluate it less favorably for other reasons, but all pros and cons must be weighed in arriving at a final evaluation of an organization's strategy, including its consistency with the personal values and objectives of the major policy makers.

Taking Advantage of Market Opportunities

A second *raison d'être* for a particular strategy may be that an organization is taking advantage of a selected opportunity in the environment. It may have, through luck or good marketing research, developed information as to one or more opportunities which existed or could have existed, and thus adapted or fashioned a strategy to pursue one or more such opportunities. In essence, the strategy may have received its impetus from an external force of the environment in which the organization operated; the technical, economic, social, or even the political environment. As was developed extensively in a previous chapter, the changes in these environments destroy some opportunities and create others. A major reason for following a strategy is in response to or in anticipation of such changes. The strategy of Hugh Hefner which centered around the "Playboy" concept, was largely a response to a perceived opportunity which existed only because of changing conditions within the social environment.[9]

Seemingly more opportunities have developed because of changes in the technological environment than in any other. The development of solid state electronics, and then of microelectronics, are outstanding examples. The strategies of many companies owed their genesis to a recognition of such changes. Xerox Corporation, IBM, and many "space age" companies are the beneficiaries of major developments in the technological environment, and their strategies are geared sensitively to the constant change inherent therein. Because the present strategy capitalized upon an opportunity in the firm's environment, or even created the opportunity such as with Xerox and Polaroid Corporation, the major question of the evaluation at this point is whether the present strategy is appropriate for the future environment. The Volkswagen strategy of

---

[9] "H.M.H. Publishing Company, Inc." Case, Intercollegiate Case Clearinghouse, Harvard Business School, Boston, Mass.

emphasizing the unchanging design of the "beetle" was thought by some in that company to be inappropriate for the future, as lagging sales might indicate.[10]

Taking Advantage of Organizational Competence

Just as the quest of an opportunity may have been the basis for the present strategy, or the needs and values of major strategists, the rationale for the strategy may have stemmed from a third source; taking advantage of a special competence or resource within the institution. An organization might utilize its managerial background or a technological strength to create, at least in part, an opportunity to be sought by its strategy. It is often difficult to make a distinction between creating a market and seizing an opportunity, but the idea here may be expressed as "invention being the mother of necessity." It seems unlikely, for instance, that a market or recognized opportunity existed for the electric toothbrush before it was developed by companies with a particular competence in making electrical products and marketing them to consumers. In another situation familiar to the authors, a chemical manufacturer had expensive plant and equipment in excellent repair but was limited as to the type of product it could produce. A strategy was developed in this company to pursue the development of as many uses as possible for the product in order to exploit the particular plant resource. Another company may realize that it has an excellent, well-trained and highly competent sales force but does not have enough products to produce the desired financial results for the firm. It may then follow a strategy based on its competence as a "marketing-oriented" company, and pursue a strategy of developing products, or in other ways gaining products for its organization to sell.

In evaluating strategy, a question that must be answered is whether the strategy is consistent with the resources of the firm. It must be determined whether the firm has the right amount and kind of human, physical, and financial resources to follow through on its selected strategy, or whether it can acquire the requisite resources. Even if the resources are presently adequate for accomplishing the strategy, will they be adequate in the future? The resources of Winnebago Industries and other companies in the motor home field were adequate to pursue their strategies through many years. The announcement of General Motors that it would be entering this field, however, may well have called for a change in strategy by Winnebago and other companies since their re-

---

[10] "End of an Affair: Volkswagen Output May or May Not Set Mark Today; Anyway, Many Bug Fans Are Becoming Disenchanted," *Wall Street Journal,* February 17, 1972, p. 36.

sources may be inadequate to compete with General Motors under their present set of objectives, plans, and policies.[11]

The danger in basing strategy on organizational resources is that management will look only at resources and competencies, and do best or make best that in which no one is interested. Although this danger is very real, some organizations base their strategies primarily and even exclusively on such an inward view. Some survive and some prosper, but others fail. The risk of failure certainly is great in such situations. Hopefully, managements which look inwardly, at the same time scan the environments and opportunities which seem to fit with organizational competencies, potential strengths, and with personal values of the major strategists. The strategy in such situations is the product of these various rationales and draws to some degree from each one. Such a strategy is likely to be evaluated favorably by the student or analyst.

Combination of Reasons

The evaluation, then, should determine which one of these three major factors (personal values and objectives, external opportunity, or internal competence) is the basic reason for the present strategy, or whether a combination of such factors gave logic to the strategy. In the case of the chemical company mentioned above, the company was working hard at marketing to uncover new product opportunities which its technical staff could develop, regardless of the particular equipment in question. Simultaneously, this company was pursuing a strategy of growth through acquisition and diversification as opportunities arose in the environment. In essence, an appropriate strategy will often reflect various reasons for being. Management will have looked to the environments for opportunity, looked internally to its resources, and looked to owners and themselves for values and other personal inputs. In any given case, one of these may be predominant, either rightly or wrongly. A proper blend, though, which will depend upon these several variables is more realistic in the development of appropriate strategy. In an appraisal of the reasons for the existence of the present strategy, such considerations are important and enlightening. Insight into the rationale will improve the evaluation, and will thereby facilitate the process of determining what changes in the strategy may be feasible or desirable.

CONSIDERING CHANGE IN THE STRATEGY

The concept of strategy has been explored thus far in the context of a going concern, a company with an existing strategy. Strategy has been

---

[11] "G.M. to Enter Motor Home Market in 1973; Sources Say Step Could Hurt Small Firms," *Wall Street Journal*, February 7, 1972.

viewed from the vantage point of a student or manager interested in analyzing a strategy. This has involved understanding what a strategy is and does, identifying and describing a particular strategy and its effects, evaluating that strategy, and determining why it has existed as the major directional guide of an institution.

Having gone this far in the analysis of strategy, the manager-analyst can consider changes in the present strategy. He may be tempted to recommend changes for various reasons which emanate from the process he has gone through earlier. He should have pondered the "whats," the "whys," and the results, and should have decided whether the strategy (in whole or in part) has been a viable one for the organization. However, he must go even further and decide whether the strategy is an appropriate one *now*, and even more importantly, whether it will be the best one to serve the organization in the *future*. To assess the future is difficult at best, but to do so is a vital element in the strategic process. If the manager or the student is to be realistic, information must be gained in appropriate amounts to allow timely decisions to be arrived at intelligently. Information concerning the future will be of a less certain nature than information relating to the present and past. But if any change in strategy is to be considered, all available projections, forecasts, and estimates of the future must be gathered, analyzed, and utilized in the process.

Changes may be suggested for a variety of reasons, among which the most obvious will be to correct problems which have become apparent. In looking at results, they may be less impressive than might have been expected. The change called for may be in the strategy itself or in the implementation of the strategy. In either case, results of operations will be a tip-off that all is not well. Another reason to suggest strategy changes is a recognition of internal changes in the organization; in its human, financial, or productive resources. Gains or losses may well demand an adjustment in the strategy. It may be that the institution's size has changed substantially and a strategy once appropriate is no longer viable. Changes in the environment are often the most dramatic agents of change, as was noted earlier, and this is particularly true of the technological environment. Others change more slowly, or perhaps the changes are more difficult to perceive. In many cases, change is prompted by some combination of these factors; results not measuring up to expectation in sales and profits; competition getting stiffer from present and new products, and the motivation of consumers changing because of a modification in social values.

The Gillette Company

An illustration of change being required by a combination of forces is the Gillette Company which for many years reaped handsome profits on ever-increasing sales of razors and razor blades, with more than half its earnings coming from overseas. Because of the fierce competition from Britain's Wilkinson Company (whose stainless blades are now distributed by Colgate), and pressure from Warner-Lambert via Schick, Gillette's share of the U.S. razor and blade market fell from 90 percent in 1962 to 65 percent in 1971. Likewise, overseas sales gains have been at ever-decreasing rates in the last several years.

Gillette changed its strategy in the last decade in response to these pressures and results, to the effect that razors and blades accounted for only 56 percent of corporate sales in 1971. To replace declining blade sales, Gillette introduced such products as men's and women's toiletries, with men's toiletries being partially a response to the changes in social values which caused sales of men's personal products to achieve dramatic growth. A further change in strategy might well be required as indicated in the following statement: "Gillette's skill has not always been innovation, but its ability to exploit new products introduced first by others. In a market environment where the competition that introduces a new product is more and more likely to be as big and tough as you are, it will be ever harder for Gillette to make off with the big share of the profits by dint of sheer marketing muscle. In fact, unless it develops a new knack for coming up with important new products, it could well need all its marketing strength just to stay where it is."[12]

Whatever the immediate impetus, the process of identifying and evaluating the strategy which has been offered here should uncover any reasons for changing the strategy, or its implementation. This is, after all, the basic reason for the entire analytical process; to allow intelligent decision making based upon the best available information, evidence, and interpretation. In viewing the overall operations of an organization to formulate business policy, the framework of strategy is useful. Understanding the concept of strategy, identifying and evaluating the present strategy, and proceeding through the other phases of this process described in earlier chapters will equip the manager and student to engage in recommendations and decisions. This is the value of mastering the concept of strategy and of identifying, analyzing, and evaluating the present strategy of an organization. If this part of the managerial job is well done, the refinement of a present strategy or the development of a new strategy will be better accomplished. It is this type of strategy development, changing from or modifying a present strategy, that is the usual job of management in an "ongoing" situation. The decisions faced are whether to modify or change the strategy, and in what ways. A solution

---

[12] The source for this quote and other data regarding the Gillette Company is *Forbes* Magazine, July 15, 1971, p. 29. More information is detailed in "Gillette Company Struggles as Its Rivals Slice at Fat Profit Margins," *Wall Street Journal,* February 2, 1972.

may sometimes require better articulation of the strategy being followed, or other provisions for more effective implementation of a strategy. Almost never in the going concern is the decision to have a strategy or not, or to develop a strategy or not.

CHANGING THE STRATEGY: STRATEGY FORMULATION[13]

Value of Analyzing the Present Strategy

Having identified and analyzed the present strategy through the process described earlier, and having considered reasons to change or not to change, the managers or students are better able to make intelligent decisions in the area of strategy development. They are informed to the best extent possible about what has been considered during the past and present in the strategy. They have noted problems, strengths, weaknesses, and opportunities. They have gained insights and reached conclusions concerning deficiencies in the present strategy which may also have pointed to directions for changes in strategies or substrategies. This is reasonable since the decision-making process must contain, or be preceded by, an analytical phase which results in problem identification and description. Thus, although the final task of the strategists is to develop strategy for the future, to do so they must depend heavily on a study and evaluation of whatever strategy already exists in their organization.

The executives who have run Walt Disney Productions, Inc. since the death of Disney evidently have adhered to this philosophy of strategy formulation. "His corporate heirs remain harnessed to his ideas. . . . We took advantage of Walt's concepts but we haven't gone in any new directions, says E. Cordon Walker, President. He and other executives make it clear that they don't intend to make any radical departures; instead their

---

13 The following view on approaches for strategy development is taken from a work of George A. Steiner, "Comprehensive Managerial Planning," The Planning Executives Institute Research Series, 1972, p. 16. Dr. Steiner in a comprehensive paragraph suggests some specific approaches to strategy development. "A systematic planning process in a formal planning system is a preferred approach to the development of effective strategies. The following specific approaches can be incorporated in a formal planning process or can be conducted in the absence of a formal system. Intuition . . . is an excellent approach if it is brilliant. For some activities such as acquisitions, some companies use the 'ad hoc' trial and error approach. A successful invention is an unexcelled strategy. Another approach is to determine the really significant factors that are important in the success of a particular business and concentrate major decisions on it. For instance, a new imaginative toy is a critically strategic factor in the success of a toy company, but superior technical and fail-safe qualities are of dominant importance to the success of an airplane manufacturer. Finding a particular spot, a propitious niche, where a company can give a customer an irresistible value that is not being satisfied at a relatively low cost, is a strategy that has made many companies rich. Finally, some companies are satisfied to follow the lead of other companies."

goal is to skillfully manage those of Mr. Disney's dreams that are already reality and to develop those that aren't."[14]

The second director of the Peace Corps (who succeeded Sargent Shriver in that job) examined the goals and policies of the organization under his predecessor before changing the Peace Corps strategy. The new strategy was then changed by the third director who examined the strategy and found it inappropriate for the new environment in which he was to lead the organization.[15]

David Ewing has put forth a basic approach to developing corporate strategies. In his article he describes "inside-out" planning and raises the question, "Instead of being considered first in the planning process, should market forecasts be brought in later as a kind of check or constraint on strategies conceived in a thought process that has begun at some other point? That point, of course, is located in the unique talents and resources possessed by the organization."[16] Those talents and resources which may have been the genesis for a strategy should come to light in an analysis and evaluation of an organization's present strategy.

Limitations of Analyzing the Present Strategy

Although the analysis of the present strategy goes a long way toward assisting in the development of a new or changed strategy, it is clearly not the only step. The main weakness of relying solely on this analysis is what is *not* learned, *not* covered, or *not* considered in the process. This analysis does not necessarily bring to light what "might be" or what "could be." The analytical process may point out much that is helpful, but it may also leave out something that is critical. Particularly with regard to the environment and opportunities and threats therein, the analysis of the present and past falls short in providing vital information. The thorough analysis of present strategy should bring to light strengths and values not evident previously, but it may *not* expose the latent opportunities of the environment or even the problems which might well await the company because of impending changes in the environment. Failure to consider the future environment thoroughly when developing strategy could well result in the malady characterized by Theodore Levitt as "Marketing Myopia."[17] This weakness is thought by some to have existed

---

14 "Mouse That Roared: Disney Company Shuns New Ideas, Irks Critics—But Is Making Money. It Sticks to Walt's Formula of 'Creating Happiness,' Barring Sex and Violence," *Wall Street Journal,* February 16, 1972.

15 "The Peace Corps" Case, Intercollegiate Case Clearinghouse, Harvard Business School, Boston, Mass.

16 David Ewing, "Corporate Planning at a Crossroads," *Harvard Business Review,* July–August 1967, p. 85.

17 Theodore Levitt, "Marketing Myopia," *Harvard Business Review,* July–August 1960, pp. 45–56.

in the Gillette Company as evidenced above. Until the management of Gillette saw the company as something other than a razor and blade company, sales and earnings began to decline. An earlier recognition of environmental changes might have avoided the problem that eventually resulted. The critics of the Disney Company have made the same point but, as yet, they have not put together a convincing case, particularly since financial results have generally been excellent in this company. Nonprofit organizations, too, have been criticized for not looking ahead and changing strategies as the environment has changed. Churches and religious institutions have been questioned as to the relevance of many aspects of their strategies in today's changing society.

Importance of External Factors

Because of the dangers of ignoring or miscalculating the various environments, any idea of strategy change must give high priority to this area. Many would argue that environmental analysis is the most vital element in the concept of strategy. As such, it must be the first consideration in the development of strategy, or in the definition of the business that an organization is in, or should be in. This may well be the case and a strong argument can be made for it. Referring again to Ewing's article, he would likely term this the "outside-in" approach to corporate strategy formulation or change.

The Need to Consider All Elements

But as important as the environment may be, it must be analyzed in concert with the other major elements of strategy, corporate strengths and weaknesses, and motives and objectives of the personalities involved. The most fruitful apparent opportunity of the market may find the organization totally incapable of capitalizing on it. Lack of required strength, resources, or desire may prohibit seizing the most alluring of "opportunities." The authors recall an aware president of a medium-sized electronics company describing the most difficult phase of his job as *selecting* from among the opportunities open to his organization. It is here that the other elements of strategy formulation are of great help because they argue against some "opportunities," and for others. If the organizational resources, objectives, and values are interjected while searching for opportunity, the best opportunity will likely be selected. By "best" we mean that the total strategy decided upon by the organization will be appropriate to all relevant aspects of the situation, thereby maximizing the probability of its success. Corporate resources and values of decision makers, as well as the opportunities and threats of the environment, are all critical factors. Exhibit 6–1 illustrates the ideas presented in the preceding paragraphs.

EXHIBIT 6–1

Corporate Strategy: A Framework for Analysis and Development

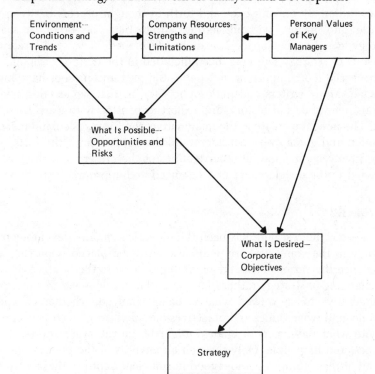

Source: Robert H. Caplan III, *Corporate Strategy: Design and Implementation*
(*A Slide Presentation*) Northeastern University, Boston, 1972.

The Importance of Balance

In all of the foregoing, there is the constant reminder of the need for balance. Here again, top managers must exercise this rare talent to be sure that all elements of the strategy are in balance, and that none are neglected or so overemphasized that an inappropriate strategy begins to take hold. If either the outside is overemphasized, or the inside, imbalance will result and problems may well occur with the strategy. So, too, problems can occur if the personal values and motives of managers or owners are allowed to weigh too heavily, relative to other realities of the situation. In the process, then, of changing strategy or introducing a new strategy, managers may well look first at the outside to the opportunities and guides which become apparent. But in the proper development of strategy, they should keep in mind all that previous analysis of the present strategy has uncovered, and should not neglect the aspects of strategy which are internal to the organization.

In the external analysis and search among opportunities, managers should refer continually to their earlier analyses of the present strategy; to the criteria, problems, strengths, ideas, values, and objectives noted in those studies. By moving back and forth in thought process between the outside and inside, without letting either bias the other, a viable strategy can be developed. It can be developed because all relevant elements of strategy will have been included in the design. Although the future is the most important viewpoint, the past and present have much to teach. Many writers and philosophers tell us that we are destined to repeat the mistakes of history, and exhort us constantly to learn from the past. The new, the creative, the imaginative, the forward-looking must be included and given every consideration. But so, too, must the facts, personal involvements, and all other realities of the present and the past be included in the development of a balanced and appropriate strategy.

SUMMARY

Since our interest here has been the identification and development of strategy in the going concern, emphasis has been placed upon the need to balance the various elements of strategy. Because the task is generally the changing of strategy rather than the initial development of strategy, it is imperative to know well what is being changed, whether change is feasible, and what values and objectives may be disrupted. It is necessary to note what the effects of change might be on the organization, its resources, and its people. Only through an analysis of the present strategy can all of these things be understood in sufficient depth so that a changed or new strategy will have the best opportunity for success. It will have that opportunity if the strategist is well enough informed to introduce among the various elements the balance that is so necessary to a viable strategy and to its proper implementation by the organization.

This chapter has as its underpinnings the material of the previous chapters and that material should be utilized in adding greater depth to understanding the process of strategy identification, evaluation and development. The three previous chapters examined in detail the basic elements of strategy identification, evaluation, and development, and thus provided material useful in this total analytical process. This chapter focused primarily upon the *process* involved in strategy identification, evaluation, and development while relying upon earlier chapters to add the depth and breadth of particular material. The important thing for the reader is to utilize all of these chapters to understand fully the identification, evaluation, and development of strategy.

The remaining chapters will be devoted to the implementation phase of the strategic process in organizations.

14. Construction of a Business Strategy[*]

BRUCE D. HENDERSON

MOST COMPANIES feel they are in a highly competitive business. Most companies regard their competitors as the principal obstacle to either higher profits or faster growth. This is natural and proper. The question is how to compete.

Strategy is the manner of using resources which is expected to provide superior results in spite of otherwise equal or superior capabilities of a competitor.

Games have been classified as: (*a*) games of chance, (*b*) games of skill, and (*c*) games of strategy. For the purpose of this discussion, assume that chance and skill are equally distributed. How can a business firm develop a superior strategy?

We can assume that each firm has a relatively free choice in choosing its businesses. This choice can be expressed in terms of product line, market segments, geographical coverage, or other elements. However, the definition of businesses also determines who it will be competing against. Therefore, freedom to choose the business means freedom to choose who the competitors will be.

Firms are never identical. They have different histories and traditions, different resources, different reputations, different management styles, and often different objectives. These differences may be either strengths or weaknesses, depending upon the strategy chosen. We can assume that such differences exist, and that they are important to the choice of strategy.

We can also assume that neither your own nor your competition's objectives are simple or obvious. There are many tradeoffs between near

[*] Bruce D. Henderson, "Construction of a Business Strategy," *Boston Consulting Group*, Series on Corporate Strategy, Boston, Mass., 1971. © The Boston Consulting Group, Inc. Reprinted by permission.

term profit and long term, between growth and profits, between growth in assets and growth in reported profits, between stability and growth, between dividends and growth, between stockholders, employees, creditors and others. It is reasonable to assume that these differences will result in different goals for different competitors.

It is also safe to assume that the future will produce a substantial amount of change. The change will be in technology, markets, and competitors. Consequently, any strategy must take this change into account.

Based upon these assumptions, the starting point for strategy development should be:

1. Definition of the business area involved.
2. Identification of the significant competitors in that business area.
3. Identification of the differences between you and the significant competitors.
4. A forecast of the changes in the environment which can affect the competition.
5. An identification of your own objectives and any known differences from those of competitors.

These are all very obvious factors, but they should be made explicit since a change in any one requires a reexamination of the entire sequence.

The difficult part of constructing a strategy is the development of the strategy concept. Any strategy of value requires that you

follow a different course from your competitors;

or initiate action which will not be effective for the competitor if he attempts to emulate you;

or follow a course which will have quite different, and more favorable, consequences for you than for your competitor.

The essential element of successful strategy is that it derives its success from the differences between competitors with a consequent difference in their behavior. Ordinarily, this means that any corporate policy and plan which is typical of the industry is doomed to mediocrity. Where this is not so, it should be possible to demonstrate that all *other* competitors are at a distinct disadvantage.

Strategy development, then, consists of conceiving of ways and means to emphasize the value of your differences when compared to competitors. The normal procedure includes:

1. Start with the present business as it now is.
2. Forecast what will happen to its environment in general over a reasonable period of years. This includes markets, technology, industry volume, and competitive behavior.

3. Predict what your performance will be over this period if you continue with no significant change in your policies or methods of operation.
4. If this is fully satisfactory, then stop there, since you do not need to develop any further to achieve satisfaction. If the prediction is not fully satisfying, then continue.
5. Appraise the significant strengths and weaknesses that you have in comparison to your more important competitors. This appraisal should include any factors which may become important: finance, marketing ability, technology, costs, organization morale, reputation, management depth, etc.
6. Evaluate the differences between your policies and strategies and those of your major competitors.
7. Attempt to conceive of some variation in policy or strategy which would produce a more favorable relationship in your competitive posture in the future.
8. Appraise the proposed alternate strategy in terms of possible risks, competitive response, and potential payout. Evaluate in terms of minimum acceptable corporate performance.
9. If this is satisfactory, then stop strategy development and concentrate on planning the implementation.
10. If a satisfactory result has not been found in the previous stages, then broaden the definition of the present business and repeat the cycle above. Ordinarily, the redefinition of the business means looking for other products you can supply to a market that you know and understand. Sometimes it means supplying existing products to a different market. Less frequently, it means applying technical or financial abilities to new products and new markets simultaneously.

The process of broadening the definition of the business to provide a wide horizon can be continued until one of the following occurs:

a. The knowledge of the new area becomes so thin that a choice of the sector to study becomes intuitive or based upon obviously inadequate judgment.
b. The cost of studying the new area becomes prohibitively expensive because of lack of related experience.
c. It becomes clear that the prospects of finding a competitive opportunity have become remote.

If the existing business is not satisfactory and no broadening of the business offers satisfactory prospects, then only two alternatives exist:

a. Lower the performance expectations.
b. Reverse the process and attempt to find an orderly method of disinvestment.

The critical element in strategy development is the development of a concept. This is inherently intuitive and cut-and-try, even though first class and skillful staff research is an absolutely essential prerequisite to success.

The process of constructing a business strategy tends to be a continuous cycle. It cannot be otherwise. Strategy development is an art, not a science.

STUDENT REVIEW QUESTIONS

1. Explain what the author means by the statement, "The essential element of a successful strategy is that it derives its success from the differences between competitors with a consequent difference in their behavior."
2. How does Henderson define "strategy development," and what do you think of his ideas regarding the procedure for strategy development?
3. Select a business organization with which you are familiar and use Henderson's procedure for strategy development to construct a strategy for that company.
4. Would the same procedure be useful in strategy development for "non-profit" organizations?
5. In what ways do you feel that intuition is helpful in strategy development, and what are the limitations of intuition in this process?

15. The Science of Strategy-Making[*]

HENRY MINTZBERG

ABSTRACT

A science of strategy-making will evolve from greater understanding of the methods used by managers to make strategy, and from the development of more powerful planning programs. Using Simon's intelligence-design-choice structure, we review two views of managerial strategy-making—"muddling through" and entrepreneurship—and six existing planning programs—forecasting, market research, systems analysis, mathematical modeling, capital budgeting, and integrated strategic planning. It is necessary to conclude (1) that planners, lacking powerful programs and the proper information, have to date played a minor role in strategy-making; (2) that planners must concentrate, in the near future, on ad hoc analyses rather than on the development of plans; and (3) that the development of useful planning programs will be preceded by more research on how the manager makes strategy.

INTRODUCTION TO STRATEGY-MAKING

MAN'S BEGINNINGS were described in the Bible in terms of conscious planning and grand strategy. The opposing theory, developed by Darwin, suggested that no such grand design existed but that environmental forces gradually shaped man's evolution.

The disagreement between the biblical and Darwinian theorists is paralleled on a more mundane level in the study of strategy-making. There are those who envision grand calculated designs for the corporate entity, and there are those who cite current practice to argue that orga-

---

[*] Henry Mintzberg, "The Science of Strategy-Making," *Industrial Management Review*, vol. 8 (1967), pp. 71–81. © 1967 by the Industrial Management Review Association; all rights reserved. Reprinted by permission.

nizational strategy evolves, shaped less by man than by his environment.

This paper is written in an attempt to review and draw together the various views of strategy-making in organizations. Strategy-making is defined simply as the process of making important organizational decisions (e.g., to reorganize, develop a new product line, embark on an expansion program). Strategy is the sum total of these decisions, and may evolve as *independent* decisions are made over time, or may result from the process of making *integrated* decision plans.

We shall begin the paper by describing the manager as strategy-maker, from both entrepreneurial and "fire-fighting" points of view. We shall then focus on the planner in order to investigate the role of formal analysis in the strategy-making process. Specifically, we shall discuss planner "programs," systematic sets of procedures to produce answers to specific strategy questions. These programs will be classified as "adaptive" or "integrative," depending on whether they are designed to help the manager make independent decisions, or to develop integrated decision plans. Four of the most common adaptive programs—forecasting, market research, systems analysis, and mathematical modeling, and two integrative programs—capital budgeting and integrated strategic planning—will be discussed.

This paper is written for two groups: the manager interested in understanding the programs and problems of the planner, and the planner interested in investigating the differences between his approach and that of the manager. A framework is developed with which to view these approaches to strategy-making.

A FRAMEWORK FOR STRATEGY-MAKING

Intelligence-Design-Choice Activity

A proper understanding of the strategy-making process will require a decision framework. We shall use the intelligence-design-choice framework:[1]

> *Intelligence activity* sets the stage for a strategic decision by discovering a problem in need of solution or an opportunity available for development. In general, intelligence activity involves scanning the environment and collecting and analyzing information on various trends.
>
> *Design activity* begins once the area of action has been determined by intelligence activity. The two stages of design activity are search—inventing, finding, and developing alternative means of solving the problem or of exploiting the opportunity—and evaluation—determining the consequences of using these alternatives.
>
> *Choice activity* is concerned with choosing one from the alternatives

---

[1] This trichotomy is presented in [9]. (Editor's note: References at end of article.)

that have been developed and evaluated. The "integration" of the various strategic decisions into a unified strategy is included in this category.

Although the intelligence, design, and choice activity are clearly delineated above, such is not always the case in practice. For example, a manager may first decide what he wishes to do and then develop alternatives and analyses to rationalize his choice. Nevertheless, the framework is a basically useful one for classifying strategy-making activity.

A working framework requires two further distinctions—that of the manager versus the planner and that of adaptive versus integrative programs.

Manager versus Planner

For purposes of illustration an overly sharp distinction is made in this paper between managers and planners. Managers will be viewed as those who must maintain the organizations that they head. They must react quickly to the variety of pressures, information, problems, and opportunities that continually bombard them, and they must, therefore, work informally. Planners are assumed to be autonomous and analytical, prepared to invoke a formal program when the need arises. Thus we shall assume in this paper that managers do not plan, and that planners do not manage.

One may compare the informal approach of the manager with the programmed approach of the planner by using the intelligence-design-choice framework. Managers are continually performing *intelligence* activity as they interpret the natural flow of information (magazines, opinions of subordinates, newspaper reports, etc.), while planners use mathematical and behavioral theories to study environmental changes (e.g., forecasting, market research). *Design* activity takes place as managers debate new alternatives in the board room, or as an operations research team delves into a problem. *Choices* may be made informally in the mind of one man, or formally, by a capital budgeting program which chooses the highest return-on-investment alternatives.

Adaptive versus Integrative Programs

Each formal planner program will be categorized as either "adaptive" or "integrative." Using an adaptive program, the planner responds to one specific stimulus and works in "real-time" with the manager. For example, a market research program may be invoked to study a new product opportunity currently facing a company, or a planner's model may be used during labor negotiations to determine the cost of various strategies.

Integrative programs are not related to specific stimuli. They are invoked by the clock (usually annually), and they draw together a large number of problems and opportunities to work out one integrated plan.

The capital budgeting procedure is an integrative program, since all proposed projects are approved, not when they are first conceived, but during the annual budget review.

Before discussing the various planner programs, we shall investigate the methods that managers use in developing strategy.

THE MANAGER AS STRATEGY-MAKER

"Intuition" and "judgment," terms we use to suggest that the mind houses some processes that are still mysterious to us, are probably the most valid words for describing the contemporary strategy-making process. In other words, the strategy evolves in the mind of the chief executive without ever being explicitly stated, and without the aid of formalized procedures. Anthony discusses possible reasons:

> Strategic planning is essentially *irregular*. Problems, opportunities, and "bright ideas" do not arise according to some set timetable; they have to be dealt with whenever they happen to be perceived. The appropriate analytical techniques depend on the nature of the problem being analyzed, and currently there is no general approach (such as a mathematical model) that is of much help in the analysis of all types of strategic problems. Indeed, any attempt to introduce a systematic approach is quite likely to dampen the essential element of creativity.
>
> Few companies have a systematic approach to strategic planning. Most companies react to changes in their environment *after* they experience the changes; they do not have an organized means of attempting to foresee changes and to take action in anticipation of them.[2]

This describes the context in which the manager operates, but it tells us little about his methods. Two pictures, one painted by Charles E. Lindblom and the other by Peter F. Drucker, provide some insight into managerial methods.

Lindblom's "Muddling Through" Manager[3]

Lindblom describes the manager who "muddles through," a passive individual with no clear goals. He acts only when forced to, and then he can only consider a few convenient alternatives, each of which will cause only small, non-disruptive changes in his organization. He is careless in evaluating the consequences of each alternative, considering only those which are important, interesting, and easily understandable. Furthermore, he examines only the marginal consequences, making no attempt to "comprehend strictly and literally present states of affairs or the conse-

---

[2] See [2], pp. 38–39.

[3] See [4], Chapters 1–6.

quences of present policies. . . . . He attempts no more than to understand the respects in which various possible states differ from each other
and from the status quo."[4] In Lindblom's opinion the analytical approach
to strategy-making—careful analysis of many alternatives in terms of explicit goals—fails because it does not recognize man's inability to cope
with complex problems, the lack of information, the cost of analysis, the
problems of timing, and the difficulties of stating realistic goals.

Drucker's Entrepreneurial Manager[5]

At the other extreme the manager is depicted as an entrepreneur, controlling his environment, actively searching for significant opportunities,
and relating them to his vision of strategy. Perhaps more than any other
management writer, Drucker speaks for the entrepreneurial manager:

> Entrepreneurship is essentially the acceptance of change as an op-
> portunity and the acceptance of "the leadership in change" as the unique
> task of the entrepreneur. Entrepreneurship in effect means finding and
> utilizing opportunity. It is opportunity-focused and not problem-focused.
> Management deals with problems. Entrepreneurship deals with op-
> portunity.
> The entrepreneur is the systematic risk-maker and risk-taker. And he
> discharges this function by looking for and finding opportunity.[6]

Although the descriptions of the entrepreneurial manager tend to be
vague, they leave little doubt about the writer's belief in his freedom
to act.

The Composite Manager

The above two views leave much to the imagination. In one case we
see the manager sitting at his desk, somewhat harassed, hoping for a
moment of relief. In the other case the manager, free of problems, roams
the world searching for grand opportunities, returning occasionally to
implement painlessly the best of his discoveries.

However overemphasized, these views do help us to piece together a
theory of managerial strategy-making:

1. Strategy evolves. An organization's strategy changes over time as
managers make new significant decisions.

2. Strategy results from two kinds of *intelligence* activity. Certain
strategic decisions are motivated by problems forced on the manager;

---

[4] See [4], pp. 85–86.

[5] See [5].

[6] See [5], pp. 8–11.

others result from entrepreneurship—management's active searching for new opportunities.

3. Strategy decisions are not scheduled; they are made when problems and opportunities happen to occur.

4. Because it is not possible to predict with accuracy what problems and opportunities will arise, it is extremely difficult to integrate different decisions into an explicit, comprehensive strategy.

5. Managers are busy people with many demands on their time. In effect, they are continually bombarded with information, ideas, and problems. Furthermore, the strategy-making environment is very complex. Therefore managers are unable to delve deeply into analysis of strategy questions. It may be concluded that *design* activity—development of alternatives to solve problems and evaluation of the consequences of these alternatives—is generally conducted without precision.

6. Managers have no rigid programs for handling given issues. Each strategic *choice* is made in a different context with new and uncertain information. The manager may have a loose vision of the direction in which he would like to take his organization, and, in an imprecise way, opportunities are evaluated in terms of this vision. But problems are not handled in terms of the vision. When a problem arises, the manager is primarily concerned with reducing the pressures that are acting. Any convenient means of solving the problem will satisfy him.

7. The manager alternates between opportunity-finding and problem-solving. To the extent that problems occur infrequently, and to the extent that the manager is effective in finding relevant opportunities, his vision of organizational strategy is turned into reality.

Once stated, these are simple, almost platitudinous notions of strategy-making. Nevertheless, we shall make practical use of them in the concluding sections.

ADAPTIVE PROGRAMS

Recognizing the manager's time constraints and the complexity of strategic decisions, planners have developed a number of programs to aid the manager in his quest for opportunities and his efforts to solve problems. In this section we discuss the adaptive programs: forecasting, market research, systems analysis, and mathematical modeling.

Forecasting

Because of the complexities of environmental changes, many large corporations have turned to forecasting as an analytical method. Using various mathematical techniques ranging from arithmetic to Markov process models, the forecaster attempts to predict economic growth, market growth, product demand, resource availability, and so on. This data is fed to the manager, who uses it to determine the problems that will face the organization, and the opportunities that are available. As such, forecasting is straightforward *intelligence* activity. The first phase of forecasting, trend determination, is a well-developed science. The second phase, analyzing the trends to determine problems and opportunities, does not appear to be highly programmed and is, therefore, often left to the manager.

Market Research

Market research, broadly defined, is concerned with the study of various aspects of a company's marketing functions. This involves *intelligence* activity—studying the product line and the company's markets to determine specific marketing problems and opportunities; and *design* activity—searching for and evaluating product, promotion, and price alternatives.

For example, a market research group in an airline company may conduct a study of the travel market and discover that the customers are discouraged by city-to-airport transportation. This defines a problem area for the management. A series of interviews may establish that passengers believe that helicopters and subways are desirable alternative means of transportation. Finally, the market researcher may partially evaluate the alternatives by determining the demand curves as a function of city-to-airport travel time.

Market research is a useful and well-developed set of programs. From a management point of view, however, market research information must first be related to a wealth of other information (e.g., finance and manufacturing information) before decisions can be made. In general, market research studies tend to be *ad hoc,* and management is left to relate them to each other and to the over-all strategy picture.

Systems Analysis

A number of organizations have developed special groups, under the title "Systems Analysis" or "Operations Research," to conduct *ad hoc* studies of individual strategy problems. These groups tend to conduct relatively intricate analyses and, thereby draw fairly tight bounds around their studies.

In the early 1950s the Rand Corporation developed the idea of applying the operations research approach of problem-solving to strategic problems. The emphasis was on military problems, and the approach came to be called "Systems Analysis." Hitch and McKean have outlined the role and methods of systems analysis in their book, *The Economics of Defense in the Nuclear Age.*[7] When Robert McNamara became U. S. Secretary of Defense, he hired Hitch to implement the book's recommendations.

Systems analysis is the natural outgrowth of the economic or "rational" approach to decision-making. The analyst takes a problem defined by management and begins by studying the objectives of the organization in terms of the problem. If the problem for a Department of Defense systems analyst is "developing a defensive strategy to protect against nuclear attack," the objectives may be defined as "minimizing death and property losses." The next step is to develop criteria to measure the consequences of alternatives. In this case the criteria might be "number of lives lost, and dollar value of property destroyed." The analyst then develops alternatives—in this case, perhaps, (1) an anti-missile system, and (2) a series of fallout shelters. Each alternative is evaluated in terms of each criterion. Thus, management would be told the extent of human and property losses given that either system was available during nuclear attack.

Systems analysis is most well-developed in the area of evaluation, where extensive use is made of statistical and economic concepts. The key concept employed is "cost-benefit," which assesses the greatest benefit for a given cost (e.g., number of lives saved for a ten billion dollar expenditure), or the minimum cost for a given benefit (e.g., cost of keeping property losses to 100 billion dollars).

Secretary McNamara has received much publicity for allowing "whiz kids" to become involved in high-level defense strategy-making, and, no doubt, this publicity will eventually influence many business organizations. However, the number of firms using systems analysis to study *strategy* problems is probably quite small at the present time. One such firm is General Electric, which has set up a group numbering 300, called "Tempo," to conduct analyses on a consulting basis for various parts of the organization.[8]

With respect to the role that systems analysts actually play in strategy-making, four criticisms may be put forth:

1. The problems to be studied are initially defined by management. No programmed procedure for problem-finding (i.e., *intelligence* activity) exists.

2. The studies are actually formal means of suboptimizing. Generally each study is independent; no means are used to interrelate various studies.

3. While it is well known that systems analysts generate alternatives, nowhere in the literature is there any mention of how search is conducted. It must be concluded, therefore, that the analyst's search procedures are no more programmed than the manager's search procedures.

---

[7] See [7].

[8] See [13].

4. Systems analysts are quick to state that they do not make choices, rather that they clarify the issues and analyze the alternatives such that management's job of making choices is easier. *Choice* activity implicitly involves trading off objectives in deciding between alternatives (e.g., the anti-missile system saves more property, but the shelter system saves more lives) and the analyst has no means of guiding the manager in these decisions.

Given these four deficiencies, it must be concluded that systems analysis is essentially *design* activity, and is concerned mainly with evaluating alternatives in the context of specific strategy problems.

Mathematical Modeling

Mathematics is a rigorous language, and the ability to use it in describing a situation indicates high-level understanding of the subject concerned. It is, therefore, not surprising that little use is made of mathematical models in the process of strategy-making.[9] Nevertheless, much research work is being done in this area, and there is little doubt that the importance of modeling will increase.

Mathematical modeling serves one basic purpose in the development of strategy. It provides to the manager a simulated environment in which he may determine the consequences of different strategies before actually implementing them, or ascertain the consequences of various environmental changes before they occur.

PERT and Industrial Dynamics represent two extremes in model building. The PERT system represents the times taken to complete, and the interrelationships among, the various activities of a project. It is used primarily as a device to plan and control the scheduling of a project. With a PERT model, NASA management is able to determine, for example, the effect of a strike on a scheduled satellite launching, or the effects of different testing procedures on the completion of the Apollo program. Industrial Dynamics employs feedback theory in the building of dynamic models of a firm's environment and operations. For example, if sales, inventory and production parameters are built into the model, management can assess the effects of a change in inventory rules on company performance.

Basically, mathematical modeling is used in the *design* phase of strategy-making to evaluate alternatives. To be accepted by management, models must be recognized as accurate. Unfortunately, at present we have so little understanding of the strategy environment that it is not possible to be optimistic about the widespread development of accurate and useful models in the near future.

In this section we have shown how certain programs are used to in-

---

[9] See [10].

crease the power of the manager while he makes strategy. Forecasting collects data on environmental trends and presents it to the manager in systematic form, leaving the manager to decide what the problems and opportunities are. Market research is used to define problems and opportunities in the marketing area and may be used as well to generate marketing alternatives and to evaluate them. Systems analysis is programmed problem solving, with its real usefulness lying in its evaluation procedures. The mathematical models that are available are used to determine the consequences of particular strategies or the impacts of possible environmental changes.

INTEGRATIVE PROGRAMS

In addition to the adaptive programs described in the previous section, programs have been designed to develop strategic plans, that is, to make a number of different strategic decisions at one point in time. In theory, these programs replace managerial intuition with fully formalized decision-making procedures. In this section this premise is investigated by analyzing two plan-producing programs: capital budgeting and integrated strategic planning.

Capital Budgeting

Capital budgeting was probably the first programmed procedure used in the determination of strategy, and it is probably the most widely used today. Ideally, the program works as follows: The various division managers of an organization determine that certain projects, such as building a new plant or marketing a new product, are worth considering. The added operating costs and revenues (or savings) which would result from the project are predicted. Net revenue for each year of the project life is determined, and this flow of funds is discounted. By comparing the resultant revenue with the investment necessary to start the project, a return-on-investment (ROI) figure is calculated. The headquarters' executives then review all the divisional proposals and accept, within the total budgetary constraint, the most profitable ones.

Two criticisms of Capital Budgeting may be presented:[10]

1. Choices are really made, not by headquarters' executives using the ROI figures, but by division executives. Knowing that the cost and revenue data are very inaccurate, they can choose to propose any project and make it look profitable.

---

[10] For two recent criticisms, see [3] and [12].

2. The one choice criterion, return-on-investment, is inadequate. It presupposes that all information relevant to the choice can be reduced to monetary terms. Social objectives, and risk and timing factors are therefore usually ignored.

One recent improvement has been "planning by mission." In the early 1960s, Theodore Leavitt[11] argued that companies should think about the service they perform rather than the products they produce (e.g., providing energy, not refining oil). Robert McNamara made popular this notion when he changed the Department of Defense budgeting system from one based on a departmental allocation (Army, Navy, etc.) to one based on a mission allocation (Strategic Retaliatory Forces, Civil Defense, etc.). This allowed for a more objective analysis of projects, since funds were no longer allocated along divisional lines.

Another variation in the McNamara system, called planning-programming-budgeting, replaces the return-on-investment criterion with a cost-benefit criterion. This aids governmental organizations, which are frequently unable to state project benefits in dollar terms. Here, systems analysis is used to compare similar projects in cost-benefit terms, and strategic choices are made on such a basis. The problem of multiple criteria is not solved, however, for no means are available to compare projects across missions. A common benefit measure (i.e., some measure of the "social good") would have to be developed first to afford a means of comparison.

Capital budgeting is an integrative program because it is designed to make a series of strategic decisions at one point in time. All major projects for the year are accepted or rejected when the funds are allocated. Unfortunately, the capital budgeting program is of marginal use in making strategic decisions. The *intelligence* activity and the search phase of *design* activity are not part of the program. The program formalizes (1) the evaluation phase, by evaluating each proposed alternative on a cost-benefit or ROI basis, and (2) in theory, the choice phase, by using the firm rule of choosing only the highest payoffs projects. The program loosely integrates the alternatives by ensuring that, taken all together, they do not violate a budgetary constraint. Other than this, however, no attempt is made to relate one project to another.

Integrated Strategic Planning

The planning process reaches its highest degree of sophistication when the planner has available a well-defined program for designing corporate strategy. He would follow his formal procedure, much as an engineer does in designing a bridge. The result would be a unified strategic plan.

---

[11] See [8].

A number of theorists have been working on such programs, and their work should, at the very least, provide more insight into the strategy-making process.

Gilmore and Bradenburg[12] propose a four-part program comprising (1) reappraisal, (2) economic mission, (3) competitive strategy, and (4) program of action phases. H. Igor Ansoff,[13] presents a highly detailed procedure for making expansion-diversification plans.

The integrated strategic planning programs usually make use of the intelligence-design-choice framework and frequently consist of some variant of the following:

1. Quantitative objectives are stated by management. For example, the organization may choose 8 percent profit and 3 percent growth as objectives.

2. The strengths and weaknesses of the organization are studied.

3. Environmental trends (e.g., economic, social, competitive trends) relevant to the operation of the organization are investigated.

4. The information collected in steps 2 and 3 is used to define problem and opportunity areas. For example, a shift in consumer tastes may indicate a problem or an opportunity for a company, and an exploitable strength may give rise to an opportunity. Thus, IBM, with its strengths in designing and selling tabulating equipment and its recognition of the trend toward high-speed computing equipment, was able to enter the computer industry at an opportune time.

5. Given the listing of problem and opportunity areas, the next step is to generate alternatives to solve the problems and exploit the opportunities. Thus, if the company organizational structure is recognized as a weakness, a number of alternative structures are proposed. If oceanography is recognized as an opportunity area, a technological company may generate a number of alternative types of sea-water recording instruments that it is capable of producing.

6. By combining the various alternatives in each of the problem and opportunity areas, a number of alternative unified strategies are developed. Thus the technological company may decide that one organizational structure suits the production of one type of oceanographic equipment, while a different structure will be necessary to produce and market another type of equipment.

7. The next step is to evaluate each unified strategy in terms of the organizational objectives developed in step 1. It may be determined, for example, that one strategy will satisfy the growth objective, but fall short on the profit objective.

8. The strategy that best satisfies the objectives is chosen.

---

12 See [6].

13 See [1].

While this description of the planning program may seem vague and inadequate, it does by and large represent the state of the art. Effective means are available to tabulate strengths, weaknesses and environmental trends, but there exist no subprograms for detailing the search (step 5) and integration (step 6) phases. The planner who applies the integrated strategic planning program finds himself using his intuition in much of his work. Indeed, asking the planner to develop strategic plans today is tantamount to letting him "muddle through" instead of the manager.

Another issue open to debate is step 1, the statement of objectives. Those who favor this step argue that explicit quantitative objectives serve to guide subsequent planning steps. The counter argument questions the stating of objectives at the outset. Management may say that it wants 20 percent profit and 10 percent growth, but analysis may indicate that these objectives are unrealistic. It may be found, for example, that one alternative strategy offers 2 percent profit and 13 percent growth, while the other offers 6 percent profit and 8 percent growth. Management determines the true corporate objectives—the relative preference for growth over profit—when it chooses one of these strategies over the other. But management cannot state this preference in the absence of actual alternatives. Thus it may be concluded that objectives cannot be inputs to the analysis, rather they result from the analysis.

In this section two integrative programs have been discussed. Capital budgeting ostensibly uses a return-on-investment (or cost-benefit) criterion to accept or reject various proposals, while integrated strategic planning presents a vaguely defined set of steps to produce unified strategic plans.

SUMMARY

Table 1 summarizes the various views of strategy making presented in this paper. A survey of the chart will show that a wide variety of organizational strategy-making behaviors are possible. The two extremes, the "muddling through" manager and integrated strategic planning, represent the difference between the totally passive, judgmental approach and the active, quasi-programmed approach. In reality, any large organization would use different mixtures of the programmed and managerial approaches, depending on the particular situation at hand. Consider the following examples:

> A problem faces the manager ("muddling through" manager). He asks a team of analysts to find and evaluate different means of solving the problem (systems analysis). Their recommendations are presented in ROI terms, and are dealt with during the annual budget review (capital budgeting).

TABLE 1

	Program	Intelligence Activity (Initiating Action)	Design Activity (Searching and Evaluating)	Choice Activity (Choosing and Integrating)
Manager	"Muddling through" manager	Problems forced on manager.	Brief search, marginal analysis.	First satisfactory alternative chosen; no integration.
	Entrepreneurial manager	Consequential opportunities actively sought by manager.	Opportunities compared to vision of strategy.	Opportunities chosen which satisfy aims.
Planner adaptive	Forecasting	Environmental changes predicted.		
	Market research	Products and markets studied to define marketing opportunities and problems.	Consumers studied to find alternatives and determine consumer preferences.	
	Systems analysis		Alternative solutions to individual problems cost/benefit basis.	
	Mathematical modeling		Alternatives tested in simulated environment.	
Planner integrative	Capital budgeting		ROI figures calculated for proposed projects.	Highest ROI projects chosen subject to overall budget constraint.
	Integrated strategic planning	Problems and opportunities identified by studying organizational strengths and weaknesses and environmental trends.	Alternatives generated to exploit opportunities and solve problems; alternatives evaluated against stated objectives.	Alternatives combined in logical sets for evaluation; set chosen which best satisfies stated objectives.

Sales predictions indicate a possible slump (forecasting). A marketing group begins to search for new products (market research), and management accepts the first reasonable alternative that the group finds ("muddling through" manager).

Management discovers a new process for saving time in constructing facilities (entrepreneurial manager). Using the PERT model, these time savings are assessed on a project basis (mathematical modeling). Valuing time, management adopts the new process (entrepreneurial manager).

Table 1 indicates that there has been little evidence of programming in *intelligence* activity, except, perhaps, in the marketing area. This activity consists primarily of managers finding opportunities and reacting to problems. Search is, by and large, an unprogrammed activity, but there has been much analytical activity in the evaluation phase of *design* activity. Unless the organization uses capital budgeting, choices are made informally by managers who satisfice, or who attempt to achieve certain strategy aims.

THE PRESENT: CONCLUSIONS

Planners play a relatively minor role in strategy-making for two reasons:

1. Their programs are loose and ill-defined. In most cases the important work is left to the manager. For example, the manager must define the projects for capital budgeting; he must interrelate the various *ad hoc* market research and systems analysis studies. In other cases, planner methods are no more formal than traditional managerial methods. For example, search is a critical part of any systems analysis study, yet there are no formal search programs. The planner "muddles through."

2. The information necessary for strategy-making flows to the manager. Much of this information—problems, opportunities, pressures, values, opinions, etc.—is unavailable to the planner.

Given the current weaknesses of planning, it must be concluded that a Darwinist evolutionary theory is more realistic than a Biblical "grand plan" theory. Strategy evolves as managers react to stimuli. It is worthwhile to do research on methods of developing integrative plans on a periodic basis, but practitioners must recognize the manager's need to react to problems and pressures as they arise and to be exposed to feedback as problems are gradually solved.

THE FUTURE: RECOMMENDATIONS

1. Until we have a fully developed understanding of the manager's strategy-making environment, and until we can develop much stronger integrative programs, planners will find the adaptive programs to be most useful. Let us return to the intelligence-design-choice framework:

If the planner can effectively tap the flow of information to the manager, he can be very helpful in the area of *intelligence* activity. Managers lack the time to analyze carefully all the information that bombards them.

Search activity, if it is to be effective, is very time-consuming. Planners can play a vital role here, not because of their analytical abilities, but simply because they have the time.

Evaluation and choice are highly complex activities. The growth of systems analysis has shown that planners can do an effective job of evaluation, given that time is available to conduct intricate analyses. However, the planner lacks the formal authority to trade off organizational objectives, and so cannot openly participate in *choice* activity.

2. Planning theorists must now concentrate on studies of current managerial methods. There is a great need to know how managers define problems, how they search for opportunities, and how (and if) they integrate *ad hoc* decisions. Currently the literature offers the reader much more on strategy-making as it should be than as it actually is.

3. The long-run future of the science of strategy-making can best be understood by turning to the past. In 1911, Frederick W. Taylor, referring to the use of analysis in physical work, used a set of arguments which could well have been used in this paper:

> It is true that whenever intelligent and educated men find that the responsibility for making progress in any of the mechanic arts rests with them, instead of upon the workmen who are actually laboring at the trade, that they almost invariably start on the road which leads to the development of a science where, in the past has existed mere traditional or rule-of-thumb knowledge. When men, whose education has given them the habit of generalizing and everywhere looking for laws, find themselves confronted with a multitude of problems, such as exist in every other trade and which have a general similarity one to another, it is inevitable that they should try to gather these problems into certain logical groups, and then search for some general laws or rules to guide them in the solution. . . . The workman's whole time is each day taken in actually doing the work with his hands, so that even if he had the necessary education and habits of generalizing in his thought, he lacks the time and the opportunity for developing these laws. . . .
>
> Planning foremen of necessity spend most of their time in the planning department, because they must be close to their records and data which they continually use in their work, and because this work requires the use of a desk and freedom from interruption.[14]

The development of the field of Industrial Engineering as a direct result of Taylor's urgings stands as a vivid example to those who support the "grand plan" approach today.

---

[14] See [11], "The Principles of Scientific Management," pp. 103–4 and 123.

REFERENCES

1. Ansoff, H. Igor. *Corporate Strategy*. New York: McGraw-Hill Book Co., 1965.
2. Anthony, Robert N. *Planning and Control Systems: A Framework for Analysis*. Boston: Division of Research, Graduate School of Business Administration, Harvard University, 1965.
3. Berg, Norman. "Strategic Planning in Conglomerate Companies," *Harvard Business Review*, May–June 1965, pp. 79–92.
4. Braybrooke, David and Lindblom, Charles E. *A Strategy of Decision* Glencoe, N.Y.: The Free Press of Glencoe, 1963.
5. Drucker, Peter F. "Entrepreneurship in the Business Enterprise," lecture delivered at the University of Toronto on March 3, 1965. Reprinted in *Commercial Letter*. Toronto: Canadian Imperial Bank of Commerce, March 1965.
6. Gilmore, Frank F. and Brandenburg, Richard G. "Anatomy of Corporate Planning," *Harvard Business Review*, November–December 1962, pp. 61–69.
7. Hitch, Charles J. and McKean, Roland N. *The Economics of Defense in the Nuclear Age*. Boston: Harvard University Press, 1960.
8. Leavitt, Theodore. "Marketing Myopia," *Harvard Business Review*, July–August 1960, pp. 45–56.
9. Simon, Herbert A. *The New Science of Management Decision*. New York: Harper & Row, 1960.
10. Starr, Martin K. "Planning Models," *Management Science*, vol. 13, no. 4 (December 1966), pp. 115–141.
11. Taylor, Frederick W. *Scientific Management*. New York: Harper & Row, 1947.
12. Tilles, Seymour. "Strategies for Allocating Funds," *Harvard Business Review*, January–February 1966, pp. 72–80.
13. "Where GE Peers Far into the Future," *Business Week*, September 11, 1965, p. 46.

STUDENT REVIEW QUESTIONS

1. What distinction does the author draw between what might be called "evolutionary" strategy and "integrated decision" strategy?
2. What is the "framework" for making strategy which the author presents in this article?
3. Discuss the "muddling through" manager, the "entrepreneurial" manager, and the "composite" manager, and explain how each deals with strategy.
4. What are the roles in strategy making of "adaptive programs" and of "integrative programs"?
5. Describe the "Integrated Strategic Planning" process discussed by Mintzberg in this article.
6. For a large, urban, teaching hospital, discuss the value of integrated strategic planning.

16. How to Evaluate Corporate Strategy[*]

SEYMOUR TILLES

No GOOD military officer would undertake even a small-scale attack on a limited objective without a clear concept of his strategy. No seasoned politician would undertake a campaign for a major office without an equally clear concept of his strategy. In the field of business management, however, we frequently find men deploying resources on a large scale without any clear notion of what their strategy is. And yet a company's strategy is a vital ingredient in determining its future. A valid strategy will yield growth, profit, or whatever other objectives the managers have established. An inappropriate strategy not only will fail to yield benefits, but also may result in disaster.

In this article I will try to demonstrate the truth of these contentions by examining the experiences of a number of companies. I shall discuss what strategy is, how it can be evaluated, and how, by evaluating its strategy, a management can do much to assure the future of the enterprise.

DECISIVE IMPACT

The influence of strategy can be seen in every age and in every area of industry. Here are some examples.

From the time it was started in 1911 as the Computing-Tabulating-Recording Co., International Business Machines Corporation has demonstrated the significance of a soundly conceived strategy. Seeing itself in the data-system business at a time when most manufacturers were still preoccupied with individual pieces of equipment, IBM developed a set

---

[*] Seymour Tilles, "How to Evaluate Corporate Strategy," *Harvard Business Review,* July–August 1963. © 1963 by the President and Fellows of Harvard College; all rights reserved. Reprinted by special permission.

of policies which resulted in its dominating the office equipment industry.

By contrast, Packard in the 1930s was to the automobile industry everything that IBM is today to the office machine industry. In 1937, it sold over 109,000 cars, compared with about 11,000 for Cadillac. By 1954 it had disappeared as an independent producer.

Strategy is, of course, not the only factor determining a company's success or failure. The competence of its managerial leadership is significant as well. Luck can be a factor, too (although often what people call good luck is really the product of good strategy). But a valid strategy can gain extraordinary results for the company whose general level of competence is only average. And, conversely, the most inspiring leaders who are locked into an inappropriate strategy will have to exert their full competence and energy merely in order to keep from losing ground.

When Hannibal inflicted the humiliating defeat on the Roman army at Cannae in 216 B.C., he led a ragged band against soldiers who were in possession of superior arms, better training, and competent "noncoms." His strategy, however, was so superior that all of those advantages proved to be relatively insignificant. Similarly, when Jacob Borowsky made Lestoil the hottest-selling detergent in New England some years ago, he was performing a similar feat—relying on strategy to battle competition with superior resources.

Strategy is important not only for aspiring Davids who need an offensive device to combat corporate Goliaths. It is significant also for the large organization faced with a wide range of choice in domestic and international operations. For instance, the following corporations are all in the midst of strategic changes, the implications of which are worldwide in scope:

> Massey-Ferguson, Ltd., with 26 factories located around the world, and vying for leadership in the farm-equipment industry.
>
> General Electric Company and Westinghouse Electric Corporation, the giant producers of electrical equipment who are recasting their competitive policies.
>
> Singer Sewing Machine Company, trying to make its vast assets yield a greater return.

DYNAMIC CONCEPT

A strategy is a set of goals and major policies. The definition is as simple as that. But while the notion of a strategy is extremely easy to grasp, working out an agreed-upon statement for a given company can be a fundamental contribution to the organization's future success.

In order to develop such a statement, managers must be able to identify precisely what is meant by a goal and what is meant by a major policy. Otherwise, the process of strategy determination may degenerate into what it so often becomes—the solemn recording of platitudes, useless for either the clarification of direction or the achievement of consensus.

Identifying Goals

Corporate goals are an indication of what the company as a whole is trying to *achieve* and to *become*. Both parts—the achieving and the becoming—are important for a full understanding of what a company hopes to attain. For example:

> Under the leadership of Alfred Sloan, General Motors achieved a considerable degree of external success; this was accomplished because Sloan worked out a pattern for the kind of company he wanted it to be internally.
>
> Similarly, the remarkable record of Du Pont in the twentieth century and the growth of Sears, Roebuck under Julius Rosenwald were as much a tribute to their modified structure as to their external strategy.[1]

Achieving. In order to state what a company expects to achieve, it is important to state what it hopes to do with respect to its environment. For instance:

> Ernest Breech, chairman of the board of the Ford Motor Company, said that the strategy formulated by his company in 1946 was based on a desire "to hold our own in what we foresaw would be a rich but hotly competitive market."[2] The view of the environment implicit in this statement is unmistakable: an expanding over-all demand, increasing competition, and emphasis on market share as a measure of performance against competitors.

Clearly, a statement of what a company hopes to achieve may be much more varied and complex than can be contained in a single sentence. This will be especially true for those managers who are sophisticated enough to perceive that a company operates in more external "systems" than the market. The firm is part not only of a market but also of an industry, the community, the economy, and other systems. In each case there are unique relationships to observe (e.g., with competitors, municipal leaders, Congress, and so on). A more complete discussion of this point is contained in a previous HBR article.[3]

Becoming. If you ask young men what they want to accomplish by the time they are 40, the answers you get fall into two distinct categories.

---

[1] For an interesting discussion of this relationship, see A. D. Chandler, Jr., *Strategy and Structure* (Cambridge, Mass.: The M.I.T. Press, 1962), pp. 1–17.

[2] See Edward C. Bursk and Dan H. Fenn, Jr., *Planning the Future Strategy of Your Business* (New York: McGraw-Hill Book Co., 1956), p. 8.

[3] Seymour Tilles, "The Manager's Job—A Systems Approach," *Harvard Business Review*, January–February 1963, p. 73.

There are those—the great majority—who will respond in terms of what they want to *have*. This is especially true of graduate students of business administration. There are some men, however, who will answer in terms of the kind of men they hope to *be*. These are the only ones who have a clear idea of where they are going.

The same is true of companies. For far too many companies, what little thinking goes on about the future is done primarily in money terms. There is nothing wrong with financial planning. Most companies should do more of it. But there is a basic fallacy in confusing a financial plan with thinking about the kind of company you want yours to become. It is like saying, "When I'm 40, I'm going to be *rich*." It leaves too many basic questions unanswered. Rich in what way? Rich doing what?

The other major fallacy in stating what you want to become is to say it only in terms of a product. The number of companies who have got themselves into trouble by falling in love with a particular product is distressingly great.[4] Perhaps the saddest examples are those giants of American industry who defined their future in terms of continuing to be the major suppliers of steam locomotives to the nation's railroads. In fact, these companies were so wedded to this concept of their future that they formed a cartel in order to keep General Motors out of the steam locomotive business. When the diesel locomotive proved its superiority to steam, these companies all but disappeared.

The lesson of these experiences is that a key element of setting goals is the ability to see them in terms of more than a single dimension. Both money and product policy are part of a statement of objectives; but it is essential that these be viewed as the concrete expressions of a more abstract set of goals—the satisfaction of the needs of significant groups which cooperate to ensure the company's continued existence.

Who are these groups? There are many—customers, managers, employees, stockholders, to mention just the major ones. The key to corporate success is the company's ability to identify the important needs of each of these groups, to establish some balance among them, and to work out a set of operating policies which permits their satisfaction. This set of policies, as a pattern, identifies what the company is trying to be.

The Growth Fad

Many managers have a view of their company's future which is strikingly analogous to the child's view of himself. When asked what they want their companies to become over the next few years, they reply, "bigger."

---

[4] See Theodore Levitt, "Marketing Myopia," *Harvard Business Review*, July–August 1960, p. 45.

There are a great many rationalizations for this preoccupation with growth. Probably the one most frequently voiced is that which says, "You have to grow or die." What must be appreciated, however, is that "bigger" for a company has enormous implications for management. It involves a different way of life, and one which many managers may not be suited for—either in terms of temperament or skills.

Moreover, whether for a large company or a small one, "bigger," by itself, may not make economic sense. Companies which are highly profitable at their present size may grow into bankruptcy very easily; witness the case of Grayson-Robinson Stores, Inc., a chain of retail stores. Starting out as a small but profitable chain, it grew rapidly into receivership. Conversely, a company which is not now profitable may more successfully seek its survival in cost reduction than in sales growth. Chrysler is a striking example of this approach.

There is, in the United States, a business philosophy which reflects the frontier heritage of the country. It is one which places a high value on growth, in physical terms. The manager whose corporate sales are not increasing, the number of whose subordinates is not growing, whose plants are not expanding, feels that he is not successful. But there is a dangerous trap in this kind of thinking. More of the same is not necessarily progress. In addition, few managers are capable of running units several times larger than the ones they now head. The great danger of wholehearted consumer acceptance or an astute program of corporate acquisition is that it frequently propels managers into situations that are beyond their present competence. Such cases—and they are legion— emphasize that in stating corporate objectives, bigger is not always better. A dramatic example is that of the Ampex Corporation:

> From 1950 to 1960, Ampex's annual sales went from less than $1,000,000 to more than $73,000,000. Its earnings went from $115,000 to nearly $4,000,000. The following year, the company reported a decline in sales to $70,000,000, and a net loss of $3,900,000. The *Wall Street Journal* reported: "As one source close to the company put it; Ampex's former management 'was intelligent and well-educated, but simply lacked the experience necessary to control' the company's rapid development."[5]

Role of Policy

A policy says something about *how* goals will be attained. It is what statisticians would call a "decision rule," and what systems engineers would call a "standing plan." It tells people what they should and should not do in order to contribute to achievement of corporate goals.

A policy should be more than just a platitude. It should be a helpful

---

[5] "R for Ampex: Drastic Changes Help Solve Big Headache of Fast Corporate Growth," *Wall Street Journal*, September 17, 1962, p. 1.

guide to making strategy explicit, and providing direction to subordinates. Consequently, the more definite it is, the more helpful it can be. "We will provide our stockholders with a fair return," is a policy no one could possibly disagree with—or be helped by. What *is* a fair return? This is the type of question that must be answered before the company's intentions become clear.

The job of management is not merely the preparation of valid policies for a standard set of activities; it is the much more challenging one of first deciding what activities are so strategically significant that explicit decision-rules in that area are mandatory. No standard set of policies can be considered major for all companies. Each company is a unique situation. It must decide for itself which aspects of corporate life are most relevant to its own aspirations and work out policy statements for them. For example, advertising may be insignificant to a company which provides research services to the Defense Department, but critical to a firm trying to mass-merchandise luxury goods.

It is difficult to generalize about which policies are major, even within a particular industry, because a number of extraordinarily successful companies appear to violate all the rules. To illustrate:

> In the candy industry it would seem safe to generalize that advertising should be a major policy area. However, the Hershey Company, which is so successful that its name is practically the generic term for the product, has persistently followed a policy of no advertising.
>
> Similarly, in the field of high-fidelity components, one would expect that dealer relations would be a critical policy area. But Acoustics Research, Inc., has built an enviable record of sales growth and of profitability by relying entirely on consumer pull.

Need to Be Explicit

The first thing to be said about corporate strategy is that having one is a step forward. Any strategy, once made explicit, can quickly be evaluated and improved. But if no attempt is ever made to commit it to paper, there is always the danger that the strategy is either incomplete or misunderstood.

Many successful companies are not aware of the strategy that underlies their success. It is quite possible for a company to achieve initial success without real awareness of its causes. However, it is much more difficult to successfully *branch out into new ventures* without a precise appreciation of their strategic significance. This is why many established companies fail miserably when they attempt a program of corporate acquisition, product diversification, or market expansion. One illustration of this is cited by Myles L. Mace and George G. Montgomery in their recent study of corporate acquisitions:

A basic resin company . . . bought a plastic boat manufacturer because this seemed to present a controlled market for a portion of the
resin it produced. It soon found that the boat business was considerably
different from the manufacture and sale of basic chemicals. After a short
but unpleasant experience in manufacturing and trying to market what
was essentially a consumer's item, the management concluded that its
experience and abilities lay essentially in industrial rather than con-
sumer-type products.[6]

Another reason for making strategy explicit is the assistance it provides
for delegation and for coordination. To an ever-increasing extent, management is a team activity, whereby groups of executives contribute to
corporate success. Making strategy explicit makes it far easier for each
executive to appreciate what the over-all goals are, and what his own
contribution to them must be.

MAKING AN EVALUATION

Is your strategy right for you? There are six criteria on which to base
an answer. These are:

1. Internal consistency.
2. Consistency with the environment.
3. Appropriateness in the light of available resources.
4. Satisfactory degree of risk.
5. Appropriate time horizon.
6. Workability.

If all of these criteria are met, you have a strategy that is right for you.
This is as much as can be asked. There is no such thing as a good strategy
in any absolute, objective sense. In the remainder of this article I shall
discuss the criteria in some detail.

1. Is the strategy internally consistent?

Internal consistency refers to the cumulative impact of individual
policies on corporate goals. In a well-worked-out strategy, each policy fits
into an integrated pattern. It should be judged not only in terms of itself,
but also in terms of how it relates to other policies which the company has
established and to the goals it is pursuing.

In a dynamic company consistency can never be taken for granted.
For example:

Many family-owned organizations pursue a pair of policies which
soon become inconsistent: rapid expansion and retention of exclusive

---

[6] *Management Problems of Corporate Acquisitions* (Boston, Division of Research,
Harvard Business School, 1962), p. 60.

family control of the firm. If they are successful in expanding, the need for additional financing soon raises major problems concerning the extent to which exclusive family control can be maintained.

While this pair of policies is especially prevalent among smaller firms, it is by no means limited to them. The Ford Motor Company after World War II and the New York Times today are examples of quite large, family-controlled organizations that have had to reconcile the two conflicting aims.

The criterion of internal consistency is an especially important one for evaluating strategies because it identifies those areas where strategic choices will eventually have to be made. An inconsistent strategy does *not* necessarily mean that the company is currently in difficulty. But it does mean that unless management keeps its eye on a particular area of operation, it may well find itself forced to make a choice without enough time either to search for or to prepare attractive alternatives.

2. Is the strategy consistent with the environment?

A firm which has a certain product policy, price policy, or advertising policy is saying that it has chosen to relate itself to its customers—actual and potential—in a certain way. Similarly, its policies with respect to government contracts, collective bargaining, foreign investment, and so forth are expressions of relationship with other groups and forces. Hence an important test of strategy is whether the chosen policies are consistent with the environment—whether they really make sense with respect to what is going on outside.

Consistency with the environment has both a static and a dynamic aspect. In a static sense, it implies judging the efficacy of policies with respect to the environment as it exists *now*. In a dynamic sense, it means judging the efficacy of policies with respect to the environment *as it appears to be changing*. One purpose of a viable strategy is to ensure the long-run success of an organization. Since the environment of a company is constantly changing, ensuring success over the long run means that management must constantly be assessing the degree to which policies previously established are consistent with the environment as it exists now; and whether current policies take into account the environment as it will be in the future. In one sense, therefore, establishing a strategy is like aiming at a moving target: you have to be concerned not only with present position but also with the speed and direction of movement.

Failure to have a strategy consistent with the environment can be costly to the organization. Ford's sad experience with the Edsel is by now a textbook example of such failure. Certainly, had Ford pushed the Falcon at the time when it was pushing the Edsel, and with the same resources, it would have a far stronger position in the world automobile market today.

Illustrations of strategies that have not been consistent with the environment are easy to find by using hindsight. *But the reason that such examples are plentiful is not that foresight is difficult to apply.* It is because even today few companies are seriously engaged in analyzing environmental trends and using this intelligence as a basis for managing their own futures.

3. Is the strategy appropriate in view of the available resources?

Resources are those things that a company *is* or *has* and that help it to achieve its corporate objectives. Included are money, competence, and facilities; but these by no means complete the list. In companies selling consumer goods, for example, the major resource may be the name of the product. In any case, there are two basic issues which management must decide in relating strategy and resources. These are:

What are our critical resources?
Is the proposed strategy appropriate for available resources?

Let us look now at what is meant by a "critical resource" and at how the criterion of resource utilization can be used as a basis for evaluating strategy.

Critical Resources

The essential strategic attribute of resources is that they represent action potential. Taken together, a company's resources represent its capacity to respond to threats and opportunities that may be perceived in the environment. In other words, resources are the bundle of chips that the company has to play with in the serious game of business.

From an action-potential point of view, a resource may be critical in two senses: (1) as the factor limiting the achievement of corporate goals; and (2) as that which the company will exploit as the basis for its strategy. Thus, critical resources are both what the company has most of and what it has least of.

The three resources most frequently identified as critical are money, competence, and physical facilities. Let us look at the strategic significance of each.

Money. Money is a particularly valuable resource because it provides the greatest flexibility of response to events as they arise. It may be considered the "safest" resource, in that safety may be equated with the freedom to choose from among the widest variety of future alternatives. Companies that wish to reduce their short-run risk will therefore attempt to accumulate the greatest reservoir of funds they can.

However, it is important to remember that while the accumulation of funds may offer short-run security, it may place the company at a serious competitive disadvantage with respect to other companies which are following a higher-risk course.

The classical illustration of this kind of outcome is the strategy pursued by Montgomery Ward under the late Sewell Avery. As reported in *Fortune:*

> While Sears confidently bet on a new and expanding America, Avery developed an *idée fixe* that postwar inflation would end in a crash no less serious than that of 1929. Following this idea, he opened no new stores but rather piled up cash to the ceiling in preparation for an economic debacle that never came. In these years, Ward's balance sheet gave a somewhat misleading picture of its prospects. Net earnings remained respectably high, and were generally higher than those of Sears as a percentage of sales. In 1946, earnings after taxes were $52 million. They rose to $74 million in 1950, and then declined to $35 million in 1954. Meanwhile, however, sales remained static, and in Avery's administration profits and liquidity were maintained at the expense of growth. In 1954, Ward had $327 million in cash and securities, $147 million in receivables, and $216 million in inventory, giving it a total current-asset position of $690 million and net worth of $639 million. It was liquid, all right, but it was also the shell of a once great company.[7]

Competence. Organizations survive because they are good at doing those things which are necessary to keep them alive. However, the degree of competence of a given organization is by no means uniform across the broad range of skills necessary to stay in business. Some companies are particularly good at marketing, others especially good at engineering, still others depend primarily on their financial sophistication. Philip Selznick refers to that which a company is particularly good at as its "distinctive competence."[8]

In determining a strategy, management must carefully appraise its own skill profile in order to determine where its strengths and weaknesses lie. It must then adopt a strategy which makes the greatest use of its strengths. To illustrate:

> The competence of *The New York Times* lies primarily in giving extensive and insightful coverage of events—the ability to report "all the news that's fit to print." It is neither highly profitable (earning only 1.5 percent of revenues in 1960—far less than, say, the *Wall Street Journal*), nor aggressively sold. Its decision to publish a West Coast and an international edition is a gamble that the strength of its "distinctive competence" will make it accepted even outside of New York.

---

[7] "Montgomery Ward: Prosperity Is Still Around the Corner," *Fortune,* November 1960, p. 140.

[8] *Leadership in Administration* (Evanston, Ill.: Row, Peterson & Company, 1957), p. 42.

Because of a declining demand for soft coal, many producers of soft coal are diversifying into other fields. All of them, however, are remaining true to some central skill that they have developed over the years. For instance:

> Consolidation Coal is moving from simply the mining of soft coal to the mining *and transportation* of soft coal. It is planning with Texas Eastern Transmission Corporation to build a $100-million pipeline that would carry a mixture of powdered coal and water from West Virginia to the East Coast.
>
> North American Coal Company, on the other hand, is moving toward becoming a chemical company. It recently joined with Strategic Materials Corporation to perfect a process for extracting aluminum sulfate from the mine shale that North American produces in its coal-running operations.

James L. Hamilton, president of the Island Creek Coal Co., has summed up the concept of distinctive competence in a colorful way:

> We are a career company dedicated to coal, and we have some very definite ideas about growth and expansion within the industry. We're not thinking of buying a cotton mill and starting to make shirts.[9]

Physical Facilities. Physical facilities are the resource whose strategic influence is perhaps most frequently misunderstood. Managers seem to be divided among those, usually technical men, who are enamored of physical facilities as the tangible symbol of the corporate entity; and those, usually financial men, who view physical facilities as an undesirable but necessary freezing of part of the company's funds. The latter group is dominant. In many companies, return on investment has emerged as virtually the sole criterion for deciding whether or not a particular facility should be acquired.

Actually, this is putting the cart before the horse. Physical facilities have significance primarily in relationship to over-all corporate strategy. It is, therefore, only in relationship to *other* aspects of corporate strategy that the acquisition or disposition of physical facilities can be determined. The total investment required and the projected return on it have a place in this determination—but only as an indication of the financial implications of a particular strategic decision and not as an exclusive criterion for its own sake.

Any appraisal of a company's physical facilities as a strategic resource must consider the relationship of the company to its environment. Facilities have no intrinsic value for their own sake. Their value to the company is either in their location relative to markets, to sources of labor, or to materials; or in their efficiency relative to existing or impending competitive installations. Thus, the essential considerations in any decision regard-

---

[9] *Wall Street Journal,* September 11, 1962, p. 30.

ing physical facilities are a projection of changes likely to occur in the environment and a prediction about what the company's responses to these are likely to be.

Here are two examples of the necessity for relating an evaluation of facilities to environmental changes:

> Following the end of World War II, all domestic producers of typewriters in the United States invested heavily in plant facilities in this country. They hypothesized a rapid increase of sales throughout the world. This indeed took place, but it was short-lived. The rise of vigorous overseas competitors, especially Olivetti and Olympia, went hand in hand with a booming overseas market. At home, IBM's electric typewriter took more and more of the domestic market. Squeezed between these two pressures, the rest of the U.S. typewriter industry found itself with a great deal of excess capacity following the Korean conflict. Excess capacity is today still a major problem in this field.
>
> The steady decline in the number of farms in the United States and the emergence of vigorous overseas competition have forced most domestic full-line manufacturers of farm equipment to sharply curtail total plant area. For example, in less than four years, International Harvester eliminated more than a third of its capacity (as measured in square feet of plant space) for the production of farm machinery.

The close relationship between physical facilities and environmental trends emphasizes one of the most significant attributes of fixed assets —their temporal utility. Accounting practice recognizes this in its treatment of depreciation allowances. But even when the tax laws permit generous write-offs, they should not be used as the sole basis for setting the time period over which the investment must be justified. Environmental considerations may reveal that a different time horizon is more relevant for strategy determination. To illustrate again:

> As Armstrong Cork Company moved away from natural cork to synthetic materials during the early 1950s, management considered buying facilities for the production of its raw materials—particularly polyvinyl chloride. However, before doing so, it surveyed the chemical industry and concluded that producers were overbuilding. It therefore decided not to invest in facilities for the manufacture of this material. The projections were valid; since 1956 polyvinyl chloride has dropped 50 percent in price.

A strategic approach to facilities may not only change the time horizon; it may also change the whole basis of asset valuation:

> Recently a substantial portion of Loew's theaters was acquired by the Tisch brothers, owners and operators of a number of successful hotels, including the Americana in Florida.[10] As long as the assets of Loew's

---

[10] See "The Tisches Eye Their Next $65 Million," *Fortune*, January 1960, p. 140.

theaters were viewed only as places for the projection of films, its theaters, however conservatively valued, seemed to be not much of a bargain. But to a keen appraiser of hotel properties the theater sites, on rather expensive real estate in downtown city areas, had considerable appeal. Whether this appraisal will be borne out is as yet unknown. At any rate, the stock, which was originally purchased at $14 (with a book value of $22), was selling at $23 in October 1962.

Achieving the Right Balance

One of the most difficult issues in strategy determination is that of achieving a balance between strategic goals and available resources. This requires a set of necessarily empirical, but critical, estimates of the total resources required to achieve particular objectives, the rate at which they will have to be committed, and the likelihood that they will be available. The most common errors are either to fail to make these estimates at all or to be excessively optimistic about them.

One example of the unfortunate results of being wrong on these estimates is the case of Royal McBee and the computer market:

> In January 1956 Royal McBee and the General Precision Equipment Corporation formed a jointly owned company—the Royal Precision Corporation—to enter the market for electronic data-processing equipment. This joint operation was a logical pooling of complementary talents. General Precision had a great deal of experience in developing and producing computers. Its Librascope Division had been selling them to the government for years. However, it lacked a commercial distribution system. Royal McBee, on the other hand, had a great deal of experience in marketing data-processing equipment, but lacked the technical competence to develop and produce a computer.
>
> The joint venture was eminently successful, and within a short time the Royal Precision LPG-30 was the leader in the small-computer field. However, the very success of the computer venture caused Royal McBee some serious problems. The success of the Royal Precision subsidiary demanded that the partners put more and more money into it. This was no problem for General Precision, but it became an ever more serious problem for Royal McBee, which found itself in an increasingly critical cash bind. In March 1962 it sold its interest in Royal Precision to General Precision for $5 million—a price which represented a reported $6.9 million loss on the investment. Concluding that it simply did not have sufficient resources to stay with the new venture, it decided to return to its traditional strengths: typewriters and simple data-processing systems.

Another place where optimistic estimates of resources frequently cause problems is in small businesses. Surveys of the causes of small-business failure reveal that a most frequent cause of bankruptcy is inadequate resources to weather either the early period of establishment or unforeseen downturns in business conditions.

It is apparent from the preceding discussion that a critical strategic decision involves deciding: (1) how much of the company's resources to commit to opportunities currently perceived, and (2) how much to keep uncommitted as a reserve against the appearance of unanticipated demands. This decision is closely related to two other criteria for the evaluation of strategy: risk and timing. I shall now discuss these.

4. Does the strategy involve an acceptable degree of risk?

Strategy and resources, taken together, determine the degree of risk which the company is undertaking. This is a critical managerial choice. For example, when the old Underwood Corporation decided to enter the computer field, it was making what might have been an extremely astute strategic choice. However, the fact that it ran out of money before it could accomplish anything in that field turned its pursuit of opportunity into the prelude to disaster. This is not to say that the strategy was "bad." However, the course of action pursued *was* a high-risk strategy. Had it been successful, the payoff would have been lush. The fact that it was a stupendous failure instead does not mean that it was senseless to take the gamble.

Each company must decide for itself how much risk it wants to live with. In attempting to assess the degree of risk associated with a particular strategy, management may use a variety of techniques. For example, mathematicians have developed an elegant set of techniques for choosing among a variety of strategies where you are willing to estimate the payoffs and the probabilities associated with them. However, our concern here is not with these quantitative aspects but with the identification of some qualitative factors which may serve as a rough basis for evaluating the degree of risk inherent in a strategy. These factors are:

1.   The amount of resources (on which the strategy is based) whose continued existence or value is not assured.

2.   The length of the time periods to which resources are committed.

3.   The proportion of resources committed to a single venture.

The greater these quantities, the greater the degree of risk that is involved.

Uncertain Term of Existence

Since a strategy is based on resources, any resource which may disappear before the payoff has been obtained may constitute a danger to the organization. Resources may disappear for various reasons. For example, they may lose their value. This frequently happens to such resources as physical facilities and product features. Again, they may be accidentally destroyed. The most vulnerable resource here is competence. The possible crash of the company plane or the blip on the president's electro-cardiogram are what make many organizations essentially speculative ventures. In fact, one of the critical attributes of highly centralized organizations is that the more centralized they are, the more speculative they are. The disappearance of the top executive, or the disruption of communication with him, may wreak havoc at subordinate levels.

However, for many companies, the possibility that critical resources may lose their value stems not so much from internal developments as from shifts in the environment. Take specialized production know-how, for example. It has value only because of demand for the product by customers—and customers may change their minds. This is cause for acute concern among the increasing number of companies whose futures depend so heavily on their ability to participate in defense contracts. A familiar case is the plight of the airframe industry following World War II. Some of the companies succeeded in making the shift from aircraft to missiles, but this has only resulted in their being faced with the same problem on a larger scale.

Duration of Commitment

Financial analysts often look at the ratio of fixed assets to current assets in order to assess the extent to which resources are committed to long-term programs. This may or may not give a satisfactory answer. How important are the assets? When will they be paid for?

The reasons for the risk increasing as the time for payoff increases is, of course, the inherent uncertainty in any venture. Resources committed over long time spans make the company vulnerable to changes in the environment. Since the difficulty of predicting such changes increases as the time span increases, long-term projects are basically more risky than are short ones. This is especially true of companies whose environments are unstable. And today, either because of technological, political, or economic shifts, most companies are decidedly in the category of those that face major upheaval in their corporate environments. The company building its future around technological equipment, the company selling primarily to the government, the company investing in underdeveloped nations, the company selling to the Common Market, the company with a plant in the South—all these have this prospect in common.

The harsh dilemma of modern management is that the time span of decision is increasing at the same time as the corporate environment is becoming increasingly unstable. It is this dilemma which places such a premium on the manager's sensitivity to external trends today. Much has been written about his role as a commander and administrator. But it is no less important that he be a *strategist*.

Size of the Stakes

The more of its resources a company commits to a particular strategy, the more pronounced the consequences. If the strategy is successful, the payoff will be great—both to managers and investors. If the strategy fails, the consequences will be dire—both to managers and investors. Thus, a critical decision for the executive group is: What proportion of available resources should be committed to a particular course of action?

This decision may be handled in a variety of ways. For example, faced with a project that requires more of its resources than it is willing to commit, a company either may choose to refrain from undertaking the project or, alternatively, may seek to reduce the total resources required by undertaking a joint venture or by going the route of merger or acquisition in order to broaden the resource base.

The amount of resources management stands ready to commit is of particular significance where there is some likelihood that larger competitors, having greater resources, may choose to enter the company's field. Thus, those companies which entered the small-computer field in the past few years are now faced with the penetration into this area of the data-processing giants. (Both IBM and Remington Rand have recently introduced new small computers.)

I do not mean to imply that the "best" strategy is the one with the least risk. High payoffs are frequently associated with high-risk strategies. Moreover, it is a frequent but dangerous assumption to think that inaction, or lack of change, is a low-risk strategy. Failure to exploit its resources to the fullest may well be the riskiest strategy of all that an organization may pursue, as Montgomery Ward and other companies have amply demonstrated.

5. Does the strategy have an appropriate time horizon?

A significant part of every strategy is the time horizon on which it is based. A viable strategy not only reveals what goals are to be accomplished; it says something about *when* the aims are to be achieved.

Goals, like resources, have time-based utility. A new product developed, a plant put on stream, a degree of market penetration, become significant strategic objectives only if accomplished by a certain time. Delay may deprive them of all strategic significance. A perfect example of this in the military sphere is the Sinai campaign of 1956. The strategic objective of the Israelis was not only to conquer the entire Sinai peninsula; it also was to do it in seven days. By contrast, the lethargic movement of the British troops made the operation a futile one for both England and France.

In choosing an appropriate time horizon, we must pay careful attention to the goals being pursued, and to the particular organization involved. Goals must be established far enough in advance to allow the organization to adjust to them. Organizations, like ships, cannot be "spun on a dime." Consequently, the larger the organization, the further its strategic time horizon must extend, since its adjustment time is longer. It is no mere managerial whim that the major contributions to long-range planning have emerged from the larger organizations—especially those large organizations such as Lockheed, North American Aviation, and RCA that traditionally have had to deal with highly unstable environments.

The observation that large corporations plan far ahead while small ones can get away without doing so has frequently been made. However, the significance of planning for the small but growing company has frequently been overlooked. As a company gets bigger, it must not only change the way it operates; it must also steadily push ahead its time horizon—and this is a difficult thing to do. The manager who has built a successful enterprise by his skill at "putting out fires" or the wheeler-dealer whose firm has grown by a quick succession of financial coups is seldom able to make the transition to the long look ahead.

In many cases, even if the executive were inclined to take a longer range view of events, the formal reward system seriously militates against doing so. In most companies the system of management rewards is closely related to currently reported profits. Where this is the case, executives may understandably be so preoccupied with reporting a profit year by year that they fail to spend as much time as they should in managing the company's long-term future. But if we seriously accept the thesis that the essence of managerial responsibility is the extended time lapse between decision and result, currently reported profits are hardly a reasonable basis on which to compensate top executives. Such a basis simply serves to shorten the time horizon with which the executive is concerned.

The importance of an extended time horizon derives not only from the fact that an organization changes slowly and needs time to work through basic modifications in its strategy; it derives also from the fact that there is a considerable advantage in a certain consistency of strategy maintained over long periods of time. The great danger to companies which do not carefully formulate strategies well in advance is that they are prone to fling themselves toward chaos by drastic changes in policy—and in personnel—at frequent intervals. A parade of presidents is a clear indication of a board that has not realy decided what its strategy should be. It is a common harbinger of serious corporate difficulty as well.

The time horizon is also important because of its impact on the selection of policies. The greater the time horizon, the greater the range in choice of tactics. If, for instance, the goals desired must be achieved in a relatively short time, steps like acquisition and merger may become virtually mandatory. An interesting illustration is the decision of National

Cash Register to enter the market for electronic data-processing equipment. As reported in *Forbes:*

> Once committed to EDP, NCR wasted no time. To buy talent and experience in 1953 it acquired Computer Research Corp. of Hawthorne, California. . . . For speed's sake, the manufacture of the 304's central units was turned over to GE. . . . NCR's research and development outlays also began curving steeply upwards.[11]

6. *Is the strategy workable?*

At first glance, it would seem that the simplest way to evaluate a corporate strategy is the completely pragmatic one of asking: Does it work? However, further reflection should reveal that if we try to answer that question, we are immediately faced with a quest for criteria. What is the evidence of a strategy "working"?

Quantitative indices of performance are a good start, but they really measure the influence of two critical factors combined: the strategy selected and the skill with which it is being executed. Faced with the failure to achieve anticipated results, both of these influences must be critically examined. One interesting illustration of this is a recent survey of the Chrysler Corporation after it suffered a period of serious loss:

> In 1959, during one of the frequent reorganizations at Chrysler Corp., aimed at halting the company's slide, a management consultant concluded: "The only thing wrong with Chrysler is people. The corporation needs some good top executives."[12]

By contrast, when Olivetti acquired the Underwood Corporation, it was able to reduce the cost of producing typewriters by one-third. And it did it without changing any of the top people in the production group. However, it did introduce a drastically revised set of policies.

If a strategy cannot be evaluated by results alone, there are some other indications that may be used to assess its contribution to corporate progress:

> The degree of consensus which exists among executives concerning corporate goals and policies.
>
> The extent to which major areas of managerial choice are identified in advance, while there is still time to explore a variety of alternatives.
>
> The extent to which resource requirements are discovered well before the last minute, necessitating neither crash programs of cost reduction nor the elimination of planned programs. The widespread popularity of the meat-axe approach to cost reduction is a clear indication of the frequent failure of corporate strategic planning.

---

[11] "NCR and the Computer Sweepstakes," *Forbes,* October 15, 1962, p. 21.

[12] "How Chrysler Hopes to Rebound," *Business Week,* October 6, 1962, p. 45.

CONCLUSION

The modern organization must deploy expensive and complex resources in the pursuit of transitory opportunities. The time required to develop resources is so extended, and the time-scale of opportunities is so brief and fleeting, that a company which has not carefully delineated and appraised its strategy is adrift in white water.

In short, while a set of goals and major policies that meets the criteria listed above does not guarantee success, it can be of considerable value in giving management both the time and the room to maneuver.

STUDENT REVIEW QUESTIONS

1. What are the six criteria which Tilles notes as being helpful in evaluating organizational strategy?
2. What are the dimensions of risk as a criterion in evaluating organizational strategy?
3. What is the distinction between what an organization is trying "to achieve" and trying "to become"?
4. What is meant by the internal consistency of a strategy?
5. What is meant by "competence" as a resource of an organization?

17. Formulating Strategy in Smaller Companies*

FRANK F. GILMORE

FOREWORD

While many sophisticated concepts of formulating corporate strategy are being studied with interest by large corporations, they hold little promise for medium-sized and smaller companies—at least, in the foreseeable future. For the latter, strategic planning is still more of an art than a science. A conference-table approach to strategy, based on executive judgment and intuition, is outlined in this article. The author describes six major steps in the process and lists the types of questions the chief executive should ask his management team to consider.

Mr. Gilmore was one of the early leaders in analyzing planning problems for business executives, and he has served the planning movement in a number of capacities. As Professor of Business Administration at Cornell University, he teaches in the Graduate School of Business and Public Administration, and is Director of the Executive Development Program. As a writer, he coauthored (with Richard G. Brandenburg) the Harvard Business Review article, "Anatomy of Corporate Planning" (November–December 1962), and has written other articles and books. As a consultant, he has worked closely with top executives in a variety of U.S. companies. During the past year he has been teaching at IMEDE, the well-known management development institute in Lausanne, Switzerland.

CORPORATE PLANNING, aimed at strategy formulation for the company, has now become so generally accepted that many executives are having

---

second thoughts about their approaches.[1] Indeed, the top management group of one major corporation has concluded that, since each of its members has at one time or another been in charge of his company's corporate planning department, there is little need to go through the formal planning cycle that characterized its approach for the past decade. Inasmuch as all of them think like planners, they feel that they have outgrown their initial planning approach and are groping for something better.

In other large companies, consideration is being given to possible ways in which management science and the computer may be applied to the strategy formulation problem. A suggestion recently offered by Russell L. Ackoff in the form of an adaptive approach appears to hold promise as a frame of reference within which such improvements may be developed over time.[2]

But for the medium-sized or small company that does not have planning departments, operations research groups, or large-scale computing capacity, and that simply cannot afford to engage in planning research, a more modest approach must be sought. This does not mean that the managers of such companies can afford to neglect their planning responsibilities. Today's widespread adoption of strategic planning will not permit such a course. What is needed is a simple, practical approach that is within the reach of these smaller companies. I shall try to meet that need in this article.

EVOLUTION OF APPROACH

Prior to the middle 1950s, the major task of the chief executive was viewed as that of adapting the company to changing conditions. This traditional approach developed during the period between World Wars I and II, when unpredictable and violent fluctuations meant adaptation or failure.

In this traditional top management approach, determination of objectives presupposed a size-up of the situation of the company as a whole. The objectives could then provide direction and unity of purpose for the development of a program of action covering the various activities of the company.

Size-ups were made in various ways, depending on the background of the management involved, the organization of the company, and the position of the company in terms of its growth and its place in its indus-

---

[1] See David W. Ewing, "Corporate Planning at a Crossroads," *Harvard Business Review,* July–August 1967, p. 77.

[2] R. L. Ackoff, *Concept of Corporate Planning* (New York: Wiley-Interscience, 1970).

try. Any one of several approaches could serve the purpose. Size-ups were most commonly conducted along departmental lines because most companies were more or less centralized then and were therefore organized by major functions, such as marketing, production, and finance. For this reason, the functional size-up approach will be examined more closely.

Exhibit 1 shows this traditional approach. It indicates the process required to reach a diagnosis of the company's prospects and problems:

EXHIBIT 1
Example of Traditional Approach to Strategy Formulation

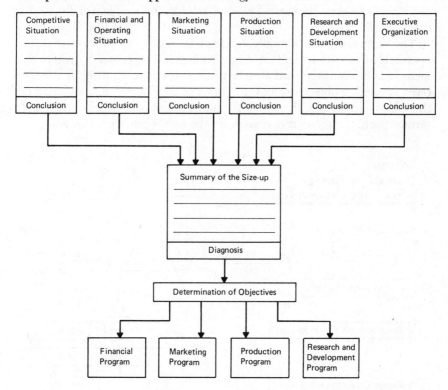

1. An analysis was made of the total picture. Its components were analyses of the competitive situation and of the various functions. (Some executives found it useful to look at the competitive situation first, and then analyze the financial and operating picture. They felt that a size-up of these two areas often provided measuring sticks or raised pertinent questions that served to sharpen the analysis of other functional areas. Moreover, many analysts found it helpful to defer the size-up of the executive organization to the last because of the light that was shed on

management performance by the examination of the functional areas.)

2. Under each topic in the breakdown, significant findings were noted and classified, and an effort was made to reach a conclusion on each major topic.

3. The separate conclusions were then combined, and an attempt was made to arrive, inductively, at the overall diagnosis. Particular attention was paid to interrelationships that might be significant for the company as a whole.

This painstaking, sizing-up, inductive process became the basis for determining objectives for the future. The chief executive then faced the task of deciding on a course of action and, in the light of the objectives, choosing between alternative ways of solving the problem diagnosed in the size-up.

This approach was actually incomplete, since the process remained open-ended, as shown in Part A of Exhibit 2. There was a definite tendency for top management to size up the situation, starting at the very base; formulate objectives and programs of action; organize to carry out the plans; and exercise executive control; but then drift along until serious problems made it necessary to size up the situation again.

EXHIBIT 2
Formulating Strategy
A. Traditional Open-Loop Process

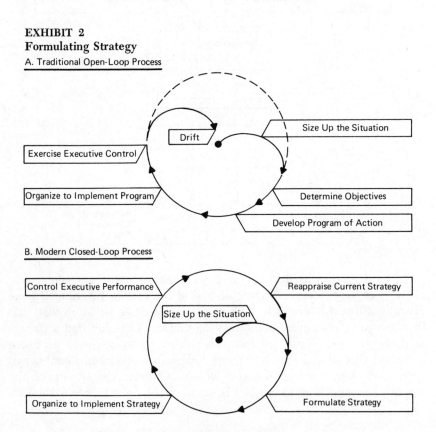

B. Modern Closed-Loop Process

Formalizing the Analysis

During the 1950s, it became increasingly clear that a new approach to policy formulation was urgently needed. It was recognized that—

concern for short-term problems would have to shift to plans for capitalizing on long-term opportunities;

sizing up the situation as a basis for a new course of action would have to give way to reappraising existing strategy in the light of the changing environment;

sporadic diagnosis would have to be replaced by constant surveillance;

concern for immediate profits and for adaptability to meet changes in current conditions needed to shift to focusing on long-range ROI, growth, flexibility, and stability.

In other words, occasional preoccupation with such questions as "Where are we?" and "Where are we going?" needed to be replaced by frequent consideration of such questions as "Are we making satisfactory progress with respect to plan?" and "Are our plans still valid?"

Not surprisingly, therefore, over the past 15 years there has been a significant shift to formal, long-range, strategic planning. The most significant distinguishing characteristic of the new approach has been that executives are now managing in accordance with a constantly updated strategic plan. Instead of just sizing up the situation at a given point of time, they schedule reappraisals of current strategy. The effect of this change is a shift from an open-loop, short-range approach to a closed-loop, long-range approach, illustrated in Part B of Exhibit 2.

As this conceptual scheme shows, the size-up of the situation can be thought of as a springboard; and as long as reappraisal of present strategy closes the loop, the system continues to cycle. Feedback and regular surveillance serve to keep the company's strategy constantly before management. Thus, after the first cycle, reappraisal of current strategy takes the place of size-up of the situation. Such reappraisal examines the same areas, but analysis is focused on the possible consequences of continuing the current strategy, given trends and developments in the external environment, and existing internal operating conditions and results.

Accompanying the change from sporadic size-up to frequent, and in many cases regular, reappraisal, there has been a shift in emphasis from size-up to formulation. In keeping with Peter F. Drucker's advice in the early 1950s, management attention has been focused more on the discovery of opportunities than on the solution of problems.[3] As a result, more emphasis has been placed on the evaluation of alternative courses of action and on maximization of performance.

---

[3] Peter F. Drucker, *The Practice of Management* (New York: Harper & Brothers, 1954).

In the formulation of strategy, management may, in time, have the assistance of tools and techniques from management science. But before significant progress along these lines can be made (as I shall discuss in the next section), there must be a better understanding of the structure of the problem itself.

Structure of Relationships

One approach to structuring the problem of strategy formulation is summarized in Exhibit 3. In this model, which was developed during a Cornell research project, the relationship between the company and its competitive environment is expressed by the strategy of the enterprise, which has three basic components:

1. *Economic Mission.*   This is concerned with the kind of business the

EXHIBIT 3
Model of New Approach

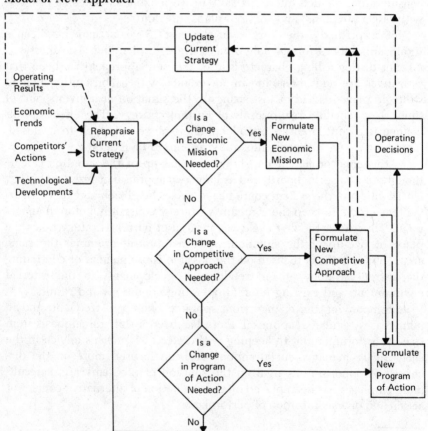

company should be in, and what its performance objectives should be.

2. *Competitive Approach.* This is concerned with finding the product-market-sales approach that will accomplish the economic mission, and with deriving pertinent goals in the various areas of the business.

3. *Program of Action.* This involves a search for efficient means of implementing the competitive approach.

In summary form, the process works as follows: Current strategy is reappraised from time to time in the light of internal operating results, economic trends, competitors' actions, and technological developments. When opportunities or threats have been disclosed, management proceeds to ask questions designed to indicate when and in what respect strategy should be changed. If a new economic mission is called for, the planners proceed to formulate a revised approach. This, in turn, calls for revision of the competitive approach and of the program of action. If the economic mission is considered sound, the competitive approach is questioned. If the competitive approach seems appropriate, the process continues until the appropriate area for revision is identified and a new strategy is formulated.

Of course, it might be concluded that the overall current strategy is sound. Then no revision would take place, and another reappraisal would be made at a later date. The broken lines in Exhibit 3 indicate the feedback of operating results (part of the control process) and the updating of current strategy as a result of formulation.

MANAGEMENT SCIENCE?

At first thought, it would appear that management science would offer several possible approaches to strategy formulation. However, the few approaches that might prove useful are in such an early stage of development that they hold little promise at this time. While a number of operations research (OR) approaches are useful in decision making at the operations level, most of these are of limited use in strategy formulation because of the large number of variables involved. For example, consider mathematical programming and simulation:

Of the various forms of mathematical programming, the best known is linear programming, which is applicable to those situations where relationships are linear and there is no uncertainty (or it may be assumed away). Under these conditions, linear programming results in optimization, but the limitations may be too restrictive for strategy formulation. Other forms of mathematical programming avoid some of the difficulties of linear programming, but computation becomes considerably more difficult and often necessitates trial-and-error approaches.

Simulation may be useful in strategy situations that do not fall within the limitations of linear programming. For example, such nonlinear relationships as those due to economies of scale may be easily incorporated, and probabilistic data reflecting the presence of uncertainty may be used. But whereas mathematical programming requires only that data be provided for an already established model, simulation requires that the model itself be constructed. This is a formidable task, involving many assumptions as to the interaction of the various components within the company and of the company with its environment. A simulation model thus requires a great deal of time and effort to construct and test, and is extremely difficult to validate. And, even if these tasks are successfully completed, there is little assurance that the same model will continue to be valid.

Other OR approaches are not relevant to the overall decision, but are applicable to parts of the strategy decision process. Among these are capital budgeting, inventory theory, scheduling theory, and so forth. They are useful as components in strategy formulation, but they cannot handle all the major aspects of the problem.

Thus, OR is only appropriate for the solution of well-defined problems where the relevant relationships can be specified and the objectives have been decided on. Under such conditions, calculations are dominant, and mathematics is often almost a substitute for judgment.

Actually, "systems analysis"—or the "systems approach," as it is often called—may offer more promise in strategy formulation than OR. Systems analysis has been defined as an approach to solving complex problems of choice under uncertainty by systematic examination of the costs, effectiveness, and risks of various alternatives. It is appropriate for use in poorly structured problems, where the relationships are not clear and where decisions must be made among alternative objectives. It became a major instrument in governmental decision making during the 1960s, and is attracting increasing attention in business as a useful way of analyzing top management planning problems.

All in all, however, the potentials of management science for strategic purposes seem limited to use in large companies that possess considerable technical resources for their development and use. For the foreseeable future, managements in medium-sized and small companies will have to use the generalizing, inductive, empirical method which has evolved out of the old, size-up approach. And this approach remains more an art than a science.

SIMPLE, PRACTICAL METHOD

I shall describe now a simple, practical planning method that can be employed by top executives in medium-sized and small companies. Several influences have shaped the sequence of steps to be suggested. John Dewey's concepts of how people think provide a useful rationale for the approach as a whole: the process of strategy formulation may be viewed as a form of reflective thinking, where one progresses step by step from recognition of the problem to solution.[4] The experience of management, teachers, and consultants during the past 50 years has also had a strong impact: the older, size-up approach has contributed to early steps in the sequence, while recent developments in strategy formulation have helped shape later steps. Finally, the need for top management to advocate its proposals, when formulated, to the board of directors has influenced the scheme to be described.[5]

The process of strategy formulation may be carried out in six progressive steps. I shall describe them in detail and illustrate them with notes made at a series of top management meetings in a small company that was applying this approach. The company, a manufacturer of insulated wire and cable, will be identified as "IWAC Co."

1. Record Current Strategy

The recording of current strategy is an important foundation for subsequent steps. In a company that is managing according to a well-defined strategy, it will be easy for the manager to record his plans. Typically today, the strategy of large corporations is a matter of record. But many medium-sized and small companies operate informally with a loosely defined strategy. In these cases, the task of recording current strategy becomes more difficult. Nevertheless, it is usually possible to infer from trends and executive behavior what strategy is implicit in the company's operations. If efforts to record current strategy fail, one can fall back on the size-up approach for the first step.

In recording current strategy, it is important to clarify top management's criteria as to the kind of company it wants to operate. These criteria will be expressed in terms of values held by the top management group. Also, what kind of company does top management think it *should* operate? Criteria for this answer will be expressed in terms of management's concept of social responsibility.

Such criteria will be important in later steps, when the core of the strategy problem is discovered, and alternative strategies are formulated and evaluated. To illustrate, in the case of IWAC Co., the top management group described the strategy that had characterized its operations for some years as follows:

> The company develops, manufactures, and sells standard telephone wire and cable to independent telephone companies. It is attempting to

---

[4] John Dewey, *How We Think* (Boston: D.C. Heath & Co., 1933).

[5] See Frank F. Gilmore, *Formulation and Advocacy of Business Policy*, rev. ed. (Ithaca, N.Y.: Cornell University, 1970).

diversify into such products as electronic connectors, printed electronic circuits, heavy-duty lighting cords, and retractile cords. The company markets all its products through distributors.

2. Identify Problems

The current strategy must be reappraised to determine whether problems exist. A strategy problem is one which may have a significant influence on the future success of the enterprise as a whole.

Management must first look at the company's environment. In order to estimate the consequences of continuing the current strategy, it needs to study external trends and developments and to make assumptions about the economic outlook, the shape of future technology, and competitors' actions. In short, it needs to establish premises about the environment on which analysis of company operations can be based. In effect, it asks, "Given the environmental outlook, is our strategy still valid? Are any opportunities or threats disclosed by this outlook?"

Then management must examine the operating situation of the company as disclosed by financial results and progress made under the current strategy in the various areas of operations. As with the old, size-up approach, a useful next step is to analyze the financial and operating picture. Meaningful reappraisal of current strategy is facilitated by a careful analysis of financial and operating trends, since, as noted earlier, useful measuring sticks for appraising other aspects of the company's operations can be derived from the financial phase of the analysis.

Executives can then proceed to reappraise the marketing, production, and research and development policies, and the management organization of the company. In particular, they must be on the alert for significant weaknesses or unutilized strengths. Throughout this part of the analysis they ask, "Is the company making satisfactory progress according to plan?"

Cutting through Symptoms. Strategy problems may take the form of threats or opportunities in the environment; failure to meet plans; signs of organizational strife; adverse trends with respect to share of market, competitive advantage, or financial results or condition; or other indications of loss of health or vigor. These problems are likely to be symptoms of a more deep-seated difficulty. To illustrate in terms of a real-life situation, let us turn back to the IWAC case.

When the top executives began analyzing the problems, risks, and opportunities of the company, they were surprised by the shape of the picture that began to emerge. I shall mention just some of the highlights of the findings management considered:

> Changes in industry structure are intensifying competition. The number of independent telephone companies is declining largely because of

acquisitions by General Telephone. Vertical integration into wire and cable insulation is taking place among both suppliers and end users. Some of the larger wire and cable companies are owned by major suppliers of wire and insulation material.

In the last five years, the number of companies making plastic-insulated telephone wires and cables has increased from 5 to 13. A slump in wire demand, along with falling copper prices early in the current year, led to price cutting in the industry. With the economy experiencing a recession, the wire and cable industry is faced with overcapacity.

Our competitors are moving toward direct selling; of 25 competing companies, 20 have sales offices, 10 have warehouses, and 13 have no distributors at all. General Cable attributes its great success to the establishment of sales offices and stock distribution centers. Yet our company continues to leave its sales effort largely in the hands of exclusive distributors. Indeed, our company is unique in its nonaggressive, competitive approach in sales.

In addition to the increase in competition as a result of changes in industry structure and the trend toward direct selling, other competitive pressures are becoming evident. Competitors are underselling us in connection with broadcast wires and cord sets because of our insistence on excessively high quality.

Despite the fact that competition is growing more intense, the company's immediate position is sound. Our sales have declined less this year (12 percent) than has been true for the insulated wire and cable industry as a whole (15 percent). Return on stockholders' investment, while sporadic, has been generally favorable. The company is financially liquid and has a reasonable long-term debt/equity ratio.

Some moves have been made to offset the impact of increased competition. First, a new works manager has been brought into the company, and already he has achieved significant operating economies. Inventory investment has been reduced 30 percent, and purchasing costs have declined significantly.

A promising outlook exists for some of the company's special products. The company holds patents on commercial applications of heavy-duty lighting cords, a recent addition to the product line. There are few competitors in this field, but the company is limiting its opportunity by selling the systems through one exclusive distributor.

The product line is being broadened through the addition of color-sheathed cords, oilproof cords, large flexible cables, and secondary power cables. But the market potential of these new products is not known by the company. Prospects in the power cable field look attractive, with only a few manufacturers currently competing. But the company is moving very slowly in this area.

Although some changes have been made in the executive organization, among them the appointment of the new works manager, several long-term employees are still entrenched in established ways of doing business which will have to be changed in light of competitive trends. Particularly notable are broadly held values about the desirability of extremely high-quality products and the feeling that the present method of selling through distributors can be changed only at great cost.

3. Discover the Core Elements

If the reappraisal discloses that major problems exist, it is necessary to discover their core. The basic difficulty may take many forms. For example, the current strategy may require greater competence and/or resources than the company possesses; the strategy may fail to exploit adequately the company's distinctive competence; the company may lack sufficient competitive advantage, or it may fail to exploit opportunities and/or meet threats in the environments; or the strategy may not be internally consistent. Diagnosis with respect to the company's performance against plan and prognosis as to the future consequences of continuing the current strategy are both involved in this step. To return to IWAC:

Management concluded that a shift in strategy was needed. It saw that IWAC could not continue on its traditional course and keep growing profitably. Two major considerations were involved. "First, the company can no longer concentrate on *standard* wire and cable products," it was reported. "All signs point to a loss of market share in this area. There appear to be better opportunities in *specialized* wire and cable products, where the company possesses distinctive competence. Second, the current policy of selling through distributors no longer appears appropriate as it is neither consistent with industry practice nor compatible with specialization."

4. Formulate Alternatives

Once the core of the strategy problem has been discovered, management can formulate alternative ways of solving the problem. It is characteristic of modern planning approaches that one must try to conceive of all alternatives that might offer some possibility of providing a solution. Then consideration must be given in a preliminary way to limitations imposed by the company's competence and resources. Also, management's values and sense of social responsibility will set some boundaries.

But this is more the time for imagination and innovation than for logic. More rigorous evaluation can come in the next step. In the IWAC case, the thinking of executives was summarized as follows:

The company has three alternative strategies it might follow. First, it could merge with a supplier or end user of insulated wire and cable. Second, it could specialize in insulated wire and cable products that require strict quality specifications and technological expertise, and at the same time improve its marketing effectiveness by distributing its products directly through its own sales force. Third, it could become an aggressive marketer of a relatively full line of insulated wires and cables with an extensive direct-sales organization.

The first alternative is a distinct possibility. Current trends toward vertical integration in the industry make the company a possible investment opportunity for an end user or supplier. The company's research capabilities, manufacturing know-how, and capacity to produce telephone wire and cable might make it an attractive acquisition for a company such as General Telephone.

The second alternative would require a closer relationship with our customers. In particular, a technical sales force would be needed that could work directly with customers in determining the end user's needs, product quality, technical characteristics of the product, and new systems applications.

The third alternative would emphasize an aggressive competitive approach embracing a full line of products and extensive marketing organization, not unlike that used by General Cable. The company would become a manufacturer of a wide line of insulated wires and cables, utilizing its technological know-how to develop new products. Increased marketing expenditures would be required in advertising and in the development of a sizable sales organization, establishment of warehouses, maintenance of inventories in the field, and development of sales branch offices.

5. Evaluate Alternatives

In this step, management looks at the bearing of the various vital factors on the choice of a strategy. The alternatives must be compared in terms of:

Relative effectiveness in solving the strategic problem.

The degree to which each matches the company's competence and resources.

Their relative competitive advantage.

The extent to which they satisfy management's preferences and sense of social responsibility.

Their relative ability to minimize the creation of new problems.

In strategy problems, more than in other types of problems, executives would like to be able to optimize with respect to *several* relevant factors. Therefore, trade-offs are necessary, for optimization with respect to one factor will be at the expense of another. This is a characteristic of business strategy problems which, along with the premium placed on discovering the core elements, makes them the most difficult challenges facing management. Probably the best one can hope to do at this time is to choose that alternative which, in his judgment, offers the best blend of advantages. If the reasoning of the IWAC executives were to be reconstructed, it might run as follows:

All three alternatives would meet the strategic challenge presented by the increasing competition in the industry. The merger route might involve the risk of lengthy and costly litigation under antitrust laws. Merger would also raise a question as to how much basic research the company as a "captive shop" would be encouraged to do. It would probably limit the scope of technological problems considered by the laboratory. This alternative would meet the threat of the declining market in telephone wires and cables more effectively than the other two alternatives, but would provide less of an outlet for management's innovativeness or entrepreneurship.

The success of the second alternative, the specialization approach, would depend largely on the company's ability to continue as an innovator. It would capitalize on the organization's capabilities in solving customers' needs. To be successful under this approach, the company would have to carve out a special niche in the insulated wire and cable market. This approach could constitute a good match between the company's capabilities and resources and the opportunities in the industry. But considerable expenditure would be needed for the development of the technically expert sales force that would be required.

The third alternative, an aggressive marketing approach involving a full line of products and a greatly enlarged marketing organization, would tax the innovative capabilities of the laboratory and would set the company into direct competition with larger companies, such as General Cable. Compared with the other two alternatives, this would require the largest additional investment. The risk involved in this alternative would center on financial problems, with the possibility of overextension with respect to long-term debt or loss of control through sale of common stock to outsiders.

We conclude that the second alternative is superior to the third, but the choice between merger and specialization is less apparent. The merger alternative might be rejected largely on the basis of management's implied emphasis on quality, innovation, and entrepreneurship.

6. Choose the New Strategy

In this last step, management identifies those factors which are of overriding importance. These are the factors on which the decision turns. In a strategy problem, where there may appear to be five or six relevant factors of significance, one or two of them may seem pivotal, and the relative standing of the alternatives with respect to these factors provides the basis for the final choice. Here is what happened in the IWAC case:

Management concluded that the best strategy was the second of the three possibilities considered—specializing in insulated wire and cable products which required high-quality specifications, and marketing its products directly through its own sales force. This meant eliminating products that did not utilize the company's distinctive competence in insulation, such as printed circuits and electronic connectors, and ceasing at the earliest practical moment to rely on distributors. Under this strategy, the company would undertake aggressive development and marketing of power cable and heavy-duty lighting cords.

EXHIBIT 4
Questions to Use in Formulating Strategy

1. Record current strategy:
    a. What is the current strategy?
    b. What kind of business does management want to operate (considering such management values as desired return on investment, growth rate, share of market, stability, flexibility, character of the business, and climate)?
    c. What kind of business does management feel it ought to operate (considering management's concepts of social responsibility and obligations to stockholders, employees, community, competitors, customers, suppliers, government, and the like)?

2. Identify problems with the current strategy:
    a. Are trends discernible in the environment that may become threats and/or missed opportunities if the current strategy is continued?
    b. Is the company having difficulty implementing the current strategy?
    c. Is the attempt to carry out the current strategy disclosing significant weaknesses and/or unutilized strengths in the company?
    d. Are there other concerns with respect to the validity of the current strategy?
    e. Is the current strategy no longer valid?

3. Discover the core of the strategy problem:
    a. Does the current strategy require greater competence and/or resources than the company possesses?
    b. Does it fail to exploit adequately the company's distinctive competence?
    c. Does it lack sufficient competitive advantage?
    d. Will it fail to exploit opportunities and/or meet threats in the environment, now or in the future?
    e. Are the various elements of the strategy internally inconsistent?
    f. Are there other considerations with respect to the core of the strategy problem?
    g. What, then, is the real core of the strategy problem?

EXHIBIT 4 (continued)

4. Formulate alternative new strategies:
   a. What possible alternatives exist for solving the strategy problem?
   b. To what extent do the company's competence and resources limit the number of alternatives that should be considered?
   c. To what extent do management's preferences limit the alternatives?
   d. To what extent does management's sense of social responsibility limit the alternatives?
   e. What strategic alternatives are acceptable?

5. Evaluate alternative new strategies:
   a. Which alternative *best* solves the strategy problem?
   b. Which alternative offers the *best* match with the company's competence and resources?
   c. Which alternative offers the *greatest* competitive advantage?
   d. Which alternative *best* satisfies management's preferences?
   e. Which alternative *best* meets management's sense of social responsibility?
   f. Which alternative *minimizes* the creation of new problems?

6. Choose a new strategy:
   a. What is the *relative significance* of each of the preceding considerations?
   b. What should the new strategy be?

CONCLUSION

The approach described in this article is most valuable for medium-sized and small companies. Top executives of these companies, working at the conference table, can approach strategy formulation as a joint effort. In such group problem solving, one of the principal tools contributing to effective leadership by the president is a carefully prepared outline for guiding the discussion. The six-step approach I have described can be the starting point for such an outline. Exhibit 4 exemplifies the kinds of questions that might be asked. The president, as chairman of the meeting, can phrase the questions in terms of the situation under discussion, note pertinent additional questions at appropriate points, and thus guide the meeting. Each of the six main tasks becomes a milepost to be passed in the progress toward a solution.

The chairman can advance group thinking by offering interpretive summaries, and, using transitional statements, he can lead the group from one major step to the next. The constant challenge for him is to maintain that balance between freedom and control which makes for progress and yet does not act to stifle creative thinking.

The job of top executives has undergone substantial change during the last 15 years. Corporate strategy has become their dominant concern. But strategy is not yet a science even in large corporations, despite recent developments in management science and computers. And for the medium-sized or small company which cannot afford OR, planning departments, or large-scale computer capacity, the task is likely to remain an art during the foreseeable future. In such circumstances, strategy should be formulated by the top management team at the conference table. Judgment, experience, intuition, and well-guided discussions are the key to success, not staff work and mathematical models.

STUDENT REVIEW QUESTIONS

1. Why does Gilmore feel that the use of management science and its application for strategy will be limited to larger organizations?
2. Describe the method for planning that the author recommends for medium-sized and small companies. What do you think of this method?
3. In what ways can meetings be useful in the smaller organization planning process?
4. Why is it important to record the current strategy as a first step in the overall strategic planning process?
5. Discuss Gilmore's list of questions to use in formulating strategy. Why do you feel this list would be helpful to managers in smaller sized organizations? What weaknesses does the list have for such managers?

chapter 7

Implementing Strategy: Organizational Structure and Behavior

Introduction

Importance of Implementation

Elements of Implementation: Securing, Organizing, and Directing the Utilization of Resources

Interrelated Activities and the Art of Management

Organizational Structure and Strategy Implementation

Organizational Behavior and Strategy Implementation

The Process of Organizing: A Dilemma in Implementing Organizational Strategy
   Breaking down the Tasks to Be Performed
   Coordination toward the Overall Goal
   Dilemmas and Some Examples
   Other Elements of the Process
   Principles and Situational Analysis
   Communication and Information

Analyzing and Changing Organizations: A Challenge in Strategy Implementation
   Emphasis on the Going Concern
   Structural Aspects of Change
   Behavioral Aspects of Change
   Need to Consider All Aspects When Implementing or Formulating Strategy

Implementation, Interrelationships, and Leadership

Summary

Readings

INTRODUCTION

THE DISCUSSION of strategy formulation in previous chapters emphasized that this process includes the identification and evaluation of existing strategies in ongoing organizations. The ultimate result of the process is usually a change in present strategy rather than a totally new strategy. Upon initial development or modification, the strategy or strategic plan of the organization is often set down in writing, but it is always subject to further modification of the objectives, major plans, or major policies which are incorporated in the overall strategy.

IMPORTANCE OF IMPLEMENTATION

Developing a strategy to guide the institution, as valuable a function as this may be, is not in itself sufficient for an organization. Beyond the task of keeping the strategy continually appropriate and useful, it is also the job of top management to ensure that the strategy is *implemented* effectively within and outside of the organization. Without suitable implementation the most precise and appropriate strategy cannot be very useful to the organization. The task of implementation requires the full measure of top-management skills and capabilities as well as the talents of all other managers, and the cooperation of all members of the organization. It is significant that in most lists of managerial functions, those pertaining to *implementation* far outnumber those involved in the *development* of strategy. Included in various lists are from 5 to 20 generally recognized functions. One summary categorization lists planning, organizing, assembling resources, supervising, and coordinating as basic administrative functions.[1] All of these topics may be divided into subcategories but only planning (in some of its aspects) is actually involved in what could be called strategy development. The point here is not to minimize the importance of the strategy formulation process, but only to dramatize the wide range of managerial activities involved in the task of strategy implementation. Most of the time and effort of most managers is spent on strategy implementation, with the amount of this activity increasing as one moves from top management to lower levels. Chester Barnard defines three major functions of executives as developing and maintaining a system of communication, promoting and securing the personal services that constitute the material of organizations, and

---

[1] William H. Newman, *Administrative Action* (Englewood Cliffs, N.J.: Prentice-Hall, Inc., 1963), pp. 4–5. Other examples of such lists can be found in various texts dealing with management. Two such texts are Dalton E. McFarland, *Management: Principles and Practices* (New York: The Macmillan Co., 1958); and Lyman Keith and Carlo Gubellini, *Introduction to Business Enterprise* (New York: McGraw-Hill Book Co., 1971).

formulating and defining the purposes of the organization.[2] Only the last is particular to the formulation of strategy. The other two focus on implementation.

The implementation of strategy is so vital to the organization, it is important that the student and manager understand its nature, activities, and place in the overall strategic framework. In analyzing an ongoing situation, it is necessary, as has been noted earlier, to conceptually differentiate the implementation phase from other phases of the strategic process. However, the thorough strategic analysis developed earlier does include much that is associated with strategy implementation rather than with the strategy itself. For instance, the internal analysis, which was the subject of Chapter 3, includes an analysis of management which contains much information about strategy implementation.

As will be emphasized later in this chapter, both strategy formulation and implementation are linked closely together since they are the two major parts of the overall strategic process. As such, a manager in practice or a student in analysis is always dealing with them simultaneously. Actually, when involved in management or the analysis of management situations, the individual moves constantly back and forth between the strategy and its implementation. Yet, being able to separate conceptually the parts of the strategic process allows a manager more precise judgment in actions and decisions, since the concept helps to organize one's thinking when facing specific situations, thereby increasing the likelihood of dealing with the right problem or issue and doing so with better perspective.

ELEMENTS OF IMPLEMENTATION: SECURING, ORGANIZING, AND DIRECTING THE UTILIZATION OF RESOURCES

Generally, the implementation of strategy consists of securing resources, organizing those resources, and directing the use of these resources within and outside of the organization. These activities are different from those of strategy formulation which are concerned with defining the objective to be achieved and the plans to be executed through the utilization of organizational resources.

More specifically, securing resources includes staffing the organization and providing the development, educational opportunities, compensation, and personnel policies to attract and keep the required resources. It includes, also, the functions necessary to provide the organization with essential financial and physical resources in timely fashion and at appropriate cost.

---

[2] Chester I. Barnard, *The Functions of the Executive* (Cambridge, Mass.: Harvard University Press, 1938), p. 215.

The very complex job of organizing resources, particularly human resources, will be the focus of this chapter. At this point, it will suffice to mention that organizing resources includes the philosophy of the management including the view of human nature underlying it, the formal and informal organizational structures, the overall climate of the institution, and the role of communications and information of both a formal and informal nature.

Directing the utilization of resources will be the major content of the two subsequent chapters. In summary, this function includes the managerial activities associated with coordinating the use of all resources. These tasks include the planning and control needed to motivate organizational members and monitor their activities in the use of other resources, and the provision of the personal and moral leadership needed for the organization to sustain itself, and to change as required over time.

INTERRELATED ACTIVITIES AND THE ART OF MANAGEMENT

In reviewing the various elements of strategy implementation discussed thus far, a series of interrelated activities are apparent which conceptually can be set forth in a logical order, but which actually occur simultaneously in an ongoing concern. The practicing manager seldom has the luxury of dealing with only one phase of this series for very long, and the order of his activity depends upon the priority of circumstances rather than upon the logic of the conceptual framework. The job always is to perform the function or functions that best achieve the strategy, or that secure commitment of organizational members to the strategy.

The priorities and views of the manager will depend upon his judgment, values, experience, power, information, and overall assessment of the situation at the time. In such a light, management or administration is seen as an art by many. One leading authority conceives of the managerial process as the necessary activities of individuals in an organization who are charged with ordering, forwarding, and facilitating the associated efforts of a group of individuals brought together to realize certain defined purposes.[3] Because management is an art and few rules can be applied consistently in all situations, the manager or student who would rely upon "principles" to guide his actions in all circumstances would inevitably be faced with the "Conflicts of Principle" expounded so forcefully in a book of that title.[4] Lowell states that what seem to be

---

[3] Ordway Tead, *The Art of Administration* (New York: McGraw-Hill Book Co., 1951), p. 3.

[4] Abbott L. Lowell, *Conflicts of Principle*, rev. ed. (Cambridge, Mass.: Harvard University Press, 1956).

universal principles are in fact only true within the limits of conditions in which they are properly applied, but not necessarily under other circumstances. We strongly subscribe to this conclusion as implied in our first chapter which advocates the use of cases, discussions, simulations, and actual experience as necessary training for managers, and notes that simply learning principles would not suffice as managerial training.

Thus, students and managers are advised not to rely upon principles but to develop a framework within which to analyze and practice the functions of management. Understanding the interrelatedness of the various elements of strategy implementation will facilitate achieving this framework. Beyond that, the manager should see in his practice and experience that the entire implementation process is interrelated with the process of strategy formulation. It is our view that both strategy formulation and its implementation constitute the strategic process. A clear understanding of that process and the interrelationships inherent within it, will serve the student or manager well when evaluating or managing an organization. Seeing the totality of the process will establish an understanding of the range of necessary activities involved in the complex job of developing and implementing an organizational strategy.

ORGANIZATIONAL STRUCTURE AND STRATEGY IMPLEMENTATION

"Structure can be defined as the design of organization through which the enterprise is administered. The design whether formally or informally defined has two aspects. It includes, first, the lines of authority and communication between the different administrative offices and officers and, second, the information and data that flow through these lines of communication and authority. Such lines and data are essential to assure the effective coordination, appraisal, and planning so necessary in carrying out the basic goals and policies and in knitting together the total resources of the enterprise."[5]

Here Chandler introduces both the nature of organizational structure and its interrelatedness with the organizational strategy. This view of organizational structure concentrates on what is to be done, who is to do it and how, what information is needed and when, and who needs to know and when. Finally, his concept includes the interrelationships among these elements of structure whether formal, informal, or both. But Chandler's statement also suggests another important idea; the proposition that the structure is dependent upon and should follow from the strategy of the organization. As explained earlier in this chapter, strategy

---

[5] Alfred D. Chandler, Jr., *Strategy and Structure* (Cambridge, Mass.: The M.I.T. Press, 1962), p. 16.

formulation and implementation are interrelated phases of a total process with strategy preceding structure. The organizational phase, the structuring of the enterprise, should be dependent upon the strategy for its form. As expressed by one notable school of thought in the field of architecture, "form follows function." This idea of organizational structure is viewed by the authors as more valid than others which would base organizational form upon preconceived notions of "principles" or "best" ways of organizing, and which do not recognize strategy as the basic determinant of organizational design.

The main purpose of organizing is to move toward the attainment of organizational objectives, and the structural design should facilitate this purpose. Managers must understand that achieving their objectives requires attention to the entire range of organizational and administrative functions which constitute the work of the managers in strategy implementation. Beyond the activity required in organizational structuring, the other tasks included in strategy implementation also follow from the strategy of the organization. The ways in which these various implementation activities are put into practice depends to a large extent upon the structural design of the organization. A well-conceived design, based upon the strategy, facilitates eventual commitment of various organizational members to the objectives and policies of the organization.

The Dennison Manufacturing Company during the decade of the mid-1950s to the mid-1960s is an example of an organization attempting to modify its organizational structure in order to be consistent with its strategy and serve to implement that strategy. For years prior to 1955, Dennison had been known as an unaggressive producer and marketer of paper products with no particularly ambitious profit motivation. A change in management philosophy and objectives accompanied by related product-market policies signaled a change in strategy toward objectives of emphasizing profits, while exercising corporate social responsibility. New products were added and acquisitions were made as elements of the new strategy. The existing organizational structure, however, was recognized as being unsuitable to the new strategy since it was organized functionally and did not fix profit responsibility. Accordingly, a new organization evolved over a decade resulting in a product line orientation with full responsibility for profit given to the manager of each product division. Top management, in designing this structure, felt that it would better serve the new strategy formulated for the corporation's direction during the ensuing years.[6] The 3M Corporation also has been structured by its top management to be what the company's 1974 advertising describes as a lot of small companies having "the kind of climate

---

[6] "Dennison Manufacturing Company (A) and (B)" Cases, Intercollegiate Case Clearinghouse, Harvard Business School, Boston, Mass.

that grows good products." This company's strategy focuses on new product development and the management believes this strategy is best achieved with a highly decentralized organization.

ORGANIZATIONAL BEHAVIOR AND STRATEGY IMPLEMENTATION

If organizational commitment to a strategy is to be attained, the organization's members must subscribe reasonably well to the visible aspects of the strategy; those elements of the objectives, plans, and policies that are apparent and visible to them, and which individuals are able to influence by their activities. Without going into a lengthy consideration of human behavior and organizational theory, it is obvious that managers must deal extensively in this very complex area. In earlier chapters, it was suggested that strategy be formulated with consideration given to the values and objectives of various interest groups, but these can often be in conflict with one another. Herbert Simon has viewed organization as the complex pattern of communications and other relations in a group of human beings, each member having assumptions, goals, and attitudes which enter his decisions.[7] This perspective emphasizes the role of individuals in the organization, and it is the complexity of individual and group behavior that makes management and administration a most challenging art.

Chester Barnard emphasized essentially the same points in stating that an organization is a composition of "cooperative acts" and concluded that a manager cannot deal effectively with people without knowing their points of view and the influences that govern their behavior.[8] It is enough at this point to state that the behavioral aspect of organizations must always remain important to the strategic process, during both the formulation and implementation phases. If behavioral considerations have been included during strategy formulation, they can be built upon during implementation. If they have been ignored earlier, the job of implementing strategy can hardly be accomplished well.

Referring again to the Dennison Company, top management was aware of and took seriously the people in the organization, both when it defined its strategy and during the implementation phase. Recognizing the difficulty which many long-time managers and employees would have in undertaking and accepting the new strategy, as well as in working within a dramatically different structure and organizational climate, top management introduced both the new strategy and the related structure over a fairly lengthy period. It was almost ten years in developing both

---

[7] Herbert A. Simon, *Administrative Behavior* (New York: The Free Press, 1965), p. xvi of Introduction.

[8] Chester I. Barnard, *Organization and Management* (Cambridge, Mass.: Harvard University Press, 1948), pp. 115–18.

the strategy and structure to a stage entirely different from the situation of the mid-1950s. Although this may not have been an ideal approach, management was well aware of the behavioral consequences of their actions and acted cautiously as they implemented the new strategy.

THE PROCESS OF ORGANIZING: A DILEMMA IN IMPLEMENTING ORGANIZATIONAL STRATEGY

A dilemma in organizing often arises. Strategy's role is to guide the organization as a totality. Yet, the organization seemingly ceases to operate as a "totality" as soon as it moves beyond a very small size and authority and responsibility are dispersed among members. Strategy must be implemented through the process of organizing the institution in a manner that best serves to accomplish the strategy. Although this accomplishment is the basic objective of organizing, the organizational process establishes subgroups composed of departments, divisions, groups, and others which may have or may develop their own sets of goals and objectives which often are not congruent with those of the overall organization. If strategy is to be implemented successfully, organizing is necessary, but ironically, it also develops many problems and limitations to the accomplishment of the strategy.

Breaking down the Tasks to Be Performed

"Basically, organization is dividing up work to achieve the short and long term goals of the enterprise. It includes the development of people and must be related to profits and other goals. But basically, it is dividing up the work."[9] As any entity grows in size and complexity, the things to be done to achieve objectives and implement strategy grow beyond the limits of one or two people. The larger the volume of work and the more varied the activities involved, the larger and more complex becomes the job of getting things done. As the leaders begin to break down the total job into parts and assign these to individuals, the process of organizing begins. It continues through the life of an organization as it grows and changes, if the organization and its leaders are responsive managers.

Coordination toward the Overall Goal

It is inherent in the function of organizing that in addition to breaking down and subdividing tasks into a network of role prescriptions for individual positions, it is also necessary to coordinate and pull together these

---

[9] William F. Glueck, *Organization Planning and Development*, Research Study 106 (New York: American Management Association, Inc., 1971), p. 11.

subdivided positions or groups of positions and roles, in order that the overall good of the institution be served: this as opposed to the divided interests of the subareas. Yet, the very act of organizing toward the achievement of organizational goals and strategy, contains in the process the seeds for activity on the part of organizational members which may be contrary to the goals of the organization. This situation is one important reason that the behavioral school of thought emerged in the field of organizational theory with its vital implications for the manager or student interested in strategy.

Dilemmas and Some Examples

Dilemmas are well documented by March and Simon who, in researching the work of various students of structured or bureaucratic organizations, concluded that these forms "contain important dysfunctional consequences," as well as "consequences anticipated by the organizational leaders." March and Simon note that the organization structure and particularly a "demand for control . . . made upon the organization by the top hierarchy . . . takes the form of an increased emphasis on the reliability of behavior . . . within the organization. . . . There is a reduction in the amount of personalized relationships. . . . The bureaucracy is a set of relationships between offices, or roles. . . . [This phenomenon] facilitates the development of an esprit de corps—that is, increases the extent to which goals are perceived as shared among members of the group. Seeking a commonness of purpose, interests, and character increases the propensity of the members of the organization to defend each other against outside pressures. . . . Thus it meets an important maintenance need of the system." But another unanticipated consequence also emerges which is dysfunctional to the goals of the organization as noted in the following statement: ". . . the rigidity of behavior increases the amount of difficulty with clients . . . of the organization . . . and complicates the achievement of client satisfaction—a near universal organizational goal."[10] Noting the strategic importance ascribed earlier in this book to the client or customer, the conclusion reached by March and Simon has major importance when establishing organizational design and controls. The implementation of strategy, in addition to recognizing the possible effects of organizational design decisions on institutional members, must also provide for the direct and indirect effects on customers. The management of Aerosol Techniques, Inc., for example, organized the R.&D. effort in such a way as to max-

---

[10] James G. March, and Herbert A. Simon, *Organization* (New York: John Wiley & Sons, Inc., 1958). The quotes contained in this chapter may be found within pages 36–47.

imize communications with its marketing groups and even with its customers in order to prevent internal interests and values from dominating the firm's efforts in research and development.[11]

In their work, March and Simon emphasize the dysfunctional consequences of delegation, one of the basic activities of organizing. Allowing that in some ways, "delegation tends to decrease the difference between organizational goals and achievement, . . . at the same time delegation results in departmentation and an increase in the bifurcation of interests . . . among the sub-units in the organization. . . . The maintenance needs of the sub-units dictate a committment to the sub-unit goals over and above their contribution to the total organizational program. . . . The bifurcation within the organization leads to increased conflict among organizational sub-units . . . as a consequence, the content of decisions . . . made within the organization depends increasingly upon considerations of internal strategy, particularly if there is little internalization of organizational goals by participants . . . as a result there is an increase in the difference between organizational goals and achievement . . ." An example of this problem occurred in the Dennison Company situation discussed earlier, when two division managers were unable to agree upon which division should sell a particular product to the firm's customers, how a limited supply of product should be allocated between the two divisions, or how transfer prices should be arranged. In this case, the two managers were interested more in their own profit performance (and bonuses) than in the overall corporate achievements.[12]

March and Simon, then, utilize the research of organizational students to show how organizing in the formal sense contains within it the potential for behavior dysfunctional to the achievement of organizational objectives and strategy, and that this condition is exaggerated when there is little internalization of organizational goals. These two conclusions are especially important to both the formulation and implementation of strategy. They serve to emphasize the dilemmas of managers in organizing to implement a strategy for the organization, but further they emphasize that a strategy, or at least objectives, must be formulated and communicated to the organization, and be accepted by members, if there is to be effective organizational guidance through the process of organizing.

For the student and manager interested in policy and strategy, these dilemmas dictate an understanding of organization on the part of anyone who would formulate or implement strategy for the benefit of the total

---

[11] "Aerosol Techniques, Inc." Case, Intercollegiate Case Clearinghouse, Harvard Business School, Boston, Mass.

[12] "Dennison Manufacturing Company (C)" Case, Intercollegiate Case Clearinghouse, Harvard Business School, Boston, Mass.

organization. Some key conclusions about the relationships between strategy and organization, which will aid strategists are summarized below and are amplified in the following pages.

1. Strategists must understand the "dilemmas" referred to earlier.
2. They must have in mind an organizational structure which can best serve their strategy.
3. They must understand the behavioral consequences within the organization (as well as outside) of strategic decisions.
4. They must analyze the present organization, its structure, and its people to determine whether these support their strategy, or whether revisions are required in these organizational elements.
5. They must determine whether a new strategy, or a changed one, can be implemented without a major change in personnel.
6. They must implement a strategy by structuring the organization and affecting the behavior of individuals and groups in ways which will best bring about the achievement of overall plans, policies and objectives.

Other Elements of the Process

It should be helpful to analyze further Chandler's definition of "structure" in order to understand the major components within organizational structure, and other elements of the organizing process. Chandler spoke of organizational design (whether formally or informally defined) and its two components; first, the lines of authority and communication; second, the information that flows through these lines. Other elements of the organizing process described earlier were the breaking down of the whole task into a complex of role prescriptions or offices, and the coordination of the various parts toward the end of achieving the overall objectives of the organization.

A full consideration of organization and the process of organizing, however, must exceed Chandler's definition of "structure," and include more elements involved in the organizational side of strategy. Organizational planning and organizational development are two such important elements. "Organizational planning is involved with reviewing and evaluating, on a continuing basis, all organization entities to determine whether the missions, structures, functions, and responsibility relationships are clearly defined and understood and effectively coordinated to facilitate the overall objectives of the company. Organization development is providing counsel and guidance that aid and encourage management to develop and clarify its organizational missions; to delineate and effectively group the work to be performed; and to clarify and resolve responsibility relationships that will enable both the organization and its people to realize their mutual objectives. In summary, organizational planning is an approach to organizational problems that places primary emphasis on structured activities and formal analysis of the structure as a way to improve or maintain an effective organization for the company. Organization development is an approach to organization problems that places primary emphasis on behavioral or people activities in attempting to integrate the informal and formal organizations for corporate effectiveness."[13] Our concern with the totality of these ideas is inescapable given the dilemmas described earlier. The organizational strategist must continually deal in both the areas of organizational planning and development since each is so vital to the successful implementation of an organization's strategy. Focusing on one without the other diminishes seriously the opportunity to make strategy a really effective guide for the organization.

Principles and Situational Analysis

The classical view of organizations emphasized organizational planning which involves breaking down the total job into various tasks, positions, offices, or role prescriptions, which together constitute much of the subject known as formal organizations. Included in these broader categories are topics such as departmentation, centralization and decentralization of authority, delegation of authority, horizontal and vertical structure, line and staff positions, formal lines of authority and communication, and span of control or supervision. Additionally, various coordinative elements are emphasized such as communication, supervision, organization charts, and committees. In more recent times, project management and matrix type organization forms have emerged.

Most of the early ideas were put forward as "principles" in the classic work of Mooney and Reiley in the late 1930s. Two major assumptions behind the "principles" espoused were that organizing was an orderly and rational process which preceded administration, and emphasized that administration dealt with humans and human behavior. In short, the human behavioral aspects seemed to be separated from the structural aspects when discussing the process of organizing; this in spite of their definition of organization as "the form of every human association for the attainment of a common purpose."[14] Their second major assumption was that authority rests on moral rights, and is the coordinating power in organizations. The limitations of these "principles" were recognized by some, particularly Chester Barnard, who had fostered such ideas as informal organizations as early as 1938 in his work, *The Functions of the*

---

[13] Glueck, *Organization Planning and Development*, pp. 10–11.

[14] J. D. Mooney, and A. C. Reiley, *The Principle of Organization* (New York: Harper & Brothers, 1939), pp. 1–10.

Executive.[15] He further proffered the view of authority which states that *effective* authority lies within the person to whom a communication or directive is aimed, rather than resting in the one doing the directing. These views of Barnard's have greatly influenced organization-oriented thinking since, and have been very influential in the behavioral theory of organizations which focuses upon the individual and groups, and their behavior in organizations, as well upon as the objectives, needs, and satisfactions of these people.

But even in the relatively flexible thinking espoused in behavioral theory of organizations, principles or panaceas are sometimes put forth and overdone, just as was true of the classical schools of organizational theory. This point has been thought-provokingly expressed as follows: "Blind reverence for principle in organization planning is not confined in the classical school of thought which considers organizations as mechanisms for the accomplishment of work. Much the same approach can be taken with equally as unfortunate results by proponents of the more contemporary theoretical approaches, such as these: The behavioral science school, which sees organizations in terms of the interactions of individuals and groups, takes personal development and satisfaction as its key parameters, and often seeks to remove structural constraints on this fulfillment."[16] We agree that there is danger in blind adherence to principles, rather than developing theories and frameworks for use in analyzing situations, followed by employing sound analysis and decision making in these situations. Students or manager strategists must be cognizant of generally accepted ideas in the field of organization, but must analyze and act within individual situations utilizing their background, experience, and knowledge as appropriate in each situation. Many would agree with the president of a small company who felt that the feelings of nobody should be spared in his company when he assumed the job because the company was on the verge of bankruptcy, and no one would have a job unless drastic and impersonal actions were immediately taken. In such crisis situations, strategy implementation for survival may well ignore many behavioral lessons that are very appropriate in less critical circumstances.

Communications and Information

Regardless of the particular school or theory, most writers on organization have emphasized the necessity for good communications in organizations. Although early emphasis stressed formal channels, more

---

[15] Barnard, *The Functions of the Executive.*

[16] D. Ronald Daniel, "Reorganizing for Results," *Harvard Business Review,* November–December 1966, p. 97.

recent attention has been aimed at both the formal and the informal communications as vital to understanding organizational processes. As mentioned earlier, Barnard recognizes the maintenance of a system of communication as one of the three basic functions of the executive. Indeed, the very fact that organizations are made up of various subgroups necessitates the establishment of a system of communication and information flows. The formal organization utilizes the formal lines of authority as the basis of the communications network but most writers and managers now also recognize the vital role of the informal channels.

If the work of the organization is to be accomplished and coordinated, information must flow in order that organizational members know the goals, strategy, and all else that they need to know if they are to perform in their own roles for the attainment of organizational aims. The planning and control system described in subsequent chapters is a major element of the formal information network in organizations. It communicates much of what is to be done, by whom, and when; as well as whether things are accomplished and how well: further, this system is often linked to the rewards and negative motivators associated with performance or the lack of it. All of these topics are covered more fully in the next two chapters.

ANALYZING AND CHANGING ORGANIZATIONS: A CHALLENGE IN STRATEGY IMPLEMENTATION

Emphasis on the "Going Concern"

At the beginning of the previous chapter, it was noted that the usual interest of most managers and students is the going concern, and thus an existing situation, strategy, and organization. Consistent with this perspective, we concentrate here on existing organizations and upon analyzing and changing such organizations. This section of the chapter, with previous discussion as background information, looks at organizations from the particular view of the student analyzing an organization to suggest changes, or the manager doing the same thing in the performance of his managerial role.

Structural Aspects of Change

The concern with changing organizations is widespread because of the rapid change in all aspects of organizational environments, the natural growth of organizations, and the development of new ideas in organizational theory. Likewise, a change in strategy often requires drastic or some lesser change in the organization's structure, behavior, or both. One noted scholar discusses these aspects while emphasizing the necessity to adapt structure to changing environmental factors. "The business planner who seeks to structure the internal organization of his company in support of its objectives and strategy must deal not only with the numerous large-scale questions previously outlined, but also with more mundane technical and economic problems. As a practical matter he deals with technological change and with economics almost simultaneously. We list below a few of the technical and economic factors that management must take into account in adjusting organizations to strategic considerations."[17] Learned then mentions product development, how customers want to buy, legalistic implications, risk, and personal factors as various subjects which affect structure as well as strategy.

Another writer also relates the structure to the strategy of the organization, emphasizing the future, but he adds a most important idea when he proposes that the "right" structure may differ from the "ideal" structure (ideal in relationship to the strategy), because of the realities of the existing organizational situation. "This key input includes the entire range of 'givens' that add up to the current situation of the enterprise. The givens that will influence organization design can be considered as (a) present structure, (b) present style of leadership, (c) present managerial processes, and (d) present manpower resources. Together they define the position from which any changes must begin. Any or all of them may call for modifying the ideal structure into some different form that is more feasible to attain and more likely to be successful."[18] This statement articulates a most important dimension to the proposition of changing organizations to follow strategy; the view that an ideal structure (relative to the strategy) is not always a realistic change for an organization.

Learned makes essentially the same point: "The design of organizational structure for effective implementation of strategy requires some examination of personal factors. Implicit in the task of building an organization is the task of assigning and developing personnel. Rarely do the 'on hand' strengths and the readily obtainable people exactly match the logical requirements for tasks and job descriptions. Thus, management faces the age-old problem of adapting or restructuring the organization around the strengths and limitations of the individuals available. Few ideal organizations exist because of this manning problem."[19]

Thus the student in his analysis evaluates the situation and the management, and recommends actions, but in so doing must recognize the limitations to ideal solutions described above. The manager seeking to change organizational structure must also recognize these factors as

---

[17] Edmund P. Learned, "Organization and Strategy," International Case Clearinghouse, Harvard Business School, 1965, p. 10.

[18] Daniel, "Reorganizing for Results," p. 101.

[19] Learned, "Organization and Strategy," p. 12.

limitations to his views of an ideal structure. Although the strategy of the organization should be the basic guide to the development of the organizational form, the resulting ideal structure must be modified by the realities of the particular situation at hand. The management of the Dennison Manufacturing Company recognized these limitations as noted above. They tempered both the strategy and the implementation of it, in recognition of the human resources available and the management's own sense of responsibility to its employees which derived from the personal values of the management.[20]

In making an analysis, it is helpful to see how the organization's management goes about changing or attempting to change the organization. The analyst should note whether there is any formal mechanism, group, or individual assigned the task of evaluating the organization in light of changing conditions as described earlier in this chapter? Many large organizations have formed organization planning and development departments since the late 1950s. One study noted that the chief executive and the board of directors can get advice and information in this vital area from many sources including the specialized departments just mentioned. The study also suggests that important information can come from those who will be affected by change, and also from consultants. In introducing change, Smith presents the following as desirable approaches to changing organizations: (a) experimenting with individual units as pilots; (b) explaining the revised organization chart to subordinates; (c) recognizing and coping with the expected resistance to change; (d) carefully determining the pace of change; and (e) preserving an experimental attitude or climate in the organization.[21] In analyzing situations, it is appropriate to determine whether any such aids and techniques are available for use by the management of the organization, or whether they should be.

Behavioral Aspects of Change

Although the previous areas suggested for analysis did recognize the importance of individuals in organizational change, behaviorists would pay much more attention to those aspects dealing with individuals, groups, and the effects of change on behavior, rather than to the structure which has been the major focus of much of this section. There is no intent here to minimize the importance of the behavioral aspects, but it is difficult to present clearly all areas at once. It is the behavior of individuals that ultimately determines the success or failure of organizational en-

---

[20] "Dennison Manufacturing Company (A) and (B)" Cases.

[21] G. A. Smith, *Managing Geographically Decentralized Companies* (Boston: Harvard Business School Division of Research, 1958), pp. 141–55.

deavors. Top management concerned with strategy and its implementation must realize this. Learned's work summarized well many propositions concerning people in organizations. Their importance in effecting real change in an organization, to implement a strategy, becomes self-evident upon study of his remarks.

> The impact of people on organizations and organizations on people are topics far too broad to summarize here. Even so, it seems useful at this point to highlight some general propositions in this area that may be useful in the analysis of a particular company's situation: (1) the cooperation of management units and of the people in each is essential to the achievement of organization purposes; (2) the purpose of formal organizations is to provide a framework for cooperation and to fix responsibilities, delineate authority and provide for accountability; (3) the informal organization with its non-prescribed relationships and *de facto loci* of influence and power, is another important factor in determining success or failure; (4) the varied motivations, activities, interactions, attitudes, and values of members of the organization frequently give rise to goal conflicts, with individuals and sub-groups diverging from one another and from overall company objectives; (5) despite their high potential for conflict, organization members also manifest a drive for orderly relationships; thus people in organizations, at various levels of management or at the working level, like to know for what they are responsible, to whom they are responsible, and by what standards their work is to be judged; (6) many people believe that their intimate familiarity with their jobs gives them a degree of expertness about the job that might be utilized by management in organizing and operating the enterprise; and (7) lower echelon personnel quite generally realize they have a need for certain types of direction from higher levels. They will seek it out if it is not provided and they will resent unnecessary delays in meeting their needs.[22]

Perception of the informal organization as inevitable and even necessary to the successful functioning of the formal organization is recognized by many writers. One has noted: "The term 'informal organization' refers to interpersonal relations in the organization that affect decisions within it but either are omitted from the formal scheme or are not consistent with that scheme. It would probably be fair to say that no formal organization will operate effectively without an accompanying informal organization."[23] The president of a relatively small company producing relays and other control mechanisms utilized an informal organization to a high degree.[24] Although it was not clear in this situation why the president

---

[22] Learned, "Organization and Strategy," pp. 3–4.

[23] Simon, *Administrative Behavior*, p. 148.

[24] "Patterson & Swift, Inc." Case, Intercollegiate Case Clearinghouse, Harvard Business School, Boston, Mass.

did not change the formal organization to conform more to the reality of the informal one, it may be that he recognized many of the problems mentioned in this chapter that can be encountered in changing organizational structure. For these or other reasons, he preferred in most cases to leave the formal organization as it was, but recognized that the informal organization was functioning effectively in carrying out the strategy of the company. He apparently was less interested in formal structure and more in actual behavior and in the results achieved. In a company as small as his, this approach seemed to function well enough but was not without problems. How this approach would work in another situation is not at all clear, but it is doubtful if this approach would be effective in a large organization because of the difficulty the president would have tying into the informal network.

Need to Consider All Aspects When Implementing or Formulating Strategy

In our view, then, a thorough analysis of the organizational situation, or a plan to change the organization, calls for attention to be devoted to both the structural aspects of the organization, and the behavioral. In some cases, a decision may be made to keep the organization as it is, after analysis has indicated that such a course is best under the circumstances. In other situations, changes may be called for. Only a thorough review of both the structural and behavioral organizational aspects will encompass the overall organizational situation in enough depth to reach valid conclusions about the organization and its appropriateness for attaining objectives and strategy, and whether thought should be given to changing the present organizational structure and behavior. This deep understanding of organizations is required of organizational strategists who would change or modify strategy, as well as of students who would analyze organizational situations. Since it is a proposition of this chapter and book that organization structure and behavior should be in accord with the strategy, a change in strategy often necessitates modification or change in the organization. Thus management cannot engage in developing and changing strategy without understanding and preparing for ensuing changes in the organization.

Members of nonprofit organizations must also see the relationship between strategy and structure. The Catholic Church changed policies and some objectives in the 1960s during its second Vatican Council. The changes were seen by many as requiring detailed explanation and clarification to the millions of members of this worldwide organization, if the changes were to be understood, and if the changed strategy was to be implemented. This was thought to be needed because the Catholic Church's policies and objectives had been especially stable for years.

Some members argued for revisions in organizational structure to better communicate and effectuate strategy changes. No such formal organizational changes were forthcoming and many believed that confusion and misunderstanding resulted because the new and more complex strategy was not accompanied by formal organizational change which might have smoothed the transition. During the ensuing years, some clergy developed informal channels and organizational elements which did not always lead to the achievement of the formal organizational goals. Such problems can often be prevented if managers recognize and deal with the relationships between strategy and its implementation.

The central concern of policy is inextricably tied to change and to planning for continuously improving performance. But policy makers, while stressing clearly that growth and change should be planned and controlled, often underemphasize the purely organizational considerations of growth and change. In light of the previous paragraphs, however, it is clear that strategy development must be undertaken with implementation always in mind. To change the strategy is not necessarily a useful practice regardless of the logic or merits of the change, unless there is reason to believe that it can and will be implemented in a reasonable time frame through organizational change and development, and this takes management's involvement and effort from the outset. "Where organizational change has successfully influenced behavior, it is a safe bet that considerable thought has been given to the steps involved in implementation—announcing the changes, realigning executive personnel, timing the various moves, and securing the participation of those affected as a means of building understanding, acceptance, and commitment."[25] Again in this statement, the management's task of securing effective organizational change is put forth as a complex and difficult process. Yet, we recognize it as vital to the strategists who would successfully implement new or changed strategy in an organization.

IMPLEMENTATION, INTERRELATIONSHIPS, AND LEADERSHIP

The analysts or managers, if either are to do well in their job, must understand the complexity of the subject with which they are involved. To manage effectively, they must understand the interrelationships involved. In short, they must have an understanding of a framework useful to their tasks. Then practice will sharpen their skills in the utilization of that framework. It is the purpose of this book to provide that framework in the concept of corporate strategy. This chapter serves as the bridge between strategy development or modification, and the implementation of

---

[25] Daniel, "Reorganizing for Results," p. 99.

planned strategy, and emphasizes the idea that implementation usually follows formulation in what is essentially a continuous process. Organizational structure and behavior are recognized as critical, and as the prime vehicles for strategy implementation.

But in addition to following the strategy development phase, organizational considerations precede and largely set the stage for and influence greatly all other elements of the implementation phase. Included among these elements are the planning and control system including the rewards and negative motivators utilized within the organization, and other aspects of the administrative process involved in directing the efforts of the organization. All such administrative activity must be attentive to the behavioral aspects put forth in these pages, as well as to the more formal and logical elements of administering the organization. Exhibit 7–1 is an illustration of a framework which depicts the relationships described in this chapter. Although we have emphasized that organizational structure normally follows from the strategy, the more important point is that the structure should support the organizational strategy. In some cases, the structure of the organization may limit the strategies that may be undertaken, and conditions may make changes in the structure unfeasible. In other cases, the structure itself may be a resource that opens strategic opportunities to the organization. Both of these circumstances are noted in an important work dealing with the relationships between strategy and structure in multinational organizations.

> Organizations that have a single or a few related product lines and a high degree of vertical integration tend to be capital intensive, and to be organized in a centralized, functionally departmentalized structure. Organizations that have a diversified product line tend to have a decentralized divisional structure. This paper indicates that the first type tends to concentrate on domestic markets, while the second type accounts for most of U.S. direct investment abroad. Expansion abroad requires diversification, reorganization, and the training of general international managers. The evidence suggests that the organizations that have been most successful in meeting this new challenge have been those that had previously acquired the ability to develop general managers capable of controlling and guiding a heterogeneous, diverse enterprise.[26]

At this point, some specific recognition should be given to the role of leadership in organizations. The importance of that somewhat magical quality and force in the development of strategy has been emphasized earlier in this book and is evident from the central position afforded it in Exhibit 7–1. The leadership required in understanding and implementing organizational change has also been implicitly considered in this chapter.

---

[26] L. E. Fouraker, and J. M. Stopford, "Organizational Structure and the Multinational Strategy," *Administrative Science Quarterly*, vol. 13 (1968), p. 47.

EXHIBIT 7–1
Strategy Design and Implementation: Interrelationship of Elements

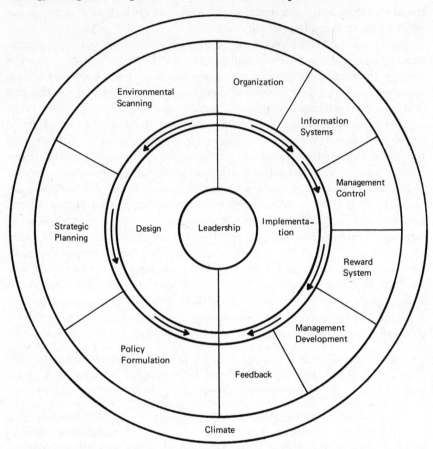

Source: Robert H. Caplan III, *Corporate Strategy: Design and Implementation* (*A Slide Presentation*) (Boston: Northeastern University, 1972).

"Leadership," which Barnard defines as "the quality of the behavior of individuals whereby they guide people or their activities in organized effort,"[27] encompasses the qualities required to participate in the entire strategic process; both in the formulation and implementation phases. Barnard has defined the four areas of leadership behavior as the determination of objectives, the manipulation of means, the control of the instrumentality of action, and the stimulation of coordinated action.[28] These tasks closely parallel the elements that comprise strategy development and implementation as developed in this book.

---

[27] Barnard, *Organization and Management*, p. 83.
[28] Ibid., pp. 85–91.

While the chief executive and/or other top managers may not individually be the ideal leader(s) in all aspects of the strategic process, they must collectively exhibit the necessary qualities of leadership in all areas of the process. This requirement encompasses a wide range of skills and abilities which seldom are to be found in one individual. But it remains for the chief executive and board of directors to ensure that all of the necessary qualities of leadership are found in sufficient quantity in the organization, to facilitate its survival and health as an entity. This crucial task of staffing the organization is facilitated if the concept of strategy and its implications are understood at the top level of the organization. If such awareness is present, the needs of the organization become clear and the task of filling those needs becomes more manageable.

Thus, the major leader or chief executive may exercise his influence in various ways depending upon him and upon the organization with which he is involved, as well as upon the particular situation facing him and the organization at the time. One leader, for instance, may focus on strategy development or more particularly upon the environment of the organization, while another or the same individual under other circumstances, may focus upon the internal aspect of organizing or changing the organization. But usually, the chief executive must lead in all phases of the strategy. At the least, he must be aware of and supportive of necessary action in all phases of the strategic process given conditions, barriers, and opportunities, not all at once necessarily but often it must appear to be so to the leaders of many organizations. Without attempting to cover the seemingly unlimited qualities and attributes required of effective leaders in organizations, we can say that effectiveness may come from filling different roles in different situations. This important topic is presented in an interesting and provocative article which highlights the need for new leadership style as situations change.[29]

Leadership style, although analyzed incessantly, emerges as a personal thing. Some leaders will be effective in ways that would spell failure for others. Understanding the concept of strategy, however, will clarify for any leaders the necessary elements of the total managerial task. Based upon this understanding, they can undertake the leadership role with an increased potential for success through the exercise of their own style of leadership.

SUMMARY

This chapter has emphasized the idea that organizational structure and behavior within organizations should be in harmony with and supportive of the strategy of the organization. It was recognized also, that the

---

[29] Robert Mainer, "The Case of the Stymied Strategist," *Harvard Business Review,* May–June 1968.

organization which would be most ideal for a particular strategy often is unrealistic given the human and other resource constraints of the organization. It is a major advantage for managers to understand and utilize a strategic framework to aid them in the implementation of strategy, and in its development. As such, they will deal with organizational situations from a point of view which encompasses all organizational realities and ties them together in a logical form. Beginning with an understanding of the various elements of strategy and its implementation, they will be better able to pursue courses of action which will lead the organization toward the achievement of its objectives.

The remaining chapters will deal further with the implementation of strategy and, while they emphasize the planning and control process, the importance of leadership will remain apparent. Further, the relationships of planning, control, and motivational aspects to the organizing process will be emphasized. These should stem from the organizational structure and its related communication and information flows, and thus are also dependent upon the behavioral climate of an organization.

18. Strategy and Structure ("Some General Propositions")[*]

ALFRED D. CHANDLER, JR.

SOME GENERAL PROPOSITIONS

IF USEFUL COMPARISONS are to be made among four companies and then fourscore more, and if decisions and actions in these firms are to indicate something about the history of the industrial enterprise as an institution, the terms and concepts used in these comparisons and analyses must be carefully and precisely defined. Otherwise comparisons and findings can be more misleading than instructive. The following set of general or theoretical propositions attempts to provide some sort of conceptual precision. Without reference to historical reality, they try to explain in fairly clear-cut, oversimplified terms how the modern, "decentralized" structure came into being.

Before developing these propositions, the term *industrial enterprise* needs to be defined. Used in a broad sense, it means here a large private, profit-oriented business firm involved in the handling of goods in some or all of the successive industrial processes from the procurement of the raw material to the sale to the ultimate customer. Transportation enterprises, utilities, or purely financial companies are not then included in this study, while those firms concerned with marketing and with the extraction of raw materials as well as those dealing with processing or manufacturing do fall within this definition. An industrial enterprise is thus a subspecies of what Werner Sombart has described as the capitalistic enterprise, which as "an independent economic organism is created over and

---

[*] From the "Introduction," to *Strategy and Structure*, by Alfred D. Chandler, Jr. (Cambridge, Mass.: The M.I.T. Press, 1962) (Doubleday Edition, 1966, pp. 8–21). Copyright © by Massachusetts Institute of Technology; all rights reserved. Reprinted by permission.

above the individuals who constitute it. This entity appears then as the agent in each of these transactions and leads, as it were, a life of its own, which often exceeds in length that of its human members."

While the enterprise may have a life of its own, its present health and future growth surely depend on the individuals who guide its activities. Just what, then, are the functions of the executives responsible for the fortunes of the enterprise? They coordinate, appraise, and plan. They may, at the same time, do the actual buying, selling, advertising, accounting, manufacturing, engineering, or research, but in the modern enterprise the execution or carrying out of these functions is usually left to such employees as salesmen, buyers, production supervisors and foremen, technicians, and designers. In many cases, the executive does not even personally supervise the working force but rather administers the duties of other executives. In planning and coordinating the work of subordinate managers or supervisors, he allocates tasks and makes available the necessary equipment, materials, and other physical resources necessary to carry out the various jobs. In appraising their activities, he must decide whether the employees or subordinate managers are handling their tasks satisfactorily. If not, he can take action by changing or bringing in new physical equipment and supplies, by transferring or shifting the personnel, or by expanding or cutting down available funds. Thus, the term, *administration*, as used here, includes executive action and orders as well as the decisions taken in coordinating, appraising, and planning the work of the enterprise and in allocating its resources.

The initial proposition is, then, that administration is an identifiable activity, that it differs from the actual buying, selling, processing, or transporting of the goods, and that in the large industrial enterprise the concern of the executives is more with administration than with the performance of functional work. In a small firm, the same man or group of men buy materials, sell finished goods, and supervise manufacturing as well as coordinate, plan, and appraise these different functions. In a large company, however, administration usually becomes a specialized, full-time job. A second proposition is that the administrator must handle two types of administrative tasks when he is coordinating, appraising, and planning the activities of the enterprise. At times he must be concerned with the long-run health of his company, at other times with its smooth and efficient day-to-day operation. The first type of activity calls for concentration on long-term planning and appraisal, the second for meeting immediate problems and needs and for handling unexpected contingencies or crises. To be sure, in real life the distinction between these two types of activities or decisions is often not clear cut. Yet some decisions clearly deal very largely with defining basic goals and the course of action and procedures necessary to achieve these goals, while other decisions have more to do with the day-to-day operations carried out within the broader framework of goals, policies, and procedures.

The next few propositions deal with the content of administrative activities handled through the different types of posts or positions in the most complex administrative structures. The executives in a modern "decentralized" company carry out their administrative activities from four different types of positions (see Chart 1). Each of these types within the

CHART 1
The Multidivisional Structure

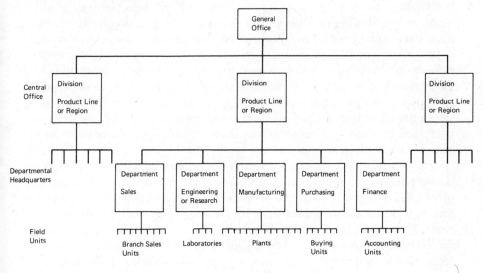

enterprise has a different range of administrative activities. Normally, each is on a different level of authority. At the top is a *general office*. There, general executives and staff specialists coordinate, appraise, and plan goals and policies and allocate resources for a number of quasi-autonomous, fairly self-contained divisions. Each division handles a major product line or carries on the firm's activities in one large geographical area. Each division's *central office,* in turn, administers a number of departments. Each of these departments is responsible for the administration of a major function—manufacturing, selling, purchasing or producing of raw materials, engineering, research, finance, and the like. The *departmental headquarters* in its turn coordinates, appraises, and plans for a number of field units. At the lowest level, each *field unit* runs a plant or works, a branch or district sales office, a purchasing office, an engineering or research laboratory, an accounting or other financial office, and the like. The four types of administrative positions in a large multidivisional enterprise are thus: the field unit, the departmental headquarters, the division's central office, and the general office. These terms are used throughout this study to designate a specific set of administrative activities. They do not, it should be stressed, refer to an enterprise's office buildings or rooms.

One office building could house executives responsible for any one of the positions or conceivably those responsible for all four. Conversely, the executives in any one of the posts could be housed in different rooms or buildings.

Only in the first, the field unit, are the managers primarily involved in carrying on or personally supervising day-to-day activities. Even here, if the volume of activity is large, they spend much of their time on administrative duties. But such duties are largely operational, carried out within the framework of policies and procedures set by departmental headquarters and the higher offices. The departmental and divisional offices may make some long-term decisions, but because their executives work within a comparable framework determined by the general office, their primary administrative activities also tend to be tactical or operational. The general office makes the broad strategic or entrepreneurial decisions as to policy and procedures and can do so largely because it has the final say in the allocation of the firm's resources—men, money, and materials— necessary to carry out these administrative decisions and actions and others made with its approval at any level.

It seems wise here to emphasize the distinction between the formulation of policies and procedures and their implementation. The formulation of policies and procedures can be defined as either strategic or tactical. *Strategic* decisions are concerned with the long-term health of the enterprise. *Tactical* decisions deal more with the day-to-day activities necessary for efficient and smooth operations. But decisions, either tactical or strategic, usually require *implementation* by an allocation or reallocation of resources—funds, equipment, or personnel. Strategic plans can be formulated from below, but normally the implementation of such proposals requires the resources which only the general office can provide. Within the broad policy lines laid down by that office and with the resources it allocates, the executives at the lower levels carry out tactical decisions.

The executives who actually allocate available resources are then the key men in any enterprise. Because of their critical role in the modern economy, they will be defined in this study as entrepreneurs. In contrast, those who coordinate, appraise, and plan within the means allocated to them will be termed managers. So *entrepreneurial* decisions and actions will refer to those which affect the allocation or reallocation of resources for the enterprise as a whole, and *operating* decisions and actions will refer to those which are carried out by using the resources already allocated.

Just because the entrepreneurs make some of the most significant decisions in the American economy, they are not all necessarily imbued with a long-term strategic outlook. In many enterprises the executives responsible for resource allocation may very well concentrate on day-to-day operational affairs, giving little or no attention to changing markets, technology, sources of supply, and other factors affecting the long-term health of their company. Their decisions may be made without forward planning or analysis but rather by meeting in an *ad hoc* way every new situation, problem, or crisis as it arises. They accept the goals of their enterprise as given or inherited. Clearly wherever entrepreneurs act like managers, wherever they concentrate on short-term activities to the exclusion or to the detriment of long-range planning, appraisal, and coordination, they have failed to carry out effectively their role in the economy as well as in their enterprise. This effectiveness should provide a useful criterion for evaluating the performance of an executive in American industry.

As already pointed out, executives in the large enterprise work in four types of offices, each with his own administrative duties, problems, and needs. The four types operate on different scales, and their officers have different business horizons. The managers in the field unit are concerned with one function—marketing, manufacturing, engineering, and so forth—in one local area. The executives in the departmental headquarters plan, administer, and coordinate the activities of one function on a broad regional and often national scale rather than just locally. Their professional activities and their outside sources of information concern men and institutions operating in the same specialized function. The divisional executives, on the other hand, deal with an industry rather than a function. They are concerned with all the functions involved in the over-all process of handling a line of products or services. Their professional horizons and contacts are determined by industry rather than functional interests. Finally, executives in the general office have to deal with several industries or one industry in several broad and different geographical regions. They set policies and procedures and allocate resources for divisions carrying out all types of functions, either in different geographical areas or in quite different product lines. Their business horizons and interests are broadened to range over national and even international economies.

While all four types of offices exist in the most complex of industrial enterprises, each can of course exist separately. An industrial enterprise can include one, two, three, or all four of these offices. Many small firms today have only a single office managing a single plant, store, laboratory, financial operation, or sales activity. Larger companies with a number of operating units carry out a single function—such as sales (wholesale or retail), manufacturing, purchasing, or engineering. Their overall administrative structure comprises a headquarters and field offices. So also today there are integrated industrial enterprises that handle several economic functions rather than just one. Finally, there are the great diversified industrial empires, carrying on different functions and producing a variety of goods and services in all parts of the globe.

Since each type of position handles a different range of administrative activities, each must have resulted from a different type of growth. Until the volume or technological complexity of an enterprise's economic activities had so grown as to demand an increasing division of labor within the firm, little time needed to be spent on administrative work. Then the resulting specialization required one or more of the firm's executives to concentrate on coordinating, appraising, and planning these specialized activities. When the enterprise expanded geographically by setting up or acquiring facilities and personnel distant from its original location, it had to create an organization at a central headquarters to administer the units in the field. When it grew by moving into new functions, a central office came to administer the departments carrying on the different functions. Such a central administrative unit proved necessary, for example, when in following the policy of vertical integration a manufacturing firm began to do its own wholesaling, procuring of supplies, and even producing raw materials. Finally, when an integrated enterprise became diversified through purchasing or creating new facilities and entered new lines of business, or when it expanded its several functional departments over a still larger geographical area, it fashioned a number of integrated divisional units administered by a general office.

The thesis that different organizational forms result from different types of growth can be stated more precisely if the planning and carrying out of such growth is considered a *strategy*, and the organization devised to administer these enlarged activities and resources, a *structure*. *Strategy* can be defined as the determination of the basic long-term goals and objectives of an enterprise, and the adoption of courses of action and the allocation of resources necessary for carrying out these goals. Decisions to expand the volume of activities, to set up distant plants and offices, to move into new economic functions, or become diversified along many lines of business involve the defining of new basic goals. New courses of action must be devised and resources allocated and reallocated in order to achieve these goals and to maintain and expand the firm's activities in the new areas in response to shifting demands, changing sources of supply, fluctuating economic conditions, new technological developments, and the actions of competitors. As the adoption of a new strategy may add new types of personnel and facilities, and alter the business horizons of the men responsible for the enterprise, it can have a profound effect on the form of its organization.

Structure can be defined as the design of organization through which the enterprise is administered. This design, whether formally or informally defined, has two aspects. It includes, first, the lines of authority and communication between the different administrative offices and officers and, second, the information and data that flow through these lines of communication and authority. Such lines and such data are essential to assure the effective coordination, appraisal, and planning so necessary in carrying out the basic goals and policies and in knitting together the total resources of the enterprise. These resources include financial capital; physical equipment such as plants, machinery, offices, warehouses, and other marketing and purchasing facilities, sources of raw materials, research and engineering laboratories; and, most important of all, the technical, marketing, and administrative skills of its personnel.

The thesis deduced from these several propositions is then that structure follows strategy and that the most complex type of structure is the result of the concatenation of several basic strategies. *Expansion of volume* led to the creation of an administrative office to handle one function in one local area. Growth through *geographical dispersion* brought the need for a departmental structure and headquarters to administer several local field units. The decision to expand into new types of functions called for the building of a central office and a multidepartmental structure, while the developing of new lines of products or continued growth on a national or international scale brought the formation of the multidivisional structure with a general office to administer the different divisions. For the purposes of this study, the move into new functions will be referred to as a strategy of *vertical integration* and that of the development of new products as a strategy of *diversification*.

This theoretical discussion can be carried a step further by asking two questions: (1) If structure does follow strategy, why should there be delay in developing the new organization needed to meet the administrative demands of the new strategy? (2) Why did the new strategy, which called for a change in structure, come in the first place?

There are at least two plausible answers to the first query. Either the administrative needs created by the new strategy were not positive or strong enough to require structural change, or the executives involved were unaware of the new needs. There seems to be no question that a new strategy created new administrative needs, for expansion through geographical dispersion, vertical integration, and product diversification added new resources, new activities, and an increasing number of entrepreneurial and operational actions and decisions. Nevertheless, executives could still continue to administer both the old and new activities with the same personnel, using the same channels of communication and authority and the same types of information. Such administration, however, must become increasingly inefficient. This proposition should be true for a relatively small firm whose structure consists of informal arrangements between a few executives as well as for a large one whose size and numerous administrative personnel require a more formal definition of relations between offices and officers. Since expansion created the need for new administrative offices and structures, the reasons for delays in developing the new organization rested with the executives responsible for the enterprise's long-range growth and health. Either these administrators were too involved in day-to-day tactical activities to appreciate or understand the longer-range organizational needs of their enterprises, or else their training and education failed to sharpen their perception of organizational problems or failed to develop their ability to handle them. They may also have resisted administratively desirable changes because they felt structural reorganization threatened their own personal position, their power, or most important of all, their psychological security.

In answer to the second question, changes in strategy which called for changes in structure appear to have been in response to the opportunities and needs created by changing population and changing national income and by technological innovation. Population growth, the shift from the country to the city and then to the suburb, depressions and prosperity, and the increasing pace of technological change, all created new demands or curtailed existing ones for a firm's goods or services. The prospect of a new market or the threatened loss of a current one stimulated geographical expansion, vertical integration, and product diversification. Moreover, once a firm had accumulated large resources, the need to keep its men, money, and materials steadily employed provided a constant stimulus to look for new markets by moving into new areas, by taking on new functions, or by developing new product lines. Again the awareness of the needs and opportunities created by the changing environment seems to have depended on the training and personality of individual executives and on their ability to keep their eyes on the more important entrepreneurial problems even in the midst of pressing operational needs.

The answers to the two questions can be briefly summarized by restating the general thesis. Strategic growth resulted from an awareness of the opportunities and needs—created by changing population, income, and technology—to employ existing or expanding resources more profitably. A new strategy required a new or at least refashioned structure if the enlarged enterprise was to be operated efficiently. The failure to develop a new internal structure, like the failure to respond to new external opportunities and needs, was a consequence of overconcentration on operational activities by the executives responsible for the destiny of their enterprises, or from their inability, because of past training and education and present position, to develop an entrepreneurial outlook.

One important corollary to this proposition is that growth without structural adjustment can lead only to economic inefficiency. Unless new structures are developed to meet new administrative needs which result from an expansion of a firm's activities into new areas, functions, or product lines, the technological, financial, and personnel economies of growth and size cannot be realized. Nor can the enlarged resources be employed as profitably as they otherwise might be. Without administrative offices and structure, the individual units within the enterprise (the field units, the departments, and the divisions) could undoubtedly operate as efficiently or even more so (in terms of cost per unit and volume of output per worker) as independent units than if they were part of a larger enterprise. Whenever the executives responsible for the firm fail to create the offices and structure necessary to bring together effectively the several administrative offices into a unified whole, they fail to carry out one of their basic economic roles.

The actual historical patterns of growth and organization building in the large industrial enterprise were not, of course, as clear-cut as they have been theoretically defined here. One strategy of expansion could be carried out in many ways, and often, two or three basic ways of expansion were undertaken at one and the same time. Growth might come through simultaneous building or buying of new facilities, and through purchasing or merging with other enterprises. Occasionally a firm simultaneously expanded its volume, built new facilities in geographically distant areas, moved into new functions, and developed a different type of product line. Structure, as the case studies indicate, was often slow to follow strategy, particularly in periods of rapid expansion. As a result, the distinctions between the duties of the different offices long remained confused and only vaguely defined. One executive or a small group of executives might carry out at one and the same time the functions of a general office, a central office, and a departmental headquarters. Eventually, however, most large corporations came to devise the specific units to handle a field unit, a functional department, an integrated division, or a diversified industrial empire. For this very reason, a clear-cut definition of structure and strategy and a simplified explanation or theory of the relation of one to the other should make it easier to comprehend the complex realities involved in the expansion and management of the great industrial enterprises studied here, and easier to evaluate the achievement of the organization builders.

A comparative analysis of organizational innovation demands, however, more than an explanation of the terms, concepts, and general propositions to be used in assessing comparable experiences of different enterprises. It also calls for an understanding of the larger historical situation, both within and without the firm, during which strategic expansion and organizational change took place. The executives at du Pont, General Motors, Jersey Standard, and Sears, Roebuck did not solve their administrative problems in a vacuum. Other large enterprises were meeting the same needs and challenges and seeking to resolve comparable administrative problems. Their responses had an impact on the history of these four companies, just as the experience of the four affected that of many others.

The administrative story in each of the case studies falls into two basic parts: the creation of the organizational structure after the enterprise's first major growth or corporate rebirth, and then its reorganization to meet the needs arising from the strategies of further expansion. In developing their early administrative structures, these four firms were following accepted practices in American industry. Here the organization builders could learn from others. In fashioning the modern, multidivisional structure, they were, on the other hand, going beyond existing practices. Here others learned from them. An evaluation of the measures each took to improve the administration of its business requires therefore some knowledge of the methods and practices of business administration at the time when each built its major structure and began the reorganization that led to the fashioning of the multidivisional form.

STUDENT REVIEW QUESTIONS

1. What is the major proposition that Chandler puts forth in his work?
2. What are the relationships among strategic decisions, tactical decisions, and implementation, according to Chandler?
3. Explain what Chandler means by the statement, "different organizational forms result from different types of growth."
4. Give an example to support the thesis noted in Question 3 above.
5. What happens if strategic growth on the part of an organization is not accompanied by adjustment of the organization's structure?
6. Discuss the organizational structure of one nonprofit organization and comment on whether you feel the structure supports the organization's strategy.

19. Organizational Structure and Multinational Strategy*

LAWRENCE E. FOURAKER and
JOHN M. STOPFORD

Organizations that have a single or a few related product lines and a high degree of vertical integration tend to be capital intensive, and to be organized in a centralized, functionally-departmentalized structure. Organizations that have a diversified product line tend to have a decentralized, divisional structure. This paper indicates that the first type tends to concentrate on domestic markets, while the second type accounts for most of U.S. direct investment abroad. Expansion abroad requires diversification, reorganization, and the training of general international managers. The evidence suggests that the organizations that have been most successful in meeting this new challenge have been those that had previously acquired the ability to develop general managers capable of controlling and guiding a heterogeneous, diverse enterprise.

ONE OF THE landmark studies in the field of business administration is *Strategy and Structure* by A. D. Chandler, Jr. A central proposition in Chandler's book is that the strategy of diversification led to organizational problems and eventually to the emergence of a new corporate structure. The purpose of this article is to see if Chandler's proposition is useful in examining recent organizational changes in the international field.[1]

* L. E. Fouraker and J. M. Stopford, "Organizational Structure and Multinational Strategy," *Administrative Science Quarterly*, vol. 13 (1968), pp. 47–64. Reprinted by permission of the publisher.

[1] A. D. Chandler, Jr., *Strategy and Structure* (Garden City, N.Y.: Anchor Books, 1966). We have received, and greatly appreciate, the help of J. Berman, C. R. Christensen, J. H. McArthur, B. R. Scott, and R. Vernon. This research was financed by a grant from the Ford Foundation for the study of the multinational corporation.

International business activity is a form of diversification that has become increasingly important for many large American companies in the last two decades. In some sense, this development may be considered a replication against which Chandler's thesis may be tested. That is, this new form of diversification should be dominated by firms with experience in managing diversified activities. Furthermore, the new diversification should lead to new problems of organization and, finally, to different structural accommodations.

MODEL

Chandler states: "Historically, the executives administering American industrial enterprises have followed a recognizable pattern in the acquisition and use of resources."[2] This process consists of a developmental transition through several distinct phases: "Thus four phases or chapters can be discerned in the history of the large American industrial enterprise: the initial expansion and accumulation of resources; the rationalization of the use of resources; the expansion into new markets and lines to help assure the continuing full use of resources; and finally the development of a new structure to make possible continuing effective mobilization of resources to meet both changing short-term market demands and long-term market trends."[3] These four phases produced three fairly distinct organizational structures:

Type I. The organization is an extension of the interests, abilities, and limitations of its chief executive, who is often the creator and owner of the organization. This structure is generally limited to a single product line and often emphasizes one function (e.g., production) more than others. It is also constrained by the sequential decision-making pattern that characterizes a single problem solver. This is the entrepreneurial business organization, which serves as a building block for most economic models.

Type II. This is the vertically integrated functionally coordinated enterprise. Generally such an organization continues to be limited to one or a few related product lines. The emphasis is on rational use of resources, efficiency, and coordination of functional activities.

> Yet the dominant centralized structure had one basic weakness. A very few men were still entrusted with a great number of complex decisions. The executives in the central office were usually the president with one or two assistants, sometimes the chairman of the board, and the vice-presidents who headed the various departments. The latter were often too busy with the administration of the particular function to devote much time to the affairs of the enterprise as a whole. Their training

---

2 Ibid., p. 478.
3 Ibid., p. 479.

proved a still more serious defect. Because these administrators had spent most of their business careers within a single functional activity, they had little experience or interest in understanding the needs and problems of other departments or of the corporation as a whole.[4]

The type II structure might be enormously efficient in the production of some classes of products, but did not produce professional management.

Type III. The accumulation of resources by a successful type II firm often led to diversification of product lines, (1) to avoid risk, (2) to ensure continuation of the organization after the major product had completed its life cycle, or (3) to sell outside the company by some divisions due to integrated production requiring plant facilities of varying capacities at different stages.

The strategy of product diversification caused many administrative problems. The functional approach of the type II firm required that the senior marketing executive coordinate the marketing activities for all the organization's products, even though they might utilize different forms of distribution, advertising, and sales effort. The senior production officer was confronted with similar complexity. These functional responsibilities could be delegated to subordinates, most appropriately on the basis of product assignments; but profit contribution of functional specialists could not be measured against performance, so control and comparison became even more difficult. The unavoidable problems of conflict and coordination at the lowest levels of the organization would frequently have to be passed up to the highest functional levels for adjudication. And some operating issues could not be settled there, but would have to reach the office of the chief executive.

Attempts to add product lines in such an environment could lead to organizational stasis because of the limited ability of the chief executive's office to cope with the new demands on its decision-making capacity. Management would then be confronted with a choice: either abandon the strategy of product diversification, or abandon the functional form of organization.

Many organizations chose structural reorganization. This reorganization took the form of a multidivisional product structure with many functional responsibilities delegated to the division general managers. The divisions were separated on a product basis and were relatively autonomous. Generally each division served as a profit center for control purposes; coordination and control from the central office was concentrated on finance and some general staff functions such as planning and research.

"Besides allocating decision making more effectively and assuring more precise communication and control, the new structure proved to

---

[4] Ibid., p. 50.

have another advantage over the functionally departmentalized organization. It provided a place to train and test general executives."[5] This ability to produce general managers allowed the type III organization to operate successfully in unrelated product areas.

With great diversity of products, staff, technologies, and managerial talents, the type III decentralized organization could move simultaneously to exploit opportunities in a variety of independent areas. The management innovation of moving from a type II structure to type III began, in the United States, in the 1920s. As is often the case,[6] the type III structure developed independently in several organizations; du Pont, General Motors, Standard Oil, and Sears are given special attention by Chandler. Many other organizations imitated these pioneers, with most of the transitions being delayed by the depression of the 1930s and World War II, so that many companies undertook the transition in both strategy and structure in the 1950s and 1960s.

In the type III organization, new products can be added, or old ones dropped, with only marginal effect on the organization. Indeed, given the prospect of finite life expectancy for any commercial product, the management is committed to a strategy of research and development as a means of ensuring the continued life of the organization. This sort of activity is compatible with the diversity and independence of parts in a type III organization. "In fact, the systematizing of strategic decisions through the building of a general office and the routinizing of product development by the formation of a research department have, in a sense, institutionalized this strategy of diversification."[7]

Since the type III organization makes it possible to manage a variety of heterogeneous activities, it also makes it feasible for research and development activity to be incorporated in the structure. Burns and Stalker, in a study of electronic firms in England and Scotland, found that certain types of business organizations did not develop research and development departments; such activity could not normally be absorbed by their "mechanistic" structures, which closely resembled Chandler's type II organizations.[8] The organizations that were successful in establishing research and development departments ("organic" structures) were described in terms that seem characteristic of Chandler's type III. These results are reinforced by the field work of Lawrence and Lorsch.[9]

This connection between research and development, product innova-

---

[5] Ibid., p. 385.

[6] A. L. Kroeber, *Anthropology: Race, Language, Culture, Psychology, Prehistory*, rev. ed. (New York: Harcourt, Brace and Company, 1948), pp. 445–72.

[7] Chandler, *Strategy and Structure*, p. 490.

[8] T. Burns and G. M. Stalker, *The Management of Innovation* (London: Tavistock, 1961).

[9] P. R. Lawrence and J. W. Lorsch, *Organization and Environment* (Boston: Division of Research, Harvard Business School, 1967).

tion, and organizational structure is important for the thesis of this paper, because the innovative capacity may be an important source of competitive advantage in foreign markets. Vernon and others have argued that the United States tends to export products developed for the U.S. market that are not being produced abroad, and this monopoly position in world markets offsets high labor costs in the United States.[10] Furthermore, at some point the organization will invest in plant and equipment abroad in order to protect its export market, particularly if that market has grown to a size that is consistent with the most efficient current productive techniques.

The result of this chain of arguments is that type III organizations can be expected to dominate foreign direct investment. The initial structural response to this strategy of diversifying direct investment around the world is to establish an international division in the type III organization. Such a division reports to one man. This focuses responsibility and control for foreign operations and economizes on the need for general managers with broad international experience (who are inevitably in short supply when the organization first expands its foreign operations).

The international division is at the same organizational level, and will tend to receive the same general treatment, as the product divisions. This same general treatment tends to create stresses that will make the international division a transient form. It is not a product division, but is rather less autonomous, for it depends more on the cooperation and assistance of the product divisions than they typically depend on each other. As a result, the product division manager is subjected to stresses and conflicts that are not always in the best interests of the organization. The product division manager, who is judged against domestic measures of performance, is therefore somewhat motivated to (1) fill his domestic orders before extending assistance to foreign markets; (2) assign his best employees to domestic tasks and shunt the orders to the international division; and (3) argue for a larger domestic share of the capital budget.

These are natural responses that may be quite costly if foreign markets are growing faster than domestic markets, which has often been the case in the postwar period. In many organizations, top management has responded to these lost opportunities in several ways. First, it has given product and functional managers more international experience and eventually more responsibility. Second, it has replaced the international division with some new organizational structure; for example, world-wide product divisions, world-partitioning geographic divisions, or some combination of these, perhaps retaining an international division for some

---

[10] R. Vernon, "International Investment and International Trade in the Product Cycle,"*Quarterly Journal of Economics,* vol. 80 (May 1966), pp. 190–207; C. P. Kindleberger, *The Dollar Shortage* (New York: John Wiley & Sons, Inc., 1950); Staffan Burenstam-Linder, *An Essay on Trade and Transformation* (Uppsala, Sweden: Almqvist & Wicksell, 1961).

purposes, or setting up a separate international company. Indeed some companies moved directly to these new structures, avoiding the problem of a conflict of interests between product divisions and the international division, and the possibility of a coalition of product divisions against the international division. This is most common where the vehicle for growth abroad has been merged with other organizations whose foreign interests are in different product lines.

Each of the possible alternative forms of the organization of international activities has distinct characteristics. The international division is the sole profit center for foreign operations, requiring only one general manager with international expertise. The manager of the international division and his staff become the repository of all the organization's international experience, causing problems of capital allocation, transfer pricing, and especially communication.

The world-wide product division structure avoids many of these problems by containing the areas of potential conflict within each division. The division manager is responsible for the profit performance of his product line throughout the world. This structure requires at least as many international general managers as there are product divisions operating abroad.

The geographic divisions partitioning the world also require an increased number of international general managers. The predominant characteristic is that the area divisions (of which the United States of America or North America is one) are headed by general managers of equal status in the structure. Each has the profit responsibility for an area, regardless of the produce lines involved. Typically, this structure is associated with those organizations that have mature, standardized product lines for which marketing, rather than production or technology, is the critical variable.

The mixed structural form is a combination of two or all of the above forms, adapted to the particular needs of a firm. A food company diversifying into chemicals might retain its international division for all the food products and establish the chemical division with world-wide responsibilities.

The separate international company is usually a response to lack of success abroad or to an unwillingness on the part of top management to become more involved abroad. Typically, this move precedes the sale of all or part of the foreign operations. It should be noted that this response does not necessarily include the incorporation of the international division as a separate subsidiary, since such incorporation is normally used as a method of reducing taxes.

The structures that have been adopted to replace the international division may not be stable. As the foreign business grows and diversifies, further structural changes may be required. Operations within the

United States require a balance between product and functional management, with area requirements relatively unimportant. However, once the organization operates abroad to a significant degree the benefits to be gained from both regional and product line control or coordination may become large. This has led a few organizations to adopt a "grid" structure, where product, area, and functional responsibilities are linked in what may be viewed as a three-dimensional organization structure. There are serious problems associated with this form, but the ability of an organization to learn to operate within such a structure may be the key to the maintenance of the flexibility of administration necessary for continued growth and prosperity abroad.

DATA

Chandler classifies the 70 largest American industrial companies in 1959 into three categories: (1) industries consisting of companies that tended to remain as type II organizations: steel and nonferrous metal; (2) industries partially accepting the type III structure: agricultural processing, oil, rubber, and mass merchandising; and (3) industries consisting of firms that had generally adopted the type III structure: electrical, automobile (transportation), power machinery, and chemicals.

The last four industries have clearly played a prominent role in the economic processes that we have been discussing. They are quite diversified, supporting Chandler's thesis that diversification leads to the adoption of the type III structure.[11] They are leaders in research and development activity, supporting the Burns and Stalker propositions.[12] They are the source of most of the U.S. export strength, as indicated by Gruber and others.[13] And they are among the leaders in foreign direct investment in plant and equipment.

A crude measure of aggregate diversification is the number of manufacturing employees outside the primary industrial activity in which the firm has been classified. Of the 17 manufacturing industries of interest,[14]

---

[11] Chandler, *Strategy and Structure*, pp. 16, 17.

[12] Burns and Stalker, *The Management of Innovation*.

[13] W. Gruber, D. Mehta, and R. Vernon, "The R&D Factor in International Trade and International Investment of United States Industries," *Journal of Political Economy*, vol. 25 (February 1967), pp. 20–37.

[14] There are 21 two-digit Standard Industrial Classification (SIC) manufacturing industries. However, the Department of Commerce presents data for foreign direct investment on a combined basis for primary and fabricated metals industries (SIC numbers 33 and 34), excludes petroleum from manufacturing, and provides foreign trade data that omit petroleum and furniture. We have comparable data for 17 two-digit industries. These are: 20 (food), 21 (tobacco), 22 (textiles), 23 (apparel), 24 (wood products), 26 (paper), 27 (printing), 28 (chemicals), 30 (rubber), 31 (leather), 32 (stone, clay, and glass), 33–34 (primary and fabricated metal), 35 (machinery), 36 (electrical), 37 (transportation), 38 (scientific and similar instruments), 39 (misc.).

TABLE 1

Employment Outside Primary Industry and in Research and Development; Export Surplus and Direct Foreign Investment for Major Industries

Industry (and SIC number)	Number of Employees		Export Surplus 1958–1964 (millions of dollars)†	Direct Foreign Investments 1959–1966 (millions of dollars)‡
	Outside Primary Industry 1958°	For Research and Development 1958°		
Transportation (37)	474,095	27,094	+493.6	4,870
Primary and fabricated metals (33–34)........	342,284	–	–	1,962
Electrical (36)	265,473	36,305	+486.3	1,401
Machinery (35)	254,160	4,526	+2,063.0	2,698
Chemicals (28)	170,875	14,667	+752.7	4,130

° U.S. Bureau of the Census, *Enterprise Statistics 1958* (Washington, D.C.: Government Printing Office, 1963).

† Trade Relations Council of the U.S., *Employment, Output, and Foreign Trade of U.S. Manufacturing Industries, 1958–1964/65* (New York, 1966).

‡ U.S. Department of Commerce, *Survey of Current Business* (Washington, D.C.: Government Printing Office, various dates).

the five leaders are shown in Table 1. It should be noted that this is a measure of domestic diversification, and that Chandler's four industries are among the five leaders.

Table 1 also shows an aggregate measure of research and development activity provided by total employment figures for people placed in these categories by their employers. Chandler's type III industries dominate the research and development activity of U.S. manufacturing establishments. The leading manufacturing contributors to the U.S. trade balance are also identified. Eight of the seventeen manufacturing industries had export surpluses on an industry basis; nine had deficits. Chandler's four represented 96.4 percent of the total export surplus by industry category of the United States in 1964. This is consistent with the Vernon position, as is the evidence that these same industries tend to follow their trade advantage with direct foreign investment as shown in Table 1.[15]

The evidence is summarized in Table 2, which relates the four industries Chandler identified as having generally accepted the type III structure and the four activities under discussion. The numbers in the body of the table indicate the rank of the organizations in these activities among the 17 industries.

From these two tables, it seems evident that the American manufacturing company with extensive international interests is likely to be: (1) diversified in its domestic business activities; (2) type III in organizational structure; (3) a leader in research and development; and (4) a

---

[15] Vernon, "International Investment and International Trade in the Product Cycle."

TABLE 2

Rank of Chandler-Type III Industries (out of 17) as to Diversification, Research and Development, Export Surplus, and Foreign Investment

	Chemical	Machinery	Electrical	Transportation
Diversification	5	4	3	1
Research and development	3	4	1	2
Export surplus	2	1	4	3
Foreign investment	2	3	5	1

major exporter from the United States. These propositions can be investigated in greater detail by using relative measures and data on individual companies.

Chandler distributed the 70 largest industrial companies (1959) in his three categories. Joan Curhan,[16] under the direction of Raymond Vernon, compiled a list of 170 companies that were in the 1964 or the 1965 *Fortune*[17] classifications and that had manufacturing subsidiaries in six or more foreign countries at the end of 1963 where the parent company owned 25 percent or more of the subsidiaries. The Curhan list represents most of the American-controlled manufacturing activity abroad.

Comparison of the Chandler and the Curhan lists shows that only 35 percent of Chandler's first group (predominantly type II organizations) were also on the Curhan list. The only steel company on both lists was the most decentralized of the steel companies. In Chandler's mixed second group, 45 percent of the companies were also on the Curhan list, (54 percent if merchandising was excluded from Chandler's group, as it was from the Curhan list). Chandler's third group of companies were all on the Curhan list except for one company which had gone out of existence through merger.

The mechanism by which this relationship is maintained was examined in more detail. The 170 companies of the Curhan list were sorted into the following categories: (1) Type II organizations, (2) Type III with an international division, and (3) Type III with the other forms of organized international activity that were described earlier. This sorting was done on the basis of annual reports, interviews, and secondary sources.[18] The large sample size made it inevitable that most of the information was gathered from published material. As a result, the classification reflects the formal structure and ignores possible discrepancies between the formal structure and informal control. No discrep-

---

[16] J. Curhan, Private communication.

[17] "The 500 Largest U.S. Industrial Corporations," *Fortune,* June 1965 and June 1966.

[18] For example, E. B. Lovell, *The Changing Role of the International Executive* (New York: National Industrial Conference Board, 1966).

ancies were found between the analyses from published materials and the evidence gained from the interviews with a limited number of the companies. Therefore, the classification may be considered to be sufficiently accurate for the purposes of this paper. The main possible source of error is for those companies in transition between the categories, since the formal organization may often lead or lag behind actual administrative practices. This, however, was not considered a serious source of error.

The classification of each company on the basis of only a few structural forms was aimed at recording the central tendency of the structure observed. Various rules were developed to allow for the many possible minor variations in the control procedures. The most important of these rules were:

1.   Foreign mining, agricultural, or service operations were not considered to be part of the manufacturing activities and were therefore ignored for the purposes of the structural classification.

2.   Given an international division, the presence of one or two foreign joint-ventures reporting directly to a product division and accounting for an insignificant volume of the foreign business did not constitute a "mixed" form.

3.   The international division did not have to control exports from the U.S.

4.   Canadian subsidiaries were classified as part of the U.S. operations.

Each company was also classified by the two-digit Standard Industrial Classification number of its largest product line.[19] The result of these classifications is summarized in Table 3 which shows that only 18 of the 170 companies in the sample have type II structures. This finding immediately suggests that foreign investment is dominated by type III organizations, which is the thesis of this paper.

From Table 3 a structural index for eight industries was calculated as follows:

1.   A ratio of the number of type II companies to all type III companies was calculated and normalized by assigning the value 1.00 to the industry with the largest proportion of type II companies.

2.   A ratio of the number of type III companies with an international division to all type III companies was calculated and normalized, with a value of 1.00 assigned to the industry with the highest ratio.

3.   The two normalized ratios were summed to form the index which is shown in Table 4. Low values of this index indicate the predominance of type III structures, particularly type III with some relatively complex form of organized international activity. Low values of the index therefore

---

[19] The source of this classification was the Securities Exchange Commission, *1965 Directory of Companies Filing Annual Reports with the Securities Exchange Commission* (New York, 1966).

TABLE 3
Structural Classification of Companies by Industry

| Industry SIC Number | Number of Companies in Sample | Stage II | Structure | |
			Stage III with International Division	Stage III with Other Forms of International Structure
20	28	5	16	7
21	1	–	1	–
22	2	–	2	–
25	1	–	1	–
26	5	1	3	1
27	1	–	1	–
28	41	1	21	19
29	8	–	2	6
30	5	–	5	–
31	1	–	1	–
32	7	1	5	1
33	8	4	2	2
34	8	1	4	3
35	19	4	9	6
36	17	1	8	8
37	11	–	4	7
38	5	–	4	1
39	2	–	1	1
Total	170	18	90	62

indicate the relative abundance of both general management in the United States and international general management.

This method of calculating a structural index is purely arbitrary. It is clear from Table 3, however, that any index reflecting the proportions of the structures of the sample of companies within an industry will provide approximately the same ranking as that shown in Table 4.

Also to be found in Table 4 is an index of diversification as calculated by Michael Gort.[20] Gort's index is derived from a sample of 111 large manufacturing companies, drawn from the 200 largest companies in 1954. This particular index (Gort does present other measures of diversification) represents the ratio of domestic employment in the primary two-digit SIC industry divided by total domestic employment, adjusted for employment associated with vertical integration.[21] These relationships tend to be stable over time, so that they should retain some relevance for the present problem; also the time difference is in the direction re-

---

[20] M. Gort, *Diversification and Integration in American Industry* (Princeton, N.J.: Princeton University, 1962).

[21] Gort's index is based on data in U.S. Bureau of Census, *Company Statistics: 1954 Census of Business, Manufacturing, Mineral Industries* (Washington, D.C.: Government Printing Office, 1958), Table 2.

TABLE 4

Structure and Diversification; Foreign Investment, Employment in Research and Development, and Export/Import Ratio in Major Industries

Industry (and SIC Number)	Index of Struc- ture	Gort's Index of Diversifi- cation*	1959–1966 Direct Foreign Investment Relative to Domestic†	Reaserch and Development Employees as Percentage of Central Administrative Employment‡	Export/ Import Ratio 1958– 1960§
Food (20) 1.175		.933	13.2%	3.10	.79
Paper (26) 1.300		.893	16.7	2.21	.31
Chemicals (28) 0.580		.752	27.7	22.49	2.79
Rubber (30) 1.000		.697	41.3	16.46	1.19
Primary and fabricated metals (33–34) 1.545		.810	20.3	6.37	.67
Machinery (35) 1.188		.807	21.8	12.56	6.37
Electrical (36) 0.638		.667	23.7	47.00	3.85
Transportation (37) ...0.364		.728	35.3	34.32	1.49

* Michael Gort, *Diversification and Integration in American Industry* (Princeton, N.J.: Princeton University, 1962), Table 8, p. 33.

† U.S. Department of Commerce, *Survey of Current Business* (Washington, D.C.: Government Printing Office, various dates).

‡ U.S. Bureau of the Census, *Enterprise Statistics: 1958* (Washington, D.C.: Government Printing Office, 1963).

§ Trade Relations Council of the U.S., *Employment, Output, and Foreign Trade of U.S. Manufacturing Industries, 1958–1964/65* (New York, 1966).

quired for Chandler's thesis. The eight industries in Table 4 are those for which data are available on foreign direct investment. This implies that they are the leading manufacturing industries in this respect, since the others have too little foreign direct investment to be reported separately. Gort's diversification index for SIC 33–34 is an average of his figures for those two industries, weighted by their respective employment sizes and representation on his sample.

Table 4 discloses some relationships immediately; that is, the four most diversified industries are four industries with the lowest structural index: chemicals, rubber, electrical machinery, and transportation. The four least diversified industries are four industries with the highest structural index: food, paper, primary and fabricated metals, and machinery. The Spearman coefficient of rank correlation between diversification and structure is 0.64. This result provides additional support for Chandler's thesis that there is a relationship between diversification and structure.

Table 4 also shows the importance of foreign direct investment in plant and equipment relative to domestic direct investment in plant and equipment, for the period 1959–1966. Again a relationship is apparent; that is, the four industries with the greatest relative direct foreign investment are the four most diversified (also with lowest structural index):

chemicals, rubber, electrical machinery, and transportation. The four industries with the least foreign investment are the four least diversified (also with the highest structural index): machinery, primary and fabricated metal, food, paper. The coefficient of rank correlation between the relative direct investment measure and Gort's diversification index is .86; between the relative direct investment measure and the structural index it is 0.69.[22]

A relative measure of research and development activity is shown in Table 4 for 1958. The four leading research and development industries are those that are the most diversified, have the lowest structural indexes, and are the most international in their investment practices. The coefficient of rank correlation between research and structure is 0.81; between research and diversification it is .90. The relationship between research and diversification is also apparent when the analysis is made at the more detailed three-digit SIC industry level. The median specialization ratio for organizations with research and development employees is .814 in 1958, and .939 for organizations without research and development employees. The specialization ratio measures the number of manufacturing employees classified in a primary three-digit SIC industry divided by total manufacturing employment in that industry.[23]

The export/import ratio for 1958–1960 is also shown in Table 4. Here the four leading industries are the same as in the case of the trade balance (rubber ranks fifth and is replaced by machinery among the leading four). The coefficient of rank correlation between the export/import ratio and structure is 0.52. The correlation between the research and development measure and the export/import balance is .71, which is consistent with the findings of Gruber and associates.[24]

CONCLUSION

It may now begin to appear that the evidence would support *any* hypothesis about the industry characteristics of the organizations that have led the movement abroad, simply because those industries are outstanding on all relevant scales for measuring business performance. This is not the case, however. Consider the not unusual statements that it is the largest, most capital intensive and most integrated organizations that dominate foreign activity. If size is measured by assets per organiza-

---

[22] The structural and diversification indexes were ranked from the lowest to the highest values, so that the "most diversified" industry was given first rank on that scale.

[23] U.S. Bureau of the Census, *Enterprise Statistics: 1958* (Washington, D.C.: Government Printing Office, 1963).

[24] Gruber et al., "The R&D Factor in International Trade and International Investment of United States Industries."

tion, this view is not supported by census data.[25] The rank correlation between assets per organization and the structural index is .40; between assets per organization and relative importance of foreign direct investment the correlation is .33. Gort also found that there was little association between size and diversification, as measured by the ratio of primary to nonprimary employment.[26] The correlation between the measure of size used here and Gort's diversification index is .29.

The measure of integration, taken from Gort, has a *negative* correlation with foreign activity, diversification (which agrees with his results), and decentralization for the eight internationally important industries.

Finally, the ratio of capital per production worker is negatively correlated with relative foreign activity ($-.14$). There is also a negative correlation between capital per production worker and the export/import ratio ($-.40$), as first suggested by Leontief.[27] The negative relationships carry over to the measures of structure ($-.21$) and diversification ($-.36$) used here. U.S. strength in international competition is concentrated in products with a relatively large labor content—probably the highly skilled technical labor required for product innovation and development, according to Vernon.[28]

The organizations that are left at home may be among the largest, most integrated, most capital intensive, and most profitable firms in the economy. Furthermore, they are not as likely to have problems of organization, management recruitment and training, staff-line conflicts, or of identifying what business the organization is really engaged in, or should be engaged in.

So, in the end, the question of the characteristics of the organization is a question of management's choice between sets of problems. Some business leaders have decided to make their organizations more cohesive by making them more integrated, capital intensive, and often more profitable. They have retained type II structures, and have tended to concentrate on domestic markets. Other business leaders have undertaken the difficult task of transforming an institution, of moving from a type II to a III structure. Many problems arise in this transition; for example, new systems of evaluation, reward, and control must be constructed. A critical aspect of the transition is teaching men to accept new roles—in this case roles as general managers. Once the organization had developed this educational capability, it could continue to diversify in an effective and efficient manner. It may be that the same pattern is being repeated in the

---

[25] *Enterprise Statistics.*

[26] Gort, *Diversification and Integration in American Industry*, p. 74.

[27] W. Leontief, "Domestic Production and Foreign Trade: The American Capital Position Re-Examined," *Proceedings of the American Philosophical Society* 97 (September 1953), pp. 332–49.

[28] Vernon, "International Investment and International Trade in the Product Cycle."

international field: when the company has small foreign interests, it economizes on competent international management by having one man coordinate foreign activities. The growth of foreign markets and opportunities requires diversification, reorganization, and the training of many more general international managers. The organizations that have been most successful in meeting this new challenge have been those type III organizations that had already developed the ability to produce general managers capable of controlling and guiding a heterogeneous, diverse enterprise.

STUDENT REVIEW QUESTIONS

1. What ideas of Alfred Chandler were the authors of this article attempting to test?
2. Describe the major forms of organizational structure which Fouraker and Stopford cover in this article.
3. Which type of organizational structure has been characteristic of companies which have successfully expanded into multinational operations? Why has that organizational form aided in this international expansion?
4. What organizational structure do you think is appropriate for those non-profit organizations that are multinational in their operations? (Consider the Peace Corps or Catholic Church as examples.)

chapter 8

Implementing Strategy: Planning and Budgeting

Introduction

The Planning Process
Objectives, Strategic Planning, and Period Planning

Implementing Plans

The Budgeting Function: A Management Approach
The Kinds of Budgets
The Advantages of Budgeting
Disadvantages of Budgeting

Implementing Strategy through the Budgeting Process
Planning Element of the Budget
Coordination Element of the Budget
Control Element of the Budget
Replanning Element of the Budget
The Look Backward
The Look Ahead

Summary

Readings

INTRODUCTION

PREVIOUS CHAPTERS of this book have emphasized that an organization's direction is influenced by a composite of critical factors, both tangible and intangible, occurring internally and externally. The courses of action an institution follows are complex, and are not always successful despite what could be judged as "sound" management and "proper" actions under the circumstances. There is no success formula for action which managers of organizations competing in a dynamic environment can have; only a useful framework for action which is supported by a continuous process of critical analysis, continuous justification for (or adjust-

394

ment of) goals, and constant revitalization of policies for achieving long- and short-range objectives in response to environmental changes. A useful strategic framework is presented in this book. This chapter and the next develop those aspects of the strategic framework which deal with the planning and control facets of the top-management job, as well as the related functions of other levels of management involved in the implementation of strategy in organizations.

THE PLANNING PROCESS

Strategy formulation, discussed in the previous chapter, stressed that the top managers in any organization must decide what is most desirable and yet achievable, not merely by *responding* to events as they occur, but by *causing* things to happen for the organization's benefit. Once objectives are set commensurate with the energies or resources to be expended, steps are taken to achieve the objectives by planning for and controlling the use of institutional resources, with the full realization that certain forces are always working against such efforts and achievement.

The marriage of explicitly stated objectives and the plans for their accomplishment is enhanced by policy statements, and all of these factors have broad influence on the more specific future goals of an organization. These major policy statements, plans and objectives constitute the formal, planned strategies discussed in previous chapters. The encompassed statements regarding desired growth, product quality, image, market, and so forth, *guide* the formulation of the period plans which serve as the specific directional and evaluative devices of an organization. The stated objectives, policies, and plans include "what we want to achieve" and "how we want to achieve"; the feedback comparison of actual results to the planned strategies identifies "what we have achieved," and also identifies desired changes which might be made in our objectives, plans, and policies, or in the implementation of these.

As should be evident, this "planning" system is by its very nature actually a planning and control system. Robert Anthony has recognized this in explaining his framework for a planning and control system. "In particular, in the important system we have labeled 'management control,' both aspects of planning and aspects of control exist, and are roughly equal in importance."[1] Anthony's framework integrates fully the two aspects of planning and control. In this book the two functions are presented separately, but recognized and emphasized here are the continuous interrelationships in operation of what is essentially one overall system. Additionally, this planning and control system is recognized as a

---

[1] Robert N. Anthony, *Planning and Control Systems: A Framework for Analysis* (Boston: Harvard Graduate School of Business Administration, 1965), p. 109.

part of the total concept of strategy—a segment of the strategic implementation phase.

Objectives, Strategic Planning, and Period Planning

The importance of objectives was discussed at length in Chapter 5. Broad objectives must be translated into specifics, and must be communicated and clearly understood throughout the organization, since eventually results at all levels must be compared against these objectives. Furthermore, objectives should be attainable, should motivate, and should generate appropriate action throughout the organization. The planning-control system in the organization is the major medium through which the *strategic* objectives, policies, and plans are translated into more specific, measurable, attainable, and meaningful (to the entire organization) goals and plans. This is not to say that planning has not taken place at earlier stages in the organization, but actually is to emphasize that much planning has already occurred. However, the nature of that earlier planning was strategic; of broad dimension and long-range implication. It was part of the process of strategy formulation—that essentially creative planning process discussed in a previous chapter. The type of planning which is the major focus of this chapter, by contrast, is a means of *implementing* the formulated strategy and its encompassed policies and plans toward the achievement of its objectives. The second side of the system, the control phase, is also a vehicle for the implementation of the preordained strategy. Anthony would define the two different types of planning as "strategic planning" and "management control."[2] We use the term "period planning" to describe the more specific and shorter range planning.

The period planning emphasized at this point involves making appraisals of and decisions about the future, just as did strategic planning, and both types require the development of policies and goals for the organization. However, the future of concern in period planning is not the longer term future considered when formulating the strategy, but is a more immediate future which can be seen with greater clarity and planned for more conclusively and specifically. This planning phase in a narrow sense does not set new objectives for the organization since this was done in broad terms while formulating the strategy. Rather, this phase involves the interpretation of the broader strategic objectives, policies, and plans, and the translation of these into more specific and shorter range goals which are essentially more specific aspects of the broader strategic objectives, policies, and plans. The entire planning process described in previous paragraphs is illustrated in Exhibit 8–1, which depicts the different types

---

[2] Ibid., pp. 16–17.

EXHIBIT 8-1

A Structure and Process of Business Planning

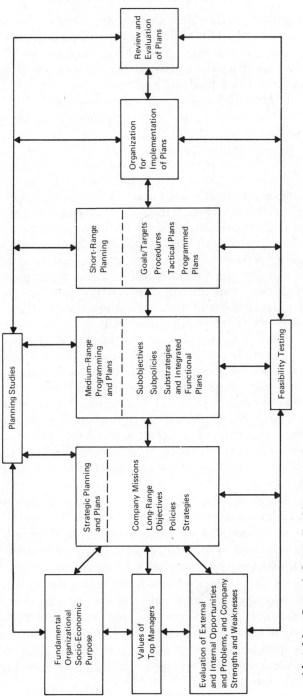

Adapted from George A. Steiner, *Top Management Planning.*

of planning from the broadest and longest range to the narrowest and shortest range, and additionally shows the major influences upon strategy and strategic planning.[3] The period planning which implements strategy and consequently is the primary topic of this chapter is shown in the center of the exhibit as "medium-range programming and plans, subpolicies, substrategies, and interrelated functional plans." Short-range planning is also covered later in this chapter during the discussion of annual budgets.

Medium-range planning is primarily the province of the various line managers. Ideally, the plans will be constructed by line managers at all levels of the organization, with appropriate staff assistance. Strategy implementation, after all, is a job of significant detail and demands broad organizational involvement. Within the planning process, inputs of information must come from all areas of the organization. In a business organization this includes sales, production, engineering, research and development, personnel, accounting, and finance as a partial list of participating functions. Each area has its ideas, hopes, plans, and aspirations, and usually, information of various sorts to justify its view.

Yet, the higher levels of management must, within the framework of the strategy, receive information, analyze it, draw conclusions, and make decisions as to what is appropriate for inclusion in medium-range plans. Top management, in cooperation with other levels of operating management thus translates strategic considerations into management considerations for specific time periods. These top level managers decide what things are to be done, in what time frames, and who is responsible for the actions and results. In short, they formulate the broad plans which middle level managers refine and reformulate for more specific guidance to all areas and functions of the organization. Finally, the end result is "short-range planning," goals, targets, and the like which are shown in Exhibit 8–1.

The planning process as it has been advanced here calls for the participation of managers throughout the various levels of an organization. One of the most important functions of the higher level management job is to encourage and achieve this participation—in short, to exercise leadership. The planning-control system which includes the budget as its major vehicle of translation within the organization should be structured to gain the involvement of the organizational members. By utilizing a budgeting process which requires various levels of management to participate in the development of future plans and goals, an important motivational force is built into the planning-control process within an organization. If a planned strategy is to be implemented suc-

---

[3] The source of this exhibit is "Comprehensive Managerial Planning" by George A. Steiner, Research Series of The Planning Executive's Institute, Oxford, Ohio, 1972, p. 6.

cessfully, such motivation is vitally required. This is consistent with the basic theme of "management by objectives" called for so often in the literature of management, and expounded in the works of Drucker and McGregor.[4]

In this context, many of the behavioral considerations covered in the previous chapter can be recalled with value. For what was deemed important in the discussions of organizational structure and behavior applies throughout the implementation phase of the strategic process. In short, attention must be paid constantly not only to the formal and logical aspects of strategy implementation, but also to the informal group and individual behavioral aspects. In the end, it is the activities of *individuals* which determine what is accomplished by the organization which seeks to implement strategy.

IMPLEMENTING PLANS

The management planning and control process, then, is a system which exists to inject into the institutional bloodstream an articulation of the strategy and the encompassed objectives, plans, and policies. This system ultimately utilizes subsystems such as information flows, motivation, and compensation systems to get the job done.

The system and subsystems which accomplish these tasks do not necessarily take the shape of formal written plans. In some cases, a less than formal system may be adequate. But managers should be acutely aware of the dangers of the "grapevine" being accepted as the indicator of the ways in which things should be done. A lack of respect for formal written plans may develop in an organization which could lead to a potentially dangerous suboptimization of organizational goals. This danger places a burden on the planners and managers, not only to *make* plans for the achievement of objectives, but also to *utilize* the plans and *let it be known* throughout the organization that they are being used. The stated goals should be the actual goals and no other goals should remain implicit unless one is willing to risk confusion and misunderstanding. Although changes will be made in goals and plans, these should be articulated and communicated to the organizational members rather than assuming that they will somehow "get the word," or even worse, assuming that the members do not need to know.

A planning system should be established which (1) communicates a well-defined plan of reasonably attainable goals; (2) engages the participation and support of all levels of management and supervisory personnel; and (3) provides feedback through a reporting system for

---

[4] Peter Drucker, *The Practice of Management,* (New York: Harper & Row, Publishers, 1954); and Douglas McGregor, *The Human Side of Enterprise* (New York: McGraw-Hill Book Co., 1970).

evaluation of results as a basis for appropriate subsequent action. This type of system requires that top executives, with participation from other managerial levels, break down the institutional objectives into functional and divisional objectives. The result should be a coordinated statement of expectations which should materialize under the predicted set of circumstances. A most effective and commonly used planning device which can be used to implement strategy is a budget that is tailored to this specific task. The remainder of this chapter discusses budgeting as an instrument for putting plans and policies into effect for the achievement of objectives, thereby functioning as a major vehicle for implementing organizational strategy.

THE BUDGETING FUNCTION: A MANAGEMENT APPROACH

Budgeting, in its broadest definition, is the function of coordinating into a plan or course of action all data and opinions of many people in an organization based on:

Future expectations regarding the environment of the organization during the budgetary period ahead.
Past experiences which can be used to shape projections of likely performance.
Expected influences of past and future upon each other.

The budgeting function as seen here creates formal, written statements called budgets, or more accurately "planning budgets," which convert organizational strategy into a course of action, and which require (1) planning, (2) coordination, (3) control, and (4) replanning. The budgeting function must have these four ingredients to be successful. Planning without coordination, coordination without control, or control without replanning are insufficient if a unified system is the goal.

The budgeting function strives to specify and to communicate organizational plans so as to adjust the internal pressures of the organization to complement or offset external pressures, with specific objectives in mind. It is the thrust which initiates and directs organizational activity in a definite manner for definite purposes. It combines forecasted expectations of what *might* happen with what management *wants to* happen.

The reason that the budgeting function has emerged as indispensable in the vitally important planning process is that this vehicle converts all elements of an organization's plans into a common financial denominator. This is an essential characteristic if results are to be compared to plans in an organization consisting of differing areas, elements, functions, resources, and so forth. This characteristic is also the reason that nonprofit institutions as well as business organizations have been able to utilize budgets on a broad scale.

The Kinds of Budgets

Certain parts of the budget system are very popular and receive more attention than other parts. When key managers talk about budgets they tend to discuss the income budget, production budget, capital budget, or cash budget. These are the obvious items that have connotations for action. However, other types such as personnel and inventory budgets are, in the final analysis, just as important since every supporting budget must be tied into the overall plan or Master Budget. The Master Budget consolidates the individual plans of the organization, usually on an annual basis, and is an integral part of the Long-Range Budget which is often called the Capital Budget.

The Master Budget, although consolidated as an annual budget, is in its detail a monthly budget and a series of continuous budgets which perpetually add a future month as each month expires. It is broken down into two categories:

1. The Operating Budget. This is comprised of many functional budgets which include the income or sales, production, selling expense, and administrative expense budgets. Even these subbudgets are broken down into smaller segments. For example, the income budget may be prepared by area, product, division, department, and so on; the production budget may be segmented by shifts, materials, labor, and so forth.

2. The Financial Budget. The influence of the operational aspects of the organization are reflected in cash, inventory, machinery, and fund budgets. These, in turn, are used to prepare pro forma or projected statements of future financial position and income. Usually a source and application of funds statement is developed, as is a cash flow statement. Special budgets also are often prepared which are not readily classified as being either Operating or Financial although they may be related to either or both types. Personnel requirements, PERT charts, and capital budgets for particular projects are examples. And underlying all such special budgets are the necessary operations specified in an advanced plan to guide the future actions of organizational members.

The Advantages of Budgeting

In the past, executives used budgets mainly for control purposes and accepted the concept that effective management must *restrict* the actions of subordinates so that their performance would reflect the predetermined plan of operations. Although this limited use of budgets may have seemed desirable at one time, it is quite clearly inappropriate in today's organizational world. The planning budget must *encourage* action as well as selectively restricting it. Budgeting must encourage individuals to start "planning within a plan," thus aiding in the development of goal congruence throughout the organization. The advantage of this type of climate is immediately apparent from earlier discussions of the importance of individual behavior in achieving effective action.

A properly conceived planning budget results in new ideas being called to the attention of key people, and permits subordinates to make day-to-day decisions consistent with longer range objectives. In addition, such a budget highlights the managers' ability to plan, to organize, and to control their areas of responsibility. Weaknesses, under a well-coordinated budgeting system, can be quickly identified for appropriate action. Additionally, capital can be directed into productive and profitable channels when a feasible, attainable, efficient system is established and accepted by motivated individuals. A feedback system permits budgetary replanning and course alteration, often before serious problems have occurred. Data for the evaluation of managers are also generated by the feedback system.

Although these advantages may appear somewhat optimistic, they are distinctly more realistic under a proper system of planning and budgeting than may be expected in a less well-managed situation. Since the budget is so central to good planning and management, it is not unrealistic to claim many of the advantages of good managerial practice for the planning budget which is well conceived and implemented in a particular organizational situation. Clearly, this planning and budgeting system is a necessary element in the implementation of corporate strategy.

Disadvantages of Budgeting

Dynamic budgeting is, as indicated above, worthy of much praise when properly used. However, some problems are inherent in the process and should be mentioned. First, budgets, as all aspects of planning, cost money and take time. Not only are there the obvious costs of personnel hired specifically for this function, but other less obvious costs also exist. Production supervisors and sales managers spend time away from direct output when involved in budgeting. Files take up costly and useful space, and paper work, reproduction, and the like become habit-forming, and fancy reports at more frequent intervals creep into the process. Executives must keep in mind that *budgeting is overhead.* The process justifies itself only insofar as it leads to actions which are more valuable or profitable than actions which would have taken place had no budgeting been involved.

Second, the results of the budgeting process are too often misused. The planning budget is designed to coordinate efforts and to develop goal congruence within the guidelines of the overall institutional strategy. This may mean, for example, that a small division of a company may be directed to maintain less inventory so that a larger division which has a higher out-of-stock cost can increase its inventory. If the first division manager takes action to accomplish this result in the interest of organizational goal congruence and his sales decline as a result, any comparisons which highlight the decline in sales must recognize that the division manager may well have done a better job and not a poorer one. This overall approach is often lacking, particularly in evaluation of results. Yet results must be interpreted and utilized properly in evaluation, as well as in replanning, coordination, and motivation.

Finally, planning and, thus, budgeting depend heavily on all predictions about the future, including those based upon historic data. This means that judgment which is subject to error is inherent in the process. Budgeting is not an exact science which can replace sound management. It should not be viewed as an inflexible device, but as one which facilitates the possible modification of plans and strategies as action takes place, results occur, and new information is generated. But experience shows that the budget, which has been based on assumptions about the future and certain events of the past, is too often utilized to stifle change and creativity, even when such change is badly needed as in the case when assumptions are shown to be in error. One must always keep in mind Robert Burns's "The best laid plans of mice and men," when dealing with planning budgets.[5]

There are, then, inherent disadvantages in the use of budgets. But on balance these weaknesses lie not in the budget itself but in the improper use of the process. Regardless, a budget carries with it potential problems and managers must be aware of the possible avenues to problems through misuse of a valuable management technique.

IMPLEMENTING STRATEGY THROUGH THE BUDGETING PROCESS

The nature of the budget as well as its major advantages and weaknesses in operation provide to the manager or student much insight as to how this tool is used in organizations. The purpose here is to focus on the budget as a prime vehicle for implementing strategy. As noted, the budget as a major planning device in most organizations, translates the strategy into medium-range and shorter term goals, policies, and plans. These more specific and timely translations of broader and longer term strategic plans are communicated through the organization in the form of the various budgets described earlier.

---

[5] The reader is referred to Charles F. Granger's article, "The Best Laid Plans . . . ," *The Controller* (now *Financial Executive*), vol. 30 (August 1962), pp. 373–76.

If budgets are to motivate organizational members as they should, however, these individuals must have an appropriate voice in the translation of strategy into the specific planning budgets. In this way the budget has already begun to serve as a major method of implementing strategy. The budgeting process continues this function as its various elements operate within an organization. These elements of planning, coordinating, controlling, and replanning are discussed below.

Planning Element of the Budget

The budget is the primary planning document and should not be merely a conservative estimate of next year's results based on last year's efforts. One does not drive a car forward by looking only through a rear view mirror. The past does have its place in aiding forecasters. However, the budget should be the articulation of the organization's future plans, in financial terms, and past data should be utilized only insofar as it helps to achieve this end.

Initially, period planning involves the accumulation of future-oriented data without particular regard for past data. Since a budget is an articulation of plans for the future, it is future-oriented data that are most precious. These data may be accumulated from market research, industry forecasts, suppliers, production managers, and so on. Some of these data can be obtained at low cost, and are much more valuable than past data. A major obstacle to reliable budget plans, as well as to strategic plans, is the scarcity of information concerning what competitors will do, how customers will behave, and what major environmental changes will take shape. Other types of future-oriented external data are also difficult to obtain.

When reliable sources for future-oriented data are exhausted, past data must be sought. Examination of such data is useful primarily because it aids in the prediction of costs. The historical facts must be critically analyzed to form a hypothesis as to how these data behaved relative to each other in the past, so that these relationships can be projected into the expected future environment. This forecast does not involve merely running a trend line out into the future, but requires an in-depth study of which costs are fixed, semivariable, variable, and also which income areas respond to advertising or sales service, which production areas have contracts that are about to expire, and many other such considerations which can affect costs differently in the future.

A segmented analysis must also be made which permits classification of all elements into controllable and noncontrollable cost categories. Those which can be controlled should be set at the level desired. Typically, these are managed or *programmed* costs such as advertising, research and development, and *committed* costs such as depreciation and managerial salaries.

The noncontrollable elements must be studied to establish how they vary as the controllable items vary, or if, in fact, they are fixed. Multiple regression analysis can be used effectively to help identify relationships which answer such typical questions as:

How does a decrease in the sales price influence sales, net income, bad debts, inventory turnover, cash flow, or number of days receivables outstanding?

What is the relationship between a hospital's patient census and its variable costs such as its cost of nursing service?

What part of a university's total costs of operation is fixed; which costs vary with student enrollment and at what rate do these vary?

If a portion of a noncontrollable cost is known to be fixed, then one can project this historic information into future budgeted amounts. If the cost category is partly or wholly variable, the causal relationship established between that category and the controllable element can be used to predict cost levels for the category. For example, if hospital laboratory costs are not controllable but they vary directly with patient census which is controllable, then, once the patient census is estimated, the laboratory costs can be estimated since there is a clear relationship between them.

The last stage of the initial budget-planning phase requires that the impact of projected costs and revenues on the available resources be demonstrated. Pro forma or estimated statements of financial position and income are the results. These projections could be analyzed as to acceptability in the light of financial criteria such as return-on-investment objectives. Projections also can be immensely useful parts of the management information system, and should be a widely utilized planning tool. For example, the broad objectives of the organization's strategy will usually have determined the overall financial objectives such as desired rate of return on investment, profit levels before or after tax, proportions of debt and equity in a firm's financial structure, or the break-even level of income for a nonprofit institution. The budget tools described here can estimate the impact of future decisions on such objectives and thereby assist decision making toward the achievement of strategic organizational goals.

Coordination Element of the Budget

In order for the best of plans to assist in the accomplishment of desired tasks, the timeliness of all relevant variables must be noted and acted upon. Short-range budgets should act in unison with long-range budgets. Production must be coordinated with sales in a relationship which permits efficient use of personnel, financial resources, facilities, plants, inventories, and so forth. The resources of the organization should be detailed in proper form as needed to guide action. The desirable events call for coordinated activity in an organization.

The planning budget helps to accomplish a meshing of all productive, promotional, financial, and administrative functions by indicating interrelationships and by fixing responsibility for a segment of each function to a department or division manager. The budget is the communication link between line and staff which helps to transmit the desired, attainable, and hopefully congruent goals. It forces the responsible individuals to perceive the relationships their unit holds to others, as well as to the total organization. For example, the sales department manager must attempt to coordinate orders so that products can be produced and delivered in a reasonable and acceptable period of time. Credit sales must be made within the limitations imposed by the working capital. For the sales manager, a desired level of sales as indicated on the Master Budget should act as an influencing and constraining mechanism. Significant deviation from a relevant range in the desired level of sales requires a revamping of the entire network of resources. In a hospital or university, the projected number of patients or students should also affect requirements for financial, human, and physical resources.

Thus, the budget serves as a coordinating element in the implementation of strategy by helping to bring together the divided groups which the process of organizing helped to bring about. A coordinated planning budget creates the means to assign responsibility and ideally the willingness to accept responsibility. When an appreciation for a properly constructed overall plan is ingrained in responsible personnel, they usually are highly motivated since a guideline for action is offered which integrates the operational resources of organizational units into a logical overall pattern. As a result, goal congruence between members and the organization is much more likely to develop. This motivational aspect of the budget is too often neglected in explanations of the budgetary process. It is, however, a basic objective and characteristic of a properly coordinated budget system. As noted in the previous chapter, such coordination is a vitally needed element if strategy is to be well implemented in an organization.

Control Element of the Budget

Probably the most widely accepted function of the budgeting process is control. But at the outset, it should be noted that the budget does not control; people control. The control aspect of budgeting demands that sufficient planning and coordination already have been accomplished. Only then is it time for "control" action on the part of managers.

Adherence to a plan must be achieved in an environment composed of a delicate balance between motivation and constraint. The budget should not shunt enthusiasm and creativity, but by the same token, it should not let developing problems or windfall successes occur without encouraging the organization to adjust to these events in a fashion which yields improved utilization of resources. Control is accomplished by having responsible individuals reviewing periodically the operational aspects and results of their units' activities. An efficient system of information gathering must be instituted and utilized. A caveat is in order here insofar as the information system and frequency of communications are concerned. Remember that a budgeting system is *overhead*. It consists of information generated over and above basic, legal reporting requirements. The benefits of this additional information must be more than would have been experienced without the additional information. The budget always should remain the instrument of the planning-control process, and not become the end in itself.

Too often a good budgeting system becomes a bad one because too many and too frequent reports are generated which are inherently useless, or just are never utilized by management. Only significant variances should be reported as indications that differences between forecasted and actual results have appeared. The task then is to analyze the significant deviations from the expected results, in order to see if the organization or particular unit should alter its course in the light of this experience, and in what ways. Deviations from the budget should be expected since the budget is a forecast. Therefore all deviations should not be reported, but only those deviations which might not have been reasonably expected. In essence, significant deviations or those which were caused by other than random events are of interest and should be reported. Such a screening process can be established with a basic knowledge of statistics supported by an input of experience and good judgment.

Management need not be as concerned with reports which show how right their forecast has been. Focus should be on unexpected results. Contrariwise, an organization that has no deviations from budgeted goals, or very few, may actually have motivational problems. Its members may achieve targets as set; no more, no less. Stedry[6] and Parkinson[7] have reported much that helps us to understand the potential weakness in always being right on target as far as budgets are concerned.

At each organizational level, deviations which are controllable must be studied for explanations of why they occurred. The responsible individuals should understand and explain the cause of such variances so that they and other managers can act to correct those which are unfavorable, take advantage of favorable ones, get new insights, or adjust with a revised budget plan.

In summary, control through the budget relies on having coordinated

---

[6] Andrew Stedry, *Budget Control and Cost Behavior* (Englewood Cliffs, N.J.: Prentice-Hall, Inc., 1960).

[7] C. Northcote Parkinson, *Parkinson's Law and Other Studies in Administration*, Sentry ed. (Boston: Houghton Mifflin Co., 1957).

plans at the start of the budgeting cycle. The final element of the cycle, by the same token, leads once more to a new beginning, to recycling, to the replanning phase.

Replanning Element of the Budget

To many experienced managers, the most critical aspect of the entire budget-planning process is the replanning function. It is important in that it involves utilizing the budgeting tool for (1) a look backward, and (2) a look ahead, thereby closing the loop of the continuous budget-planning process.

EXHIBIT 8-2
The Budget-Planning Process

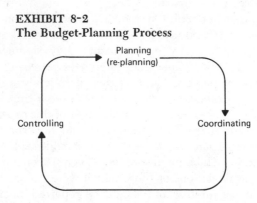

The Look Backward. When the budget-planning system is operating properly, a study of significant deviations permits the focus to be placed on performance, both good and bad. Reward and punishment mechanisms must be an integral part of the system to provide motivation. Those responsible individuals who perform well must be given some form of recognition, whether it be subtle or obvious. The proverbial carpeted office may not be so necessary for some as a picture in the organization's magazine, or a raise in salary. Positive motivation is undeniably a necessity, but negative motivation continues as a legitimate method of motivation in appropriate circumstances. Fixed rules of when to use either type of motivation seldom have a valid basis, and judgment is required for this decision.

For those who fail to achieve the planned objectives, some adjustment may be necessary. The controllable deviations should be explained and their causes pinpointed. Conclusions should be reached regarding performance in the light of the individual's available resources, experience and accountability. Only then can an informed decision be made as to what action to take and what motivational approach to utilize. At times, the review of results and causes may indicate that planning assumptions were wrong, or that unexpected events interfered with accomplishing plans. Interpretation of results is an area for astute analysis and good judgment. Often, the managers whose performance is being evaluated by comparison with expected results may be excellent sources to recommend future improvements in the plans and budgets, as well as sources of improvements in operations.

The look back encompasses many areas of interest to managers. For instance, this view may have important implications for future implementation of the organization's strategy, or it may even call for a change in the overall strategy being followed, or in some aspect of the strategy. Review of results and their causes may well indicate that the specific goals of the plan were inappropriate. This conclusion may lead to a further one which notes that some broader strategic goal, plan, or policy was not appropriate. It is in reviewing results that cautious and informed judgment must be utilized by management, because decisions are made which might or should affect the strategy of the organization. Or the review might signal the need for change only in implementation of the particular budget, in the actions of managers as they operate toward achieving budgeted and/or strategic plans. The look back, then, and the actions of management which follow, are vitally important to carrying out the strategy of an organization, and in some instances, to reformulating the strategy.

The Look Ahead. A review is made of results achieved by making a comparison between the results expected and actual performance in order that a reformulation of a new plan or new element of the strategy may transpire. Strategic considerations always are paramount; environmental changes again shape the course for future action, and "new" historic data are used to improve forecasts. New medium- and short-range budgets are prepared and shaped within a framework which includes changes made in the long-range forecasts, plans, and strategies. These shorter range budgets influence the speed with which long-range objectives are achieved. They mesh as gears; one moving as the others move, each driving the others.

Seeing this interdependency of shorter range and long-range plans is a critical aspect in the understanding of the overall planning-budgeting process. Both long and shorter range considerations are always involved in decisions, and the proper utilization of the budgetary process greatly facilitates the meshing of gears described above. As the organization looks ahead for its continued survival and prosperity with new strategies, policies and plans, these broad guidelines will set the directions for the replanning phase of the budget-planning cycle. All that was learned throughout the organization during the previous cycle should be integrated into management's thinking and decisions at the outset of this new cycle. Once again, all of this experience will be synthesized for the upcoming period in the planning budget and, once again, this new budget will become a prime vehicle for the translation and communication of goals throughout the organization. Planning, then, including the vital budgeting system, is a continuing process that is an indispensable management function in the implementation of corporate strategy.

SUMMARY

The planning described in this chapter is observably a planning and control system which is a continuous process in an organization that is truly being *managed*. The planning aspect of the system was emphasized here only as a convenience and not to indicate that it is in actuality separable from the overall planning and control system. Indeed, much of the chapter, of necessity, dealt with the control element in order to explain more clearly the planning aspects of the system.

A basic premise of the chapter is that the type of planning emphasized here is concerned with the implementation of planned strategy in an organization. The formulation of that strategy and resulting plan conceptually precedes the planning and control system described here. The system utilized in any institution will depend greatly upon the organizational structure, and upon the organizational behavior ideas embodied in the management's philosophy.

The budget as a planning device for management is discussed in detail and recognized as the articulation in financial terms of the plans of the organization. The budget system when used properly, then, is a most effective method for implementing strategy. The managerial voice is communicated in a network of plans which seeks to promote teamwork, responsibility and desirable action. The process is a perpetual one and demands a suitable information system which not only communicates objectives, policies, and plans throughout the organization, but also provides feedback responses so that actions can be controlled or influenced on a continuing basis toward the achievement of stated goals. Future information is the most desirable input to the budget which is to guide actions in future periods. Past data, however, are relevant, but must be employed judiciously and for proper purposes.

In the next chapter, the control and motivational aspects of the planning and control system will be considered in depth. The replanning phase of the cycle will again be noted as being closely allied with the process elements of control and motivation. Finally, the interdependency of all planning-control elements and the strategy of the organization will be emphasized and articulated by means of a case situation.

20. Selection of a Framework[*]

ROBERT N. ANTHONY

THE NEED FOR A FRAMEWORK

To BE USEFUL, material dealing with any broad subject needs to be organized within a framework of topics and subtopics. If the topics and subtopics are well chosen, the available material can be so arranged as to make it possible for one to reach conclusions generally applicable to each classification but not applicable to the other classifications. Such conclusions or generalizations, furthermore, will have validity and significance impossible in the absence of such a framework.

For example, the nervous system is a main topic in human biology; its two major subtopics are the central (cerebrospinal) nervous system and the reflex (automatic) mechanism. Certain generalizations apply to the nervous system as a whole, whereas others apply to one of the subtopics, but not to the other. Thus, the nervous system is concerned with the transmission of impulses from sense organs to muscles; the central system, to the voluntary muscles, and the reflex system, to the involuntary muscles.

Suppose an ecological study is made of a community. One way of summarizing the result would be by streets arranged in alphabetical order; another way would be by height categories of the inhabitants. Neither of these frameworks would be as useful as one based on income, race, or occupation.

Within a given subject area, different frameworks can be useful for different purposes. Thus, in biology, the classification of plants and animals by phylum, class, order, family, genus, and species is useful for some purposes. Comparative anatomy, which cuts across these classifica-

---

[*] From Robert N. Anthony, *Planning and Control Systems: A Framework for Analysis,* pages 1–23. Published by Division of Research, Harvard Business School, Boston, 1965. Reprinted by permission.

tions, provides a useful framework for other purposes. So also does the study of growth or reproduction, which cuts across in another dimension, and the study of evolution, which cuts in still another dimension. By contrast, a study of animals classified according to the color of their eyes has limited usefulness.

This book proposes a framework for the broad subject, planning and control systems. It is hoped that this framework will be useful to those who do research on such systems, to those who design them, to those who use them, and to students.

Users of the Framework

Research. The researcher needs a classification of topics and subtopics that indicates the limits within which his findings are pertinent; that is, he wants to make statements about each main topic that are valid for that topic but not for other main topics, and he wants to make statements about each subtopic that both are within the context of the general statements about the main topic and also apply to that subtopic and not to others. If these statements are in fact valid, one can apply them to a new problem (phenomenon, process, object) by deciding where this problem fits into the framework. The statements made about the appropriate subtopic plus those made about the appropriate main topic will be relevant to the new problem if it is classified properly in the framework. The foregoing statement is, of course, only approximately correct, for however carefully the topics are defined, there will be many borderline situations for which the precise classification is in doubt.

The other side of this coin is that the researcher who reports on a study of a single, narrow subtopic has a difficult job unless he has an over-all and generally accepted framework to which to relate it. Either he must work out *de novo* and explain the relevant statements for the main topic of which his subtopic is a part, or he must assume that his readers have the same understanding of the broad area that he has, which may very well not be the case.

This problem is a central one in research on planning and control systems at present, as anyone who has an acquaintance with the literature on planning and control well knows. For example, the hundreds of articles on expense control, or some aspect of expense control, generally fall into one of two categories. Either the author sets forth statements about control in general as a background to the specific idea he wants to present, in which case a large fraction of the article repeats statements made in numerous other articles; or he omits this background material, in which case his readers do not know which of several possible frames of reference he has in mind. If a proper framework existed, together with generally agreed upon definitions and concepts for the main topics, he could present new ideas relating to specific subtopics without all this repetition or likelihood of misinterpretation. As it is, many articles dealing with problems of planning and control tend to be miniature, and necessarily superficial, treatises of the whole subject, rather than thorough analyses of single aspects of it.

The job of the author or researcher who deals with some aspect of a subject is made much easier if he can show how his topic fits into a larger whole. If readers are familiar with this larger structure, authors can take the essentials of the structure for granted, rather than spend time explaining them.

Other Users. The systems designer and the systems user also need a framework. As new ideas come to their attention, they need some way of organizing them, of relating them to or contrasting them with ideas they already have accepted, and, if they accept the new idea, of knowing the limits of its applicability. The student in a subject that is new to him needs a framework for a similar reason. For most subject areas, textbooks provide such a framework, and the more highly developed the subject area, the better organized are its textbooks. The area in which we are interested, planning and control systems, is so new as an organized field of study that textbooks providing a framework have not yet been written.

Finally, a framework has collateral benefits—to companies in thinking about job descriptions and organization structure, to schools and other training programs in planning courses, and to libraries in classifying books and articles.

DEFINITIONS AND LIMITATIONS

The totality that this study seeks to break down into useful topics is labeled Planning and Control Systems. Although the approximate meaning of this term is intuitively obvious, we need to make our intended precise meaning as clear as possible before proceeding to develop the suggested framework. The words "planning" and "control" are discussed at length in a subsequent section; "system" is defined here.

Definition of System

The word system has many meanings. (Even the *American College Dictionary* lists 13 definitions.) The first definition in *Websters Unabridged* comes close to what we intend: "A complex unit formed of many often diverse parts subject to a common plan or serving a common purpose." There are two essential ideas in this definition: (1) the individual parts of a system are often diverse, and (2) the collection of parts forms a unity—or a wholeness—either because the parts are "subject to a common plan" or because they "serve a common purpose." The dictionary definition of a biological system also is relevant: "An assemblage of parts or organs of the same or similar tissues, or concerned with the same function; e.g., the nervous sytem, the digestive system." A planning and control system, then, consists of diverse parts that serve a common purpose, this purpose having to do with planning and control.

The use of the plural—systems—for the total area signifies that in our view there are more than one planning and control systems in one organization. As will be seen, we believe that this concept is more useful than the alternative of viewing the separate systems as parts of one over-all entity, that is, as a single, integrated system. The distinction is not important, however, and if the reader prefers to think of *the* planning and control system—a single entity—he is welcome to do so.

Systems and Processes

It is important to distinguish between "systems" and "processes." In brief, a system facilitates a process; it is the means by which the process occurs. The distinction is similar to that between anatomy and physiology. Anatomy deals with structure—what it is; whereas physiology deals with process—how it functions. The digestive system facilitates the process of digestion.

In one sense we are interested in both structure and process, since the structure can be understood best in terms of how it works. A description of the forms, procedures, and rules that constitute the structure considered apart from the functions they are intended to perform would be sterile.

This fact is even more relevant for our subject matter than in the case of biology. In biology, structure determines process; oxygen enters the bloodstream *because* of the structure of the lungs, and this structure must be accepted as a given. In an organization, by contrast, the structure can be modified to fit whatever seems to be the best process; within limits, the process rather than the structure is the determinant. It would be even less realistic to divorce a discussion of systems from a discussion of the related processes than it would be to discuss the digestive system without mentioning the process of digestion. Our study, therefore, will take up both structure and process, and indeed usually will give more attention to the latter than to the former.

We discuss processes in order to facilitate an understanding of systems. Such a discussion is to be distinguished from a discussion of the processes for their own sake. Planning and control systems are used to facilitate decision making, but we are here interested in the systems, rather than in the decisions. People, not systems, make decisions.

Role of the Systems Designer

The foregoing distinction is especially important in analysis of the proper role of the systems designer.

The systems designer devises planning and control systems that will provide management with help in decision making and in the implementation or control of the decisions made. It is not his function to make marketing decisions, or production decisions, or decisions in any management area other than the systems area.

One reason for making this distinction between the decision-making process on the one hand and planning and control systems on the other hand is that this permits useful generalizations to be made about the processes or systems, generalizations that are independent of any specific activity and that are, therefore, applicable to a wide range of activities. There are similarities, permitting the development of general principles, in planning and control systems as they apply to marketing, production, research, and other business functions and also as they apply to government and other nonprofit organizations, even though the nature of the decisions made varies greatly among functional areas and between profit-seeking and nonprofit organizations.

Just as there is a marketing expertise, a production expertise, a finance expertise, and a general management expertise, so is there a planning and control systems expertise, or at least one can be developed. It is essential that the two types of expertise—the expertise in a function and expertise in systems that cut across functions—should not be confused with each other. The systems specialist is presumably able to help the marketing people to devise a planning and control system that will facilitate the management of the marketing process, but he should resist the temptation to tell marketing management what the decision on a marketing problem should be. The systems specialist can suggest methods of collecting and analyzing the information needed for one to make sound decisions, as well as methods of communicating the decisions and the results obtained, but he should not do the *deciding*. He can suggest the kind of data for management to use in deciding on pricing policy, but he should not determine the policy itself; useful ways of preparing an advertising budget, but not how much to spend for advertising or in what media; useful ways of estimating the costs of various channels of distribution, but not what channels to use; and so on.

Although not everyone agrees with us, we also believe that systems design should be distinguished from—kept separate from—decisions regarding the organization structure and division of responsibilities. The way in which a company is organized obviously has an impact on its planning and control systems, but when management is thinking about the best way of organizing, this impact is only one of several factors that it takes into account. The systems designer can give useful advice on the probable impact of alternative methods of organization on the planning and control systems, but this advice relates to only one aspect of the organizational problem. Management also must consider a number of other factors, particularly the personalities of the executives involved.

Thus, the systems designer, *when he is working as a systems designer* rather than as an over-all adviser to management, does not say that decentralization is good, or that it is bad. Rather, he says that if an organization is decentralized, it should use such-and-such management control systems; and if centralized, it should use different systems. In short, in designing systems, he must be prepared to accept the organizational relationships as a given. He may point out that a different organization structure would facilitate planning and control; however, if management believes that other considerations are more important and therefore decides not to change the organization, the systems designer builds the best systems he can to fit the needs of this organization.

Formal and Informal Systems

A distinction also should be made between formal and informal systems. It corresponds to the distinction between formal and informal organizations. Although it would be short-sighted to overlook the practical importance of the informal ways in which things get done in an organization, in this study we are mostly concerned with formal systems. By definition, one does not *design* an informal system; it is created without design. And since the basic reason for our interest in planning and control systems is to design better ones, we shall tend to think in terms of formal systems—those whose structure is visible and whose operation has explicit authorization. However, we shall not overlook the ways in which informal systems impinge on formal systems and thereby affect the planning and control processes.

Limitation to Large, Human Organizations

Our discussion is limited throughout to systems in *human organizations,* that is, groups of people brought together for a common purpose. Others, principally the cyberneticists, take a broader view; they consider the common characteristics of systems in individual persons, in organs, and in cells, as well as in groups of persons. We shall draw analogies between some aspects of systems in human organizations and other systems, but they are only analogies; no attempt will be made to discuss the question of whether or not generalizations applicable to systems in organizations are also applicable in a broader context.

We use "organization" not in the broad sense of "any group of persons associated together," which includes the family and other types of small groups, but rather in the more limited sense of "administered organizations" as defined by Thompson, et al.:[1] Administered organizations consist of groups that have these four characteristics: (1) they exhibit sustained collective action, (2) they are integral parts of a larger system, (3) they have specialized, delimited goals, and (4) they are dependent upon interchange with the larger system.

The analysis is not limited to any particular type of organization. Much of our research has been with profit-seeking companies, but we have done enough work with government agencies and other types of nonprofit organizations to warrant a belief that the suggested framework and accompanying descriptions of the topics are relevant for both profit-seeking and nonprofit groups.

We do exclude *small* organizations. Systems exist, at least in rudimentary form, in all organizations, whatever their size. Nevertheless, it is quite likely that the planning and control systems of small organizations—especially those so small that the management consists of one person rather than a group—are so different from those of larger organizations that many of the generalizations that are applicable to large organizations are not applicable to small ones, at least without considerable modification.

Although the suggested framework is believed to be broadly applicable, it probably is not universally applicable. It was prepared by and discussed with people who grew up in a "Western," "well-developed" cultural environment. Possibly the environment in other cultures is such that certain conclusions are not relevant to organizations there. We have no positive evidence that such is the case, but we are mindful of the disastrous results that have sometimes occurred when an American practice was transferred without modification to some other culture.

THE SEARCH FOR THE BEST MAIN TOPICS

Because the general subject area is named planning and control systems, there is a natural temptation to use as the two main divisions: (1) planning (roughly, deciding what to do) and (2) control (roughly, assuring that desired results are obtained). Many investigators and authors have followed this practice. Fayol,[2] for example, used the following processes or functions: planning, organizing, commanding, coordinat-

---

[1] James D. Thompson, et al., eds., *Comparative Studies in Administration* (Pittsburgh: University of Pittsburgh Press, 1959), pp. 5–6.

[2] Henri Fayol, *General and Industrial Management,* translated from the French *Administration Industrielle et Générale* (Dunod, 1925) by Constance Storrs (London: Sir Isaac Pitman & Sons, 1961).

ing, and controlling, thus setting up a fundamental distinction between planning and control. Other authors have used the same or similar break-downs. . . . Usually, authors regard these functions as occurring at every management level in the organization. Some refer to the "assign-ment of these activities to various executives," as if they were discrete, separable functions. Usually, two of the functions of management that are listed are planning and control.

Our attempts to fit facts into and make generalizations on the basis of such a breakdown have led to the conclusion that the over-all title selected for the area represents a trap; it insidiously invites a classification into (1) planning and (2) control, whereas this is *not* a useful break-down. The trouble essentially is that, although planning and control are definable abstractions and are easily understood as calling for different types of *mental* activity, they do not relate to separable major categories of activities actually carried on in an organization, either at different times, or by different people, or for different situations.

Most people in an organization engage in planning—from the salesman, who decides which customer to call on next, up to the president, who is thinking about the acquisition of a new subsidiary. But the planning done by the salesman is so different in its purpose and nature from that done by the president that few generalizations can be made that apply to both, and those generalizations that are valid for both are so vague and general that they are of little help in the solution of practical prob-lems of systems design.

In organizations there also is a process called control, but the type of control that is involved in assuring that a direct production worker's performance is satisfactory differs in important respects from the control exercised over, say, a researcher or a private secretary. Therefore, if control were to be a major subdivision, few generalizations could be made that would apply to all aspects of the process.

Furthermore, most authors describe the control process as involving, among other things, decision making, whereas decision making is also clearly the essence of the planning process. Conceptually, it is possible to break the control process into its purely control elements and its plan-ning elements, but such a breakdown is not useful, since in practice the elements occur together. For example, consider the activities that are generally understood to be included in the process called budgetary con-trol. This process involves a recurring cycle of activities. The cycle starts with the preparation and approval of a budget, which clearly is a plan-ning activity. But the budget also is used as a basis for control; indeed, many contend that the budgetary preparation activity is a principal means of achieving control. During the budget year, many activities occur that clearly fit the definition of control, but, simultaneously and as a part of the same process, there may occur an activity called budget revision, which is planning. In short, planning and control activities are so closely intertwined in the budgeting process that to describe each of them separately is not only difficult but also pointless—pointless because those concerned with the process usually are involved with and interested in both its planning aspect and its control aspect.

Despite these difficulties, authors do attempt to construct a framework with planning and control as separate main topics. Koontz,[3] for example, makes a basic distinction between planning ("selection from alternatives") and controlling ("measurement and correction of activities"). Note that even these two definitions overlap, since the correction of activities certainly involves a selection from alternative possibilities for correction. He goes on to say, ". . . the control process . . . involves three steps: (1) the establishment of standards; (2) the appraisal of performance against these standards; and (3) the correction of deviations." Surely, the first of these involves the selection from alternatives and necessarily precedes both the measurement and the correction of activities; it is much more closely related to planning than it is to control. To the extent that the third step requires a revision of the program, which is one type of correction that Koontz describes, this also is planning. Thus, what is supposed to be a basic distinction between planning and control turns out, by its own definitions, not to be a distinction at all. Other authors, although also recognizing the same interrelationship, devote whole chapters or even whole sections of their books to separate discussions of planning and control.

It should be recognized that Koontz is thoroughly aware of the existence of this overlap; in the article from which the above definitions are quoted, he says that "planning and control are so closely interconnected as to be singularly inseparable," and similar statements appear in other books and articles. He nevertheless believes that a distinction between planning and control is useful, for example, in pointing up the necessity of relating controls to plans. He therefore sets forth a list of "Planning Principles" and a separate list of "Principles of Control."

Actually, Koontz' principles of planning are generally related to the broad, important types of plans that we propose to label strategic planning; they do not relate to the recurring, systematic types of planning that we shall put under the heading of management control. This focus on strategy can be seen in a comparison of Koontz' principles with the "principles of military strategy" used by the military. . . . Thus, his lists of principles seem to be based on a distinction that is not made clear in his definition.

Some writers, after recognizing the interrelationship, take the op-

---

[3] Harold Koontz, "A Preliminary Statement of Principles of Planning and Control," *Journal of the Academy of Management,* vol. 1 (April 1958), pp. 47, 48.

posite tack. Rathe,[4] for example, points out that "it is difficult to separate planning and control." This leads him to lump these activities together: ". . . the interplay of planning and control has become known as Management Control." Probably he intends management control to be used in the same sense as that in which it is used in this study.

The editors of *Administrative Control and Executive Action*[5] imply that they intend the term "administrative control" to correspond approximately to what will here be designated as management control, that is, to include a type of planning. Nevertheless, the editors' definition of control is this: "the review of actual progress by comparison with the plan and observation of the variance or deviation," and this definition excludes planning.

The confusion in the literature is reflected in company practice. There is, for example, a function that some companies call "production planning" and that other companies call "production control." There often is no difference in the activities actually performed under these labels.

Other Possible Frameworks

These considerations led to a search for a different way of organizing the material in the area—a framework that does *not* use planning and control as the main subdivisions or, on the other hand, lump together all aspects of these functions. What is needed is a framework that will permit the arrangement of useful generalizations under main topics with a minimum of overlapping. Furthermore, the organizational activities classified under a given main topic should be essentially similar to one another in some respects and essentially different from activities that are classified under other main topics.

Over the past three years, we have experimented with various possibilities for such a framework. Our first step was to draw from the literature several hundred statements about planning and control systems. We attempted to arrange these in some sort of sensible order. At one time, we used "structure" and "process" as the two main headings. Under structure, which we considered analogous to anatomy (what a system *is*), we collected comments about (*a*) the characteristics of the information contained in an organization system, broken down by operating input information (e.g., costs), capital input information (e.g., capital budgets), output information (e.g., transfer prices), and combined input/output information (e.g., return on investment), and (*b*) the structure and con-

---

[4] Alex W. Rathe, "Management Control," in *Administrative Control and Executive Action*, B. C. Lemke and James Don Edwards, eds. (Columbus: Charles E. Merrill Books, 1961), p. 27.

[5] B. C. Lemke and James Don Edwards, eds., *Administrative Control and Executive Action*, p. viii.

tent of reports. Under process, which we considered analogous to physiology (what the system *does*), our breakdown was into long-range planning, short-range planning, operating, measuring results, and acting on results.

It soon became apparent that the topics listed under "process" were artificial. Authors did write about long-range planning as a separate subject, but most of them made no sharp separation among the other topics listed. Instead, they described short-range planning, operating, measuring results, and taking action as parts of one unified process, and they preferred to discuss the process as a whole, rather than to consider any one of its parts as a separate entity.

Furthermore (and in retrospect this seems obvious), many authors who wrote about the anatomy of a system, did so in terms of physiology —how it worked. We had to classify their statements under each of our two main headings, and this was a clear indication that our classification scheme was weak. Efforts to patch up this outline proved unavailing. The basic difficulty was in the main headings, and we could correct it only by making a fundamental change in them.

THE PROPOSED FRAMEWORK

A brief description of the main topics in our proposed framework is given here, together with the considerations that led us to settle on this framework as the most useful one we can think of. . . .

Strategic Planning

To start with, we found it easy to identify two rather different types of planning activities in an organization. One is the type of planning mentioned above as associated with the control process, an activity related to the ongoing administration of the organization. The other type is identified by terms such as policy formulation, goal setting, and top management planning. The thought processes in each of these types of planning are similar, but in most other respects the two types are so different that almost no important generalizations apply to both of them.

We identified this latter planning activity as the first of our main categories and labeled it *strategic planning*. The definition we suggest is as follows:

> *Strategic planning* is the process of deciding on objectives of the organization, on changes in these objectives, on the resources used to attain these objectives, and on the policies that are to govern the acquisition, use, and disposition of these resources.

"Objectives" are what the organization wishes to accomplish (in military parlance, the "mission"), and "policies" are guidelines that are to be used in the choice of the most appropriate course of action for accomplishing the objectives.

The word "strategy" is used here in its usual sense of combining and employing resources. It connotes big plans, important plans, plans with major consequences. Some students of management restrict the word strategy to those plans that are made in response to a competitor's action or in anticipation of his probable reaction, but there appears to be no particular reason for making such a restriction, and the word is not used here in this limited sense. Others draw a distinction between strategy and "grand" strategy, but again, there seems to be no valid reason to set up separate categories for purposes of the suggested framework. . . .

Management Control

Whereas strategic planning is one type of planning, there is another type that is associated with the ongoing administration of the enterprise, but, as already pointed out, this other type is so closely associated with control activities that setting it up as a separate main category would be artificial. For our second main category, therefore, we use a concept that combines both planning and control. As a label for this concept, we use "management control."

This label has the obvious weakness of not mentioning planning. The obvious solution, to use "management planning and control," seems unnecessarily cumbersome. . . . Furthermore, there seems to be increasing use of the term management control to refer to the same combination of planning and control activities that we have in mind. The definition we suggest is as follows:

> *Management control* is the process by which managers assure that resources are obtained and used effectively and efficiently in the accomplishment of the organization's objectives.

This definition is intended to convey three key ideas. First, the process involves managers, that is, people who get things done by working with other people. Second, the process takes place within a context of objectives and policies that have been arrived at in the strategic planning process. Third, the criteria relevant for judging the actions taken in this process are effectiveness and efficiency. . . .

Operational Control

At one time, we thought that strategic planning and management control should be the two main topics of our framework. It became apparent, however, that many of the generalizations that are relevant for management control do not work well for a certain class of the organization's activities, and that there are generalizations applicable to this class that are invalid for other activities. It also is apparent that mistakes with serious practical consequences have been made when techniques and generalizations found valid for one class of activities have been applied to the other. We therefore saw the need for a third main topic.

We have groped for the most useful way of describing this third topic so as to differentiate it from management control, but even now are by no means satisfied with the results. One possibility was to draw a line between activities that required the use of judgment and those that could be completely governed by formal decision rules. We referred to these as nonprogrammed and programmed activities. However, this distinction eventually seemed to be less useful than a slightly different one, one that is based on the distinction between the activities properly referred to as management and activities that relate to the performance of specified tasks. We call the latter *operational control* and define it as follows:

> *Operational control* is the process of assuring that specific tasks are carried out effectively and efficiently.

This definition is somewhat vague. It intends to convey the idea that operational control is to be distinguished from management control in at least the following key ways: (1) Operational control is concerned with tasks (e.g., manufacturing Job No. 5687; ordering 500 units of Item 84261), whereas management control is concerned with individuals, that is, managers. (2) The tasks to which operational control relates are specified, so that little or no judgment is required as to what is to be done; the activities to which management control relates are not specified, and management decides what is to be done within the general constraints of the strategic plans. In operational control, the focus is on execution; in management control it is on both planning and execution. . . .

Classification of Business Activities

The three processes described briefly in the preceeding paragraphs are the main categories of our framework. It is unrealistic for us to expect that they are already meaningful to the reader. Our task . . . is to make them meaningful. Exhibit 1 is given as a preliminary device for this purpose. It classifies certain planning and control activities of a business organization under our three main categories. Note that the activities listed under strategic planning are almost entirely planning activities, that those listed under management control are a mixture of both planning and control, and that those listed under operational control are almost entirely control activities.

EXHIBIT 1
Examples of Activities in a Business Organization Included in Major Framework Headings

Strategic Planning	Management Control	Operational Control
Choosing company objectives	Formulating budgets	
Planning the organization	Planning staff levels	Controlling hiring
Setting personnel policies	Formulating personnel practices	Implementing policies
Setting financial policies	Working capital planning	Controlling credit extension
Setting marketing policies	Formulating advertising programs	Controlling placement of advertisements
Setting research policies	Deciding on research projects	
Choosing new product lines	Choosing product improvements	
Acquiring a new division	Deciding on plant rearrangement	Scheduling production
Deciding on nonroutine capital expenditures	Deciding on routine capital expenditures	
	Formulating decision rules for operational control	Controlling inventory
	Measuring, appraising, and improving management performance	Measuring, appraising, and improving workers' efficiency

Disclaimers

At this point, we wish to make two disclaimers.

First, we did not originate the classification described above. Others have used the same similar categories. For example, Simon's[6] distinction between programmed and nonprogrammed decisions essentially corresponds to our categories of operational control and management control. The distinction between policy formulation and policy execution or administration, which is a common one in management textbooks,[7]

---

[6] Herbert Simon, "A Framework for Decision Making," *Proceedings of a Symposium on Decision Theory* (Athens: Ohio University, 1963), pp. 1–3.

[7] See, for example, George Albert Smith, Jr., and C. Roland Christensen, *Policy Formulation and Administration* (4th ed.; Homewood, Ill.; Richard D. Irwin, Inc., 1962).

corresponds to our distinction between strategic planning and management control. And increasing numbers of researchers and practitioners are using the term management control in the same sense as that in which it is used here.[8]

Our second disclaimer is against implying an unwarranted degree of precision in our classifications. The lines between categories are blurred, and, as our colleagues have amply demonstrated in discussions of the framework, it is easy to find situations that do not fit clearly in a single category. We believe that these borderline situations and exceptions are not so numerous as to upset the essential validity of the categories, but there is room for disagreement on this point.

Information Handling

The three terms defined above comprise the three main topics in our framework. . . . [T]wo other topics are discussed which, although not viewed here as a part of the area of planning and control systems, are related to it and need to be carefully distinguished from it.

The first is called *information handling.* Planning and control systems use data, and generalizations about the uses of data for strategic planning, management control, and operational control properly belong under each of these headings. But quite apart from these generalizations about the use of data, some important generalizations can be made about handling data, generalizations that are independent of the intended use of the data. The whole body of generalizations relating to the design and utilization of computers is an example. Since these generalizations cut across our three main topics, it seems desirable to collect them in a separate category. This is defined as follows:

> *Information handling* is the process of collecting, manipulating, and transmitting information, whatever its use is to be.

❖   ❖   ❖   ❖   ❖

Financial Accounting

Strategic planning, management control, and operational control are internally oriented; that is, they have to do with activities that occur inside an organization. There is a certain amount of confusion between these processes and *financial accounting,* which has an entirely different orientation, as suggested by the following definition:

> *Financial accounting* is the process of reporting financial information about the organization to the outside world.

---

[8] See, for example, Charles P. Bonini, Robert K. Jaedicke, and Harvey M. Wagner, *Management Controls* (New York: McGraw-Hill Book Company, 1964).

. . . Our objective is not to describe fully the process or the principles governing it [financial accounting], but rather to distinguish clearly between financial accounting and management control. The difference stems essentially from the fact that society has developed certain financial accounting principles to which all businesses are expected to adhere, whereas no such externally imposed principles govern management control information.

The relationships among the five topics here defined are indicated by Exhibit 2.

EXHIBIT 2
Planning and Control Processes in Organizations

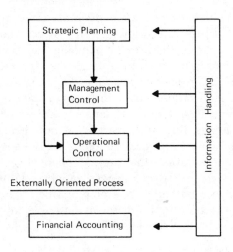

SUMMARY

The purpose of this study is to suggest a useful framework for classifying topics that fall within the general subject labeled planning and control systems. Such a framework is essential to the researcher, the practitioner, and the student.

The general area consists of formal planning and control *systems,* designed to facilitate planning and control *processes* in human organizations, without regard to whether the organizations are profit-seeking or nonprofit in character, but excluding small organizations.

The three processes designated as the main topics of the proposed framework are strategic planning, management control, and operational control. In addition, we distinguish these topics from information handling and financial accounting.

STUDENT REVIEW QUESTIONS

1. What distinction does Anthony make between the decision-making process and the planning and control system?
2. Anthony notes that "planning and control activities are so closely inter-related in the budgeting process that to describe each of them separately is not only difficult but pointless. . . ." Do you agree with this observation?
3. What is "management control," according to Anthony?
4. How does "management control" differ from "strategic planning" and from "operational control"?
5. Apply Anthony's "framework" in two situations, a business enterprise and a nonprofit organization.

21. The Planning Dilemma: There Is a Way Out[*]

JAMES S. HEKIMIAN and
HENRY MINTZBERG

STRATEGIC PLANNING increasingly is becoming an important top management preoccupation. This kind of planning, which some companies call long-range planning, establishes the direction in which the organization will go. It is a formalized procedure that considers such decisions as whether to market a new product, float a stock issue, restructure organizational responsibility, embark on an expansion program.

Many large corporations now have departments responsible for drafting their strategic plans. These departments are staffed by specialists—economists, market researchers, statisticians, operations researchers and systems analysts—who are skilled in the use of such tools as computers, game theory and mathematics. Over varying periods of time, but most often yearly, strategic plans are produced, supported by vast amounts of data that have been carefully documented and analyzed in the best scientific tradition.

Despite this systematic approach, there is some evidence that management does not always use the plans its planners have developed. Consider these cases:

1. A team of researchers recently spent a week interviewing the top executives of a large East Coast textile firm in an attempt to determine just how the company's strategic decisions are made. When their work was about completed, the researchers asked the president of the company whether he had ever considered establishing a planning department. "A planning department? We've had one for three years," he answered. "Would you like to see a copy of our strategic plans?" The researchers

---

[*] James S. Hekimian and Henry Mintzberg, "The Planning Dilemma: There Is a Way Out," *Sloan Management Review*, May 1968. © 1968 by the Industrial Management Review Association; all rights reserved. Reprinted by permission.

were somewhat taken aback. At no time during the discussions about top-level decision making had the president mentioned the existence of strategic plans drafted by the planning department.

2. Two members of the planning department of a large Canadian corporation told a colleague how frustrated they were. "We exert tremendous efforts developing the annual strategic plans. Meanwhile, management goes along making important decisions without ever referring to our plans. Last week, for instance, the president went to lunch with a friend and on the spot bought his company. If he had checked our plans, he would have seen that the acquisition was all wrong. Why do we bother making plans?" These men subsequently quit the company.

Yet it's only fair to say that if some planners are disillusioned because their plans are often contradicted or ignored, many managers are unhappy because they feel the plans frequently are impractical and irrelevant. The dilemma is often phrased this way: Planners make plans and managers make decisions and "never the twain shall meet"—at least not very often.

To a large extent the dilemma is inevitable because of the way in which the job of each group is conceived. For this reason, it is necessary to examine the nature of managerial work and the nature of the planning effort before any attempt can be made toward finding a way out of the dilemma.

THE MANAGER'S JOB

The traditional view of managerial work is contained in the writings of Luther Gulick, who, in the 1930s, presented the acronym POSDCORB— planning, organizing, staffing, directing, coordinating, reporting, budgeting. The manager is depicted as an omnipotent individual, continually pushing ahead with an ever better corporate strategy.

Compare this view with the sort of managerial day common today: The telephone rings regularly; a large and diverse group of people come in to discuss a wide range of issues; a staggering load of mail crosses the desk, some containing vital information, some requiring response or other action, and some junk; a retiring employee says good-by; the mayor sends an assistant to advise that steps must be taken to reduce the fumes coming out of the factory chimney; an article in the *Harvard Business Review* strikes a responsive note.

It is obvious that the POSDCORB image is not a very helpful one; the manager's job is far more complex and far less glamorous than this acronym indicates. The following three concepts help to explain the nature of managerial work today:

1. Organizational Nerve Center. The focal point of organizational information, whether that organization be a multibillion dollar conglomerate or a 50-man job shop, is the manager of the organization. The problems, the ideas, the pressures and the simple detail all find their way to the manager.

Some of this information is in hard form; that is, it is tabulated on paper and is available to anyone who has access to the paper. Examples are production reports, market forecasts and written customer complaints.

Much of the data, however, particularly that important in the making of strategic decisions, is never converted to hard form: the preliminary reaction of the board of directors to a proposal, the conflict between two subordinates who approach the manager for a solution, the words of suppliers as to what a big competitor is planning to do, the morale of the factory workers. All this, too, is important information, yet none of it is ever recorded, and some of it is never even verbally communicated.

The manager, in the unique position of heading the organization to which these data pertain, finds that he is the nerve center of the organization. True, he never has all the information that he wants, but he has more of it and he gets it from more sources than anyone else in the organization. As the head of his organization, he must know what each department is doing, and he selectively carries or transmits this information from one department to another. Much of the information that flows in from outside the organization flows through the manager. Directors, heads of other companies dealing with the organization, stockholders, government officials all feel that it will be most effective to deal with the president. And as long as everybody *feels* this way, they are correct!

2. *Adaptor to Time Constraints.* Managerial work is distinguished by time pressures of three kinds: the manager's lack of time, his need to react quickly to unanticipated problems and the need to time his decisions properly.

Lack of Time. It is a simple fact that the manager wishes each day could be extended. The great number of people whom he wishes to see and who wish to see him, along with the ever-increasing load of reading material, create great time pressures. The textbooks say that he should plan, but the mail will not wait and the people who want to see him cannot be delayed. In effect, the manager's most valuable resource—his time—is, to a great extent, not allocated by himself. Thus the manager cannot be depicted as relaxed and reflective. Rather, he must integrate information as it comes, must juggle a large number of issues at the same time and must make many decisions hastily. The manager is not a planner because he does not have time to delve into issues at length or reflect leisurely and carefully about his problems.

Reacting to Unanticipated Problems. Usually, the manager does not become aware of problems in time to meditate carefully about alternative solutions. Frequently, the pressures to come up with a quick answer to a problem become overriding. A company president, for example, may have to act quickly to reassure stockholders and customers when it comes to light that a subordinate officer has been engaging in unethical activities. Or consider the time pressures on a company president when a piece of equipment the company has introduced has resulted in the deaths of several people. He must come up with a fast explanation of why it happened and what is being done to prevent a reoccurrence.

Timing the Decision. Timing is the critical element in the seizing of opportunities. Decisions often cannot be carefully scheduled; effective change often depends on chance opportunities that cannot be forecast. The president of a very large manufacturing firm, for example, decided that he wanted to effect a reorganization. He knew that if he did it "right now," considerable resistance and bitterness would develop; but he also knew that it would be too long a wait until two or three "old line" vice-presidents retired. Therefore, he temporarily shelved his decision until the timing was right. When one vice-president unexpectedly resigned, he moved another to a new position and integrated the third into his new plan of organization.

And take the case of the president of the Canadian corporation mentioned earlier who went to lunch and bought a company. Perhaps the asking price was so good that he could afford to enter a market that had never before been considered.

The manager is basically an adaptive worker. He does not and cannot sit back and make formal plans. Because he is continually working under severe time constraints and because he must react quickly to unanticipated problems and chance opportunities, the manager must handle each new situation according to the realities of its time pressures.

3. Ultimate Authority. To the extent that any organization is formally structured, one ultimate authority must exist. Inherent in the manager's job is the notion of authority. He is considered responsible for the important decisions made in his organization. This is not a theoretical aspect of his job, and is not, as many behaviorists would have the manager believe, a disappearing function. Whether he is signing checks or reviewing a capital budgeting proposal, the manager is acting as a final authority.

This responsibility extends even to decisions made by subordinates. When the steel industry tried to raise prices in 1962, for example, the final onus fell on the respective company presidents.

Why, in the age of participative management, is there a need for such old-fashioned authority? The answer is twofold:

1. To ensure that an organization does not take off in a variety of opposing directions, it is necessary to have the same person authorize every major decision.

2. To take into consideration the often conflicting interests of many groups involved with the organization, such as stockholders, employees or government regulators, someone must make value judgments in the interests of some and contrary to the interests of others. Value judgments

—choosing between growth and profit or deciding whether to lay off employees for one week to decrease costs—are basically different from questions of fact. Factual decisions can be made by anyone who can get the information; choices among values are by necessity judgmental. The manager is assigned to make these judgments.

In view of these aspects of his job, what can be concluded about the manager as strategy maker? First, the manager must be the heart of the strategy making system. The process begins with information gathering, and we have seen that the manager has the information. It ends with choices among values, and we have seen that the manager has the unique authority to make these choices. Furthermore, we can conclude that strategy making is not a process of once-and-for-all planning. Rather, strategy *evolves* as the manager reacts to problems and opportunities as they arise. In essence, he works in stepwise fashion, identifying a problem or opportunity, making a decision, interpreting the feedback, moving on to the next problem and so on. This is why managers often find that they have implemented strategy before they have explicitly stated it. Gradually, the precedent-making decisions evolve into organization strategies.

THE PLANNER'S JOB

The planner's day differs considerably from that of the manager. The information, the telephone calls, the requests and the problems that constantly interrupt the manager are not a central part of the planner's concerns.

Three aspects of the nature of planning stand out vis-à-vis the nature of managing:

1. *The Single Task.* The planner has one long-range and well-defined task: to make plans. All his time is devoted to this job. Thus he is not disrupted or led astray from his main task. However, because his task is unrelated to the day-to-day operating problems of the organization, the planner is removed from the natural flow of information. He is not in touch with ongoing operations and, therefore, is unable to appreciate the daily pressures that act on the manager. As a result, he cannot understand why the manager treats planning so lightly.

2. *The Integrative Approach.* Planning is basically an integrative process. In effect, one plans in order to make many decisions at the same time so that they can be interrelated. When the cry goes up that the organization needs to plan, the cause has inevitably been a conflict between decisions made at different points in time. For example, when management discovers that the new factory is not large enough to handle the new product line, someone points out that a facilities planning effort would have taken into account the decision to embark on a new product line.

Planners make their plans by collecting information that is relevant and available to them, analyzing it and generating possible courses of action.

They attempt to collect long-run data, ignoring day-to-day fluctuations. They will investigate consumer and economic trends and look at technological change, and then define the basic problems, challenges and opportunities that will face the organization in the future. They project and evaluate the consequences of alternative courses of action. After combining various possibilities into alternative strategies, they develop explicit plans to solve the problems and exploit the opportunities. Then further plans (manpower requirements and budgets, for example) are drawn up to account for the effects of changes in basic strategy. By its very nature, planning leads to an integration of the various elements the plan comprises.

3. The Programmed Approach. In contrast to the manager who must act quickly and intuitively, the planner has the time and training to use a programmed or systematic approach to the making of strategy. "Programmed" in this context is the opposite of "intuitive," which implies an undefined procedure that takes place subconsciously in the mind of one man. The planner takes an explicit approach and he follows well-defined procedures for handling given inputs. However, the planner is still required to make many judgments at stages where steps and sequence are not clear.

Clearly, strategy does not *evolve* from planning as it often does from specific managerial actions. The methodology of planning demands that strategy be *created*. There is no recognition of the implicitness or adaptiveness associated with managerial strategy making; the planner sets forth one set of explicit plans for all to see.

THE PLANNING DILEMMA

The planning function evolved over the years in the large corporation because management recognized the need to integrate various decisions and to take a more reasoned look at the future. Furthermore, useful planning programs were becoming increasingly more available. Management realized that it would be unable to carry out this kind of planning itself because of the time pressures discussed earlier. Thus planning and managing became separate functions on the organization chart. Planners were to plan, and managers to manage. It is important to recognize that this decision was one of expediency rather than reasoned thought.

The result has been ambivalent behavior in organizations. (See Table 1.) *Unaided managing* has led to a short-run view of organizational strategy making; treating each decision as an independent step has led to uncoordinated efforts. As organizations have become more complex, fire fighting has replaced innovating. Managers continued to manage as they always had. The only difference was that someone else was doing the "necessary" planning. However, it was not readily apparent that nothing had really changed. Planning was going on, but it was *detached planning*.

Plans were made and managers filed them away because they seemed to be (and often were) unrelated to the problems at hand.

TABLE 1
Managing versus Planning

Factor	Manager	Planner
Work pressures	Many demands on time; no chance to delve.	Much free time; one job—to plan.
Decision-making method	Intuitive; implicit.	Analytical; explicit programs.
Authority	Formal and real; must choose among values.	Formal authority only with factual questions.
Information	Nerve center.	Lacks effective access to channels, but has time to collect information.
Feedback	Short-run, adaptive.	Long-run, reflective.
Timing	Needs to react to un-anticipated problems, chance opportunities.	Neglects timing factors.
Strategy making	Strategy evolves as precedent-setting decisions are made in stepwise fashion.	Integrated strategic plans created at one point in time.

This, then, is the dilemma: The manager, who has the authority and information to formulate strategic plans, has been unable to make effective use of the planner, who has the time and the skills to do this job. The manager needs to adapt to what is going on, the planner wants to integrate what will go on, and the organization desperately needs both—but not separate from each other. Managing and planning are neither easily nor logically separable functions.

COOPERATIVE PLANNING

Is there any way out of the dilemma? We believe there is, that it is possible to set up an effective strategy making system. Such a system will recognize:

The manager's access to information and his time constraints.

The planner's basic resources—time and analytical programs.

The manager's responsibility for making the final choices.

The need for organizational flexibility to adapt to unanticipated problems and chance opportunities.

The need for integrated decisions.

The planning system that we propose resolves the problems discussed earlier and meets the requirements for effective strategic planning by (1) reorienting the planning process so that timing factors are recognized, (2) including a contingency planning phase and (3) delegating one other job to the planner—that of applying his programs when unexpected circumstances create a situation requiring fast reaction. We call this *adaptive planning, contingency planning* and *real-time planning*.

TABLE 2
Cooperative Planning

Planning Method	Manager's Role	Planner's Role
Adaptive planning: Plans created in the form of decision trees, accounting for trigger events and branch decisions.	Monitors environment to define trigger events; chooses branch.	Works with manager to develop strategic plans in form of decision trees.
Contingency planning: Contingencies forecast, and means of handling them when they occur developed.	Works with planner to forecast contingencies; calls on plan or program when contingency is recognized.	Works out solution or program to handle each contingency; applies programs when necessary.
Real-time planning: Manager and planner work as man/machine system, handling unanticipated events in real-time.	Defines events to planner; chooses next course of action, using planner recommendations.	Clarifies the issue; searches for alternatives; evaluates alternatives; integrates events and solutions with existing strategic plans.

Adaptive planning recognizes the importance of timing and uncertainty in implementing plans and thus deals with *anticipated* action. There is no question that the plan will be undertaken; the question is when and how. Contingency planning is concerned with events that *may* occur. Plans are prepared in case they are needed. Real-time planning recognizes that there will always be some *unanticipated* problems, and the need for planning will arise along with the problem. (See Table 2.)

Adaptive Planning

Traditionally, strategic plans are laid out as if all planned decisions will be made with certainty at a predetermined time. In fact, such certainty seldom exists. If the plans are to be useful to the manager, they must be broad enough to give him room to adapt. Two kinds of uncertainty must be recognized:

Uncertain Timing. Events that are expected to occur at uncertain times must precede the making of decisions. For example, interest rates must fall before the go-ahead is given on a new plant; political conditions have to stabilize before the Nigerian sales branch is opened; diversification moves by a defense contractor will be signaled by moves toward peace in Vietnam.

Uncertain Events. The manager may want to be able to choose from more than one plan. The events leading up to the decision will determine which plan is, in fact, chosen, but that choice cannot be made when plans are first made. For example, the size of a marketing effort for a new product may depend on test market results; the location of a new plant may depend on impending state legislation; the mix of acquisitions may depend on the changing attitudes of antitrust division; an oceanographic firm's expansion may depend on whether the Department of Defense's post-Vietnam planning emphasizes offensive anti-submarine warfare or defensive anti-missile warfare. Thus the planner must focus not only on the decisions to be made, but also on the "triggers" preceding them, which will determine when those decisions are to be made and how they will be made. Current practice resembles Cook's tour planning—plans are represented by a determinate series of steps. In contrast, Lewis-and-Clark planning occurs when plans are represented by a decision tree showing the trigger events and the decision branches.[1] The two kinds of plans can be depicted this way:

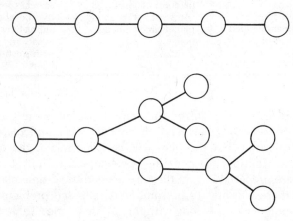

In Lewis-and-Clark planning, the planner works closely with the manager and develops strategic plans that suggest *when* it would be opportune to take action and *what* action would be called for in given recent events.

---

[1] These kinds of planning are described by James R. Schlesinger in a RAND Corporation article entitled "Organization Structures and Planning" (P-3316, February 25, 1966).

Under this approach, the plans are not so constrained that management feels that it must ignore them. The plans recognize the adaptive nature of managing and give the manager the flexibility to decide the *what's* and *when's* of the current situation.

Contingency Planning

Planners have rightly spent great amounts of effort to predict environmental trends. They have stressed quantitative projections; using mathematical techniques they extrapolate economic, market share, cost and other trends. There has been little recognition, however, of the need to predict important events that *may* or *may not* occur and to develop means of reacting to the resulting problems and opportunities. For example, a drug manufacturer may predict the future development of a birth control pill to be taken once a year; a supermarket chain may consider the possibility that a soft goods discount store will decide to market food items; a bank would be alert to possible changes in the interest rate; a large manufacturer may have reason to anticipate a strike or tariff change.

In effect, the planner is looking for possible problems and opportunities *before* they occur. Note that contingencies may be external to the organization—political occurrences, competitors' actions, economic events or internal—technological breakthroughs, strikes, project failures. The decision to plan for a contingency, and the resources committed to such planning, will be a function of the projected impact of the contingency on the organization. The manager will play a vital role in identifying those contingencies that are likely enough to occur and that, if they do occur, will have enough impact to warrant the preparation of contingency plans. He'll also denote the amount of effort that is justified in view of the likelihood and the impact of the contingency.

Once the contingencies that may throw the existing plans and the organization into disarray have been identified and analyzed, the planner prepares contingency plans. The planner assumes that each given contingency will indeed occur and studies its impact on the organization. In doing this, he also attempts to assess the lead time that the organization will have between the occurrence of the contingency and the need to act on it. He is then able to work out an approach to the potential problem or opportunity in light of this lead time.Three kinds of approaches may be used.

If the contingency will have a devastating effect on the organization, it may be necessary to hedge. For example, if a possible strike might cause great financial losses, early steps may be taken to decrease the possibility of a strike. If the probability of a sudden jump in sales is high enough, it may pay to go ahead on a new plant rather than just plan to do so. In effect, the plans are changed to avoid the contingency.

Where the nature of the contingency can be easily predicted in advance, the planner would work out a complete solution and relate it to the existing plans. Thus a bank may be able to make specific plans to handle given changes in the interest rates. Or take the dramatic example of war plans. Wherever the President of the United States goes, he has at his side a briefcase of plans outlining the steps to be taken in the event of any serious, imaginable war contingency. If the contingent event actually occurs, the plans are available for immediate implementation.

Finally, when the circumstances surrounding the contingency cannot be known exactly in advance, and when the lead time allows for it, the planner will develop a *program* to deal with the situation when it arises. For example, a company on a merger spree may not know in advance what opportunities will become available. But the planner may be able to develop a procedure in the form of checklists to aid in the quick analysis of opportunities when they arise. An organization that foresees possible labor strife may take steps to develop a real-time computer program to evaluate the cost of any wage package brought up during the negotiations.

Contingency plans, therefore, may take three forms—immediate action; solutions to handle the contingency; programs to aid in the handling of a contingency when it arises.

We have seen how the planner is able to do the groundwork necessary in helping the manager respond to contingencies. Two vital jobs remain. First, the manager must know what is available within the inventory of contingency plans, so that when the situation presents itself, he can call on the appropriate plan or program. This requires careful briefing by the planner. Second, the planner must keep in touch with events and with the manager, so that contingency plans can be updated and called into action as changes take place.

Contingency planning allows the planner to use his free time to study contingencies. He then uses his analytical programs to work out methods for handling them. Throughout the year, the manager, as nerve center, looks for the occurrence of contingencies. When they occur, however, there is no need for him to act autonomously and intuitively; he is now able to call on the planner for a carefully worked out method of handling the issue—either a specific plan or a program to develop answers.

Real-Time Planning

Obviously, not all problems and opportunities can be foreseen. Also, although some may be foreseen, management may decide the potential situation does not warrant a contingency plan. Nevertheless, the planner need not let his skills go to waste because a situation external to the planning process arises. The manager and planner can work like the much-heralded man/machine system, the manager coupling his current information and intuitive knowledge with the programs of the planner. When an issue suddenly arises, the manager begins by defining the situation to the planner. "I have a chance to get this contract if I act fast. Should I?" "Supplier X is not going to deliver a vital component on time; it may be three weeks late. What will happen?" "The government is on the verge of calling back our ambassador from that African state where our plants are located. What should we do?" The planner is thus able to get information to which only the manager has access. The planner then may conduct one of four kinds of analysis:

Conceptualization. He may clarify and conceptualize the issue, getting more information on the structure of the problem, the important variables and the related events. For example, if it is one concerning economic events, he may use input/output analysis to develop a "feel" for the magnitude of the problem.

Search. The planner may search for alternative solutions to a problem, perhaps using brainstorming techniques, perhaps scanning relevant literature.

Evaluation. He may undertake a detailed, explicit evaluation of the consequences of the opportunity or of the possible solutions to a problem. A new product invention may call for a market research study; a problem relating to tariff changes may lend itself to an operations research approach; a facilities problem may be amenable to cost-benefit or return-on-investment calculations.

Integration. Finally, the planner would study the effect of the issue and its solution on the existing strategic and operating plans. The plans would then be changed to avoid new problems and to take advantage of the necessary changes in an integrated fashion. For example, the planner might use a PERT model to study the effect of a strike in one area on the schedules of all the company's projects.

Finally, the planner comes back to the manager with the analysis, and the manager chooses the next course of action.

In part, the planner has done what the manager might do if he had the time. But he has done it more thoroughly and with far less time pressure. The manager has continued to manage as he must, giving attention to the mail and the callers, while the planner gives attention to the problem. The key to this system is leverage. The manager may spend one hour defining the issue to the planner and one hour listening to the planner's recommendations one week later. During that one week, the planner and his staff of eight may be able to put in two man-months working on the problem. The planner can put in two man-months in one week; the manager may not be able to afford even two man-hours.

Note that real-time planning is not simply a method for having intelligent people look at problems. Most managers already use intelligent assistants to advise them on the issues that arise. In this system, the manager is taking advantage of the planner's programs and skills. In one case market research is used; in another, systems analysis; in a third, input/output analysis. The manager is calling on proven management science to give him insight into problems while they are current and while he goes on managing.

This differs from traditional uses of management science programs, where only the issues devoid of extreme time pressures are given to the analyst. The planner who can succeed in this environment is the one who can do "quick and dirty" analysis; that is, one who can apply his programs with the speed necessary to give answers to the manager in "real time"— while the problem is current. This will involve cutting many corners, and will frustrate the planner who looks for elegance in his solutions. Market researchers may have to avoid tests of statistical significance, operations researchers will have to admit to themselves that many alternatives have been ignored because of lack of time, forecasters will have to use simple mathematics. But unlike the elegant solutions, these will be useful to the manager because they are timely and can be adapted to his problem.

Planner of the Future

In the years ahead we foresee the planner's playing a more active role in the actual affairs of the company. His plans are no longer elegant documents describing corporate utopia. They are concerned with *real* triggers and *real* contingencies and *real* time, and they handle these situations in the context in which the manager will have to handle them. When the anticipated problems and opportunities arise, the plans, in the form of decision trees, relate to them. When contingencies occur, the planner is close at hand, prepared to pull out the plan or program that has been especially developed for this particular eventuality. When there is an occurrence that was unanticipated, the planner does not bury his head in the sand, hoping that it will go away so that the plan remains intact. He leaves his long-range planning function temporarily and works with the manager to handle this issue, with the manager contributing his knowledge of the situation and the planner his time resources and analytical programs.

The recommendations for adaptive, contingency and real-time planning derive from one basic belief: Planning and managing must be closely integrated in all situations. When this is true, strategic planning will be a powerful tool; when not true, the inevitable planning dilemma will result.

STUDENT REVIEW QUESTIONS

1. Do managements use the plans which their organizational planners develop? What happens if they do not?

2. What are the aspects of time in the manager's work which affects his ability and willingness to plan?
3. Should planning be a line function, a staff function, or should it involve both types of managers?
4. What is the "planning dilemma," according to the authors?
5. Is "real-time" planning an answer to the planning dilemma, in your opinion?
6. Who should do the planning in universities; faculty groups, administrators, or staff planners?

22. Using the Systems Analyst in Preparing Corporate Financial Models[*]

DANIEL J. McCARTHY and
CHARLES A. MORRISSEY

PROBABLY no function in corporate or institutional management has received more attention in the past ten years than that of formal long-range planning, particularly financial planning. Top management increasingly finds that it requires more and more data on specific areas of company performance and on how to improve performance. They require even more information about their industries and product areas to aid in determining where the company is and where it should be headed. They also need analyses of external or environmental factors, such as buying patterns and emerging technologies, and logistics and supply channels as related to their objectives. For example, the commitment of construction funds for new manufacturing facilities alone is for many institutions a complex job of data collection, analysis, and presentation. It is becoming increasingly clear that long-range planning in reality has become a huge and sophisticated data collection activity requiring a thorough analysis of all phases of a company's internal and external environments.

Financial officers in many organizations are aware today of the value and even the necessity of financial planning and of producing useful financial models which fit their organizations. The vital nature of financial planning in major organizational decisions makes crucial the job of business analysis which occurs early in the planning process. This function

[*] Daniel J. McCarthy and Charles A. Morrissey, "Using the Systems Analyst in Preparing Corporate Financial Models," *Financial Executive,* June 1972. Reprinted by permission of the publisher, *The Financial Executive* (formerly *The Controller*).

involves setting proper objectives for the plan, deciding upon the most appropriate and valuable information at the least cost, avoiding duplication of effort, acting to insure the best and broadest legitimate utilization of the information being developed, and giving serious consideration to the ways in which the acquired data should be analyzed to fulfill the various objectives and uses of the plan or model.

The financial manager must consider carefully the ways in which various groups and individuals, including the computer-oriented members of the organization, may be utilized in the planning process in order to insure the best results from all quarters. Financial departments in many organizations perform all aspects of the business analysis and other functions of the planning process after gathering data from various functional departments and from within the financial department. If a computer is to be used in this process, they may go to the data processing department to obtain the assistance of a systems programmer who may not understand their needs. Or the finincial department may attempt to work with a computer programmer who doubles as a systems analyst and who is not likely to understand the users' needs. This can lead to serious problems for the financial or user department. In the vital area of financial planning and model building, where results are used regularly in top-level decision making, the systems analysis function is paramount, especially when a computer will be an element of the planning process.

Who will fulfill the various functions and where the functions should be located in the corporate organization is a matter of major concern to all involved in the planning process, but particularly to the financial officer, who is responsible ultimately for results. If a computer will be included in a planning process the financial officer will find it particularly advantageous to use a good systems analyst. Such an analyst can bridge the gaps between the financial department, various user departments, and the data processing function. A good systems analyst is capable of doing the business analysis which occurs early in the plan and which calls for a high degree of cooperation between the financial department and various other groups who must supply the required data for the plan. He also has the necessary skills to perform the computer analysis required for the project and can communicate directly with computer programmers and computer analysts if it is necessary.

Having a good systems analyst in this position is ideal, of course, since he is able to deal well with both technical computer groups and non-technical result-oriented user groups.[1] If a systems analyst is not available, it may be necessary to develop such an individual from within the financial department or from the data processing staff. The

---

[1] For a good description of the skills and capabilities required of such an analyst, see *Computerworld* articles by Milton C. Spett, May 13 and 20, 1970.

presence of such an individual will open up more opportunities for the proper construction and use of financial models and plans within an organization. The complexity of the plan makes the systems approach totally logical in this process, and this, when coupled with the fact that a computer will be used in the planning process, calls for the involvement of a systems analyst.

PLANNING MODEL

Most companies have accepted a three- to five-year period as an appropriate time frame for their plans. Planning often begins with a documented projection of company sales by product line for each of the projected years. This data base can include an analysis of each product by its cost components, such as manufacturing, marketing, and overhead. For many companies, this type of analysis reveals, perhaps for the first time, how the company makes money—and sometimes loses it! Companies must also project their sales growth and earnings targets in specific terms for the projected years. The gap between the two sets of figures, actual and projected, represents a target for management to reach through new product introduction, acquisition, cost cutting, and generally improved management.

The framework for this analysis has been well documented by Robert Anthony in *Planning and Control Systems.*[2] Simply stated, the planning systems analysis starts with a general statement of strategy, which usually encompasses what the company is as well as what it wants to become at various stages in the future. For example, "The XYZ Company intends to become the major factor in the field of manufacturing and marketing peripheral devices for the computer industry."

The next step is to document the management control level. To continue to develop the strategy set for them in the preceding paragraph, the directive would be, "The director of marketing shall implement and maintain a national advertising program to insure the proper exposure and understanding of the company's products." The management control level is the most complex since each functional area of the company must interface with others. Furthermore, if top management decides to supplement its current product line with new products, the interface between marketing, engineering, and production becomes critical, and the flow of information among these functions becomes crucial to an efficient introduction of the product.

Finally, the operational control level, which includes advertising, quality control, and inventory management, requires the specific informa-

---

[2] Robert Anthony, *Planning and Control Systems* (Cambridge, Mass.: Harvard University Press, 1965).

tion of budget, product description, and scheduling to carry out tasks directed by the management level. For example, "The advertising director will manage a budget of $400,000 with proper controls and analysis to insure the most effective use of our advertising expenditures." This subsystem flow from the advertising function to the director of marketing and then to top management represents a significant information handling problem particularly if it involves readership analysis, test marketing, direct mail analysis, and the like.

The dynamics of these plans in turn generate a great deal of the information for the finance function to plan the future in financial terms. What is the probability of success of the sales plan? Does this product decision require new financing? Should the new product area be acquired, perhaps for stock, to avoid cash disbursement?

The finance function then faces a continuous model-building process which must blend marketing, production, and sales information with the following factors:

Cash flow.
Debt/equity ratios.
Projected profitability rates.
Projected earnings per share.
Stock price.
Projected P/E multiples.
Projected interest rates.
Projected economic conditions.

ROLE OF SYSTEMS ANALYST

Experience with formal long-range plans has led to the realization that the systems analyst can play a paramount role in structuring information networks for planning models. Historically, planning groups found it difficult to collect and format the amount of data required to prepare a complete plan or model. The use of precise forms solved some of these problems, but the liaison between functions responsible for providing information for these forms was often vague. The resulting uncertainty often led to inefficient or little use of the models or plans, or, every bit as bad, they were used with erroneous and incomplete information.

The systems analyst who has dealt with the development and analysis of traditional business information systems and with their applications to the computer can relate his experience directly to the long-range planning process. But, once confronted with these areas of activity, he faces a formidable task. He must have or develop a thorough understanding of the planning sequence and must participate in preparing the documentation which will be used by managers in submitting data. He must be aware of how this data may result as a combination of the output from two functions such as cost accounting and marketing. For example, costs of products usually vary with volume. Marketing must project sales levels to give the cost accounting department data upon which to project these costs, and the systems analyst must elicit information from both groups to prepare the necessary information in timely fashion.

He must cross functional lines to insure proper timing and formatting for submittal of information and, in turn, sequence his own activity to compile and format summaries for analysis at the management control level.

He may be called on to create or modify a product numbering system so that products can be logically grouped.

He must avoid commentary or editorialism on company plans despite his feelings on their appropriateness.

And finally, he should recognize wherein computer technology can enhance the planning process and he must work with the computer programming group in developing and interpreting from the business and financial areas to the computer area.

In summary, the systems analyst is the "linking" individual who insures that the components of the plan are properly assembled and formulated and ultimately submitted for action to the director of the long-range planning program, and, if the information is to be computerized, that computer tools are properly used in this process.

ROLE OF COMPUTER

Obviously there is a high degree of identity today between this type of quantitative analysis and the computer. However, there are as yet far too few stories of successful application of the computer in this type of analysis. As in all other business information systems, the successful use of the computer depends on well documented and thorough analysis of the output required, for whom it is intended, in what format, and with what flexibility the data are to be presented.

For the most part, those computer systems which perform billing, cost accounting, payroll, or other such operational control level applications are not designed to supply the information required for planning. Unfortunately, many top managers assume that computer programs have the flexibility to arrange data in the required format and project it under various alternatives. Many bitter experiences have arisen because management has not understood these limitations of computer programs. Managements also frequently assume that the computer is another machine which is utilized best when utilized most. But it is far better when the computer is idle than when it is being utilized improperly.

The systems analyst, however, understands computer applications and can identify data in computer reports which can be utilized in the planning project. For example, the system study which led to computerization of inventory status reports may be a source of information on how data flows between marketing and production. If the inventory management program is successful, a commitment to extend the system to a three- or five-year planning cycle may seem more acceptable. However, if there are major problems with the inventory program, its use in long-range planning may be impossible under existing circumstances.

No matter how successful the current computer operation, however, without "top-down" planning, the computer's value in financial planning will be very limited. Whatever the outcome or problems associated with implementing the planning system, it should be clearly understood that its objective is to give top management a reasonable picture of the company's financial stature for the next three to five years under varying assumptions and conditions. This objective requires the participation of top management in every major aspect of the system, but in varying degrees depending upon the area.

CONVERSATIONAL COMPUTING

Once formal planning data are presented in a successful planning system, a further step is required. This step—a fairly recent management technique—is the use of quantitative analysis by computer to assist management in manipulating the data to evaluate alternatives. Immediate questions arise after the initial plan presentation, such as: "What if we reduce advertising expenditure? Can we still meet our profit objective?" "What if we acquire Company X? What happens to earnings per share?" "What if sales do not grow 7 percent in 1972? What happens to earnings and to earnings per share?" "Are our operating ratios in line with our competitors?" "Should our acquisition be made on a pooling or purchase accounting basis?" "What is the probability of certain events—wage settlement, raw material price increases—and can we apply these probabilities to our plan?"

A new opportunity to utilize the systems analyst lies in the presentation of financial forecasts to the manager on an interactive basis. Through computer time-sharing and remote access, the analyst can give management an opportunity to manipulate planning data, reformat it, change assumptions, utilize probabilities, and isolate specific areas for analysis—in short, to interact with the data and with assumptions which underlie them. This flexibility avoids the lead times and pre-planning as well as the delays that the batch processing computer environment requires and is a dramatic example of the computer finally being of specific use in the top management decision-making process.

Such utilization, however, places significant requirements on the financial systems analyst to expand his knowledge of new techniques such as time-sharing and other remote access methods. Furthermore, the analyst must be able to educate top management in such new techniques; overcome the fears on the part of users of such methods; insure the EDP function's understanding of the priorities which the long-range planning system may require; and focus on the implementation of this planning system.

IMPLEMENTATION

Since implementation is usually a time of extreme difficulty for most "planning" systems, particularly if the computer is introduced, an example of a financial planning model implemented with the use of time-sharing techniques is described below. The financial systems analyst can play a key role during the crucial stage of implementing the model.

Perhaps the most important data base in any organization is the income statement. It is the summary not only of company performance, but many times of important accounting policy decisions. This latter factor is very important in long-range financial planning, especially for publicly held companies.

Exhibit 1 presents a simple income statement of the current year for

EXHIBIT 1

SALES		732.6
COST OF GOODS SOLD	423.15	
ADVERTISING	127.8	
GENERAL AND ADMINISTRATIVE	84.5	
OPERATING INCOME		97.15
TAXES	40.13	
NET INCOME		57.02

NOTE: BASE YEAR IS 1969.

the XYZ Company. To project future years, a series of decisions is required from all levels and areas of the company about performance assumptions such as sales forecasts, pricing, cost allocations, capital expenditures, taxes, and the like. Projections of this statement for the next few years will also include such assumptions as projected economic conditions, new product decisions, acquisition moves, and even perhaps product spin-offs.

The financial systems analyst assigned to the preparation of such a data base, then, must be aware of all the functional areas involved, must know that the projected income statement will be presented to the chief operating officer, and that assumptions made in preparation must be well documented.

When the projected statement is presented, the president and the executive committee usually want to evaluate the impact of changes in external economic conditions, changes planned within the company, or proprietary information not given to the planning personnel when determining the plan. And usually top management wants the alternatives evaluated in a very short time. Here interactive computer technology is valuable in its ability to compare and manipulate the base of information and present new data almost at once. Once the base year data are established, as in Exhibit 1 for 1969, it is possible through available computer forecasting programs to manipulate the information using expected absolute changes, percentage changes, or probability changes. Actually, it is possible to use all or any combination of such changes, depending upon the nature of the assumptions to be used in the forecasted plan. In addition, some programs make it possible to use "plug figures" such as needed cash, differences between "required" profit level and projected profit, stock available for acquisitions under certain dilution levels, and other changes based on assumptions to be made. These areas are of keen interest to top management and to all financial planners interested in financial forecasts and other such models.

The advantages to managers, planners, and analysts of the time-shared computer mode is readily apparent from a review of the set of exhibits which will be discussed below. The interactive possibilities for the individual and the computer are numerous and allow nearly instantaneous "conversation," questions and answers, and changes of assumptions and responses on the part of both men and computer. Exhibit 2 for example, continues the development of the financial model, building upon the base year (1969) data. "Income" is simply the program title. Having called out the program, the analyst (or manager) is queried by the computer whether he "wants to enter base year data." He responds "no" in this case—the data had already been entered—but usually would respond "yes" and would enter the data which he had collected and summarized after consulting with many individuals and groups in the organization. (It should be noted at this time that all items on the exhibit printouts are produced by the computer answering except figures or statements which follow a question mark. These are responses of the analyst. The question marks, it should be noted, follow questions asked by the computer.)

The computer then asks whether the analyst wants to use average or individual growth rates in forecasting the results for the next few years under assumed growth rates, and tells the analyst to "type average or individual." After the analyst answers that he wants to use the individual growth rates, the computer formats projections for the next few years in sales and various expense categories. The analyst supplies the numbers which he expects to be appropriate growth rates for the items and periods. Again, it should be noted that he could supply any numbers and any combination of numbers, and if he wished, could even modify the program by adding new expense categories.

EXHIBIT 2

INCOME
DO YOU WANT TO ENTER BASE YEAR DATA? NO
DO YOU WANT TO USE AVERAGE OR INDIVIDUAL GROWTH RATES? TYPE AVG
OR INDIV? INDIV
PERCENT GROWTH IN SALES
   FOR YEARS 69–70? 50
   FOR YEARS 70–71? 8
   FOR YEARS 71–72? 10
   FOR YEARS 72–73? 5
PERCENT GROWTH IN COST OF GOODS SOLD
   FOR YEARS 69–70? 40
   FOR YEARS 70–71? 25
   FOR YEARS 71–72? –7
   FOR YEARS 72–73? 3
PERCENT GROWTH IN ADVERTISING
   FOR YEARS 69–70? 60
   FOR YEARS 70–71? 35
   FOR YEARS 71–72? 15
   FOR YEARS 72–73? 5
PERCENT GROWTH IN ADMIN & GENERAL EX
   FOR YEARS 69–70? 30
   FOR YEARS 70–71? 20
   FOR YEARS 71–72? 10
   FOR YEARS 72–73? 10

INCOME STATEMENT
$ IN THOUSANDS

YEARS	69	70	71	72	73
SALES	732.6	1098.9	1186.81	1305.49	1370.77
− CGS	423.15	592.41	740.51	688.68	709.34
− ADV	127.8	204.48	276.05	317.46	333.33
− ADM & GEN	84.5	109.85	131.82	145	159.5
= OPER INC	97.15	192.16	38.43	154.36	168.6
− TAXES	40.13	85.74	11.95	67.59	74.43
= NET INC	57.02	106.42	26.48	86.77	94.17

After all data have been entered by the analyst in response to questions from the computer, the computer automatically prints out the forecast for the next four years (based on the analyst's assumptions) under the caption, "Income Statement, $ in Thousands." As a further note, the program used in this example has the growth rates reacting with the previous year's figures and not continually reacting to the 1969 original base year. This is as would be expected by a financial analyst, but might be neglected by a less informed systems analyst who might continue to use the 1969 base year.

Exhibit 3 shows the model after Exhibit 2 or a series of Exhibit 2s had been produced by the computer and analyst working together. The first segment of the questions from the computer is a safeguard because the analyst may well have changed growth rates many times while working through the stage of the model pictured finally in Exhibit 2. If the

EXHIBIT 3

DO YOU WANT THE GROWTH PERCENTAGES [GROW] LISTED,
PERCENTAGE RELATIONSHIP [PERCENT] OF ITEMS TO SALES LISTED OR
DO YOU WISH TO TRY OTHER PERCENTAGES? [YES] OR [NO]?
PERCENT

PERCENT OF SALES

YEARS	69	70	71	72	73
SALES	100	100	100	100	100
− CGS	57.76	53.91	62.4	52.75	51.75
− ADV	17.44	18.61	23.26	24.32	24.32
− ADM & GEN	11.53	10	11.11	11.11	11.64
= OPER INC	13.26	17.49	3.24	11.82	12.3
− TAXES	5.48	7.8	1.01	5.18	5.43
= NET INC	7.78	9.68	2.23	6.65	6.87

analyst desired, the computer would list for him the last set of growth
rates which he used to produce his final Exhibit 2. In our example case,
the analyst did not need this aid and thus considered his other options:
whether he wanted, for all items and all periods, a percentage relationship to sales, or perhaps to continue changing growth rate percentages
(actually produce a new Exhibit 2). He chose the second option of listing
all items as a percentage of sales and answered "PERCENT." The computer responded automatically with a listing of all items for all periods
as a percentage of sales.

Exhibit 4 shows the analyst and computer considering the plan after
now having the information of Exhibits 2 and 3 which were produced
by the assumptions made to date and the basic program for a financial

EXHIBIT 4

DO YOU WANT THE GROWTH PERCENTAGES [GROW] LISTED,
PERCENTAGE RELATIONSHIP [PERCENT] OF ITEMS TO SALES LISTED OR
DO YOU WISH TO TRY OTHER PERCENTAGES? [YES] OR [NO]
?YES
INPUT FACTOR, [SALES, CGS, ADV, ADM] IN QUOTES, YEAR PERCENTAGE
AND WHETHER OR NOT THERE ARE MORE CHANGES, [YES] OR [NO] IN QUOTES
?"SALES",70,45,"YES"
?"SALES",71,5,"NO"

INCOME STATEMENT
$ IN THOUSANDS

YEARS	69	70	71	72	73
SALES	732.6	1062.27	1115.38	1226.92	1288.27
− CGS	423.15	592.41	740.51	688.68	709.34
− ADV	127.8	204.48	276.05	317.46	333.33
−ADM & GEN	84.5	109.85	131.82	145	159.5
= OPER INC	97.15	155.53	−33	75.79	86.1
T.L.C.F.	0	0	0	33	0
− TAXES	40.13	68.15	0	14.04	34.83
= NET INC	57.02	87.38	−33	61.75	51.27

plan which has been stored in the computer. The first part of Exhibit 4 is a repetition of the questions asked in Exhibit 3. At this point, if the analyst simply answered "no," the program would be finished and the analyst would have his data. If, however, the analyst wishes to change any previous assumptions, he is free to do so without trying the patience of the computer. In Exhibit 4, he decides to do so and proceeds to respond "yes" to the question, "Do you wish to try other percentages?" Actually, he is now repeating the process he went through in Exhibit 2 of supplying growth rates for the next few years to the base year data of 1969. The only data he changes, however, are sales growth figures for 1970 and 1971, and then tells the computer by his "no" response that there are no other changes he wishes to make. The patient computer immediately produces the new "Income Statement, $ in Thousands." Note that the analyst, by changing the 1971 sales growth rate to 5 percent from 10 percent, produced a loss of $33,000 rather than a profit of $26,000 for 1971 (Exhibits 2 and 4).

Exhibit 5 then shows the computer asking its usual questions and the analyst asking for a new listing of "items as a percentage of sales" based

EXHIBIT 5

DO YOU WANT THE GROWTH PERCENTAGES [GROW] LISTED, PERCENTAGE RELATIONSHIP [PERCENT] OF ITEMS TO SALES LISTED OR DO YOU WISH TO TRY OTHER PERCENTAGES? [YES] OR [NO]
?PERCENT

PERCENT OF SALES

YEARS	69	70	71	72	73
SALES	100	100	100	100	100
− CGS	57.76	55.77	66.39	56.13	55.06
− ADV	17.44	19.25	24.75	25.87	25.87
− ADM & GEN	11.53	10.34	11.82	11.82	12.38
= OPER INC	13.26	14.64	−2.96	6.18	6.68
− TAXES	5.48	6.42	0	1.14	2.7
= NET INC	7.78	8.23	−2.96	5.03	3.98

upon his latest set of assumptions, and the computer as usual responds with a new listing for the analyst's review. At this point, the analyst, having run out of assumptions for the time being, ends the program.

Although this model is not highly sophisticated, it is useful and of the type that managers and analysts require regularly and spend a good deal of time preparing. Any model builder or user who has the experience and the insight can improve the model and the way in which it is used. The user can be any manager or financial analyst, and members of either group can also construct such models. More realistic, though, is the use of the systems analyst in the initial model-building task, as we have discussed earlier. But, in any case, skills and knowledge from various areas are called for in constructing useful financial models, and the finanical officer must see to it that such resources are put to this important task. He thus must consider the appropriate sources for such individuals, and he must consider a systems analyst or, specifically, a financial systems analyst, for this position.

CONCLUSION

Management has often been unaware of the sophistication of information systems, particularly computer-based systems, and has not always recognized their applicability to such areas as financial modeling. The nature of long-range planning models with their complexity and organization-wide involvement presents a natural area of application for the systems approach to constructing information models. The role of the systems analyst in this function should be a vital and valuable one for the financial organization.

Generally the chief financial officer or manager will be involved in initiating the utilization of the systems analyst in the financial area. Thus, a first step must be the financial manager's recognition of the advantages of having a systems analyst; it has been the objective of this article to point out the possibilities that exist in this important area. There may well be in the data processing arm of the organization a systems analyst who could render invaluable service to the financial officer and his group. Or perhaps within the financial organization is an individual who has the required attributes to be an effective systems analyst, and who already has a high degree of skills and ability in financial things. The objective for the financial officer, at any rate, must be to discover and develop the required talents in the organization in order to fully utilize the systems approach and computer capability which can so well assist him in the job of financial planning and the preparation of other useful financial models.

STUDENT REVIEW QUESTIONS

1. What is the relationship between corporate financial models and an organization's planning process?
2. What are the advantages of utilizing a systems analyst in the overall process of planning?
3. What are the advantages of conversational or interactive computing in the organization's planning process?
4. Why do the authors feel that income statements, including "pro forma" statements, are a very important data base for planning in organizations?
5. What is the significance of "what if" questions in planning, and how does interactive computing aid managers in answering such questions?
6. Would interactive computating be useful for managers in nonprofit organizations? Why or why not?

chapter 9

Implementing Strategy: Control and Motivation

Introduction

Perspective on the Budget and Control
   Relationship of Control to Strategy

Control, Responsibility, and Reporting

Control and Exception Reporting

Motivational Considerations

Relationships among Strategy, Plans, Control, and Motivation:
A Case Study
   The Burnside Division
      Analysis of Burnside Case

The Planning Concept Illustration

Summary

Readings

INTRODUCTION

HAVING DEVELOPED a strategy for the organization, the next logical and necessary step has been described as the proper implementation of the strategy. It was suggested in previous chapters that organizing is the first step in implementing strategies, and that plans to implement the strategy are most often communicated throughout the organization in terms of a planning-budget system. We have not meant to suggest that the budget articulates all aspects of the plans of an organization. However, we emphasized that the budget does bring together in one document the specifications in financial terms of what an organization in a given period hopes to accomplish and, additionally, it serves as a standard against which actual results should be compared. Measurement of performance against the budget, furthermore, may lead to changing the plans, goals, resources, or some mix of all three, and can even be a stimulus to a review of basic organizational strategy. Finally, the planning budget is usually linked to the organization's reward-punishment system which hopefully enhances motivation to achieve the organization's goals. It is this area of measurement and motivation as elements of strategy implementation that is the principal subject matter of this chapter.

PERSPECTIVE ON THE BUDGET AND CONTROL

To place the budget and the overall control function in perspective, it is helpful to review events which happen throughout the organization prior to the budget being finally developed. Some events happen simultaneously while others build on prior events.

1. Strategy, changes in strategy, and major policies are articulated by top management, and are communicated throughout the organization in varying degrees of specificity and time horizons.
2. Goals or targets are set by top management in marketing and financial terms such as percentage of market desired in product areas or geographic areas, profit targets, return on investment desired, and others.
3. Responsible administrators in each department and division of the organization offer their inputs to various budgets and plans based on opinions and factual data concerning the environment, products, markets, research and development, new products, competition, resources needed, and countless other considerations including personal objectives and needs.
4. The organization's financial group translates resource needs into financial needs and analyzes capital resources, working capital, debt-equity structure and the like, and usually provides pro forma financial statements and determines funds needed to reach the stated goals.
5. All considerations are pulled together by financial and organizational planners and managers, and are set down as a working plan for some period of time, usually three or five years. A separate plan is developed for each year, of course, and the three- or five-year plan is revised at least annually in light of changes in environments and resources, or for other relevant reasons such as noted in the previous chapter.
6. These period plans, targets, and objectives should be consistent with and developed within the framework of the company's overall strat-

egy. Finally, the financial budget translates all other goals, plans, and budgets into dollars, and becomes the basic implementation and communications device in the planning system. The financial medium is the one available common denominator and is used in the budget to communicate to the organization in a common language the results of the entire planning process.

All planning must be undertaken with the broad perspective of strategy in mind, and with an eye on specific details, internal to and external to the organization. This combination of totality and particularity in approach is crucial for effective planning and control. A key mission of management in all organizations is to maximize or optimize certain accomplishments while at the same time minimizing the various costs necessary to achieve those ends. In the planning-control process, standards are created and utilized so that deviations may be measured, and overall results may be evaluated.

Relationship of Control to Strategy

The broader objectives, plans, and policies are utilized in defining rather general aims of an organization which are of a relatively long-term nature. Because of the general nature and longer term aspect of strategic goals and plans, it is difficult to use these as standards against which to compare results during yearly or even shorter operating periods. Thus, as discussed previously, more specific goals, plans, and policies are established for shorter periods of time, usually in the form of various organizational budgets. Specific, shorter term results can readily be compared against these more precise standards on a frequent basis. As long as these more specific standards are consistent with the broader strategic elements, they can serve as milestones against which to measure the organization's periodic progress toward attainment of its strategic goals and plans. This control aspect of the planning-control process, utilizing budgets as a prime vehicle, is an essential element in the implementation of corporate strategy.

CONTROL, RESPONSIBILITY, AND REPORTING

Management is well advised not to dictate budgets for all groups and departments. Rather, upper management should work with all organizational levels and groups in order to arrive at specific and mutually satisfactory goals for the budget period. A budget should not be looked upon as an imposed control, but ideally should be accepted by members as the organization's plan for the future, from which variations can be measured for the benefit of the enterprise and all its members. Clearly assigning responsibility and accountability is essential to an effective management control system. Responsibility accounting and reporting builds upon this principle by incorporating a system which gathers data on revenues, costs, and profits, and then organizes the data into information tailored to the authority-responsibility structure of the firm. The structure, in turn, should be developed with the organization's strategy as the basic criterion. Every person with an assigned responsibility has a set of key factors by which he is expected to judge his own operations. Since each report is addressed to a separate responsibility, different sets of facts and criteria are relevant in different reports.

Responsibility reporting emphasizes the importance of controlling costs at the level at which they are incurred, maximizing revenues at the points at which they are generated, and tying the authority, responsibility and accountability for these to specific individuals at these locations. The revenues and/or costs must be attributable to the particular person's efforts and must be under his control. Profit planning and control has as its basis the application of the *responsibility* concept. Briefly, this entails the assignment of responsibility for all significant areas of operation and the associated costs and/or revenues to specific individuals within the organization. These individuals are usually department heads, and each is responsible for the operations and costs of his department. Such departments are usually termed *cost centers*. If a manager is responsible for income as well as costs, he is also responsible for profit and thus manages a *profit center*. Once cost and profit centers have been established, each such center must develop a detailed budget which is a plan for some future period, usually one year, in which the major events and operations and the amounts of anticipated costs and revenues are estimated. In order for such budgets to be useful analytical tools, all costs and revenues should be broken down into their significant components, and a reporting system must be established which facilitates the collection, analysis, and reporting of results of operations to appropriate managers.

Problems arise in organizations, both business and nonprofit, when managers are held accountable for costs over which they have no control, or only partial control. This situation is most pronounced in organizations where allocated costs are prevalent and important. Similarly, in multi-division business organizations, transfer costs which sometimes are viewed as arbitrary, affect income of some divisions, costs of other divisions, and the profits of any division which is a profit center. In all such circumstances, the control system and related budgets must contain safeguards against such problems by assigning responsibility and accountability with special care.[1]

---

[1] For situations which deal with these particular problems of implementing strategy, see "Texas Instruments Incorporated (A) and (B)" Cases, and "Dennison Manufacturing Company (C)" Case, Intercollegiate Case Clearinghouse, Harvard Business School, Boston, Mass.

There is, of course, a time lag between budgets going into effect and the occurrence of operations within the organization. There is also a lag of some time between actual events and the reporting of those events. The reporting system should assure that this *post facto* lag is at an acceptable level. Without a reporting system to *feed back* timely results of activities in the enterprise, there can be no control function. Merely constructing and implementing the planning budget does not automatically ensure feedback of results which is necessary for a comparison of actual results to planned or standard. The control system must include a reporting element for appropriate and timely information to be fed to various managers within the organization. As was brought out in a previous chapter, the question of who gets what information and when, is a crucial one in the proper development of an organization and its control system. It is only through the establishment of an effective reporting system that the final phase of the entire planning-control system can be accomplished. By making comparisons of actual results to planned results, the loop can be closed, control can be exerted, and the replanning phase can be entered. Beyond this, the closing of the loop allows a particular opportunity for a motivational review, and for managers to communicate with one another concerning plans, policies, standards, performance, expectations, and results.

Usually, the reports received by managers at lower echelons deal with many specifics that are relatively short-range in nature. The higher the manager's level, the fewer detailed items will the reported information deal with. Correspondingly, the results and the standards against which these are compared will usually apply to things which are of broad importance to the organization. Top management will be most interested in how results and other reported information match up against their broader strategic goals and plans, and whether these and the major policies of the institution are being followed and attained. Or, they may question aspects of the organization's strategy after reviewing results of operations, or after receiving other appropriate information through the management control system. In this way top management can determine if the present strategy is being properly implemented, producing expected results, or conversely, whether the strategy is faulty or not being properly implemented. The control element of the planning process can thus be utilized as the vehicle for various levels of management to review results, assess information, and initiate appropriate action.

While recognizing the value of historical data, management reporting ideally seeks to achieve an integration of the past, the present, and the future. The cycle looks like this: managers plan and in planning consider alternatives, set objectives, and create standards for evaluation. They seek to carry out their plans and operate toward attaining objectives. Finally, they examine and evaluate results, compare them with plans, and again consider alternatives—in effect replanning for the future.

But so much of reporting is concerned with the past that there develops an almost natural tendency to view reported data in the same way one might view history. But the past is gone, the results are in, and if mistakes have been made or plans gone awry, the task is to look ahead and enter the future with a fresh perspective. A sharp distinction, then, develops between the past and the future, and this can subtly mar or enhance the perspective of management in planning, doing, evaluating and replanning. Reporting is most meaningful to management when it can influence future decisions, and this discussion has emphasized the corrective or future-oriented aspects of the control function as vital in implementing strategy.

CONTROL AND EXCEPTION REPORTING

Almost every manager tends to manage by exception; that is, he or she concentrates his time and effort on those areas of his organizational responsibility that are not operating according to plan. Although most of his time will be spent investigating and correcting disappointing results, at least some time will be devoted to determining the reasons for unexpectedly favorable developments in the hope of finding why they occurred and whether lessons can be applied to other areas.

Only when this natural tendency is converted into a system is it referred to as *management by exception*. The characteristic of this system is that each executive consciously screens the data coming to him to determine which situations constitute important exceptions, and then deliberately focuses his attention on these situations. Furthermore, he passes up the line to his superiors only information on *major* exceptions. Frequently, this last policy is based on a predetermined formula. For example, any departmental expense that exceeds the budget by $1,000 or 5 percent must be investigated and a report must be rendered to an appropriate senior manager.

Exception reporting started out as a procedure designed to implement exception management, but has grown into something more. Originally, it was designed to save the time of managers who followed the principles of exception management, by eliminating from reports to them all items that were reasonably in line with expectations. This screening was ordinarily done by hand and resulted in shorter, more meaningful reports going to higher management. Such reports were to focus attention on significant data.

However, the advent of computers has brought about a change. Computers have the power to churn out reams of detailed data not all of which is needed regularly. In fact, a frequent criticism of computers is that they spew out so much material that executives lack the time to digest it, or act upon it. To the extent that this complaint is justified, the computer is not really helping management to perform its functions.

What is required in dealing with computer-generated data, as with all other kinds, is for management to exercise its proper judgment when designing and implementing the reporting system. Information is necessary for control and in the present context, we mean management control rather than detailed control of specific tasks at the operational level. What information is needed for comparison against plans in order to control the activities of subordinate management, evaluate their performance, motivate them to improve efforts, and allow for replanning? Application of management by exception may well be applicable in some circumstances after answering this question, and reporting systems should reflect these predetermined requirements for information.

It should be evident to the student or manager interested in strategy that only limited amounts of information can be digested by the organization's strategy makers. Therefore, it should be information of a summary nature and should deal with items of broad and long-term consequences for the organization. Yet, behind such summary reports of results and information lies an enormous amount of detailed information which has been digested, analyzed, and summarized by other levels of line management or staff. The information which must filter through the various information systems of the organization will often be concentrated in the various budgets utilized in the organization's planning and control system.

Since the strategy makers in an organization must determine what information they will require to monitor the implementation of strategy, they must ensure that the planning-control system provides that information in appropriate detail and timely fashion to all levels of the organization. Then, they as managers should be able to manage by exception in their own broad spheres of responsibility and authority.

MOTIVATIONAL CONSIDERATIONS

If strategy and the more precise goals, plans, and policies which derive from strategy are to be achieved in an organization, the members of the organization must usually have a reasonable commitment to the achievement of such endeavors. To gain this commitment, an organization requires the leadership of its top management and other managers, and a concurrent motivation on the part of organizational members to achieve the desired goals and plans of the strategy, as well as more specific targets which are visible and real to them. Motivation then becomes a most important element in implementing strategy and can in large measure be accomplished by the reward-punishment system of the organization, a large part of which may be coupled with the planning-control system, specifically within the budgets which guide the institution's operations. Positive and negative incentives such as bonuses, raises, promotions, and demotions are often utilized in tandem with various budgeted goals of a financial and nonfinancial nature in a motivation system.

Achieving in an organization a motivation system that blends the attainment of personal goals with those of the institution is a decidely difficult task. In some cases excessive rewards may be offered to individuals without a corresponding achievement of organizational goals, such as can occur when targets have been set too low. The opposite case is probably an even more common occurrence. One author has criticized the management of International Telephone and Telegraph Corporation (I.T.&T.), for the way this organization's president allegedly motivates his managers.

> Geneen [President Harold S. Geneen] provides his managers with enough incentives to make them tolerate the system. Salaries all the way through ITT are higher than average—Geneen reckons 10 percent higher —so that few people can leave without taking a drop: . . . having bound his men to him with chains of gold, Geneen can induce the tension that drives the machine. "The key to the system," one of his men explained, "is the profit forecast; once the forecast has been gone over, revised and agreed, the managing director has a personal commitment to Geneen to carry it out; that's how he produces the tension on which the success depends." The tension goes through the company, inducing ambition, perhaps exhilaration, but always with some sense of fear: what happens if the target is missed?[2]

I.T.&T.'s motivation system is seen by the author of this statement as being tied to the budgetary-control process, and being utilized in a way that neglects the personal human needs of many managers by relying basically upon money, tension, and fear for motivation. Yet, all of these motivators are utilized to some degree in all profit and nonprofit organizations including organized religions, governments, hospitals, and universities. It is the careful use of various positive and negative motivation that is most likely to bring satisfaction to individuals as well as success to organizations.

The ability to provide professional and executive and other personnel with opportunities for achievement, with recognition, and with responsibility, is likely to provide an organization with truly motivated personnel. Management policies which lead in this direction include management by objectives, decentralization, delegation of authority, profit center accounting, annual performance reviews, junior boards of directors, rotating committee memberships, opportunities to meet and work directly with executives two or more echelons higher, and even a pat on the back when deserved. In some cases the encouragement of individuals to serve in community activities and subsequent recognition of this service can be

---

[2] Anthony Sampson, *The Sovereign State: The Secret History of ITT* (London: Coronet Books, 1974), p. 119.

helpful. However, it would be naïve to deny the role of negative motivation such as threats of salary reductions, loss of job, demotion, and the like. For some individuals, these forces are the only motivators to achieve organizational goals. The weakness in such motivators is that these can be overused by some managers with a resulting deterioration of the organization. But the same can also be said of positive motivation. Balance and perspective are the keys in developing a motivation system which gains commitment of individuals to organizational goals and strategy.

Maslow[3] in his work on the need hierarchy of individuals offers insights to human needs as motivators and fulfilled needs as nonmotivators. An organization of sensitive top managers will remain constantly aware of the needs and changing needs of the organization's management group, of the work force, and of their own needs. This idea was discussed in earlier chapters when personal needs and values were recognized as key elements in the process of setting objectives, developing strategy, and designing an organizational structure. In the more specific and shorter range activities of an organization, these same motivational considerations emerge as important. If objectives at any level are to be deemed desirable by organizational members, or if the process by which objectives are to be achieved is to be considered acceptable, the needs and satisfactions of these individuals and groups must be considered. Participation by members of the organization in the budgeting function is clearly a stimulus to these individuals to work toward the achievement of budgeted goals according to many research studies. Research on motivation also indicates that the higher one's management level, the greater is one's participation in the budgeting process.

> This study has examined four hypotheses in a budget setting environment. It was found that perceived participation in the budget process and motivation to achieve the budget are positively related along both the goal directing effort and evaluative effort dimensions of motivation, but more on the former. . . . Finally, a positive relationship was shown to exist between perceived participation in the budget process and organizational level. These findings support other research indicating a positive relationship between participation and motivation and an increasing level of perceived participation as an individual rises in the organizational hierarchy.[4]

Considering the budget to be a motivational instrument, it follows that the construction of the planning budget must include legitimate attention to individual and group needs and values. If these personal elements are

---

[3] A. H. Maslow, *Motivation and Personality* (New York: Harper and Brothers, 1954).

[4] D. G. Searfoss, and R. M. Monczka, "Perceived Participation in the Budget Process and Motivation to Achieve the Budget," *Academy of Management Journal*, vol. 16, no. 4 (December 1973).

included in the budgeting process, the budget which results will fulfill its function as a motivational force in the operations and activities of organization members. As such it should serve to implement the strategy of the organization. Probably the best guarantee of such a result is the real involvement of all management groups and other appropriate organizational members in the development of the budget and its related plans. Further, the desired process encompasses the careful use of the budget when evaluating reported results and performance against the plans, forecasts, and standards of the budget. If the budgeting process is properly conceived, developed, and utilized by top management, it can become an indispensable motivational element in management's job of implementing the planned strategy of an organization. The control side of the planning-control system is thus seen as part of an overall system of motivation within the organization, and should be considered in this context.

RELATIONSHIPS AMONG STRATEGY, PLANS, CONTROL, AND MOTIVATION: A CASE STUDY

The following case situation is intended to demonstrate that setting objectives, planning, control, motivation and replanning exist in a delicately balanced system that requires continuous examination and adjustment. The cycle in a going concern actually begins at the feedback stage and involves the measurement of success by comparing actual and planned results. Further action is taken as required to ensure organizational and personal goal congruence. New plans and goals are formulated, tested, and ultimately reshaped, utilizing policy and strategy as guides. Specific goals are articulated in the plans and budgets, against which results are again compared during the management control phase of the system. Motivation is recognized as a vital factor in the success or failure of the organization in accomplishing both specific results and the overall strategy.

The Burnside Division

In late 1974, Mr. Jerome Woodlawn, general manager of Burnside Division, was busily involved in a vigorous evaluation of the division's performance over the last seven years. Burnside Division produced plastic keys which are used on typewriters and other business machines. Burnside Division operated independently of Worth Manufacturing, Inc., a large diversified concern composed of more than a dozen operating divisions manufacturing a wide variety of industrial and consumer products.

The expansion of the plastic key market was very rapid after the early

1960s. Previously, the products were delicately constructed items requiring many parts and much handicraft production. About seven years ago, a new process was developed by the Worth Manufacturing research team which replaced several parts with a highly durable plastic innovation permitting more of the hand work to be done by automated processes.

The improved product was successful immediately because it had wide application and was both dependable and inexpensive to manufacture. Almost simultaneously, some competing companies working on the product developed a unit so similar in design that no patent possibilities existed. Burnside Division was established to aggressively compete in the market for the improved keys which, at that time, was about 500,000 units per year, and to assume all production and selling functions for the product.

The latest available industry estimates showed that about 100 companies utilized the improved type plastic key and represented the market for Burnside and other manufacturers. Estimated industry sales rose to 5 million units. As production and sales expanded, prices fell from nearly 50 cents per unit to about 20 cents. At the present time, Burnside competed with 15 companies and received nearly 15 percent of the available business; 4 others captured another 70 percent, and the remaining sales went to smaller firms which made the product to utilize idle capacity.

Worth Manufacturing, part of a larger conglomerate, acted practically as an independent entity. Worth executives served on the Long-Range Planning Committee and worked with divisions like Burnside, but all responsibility for operating Burnside rested with Mr. Woodlawn, subject to the quarterly review and evaluation of the committee. However, any capital expenditures over $40,000 had to be approved by Worth's Planning Committee.

At the last quarterly meeting, the reviewing executives expressed their concern over the apparently sluggish improvement in Burnside's profit/sales ratio. They contended that such a specialty item should yield a before-taxes profit of 20 percent of net sales. Furthermore, they suggested that Mr. Woodlawn pursue this percentage as a long-run objective for his division, and submit shortly a plan for accomplishing this goal within three years.

Mr. Woodlawn, a diligent manager, proud of his division and well respected within Burnside, was upset not only because of the lack of recognition for the increased profit earned in the current period, but also by the new objectives which he doubted were achievable. Immediately, he called his most responsible divisional executives: sales and production managers, research and development head, and controller. He disclosed the events that took place at the corporate meeting and indicated that he wanted the controller to take immediate action toward developing a plan for achieving a 20 percent profit/sales ratio within three years, without drastically changing present sales and production policies.

In the meantime, Mr. Woodlawn, feeling harrassed, stated that he intended to review the past performance of Burnside Division in order to critically evaluate the profit improvement and to judge the reasonableness of the goal set by the Planning Committee. Income statements for the division since its inception are shown in Exhibit 9–1. No balance sheets were available since Burnside was not separately incorporated. The division records indicated that current assets amounted to about $30,000 and that the net depreciated book value of the fixed assets was currently about $40,000 which was about 50 percent of the estimated original cost.

Analysis of Burnside Case. In retrospect, Mr. Woodlawn is justified in his concern about how he is being judged by Worth's Planning Committee. In terms of return on capital equipment invested, his performance is yielding slightly under 50 percent. Even judging his return on assets employed, the yield is in excess of 25 percent. If one assumes a 50 percent tax rate, the return is quite respectable. A glance at the profit to sales ratio, however, indicates that the goal of a 20 percent return has never been met, implying that if the situation does not radically change, such a goal is not going to be achieved.

At this point, two questions arise. First, should Burnside direct its efforts toward achieving a goal of 20 percent profit to sales? Second, if the goal is to be achieved, how should Burnside plan for its attainment?

The first question must be answered at two executive levels. From Woodlawn's position, his refusal to comply could cause him difficulty with the Planning Committee. A goal has been stated; Woodlawn could proceed ahead to achieve it since favorable or unfavorable evaluation of his performance is dependent upon it. If the goal is not attainable under present conditions, then he could seek some help through policy changes. Either the plant and equipment investment restrictions might be removed or some drastic production and marketing changes might be made. Or, he could question the goal if he had a firm basis for doing so.

At the Planning Committee level, the managers must be sure that what they are suggesting to Mr. Woodlawn is, in fact, what they want him to achieve. That is, they must be convinced in view of the overall corporate strategy that the stated goal is realistic, attainable, and consistent with the overall strategy. They will evidently judge Woodlawn favorably if he achieves the goal under the restrictions set forth; and apparently will not think otherwise, even if other measures of performance become less satisfactory. Any major questions which remain in Woodlawn's mind regarding the profit-to-sales ratio (Why the 20 percent figure? Why three years?) should also be answered. Here is an example of the need for participation of various managerial levels, even in setting the fairly long-term financial goals for the division.

The answer to the second question (How do you plan for achievement?) presumes an affirmative response to the first. There are various ways of accomplishing an improved profit-to-sales ratio. One way is to

EXHIBIT 9–1

Burnside Division Detailed Income Statements 1968–1974 (000s)

	1968		1969		1970		1971		1972		1973		1974*	
	Amount ($)	Sales (%)	Amount ($)	Sales (%)	Amount ($)	Sales (%)	Amount ($)	Sales (%)	Amount ($)	Sales (%)	Amount ($)	Sales (%)	Amount ($)	Sales (%)
Gross Sales:	52.5	105	72.8	104	96.3	107	127.2	106	117.7	107	141.7	109	162.0	108
Less:														
Sales returns and allowances	.5	1	.7	1	1.8	2	2.4	2	1.1	1	2.6	2	1.5	1
Sales discounts	1.0	2	.7	1	1.8	2	1.2	1	2.2	2	2.6	2	3.0	2
Freight-out	1.0	2	1.4	2	2.7	3	3.6	3	4.4	4	7.5	5	7.5	5
Total	2.5	5	2.8	4	6.3	7	7.2	6	7.7	7	11.7	9	12.0	8
Net Sales	50.0	100	70.0	100	90.0	100	120.0	100	110.0	100	130.0	100	150.0	100
Variable Costs:														
Materials	21.5	43	28.0	40	36.9	41	56.4	47	47.3	43	49.4	38	54.0	36
Direct labor	8.0	16	9.1	13	9.9	11	15.6	13	13.2	12	14.3	11	15.0	10
Sales commissions	5.5	11	7.7	11	12.6	14	15.6	13	14.3	13	16.9	13	21.0	14
Repairs and supplies	4.0	8	1.4	2	1.8	2	3.6	3	3.3	3	3.9	3	3.0	2
Other	2.5	5	1.4	2	.9	1	2.4	2	3.3	3	3.9	3	4.5	3
Total variable costs	41.5	83	47.6	68	62.1	69	93.6	78	81.4	74	88.4	68	97.5	65
Contribution margin	8.5	17	22.4	32	27.9	31	26.4	22	28.6	26	41.6	32	52.5	35
Fixed Costs:														
Manufacturing salaries	1.0	2	2.1	3	1.8	2	1.2	1	1.1	1	2.6	2	3.0	2
Other administrative costs	2.0	4	2.8	4	1.8	2	2.4	2	2.2	2	1.3	1	1.5	1
Manufacturing engineering	2.0	4	.7	1	.9	1	1.2	1	1.1	1	1.3	1	1.5	1
Office expenses	5.5	11	3.5	5	5.4	6	6.0	5	4.4	4	3.9	3	6.0	4
Taxes, depreciation, etc.	10.5	21	14.0	20	17.1	19	9.6	8	8.8	8	13.0	10	16.5	11
Total Fixed Costs	21.0	42	23.1	33	27.0	30	20.4	17	17.6	16	22.1	17	28.5	19
Net income (loss) before taxes	(12.5)	(25)	(.7)	(1)	.9	1	6.0	5	11.0	10	19.5	15	24.0	16

* Nine months.

increase sales; another is to lower costs; a third is some combination of the two. The economic situation of the particular industry in which Burnside is competing is oligopolistic, and is characterized by some growth and a general price leveling. This environment will be troublesome to Burnside because no product differentiation exists, and the situation does not permit long-run advantages from price increases since competition is too pronounced. These are all considerations that are important to the strategic planning of Worth Manufacturing, as well as to the particular situation of Woodlawn. This situation apparently leaves only cost reduction as a realistic approach to accomplishing Burnside's stated objective of increasing profit as a percent of sales.

Before Woodlawn and his staff begin preparing a plan for the future, a look at the income statements should reveal some information regarding the sources of improvements in the profit-to-sales ratio in the past. Woodlawn knows that Burnside has maintained its share of the market and has increased its aggregate dollar sales by increasing unit sales volume in the face of lower unit selling prices. Disregarding the year 1968 as a start-up year, the profit-to-sales ratio has improved from −1 percent in 1969 to about + 16 percent in 1974. The sources of these profit gains may be summarized as follows:

Year	Percent Change in Profit from Variable Costs	Percent Change in Profit from Fixed Costs	Total Change in Percent of Net Profit
1970	−1	+ 3	+ 2
1971	−9	+13	+ 4
1972	+4	+ 1	+ 5
1973	+6	− 1	+ 5
1974	+3	− 2	+ 1
Total	+3	+14	+17

Thus, it can be concluded that during the past five years, control over the fixed costs coupled with sales volume increases contributed most to the total profit change. In the last three years, however, the control of variable expenses has been favorable, while fixed expense percentage has increased somewhat. Over the entire five-year period the more significant changes in profit have come first from an ability to increase volume without expanding capacity, and lately from success in purchasing materials as shown by the table below:

Percent Changes in Profit by Selected Cost Categories (From Exhibit 9–1)

	1970	1971	1972	1973	1974	Total
Materials (variable)	−1	−6	4	5	2	+4
Taxes, depreciation, etc. (fixed)	1	11	0	−2	−1	+9

Considering the growth of this industry, it is likely that Burnside could attain 20 percent profit on sales by merely slowing its capital replacement and expansion rate, and cutting back on repairs, supplies, advertising, sales discounts, and the like. Sacrificing profitable growth to reach the desired profit-to-sales ratio, however, is not a policy the Planning Committee is likely to endorse. In the short run, Burnside and particularly, Woodlawn might be judged favorably, but in the long run Worth Manufacturing might well have been eliminated as a competitive force in the plastic key market. Just as undesirable, attaining the short-run goal might also have endangered the survival of a profitable corporate member, another factor of strategic importance to Worth Manufacturing and its parent company.

A major value of profit planning and control lies in involving operational managers affected by the planning process, and having them anticipate the steps which must be taken to establish and accomplish desirable and congruent corporate goals. It is not meant to be a system which forces subordinate levels of management to manipulate operations to avoid unfavorable judgment from above, particularly as a short-run expediency. Finally, it should be obvious from this illustrative case situation that the planning and control system must stem from and be consistent with the overall strategy of the organization. The system must start with the strategy if it is to serve its purpose as a major vehicle for the implementation of the strategy.

THE PLANNING CONCEPT ILLUSTRATION

The preceding case example was designed to illustrate the links between strategy, goals, planning, control, and motivation in the process of implementing corporate strategy. All levels of management must be encouraged to strive toward the basic goals. Strategic objectives, policies and plans are developed in anticipation of eventual accomplishment through shorter range and more specific goals, policies, and plans. Accordingly, the planning-control process is employed for the implementation of strategy, primarily through utilization of budgets. Finally, a basic element of the entire system must be the motivation of those organizational members involved in the process to work toward the desired achievements and accomplishments.

SUMMARY

This final chapter has discussed the control function of management and the importance of control in the implementation of strategy. Particular attention was paid to control as an integral part of the management planning and control system which was introduced in the preceding chapter.

The perspective on control in the planning-budgetary process was also emphasized, and control was described as a motivational element within the overall context of implementing strategy.

To facilitate the function of control, the necessity for accountability and responsibility reporting was discussed. The inclusion of this subsystem was recognized as the essential ingredient needed to develop and communicate the actual results of activities within the enterprise. Without such information for comparison to plans and budgets, the control function could not be exercised.

Because of its importance in being a basic reason for the control function, the subject of motivation was covered, as was the budget as a key instrument of motivation in organizations.

The case study was included to bring together in one situation the various elements which have been discussed as important in the implementation of strategy, and the crucial role of motivation was emphasized once again.

Viewing this chapter as closely interrelated with the last two chapters provides a unified look at the implementation of strategy. The planning and control system has been considered as a basic vehicle of communication and motivation in an organization. Together with the formal and informal lines of authority and communication resulting from the structure and behavior of the organization, the planning-control system constitutes the network through which the information flows that keeps an organization functioning, informing members of the objectives, plans, policies, results, and day-to-day activities of the enterprise. The important role of the planning budget in this overall network was also emphasized.

The behavioral as well as the formal and structural aspects of the entire implementation phase was emphasized throughout the three chapters, and particular emphasis was placed on the motivational aspects of formal structures and systems in organizations.

Beyond the interrelatedness of all elements within the implementation phase, that entire phase was recognized as being itself interrelated with the formulation phase of the strategic process. Because of this relationship, the logical, behavioral, and motivational aspects of the implementation phase must be subjects for consideration during the time of strategy formulation.

Throughout these pages, leadership requirements of various types were noted as being vital in organizations, considering the complexity and importance of the job of top management with its responsibility for formulating and implementing strategy.

Finally, it is hoped that the framework espoused in this book will aid managers and students in analyzing and operating in actual and simulated managerial situations with these concepts as guides to action.

23. Do Management Control Systems Achieve Their Purpose?*

DOUGLAS McGREGOR

A PRIME OBJECTIVE of management has always been to get employees to function at high levels of performance. To do this, most companies have worked out some way of letting workers know how they measure up to the standards that top management considers acceptable. This usually takes the form of some kind of administrative procedure with a built-in feedback that consists of rewards for the employee when he has complied with the standard and punishment when he hasn't.

But how well do these controls actually work?

Most managers will probably agree that they do work—but rather less well than the managers desire. Among some people they do bring about a certain amount of compliance with management standards, but they also have important unintended consequences. Among these are:

1. Widespread antagonism to the controls and to those who administer them.

2. Successful resistance and noncompliance by many employees at all levels within an organization up to the top (and sometimes there also).

3. Unreliable performance information because of employee antagonism and resistance to the administrative controls.

4. The need for close surveillance of employees. This results in a dilution of delegation, which cuts into managerial time and impedes the development of workers.

5. High administrative costs.

Most of these consequences can be readily observed within any large

* Douglas McGregor, "Do Management Control Systems Achieve Their Purpose?" *The Sloan Management Review*, February 1967. © 1967 by the Industrial Management Review Association; All Rights Reserved. Reprinted by permission.

organization. To different degrees they are characteristic of virtually all managerial control systems.

What accounts for management's inability to devise control systems that are fully effective in getting employees to comply with the company's performance standards? We, perhaps, can understand this failure better if we first take a look at how some of these control systems work.

WHAT MANAGEMENT WANTS

Occasionally, the standard management is aiming for, at least as stated, is perfection. If the concern is safety, the goal is no lost-time accidents; with certain clerical functions, the quality standard is no mistakes.

Sometimes the goal is not perfection, as in the case of turnover where usually the standard is to keep turnover below some upper limit. With variables like quality of product or level of output, standards are often expressed in terms of a specified acceptable level.

Finally, the standard may simply be improvement over present performance, as is frequently the case with sales and sometimes with cost controls.

Actual performance under any control system is significantly affected by who sets the standards and at what level they are set. Experience demonstrates that if they are too high, they will not be regarded as possible and relatively little effort will be made to achieve them. On the other hand, if they are too low, the real potential will not be achieved. However, the employee's reaction will be directly determined not by the objective standard, but by how he perceives it. Perception is influenced by feelings, needs and attitudes. The significant question is: What will be perceived to be reasonable?

Many managerial control systems are applied mechanically. Management will determine what is possible and what is reasonable or necessary, often making extensive use of professional help in the process. Then it endeavors to achieve the desired level of performance by using "legitimate" authority and extrinsic[1] rewards and punishments.

This general strategy may be qualified in many ways. For example, the process of expense budgeting usually involves various units submitting

---

[1] "One important body of knowledge has to do with two quite different kinds of motivational relationships. The first, and by far the most recognized and utilized today, involves what are called *extrinsic* rewards and punishments—they exist as characteristics of the environment, and their relationship to behavior is relatively direct. Money is the most obvious of them, but fringe benefits, promotion, praise, recognition, criticism, and social acceptance and rejection are other examples.

"*Intrinsic* rewards, on the other hand, are inherent in the activity itself: the reward is the achievement of the goal. Intrinsic rewards cannot be *directly* controlled externally, although characteristics of the environment can enhance or limit the individual's opportunities to obtain them. Thus achievements of knowledge or skill, of autonomy, of self-respect, of solutions to problems are examples."

proposed budgets that are then modified at higher levels until they are acceptable to those levels.

TRIAL AND ERROR

Such a process is subject to all the side effects mentioned at the beginning of this article. What is ultimately achieved, therefore, is the result of a trial-and-error process of coping with the consequences of the standard setting. If the standards are accepted—if they are perceived to be reasonable—the results will tend to be satisfactory. If they are not, the tactics adopted will be (1) to persuade or coerce lower levels into accepting the standards; (2) to attempt to get performance within the established standards by pressure (the threat of punishment) while accepting the negative side effects or attempting to eliminate them by increased pressure; or (3) to lower the standards or accept substandard performance.

This process, based as it is upon a mechanical conception of cause and effect, tends inevitably in practice to place strong emphasis on the threat of punishment. Except in the case of incentive plans, the extrinsic rewards for compliance tend to be long range and relatively uncertain. The manager who succeeds in meeting the standards that have been set for him can hope for long-term rewards in the form of salary increases and promotion. But the probability of punishment or of the withholding of rewards for noncompliance is much more certain. Since the basic purpose is to obtain compliance with goals and standards set by others, the individual's chief motivation is to escape punishment.

PERCEIVED THREAT

One fundamental reason control systems often fail and sometimes boomerang is that those who design them fail to understand that an important aspect of human behavior in an organizational setting is that *noncompliance tends to appear in the presence of perceived threat.*

This noncompliance takes the form of defensive, protective, resistant, aggressive behavior. Note that I have used the words "perceived threat." Feelings are facts! The question is not whether management believes the control procedures are threatening; the question is whether those affected by them feel they are.

There are several conditions under which threat is likely to be perceived. One is where punishment—as opposed to support and help in meeting standards and objectives—is emphasized. Where the feeling is generated that the employee must conform "or else," the sense of threat is common. The data cited by Rensis Likert from the many studies conducted by the Institute for Social Research at the University of Michigan consistently indicate that pressure of this kind for higher performance is rather generally perceived to be threatening.[2] The evidence of noncompliance comes from the lower performance in work units where pressure of this kind is steadily used as part of the manager's strategy, compared with the output in units where such pressure is minimal or absent.

A second condition under which threat is likely to be perceived is where trust is lacking in the relationships between superior and subordinates and between line and staff people who administer control programs.

A third condition arises when the feedback of information negatively affects the individual's self-esteem, his career expectations and his emotional security in the employment relationship.

DELIBERATE NEEDLING

Let us consider some features of conventional management control systems that may create threat. A common one is pressure for compliance with externally imposed standards. This can take the form of accounting controls, budgets, the performance standards of the boss, industrial engineering standards of work and the like. In one large organization, those responsible for an elaborate system of performance measurement are explicit in their philosophy. It is: "Measure everything you possibly can, and use the measures as needles." The management of this organization firmly believes that performance could not possibly be as high as it is without this strategy of control. All the side effects mentioned above can be observed at middle and lower levels, but the attitude of top management appears to be that these costs are probably inevitable and not very important. In a company with this viewpoint, if noncompliance continues or reappears, the reaction is to increase the pressure.

ACCOUNTABILITY

The logic of accountability within the framework of conventional managerial principles is clear. However, it takes little experience with the operation of this principle in everyday organizational life to recognize that its practical use is to discover and punish noncompliance with externally imposed standards and controls. The real meaning in practice of the principle of accountability is: "Find out who goofed."

Control through measures that stress variance from normal standards also emphasizes mistakes, failures and substandard performance.

But the concept of accountability is likely to be perceived as a threat by employees. In one company top management acquired incontrovertible

---

[2] R. Likert, *New Patterns of Management* (New York: McGraw-Hill Book Company, 1961).

evidence that many of the performance measures on which they relied were in fact unreliable because the data were "fudged" in one way or another. The evidence suggested that this phenomenon existed not only at lower levels, but well up into middle management.

STAFF/LINE RELATIONS

The attitudes and affiliations of staff specialists who devise and administer the administrative control systems for management are another substantial source of threat to many employees in the line organization. These staff groups often have a low regard for the honesty of those who are affected by the control system.

Another aspect of staff involvement in the administration of controls concerns the natural affiliations of staff groups. Typically, the manager of a staff organization reports to a line manager a level above him organizationally. Quite naturally, his conception of his role is to assist his boss, to behave in such a way as to obtain approval from the boss. In the performance of his role it is unlikely, to say the least, that he will consider it a major responsibility to support and help line managers at his level and below about whose performance he is collecting information for his boss to use.

Almost regardless of the policies that may be stated about the relationship of staff to line, the conventional organization structure and mode of operation generates these attitudes. It requires a different system structure and a different set of relationships to generate trust and support between the line and those staff groups who administer information feedback control loops.

INFORMATION FEEDBACK

Finally, consider the normal flow of information in the feedback loop. The information may flow back to the individual whose performance is being "controlled." Almost universally, however, it flows back also to the level above him, and sometimes to several higher levels. Moreover, it may flow to those higher levels in specific detail. Sometimes it goes to higher levels before it goes to him, and sometimes it goes to higher levels without going to him at all except as his boss sees fit to feed it to him.

Without arguing the logic or the necessity for these channels of information flow, I would state as a simple fact that when such information is critical of a man's performance (when it reveals mistakes or substandard performance of the individual or of those below him in the organization), *threat is involved.* Moreover, the threat is substantial because it may carry implications for his long-run career in the organization.

The principle of management by exception, under which only variances from standard are fed back to high levels, *could* be a positive motivational device if the emphasis were on recognition and reward for variances *above* standard. I have yet to encounter an organization, however, in which the principle is utilized in this manner. In practice, "control" means discovering, correcting and punishing negative variations from standard.

Let us carry the analysis one step further. If the above generalizations are sound, it would seem probable that one could successfully predict at least some forms of noncompliance that would indicate the presence of threat. What predictions can be made and what evidence is there to support them?

The first prediction would be of *simple failure to comply with demands for change* when perceived threat exists. A former Sloan Fellow at Massachusetts Institute of Technology conducted a rather simple but revealing research project to test this prediction in connection with one type of managerial control—performance appraisal.

In the company he studied, there was a standard and well-administered performance appraisal program. The general manager was strongly in favor of performance appraisal, and he had supported it openly and approved of the training of his subordinates in administering the program and conducting appraisal interviews.

Reasonably good records were made and kept centrally. Thus it was possible to go through the records over a period of time and select all the cases in which a superior had requested a change in the behavior or performance of a subordinate during an appraisal interview. The subordinates and superiors in question were then interviewed to find out whether (a) they both remembered the request for change, and (b) they agreed the change had occurred. He found that only in about 10 percent of the cases did both the supervisor and the subordinate agree that the requested change had occurred. In other words, most employees did not comply with the request or did not even remember that a request for improved performance had been made.

Another prediction would be that in the presence of perceived threat *human ingenuity will be exercised to defeat the purposes of the control system.* William Foote Whyte's *Money and Motivation*[3] presents ample evidence, in a series of case studies, of the high degree of ingenuity the average human being can display under such circumstances. In fact, the general recognition of this phenomenon under all types of control systems is sufficient to persuade many managers that a foolproof control system would be too costly if it could be devised.

The real cost, however, of such behavior is the diversion of human creativity in this direction. If half the human ingenuity now exercised in

---

[3] William F. Whyte, *Money and Motivation* (New York: Harper & Row, Publishers, 1955).

The McGregor Point of View

"Does management have any legitimate concern for individual self-actualization in an organization committed to the achievement of economic goals?

"Some managers say no. This is the concern of the individual (or perhaps more widely of society) off the job. The requirements of organized human effort, along with technological considerations, clearly prevent any meaningful degree of self-actualization on the job. These needs, even if they do exist, are incompatible with the requirements of enterprise.

"Some managers answer with a qualified yes. They see paternalistic managerial strategy as the way to encourage self-actualization. But a paternalistic strategy in fact involves control of extrinsic° rewards. It is a matter of being good to people by giving or withholding certain kinds of benefits. It is not the creation of an environment that provides opportunities for intrinsic° rewards. Therefore, a paternalistic strategy does not in my view create conditions for self-actualization.

"Some people, I among them, see a genuine potential for linking self-actualization with organizational goals. The possibilities are not equal for all people because some are prevented from self-actualization by the crippling effects of some of their early experiences. Nor are the possibilities equal on all jobs. But they are not precluded on most.

"It seems to me that strategic planning based on this recognition can lead *both* to a better society and to a more effective organization in economic terms. It is a way of tapping latent resources of creativity, skill and knowledge that are otherwise unavailable to the organization.

"A strategy that deliberately makes self-actualization one of its goals need not involve major limitations on profitability. It may involve costs, but the expectation is that these will be more than offset by the savings in costs that otherwise would be expended in overcoming neutral or passive attitudes toward organizational goals. The costs of certain kinds of control procedures and incentive plans are by no means minor.

"My view then, clearly influenced by my values, is that one of the fundamental characteristics of an appropriate managerial strategy is that of creating conditions that enable the individual to achieve his own goals (including those of self-actualization) *best* by directing his efforts toward organizational goals.

"Such a strategy is *not* permissive management, or soft or indulgent management. It includes clear demands for high performance, clear limits consistently enforced. The latter are, in fact, necessary for the individual's psychological security, for him to be able to predict what is possible and what is not. It involves clear, open communications about the pressures and limits imposed by reality. It does involve the creation of a climate of genuine mutual trust, mutual support, respect for the

---

° See footnote 1.

> individual and for individual differences. Only in such a climate can
> latent tendencies toward self-actualization find expression. Even then,
> the process may occur slowly and, at first, tentatively. It is to be ex-
> pected that some percentage of any employee group (perhaps on the
> order of 10 percent) will not respond at all or will take advantage of
> such a strategy. For such people the firm enforcement of limits, fol-
> lowed if necessary by dismissal, is the only feasible course. Otherwise,
> there is danger that indulgence toward such persons will affect the whole
> organization negatively."

this way could be tapped to increase organizational effectiveness, the
gains would be startling.

A third predictable form of noncompliance in the presence of threat
is *dishonesty*. Moreover, one could further predict that the perception
of threat would become a justification and a rationalization for the dishonest behavior. Melville Dalton's *Men Who Manage*[4] provides some
convincing documentation at *middle levels of management* for these two
predictions.

THE NATURE OF DISHONESTY

There is a common and mistaken tendency to attribute a dishonest act
by an individual to a characteristic of his personality. Implicitly we divide
the population into two categories: dishonest people and honest people.
There are individuals who display dishonesty consistently in a wide
variety of situations. Such a characteristic almost always reflects mental
illness—a form of personal adjustment that lies quite outside the normal
range. A dishonest act by the average man, however, tends to be specific
to certain circumstances and is not the manifestation of a general character trait. It is in this sense that we can say quite truthfully: "Most people
tend to be fundamentally honest."

Certain sets of circumstances, coupled with certain cultural norms
and standards, will produce behavior that is dishonest in varying degrees
on the part of many people who would, in most other aspects of life, be
scrupulously honest. Automobile traffic regulations and the federal income
tax tempt many individuals to be dishonest. So do a great many managerial control systems. The error is to seek the cause of dishonesty in the
nature of human beings rather than in the pressures to which they were
subjected. Just as individuals try to "beat the system," organizations try to
"beat the rascals."

---

[4] Melville Dalton, *Men Who Manage* (New York: John Wiley & Sons, Inc., 1959).

Human beings can distinguish between the numbers used to measure a performance and the performance itself. This ability can and does become the basis for an exciting game known as "getting the numbers." Almost everybody likes to play it, not only because it requires the exercise of ingenuity and involves risk, but also because it provides a very satisfactory outlet for hostility. And in the excitement of the game, the issue of the dishonesty involved is neatly buried.

The generalization that emerges is that conventional managerial control systems have a strong tendency to generate and accentuate the very behavior they seek to prevent: noncompliance. The reason, fundamentally, is that pressure for compliance in a climate lacking in mutual trust and support leads to the perception of threat. The reaction to threat is hostile, defensive, protective behavior. Attempts to correct control systems designed on the basis of conventional strategy by increasing the accuracy of measurement, by audits or by tighter controls serve simply to increase the threat. The consequences, as has been demonstrated above, are quite easy to predict.

Unfortunately the *absence* of threat does not guarantee compliance. It may lead merely to indifference, to a reduction in active noncompliance. The absence of perceived threat in managerial control systems is therefore a necessary but not a sufficient requirement for positive compliance. Let us consider, then, a second generalization about human behavior: *Human response to information about performance varies with commitment to goals.*

THE VALUE OF COMMITMENT

Within any organization perhaps the most fundamental difference between an employee attitude of passive compliance and employee willingness to adopt a dynamic problem-solving approach lies in top management's attitude toward the capabilities of the organization. These, of course, are not measurable in terms of specifics like industrial engineering standards, estimates of possible cost reduction, quantity in manpower requirement estimates. Such measurements if they were possible might be useful, but they wouldn't take account of the capacity of the organization for invention and innovation. They ignore the implication of the adage, "It is not how hard but how smart you work."

In fact, from this point of view the capability of the organization is *unmeasurable.* From this point of view the soundest managerial strategy is to develop an organization capable of meeting external demands and pressures in such a manner that it will compete successfully whatever the vicissitudes. The belief is that if members of the organization are identified with this goal, they can cope with reality even when such coping involves belt tightening, workforce reduction, limitations in extrinsic rewards.

To cope with reality, however, the organization must know what reality is. This requires open communication, mutual trust, mutual support and the management of conflict by working it through. The basic requirement is not mere acceptance of goals and standards, but commitment. Such commitment is necessary not only with respect to the over-all successful competition of the organization but with respect to all the specific sub-goals associated with performance.

The principle is that human beings will direct their effort, exercise self-control and responsibility, use their creativity in the service of goals to which they are committed. The managerial task is to help the organization achieve and maintain high commitment, and heavy reliance is therefore placed on the intrinsic[5] power of identification.

Identification and commitment rest on linking the individual's own goals with those of the organization. Top management, then, relies heavily on intrinsic rewards and punishments and on the achievement of equity in administering extrinsic rewards and punishments.

A MANAGERIAL STRATEGY FOR INDUCING COMMITMENT

The strategy we're talking about here is based on the assumption that although it may be possible to get acceptance by imposing goals and standards, it is not possible to get commitment. Therefore, it follows that the tactics for establishing standards that employees are willing to commit themselves to are ones that involve the joint, open exploration of organizational reality.

Given the existence of a reasonable degree of mutual trust and mutual support, the following tactics would be consistent with such strategy:

1. An open presentation and discussion of management's view of the requirements for successful competition at any given point in time. This would include an analysis of the external forces and the internal problems reflected in the information on past performance. The latter would include an examination of possible "restraining forces" preventing a realization of the organization's capability.

2. A broad analysis of changes in performance of the organization that would be required to meet the demands of external reality.

3. An analysis by each subunit of the contribution it can make to the total organizational effort. This analysis would be conducted at each level of the organization from the face-to-face subunits at the bottom through departmental and divisional units to the top.

4. A statement from each unit of the goals and standards to which the unit could commit itself relative to (1) and (2) above. Included in the statement would be an analysis of what help the unit would need in accomplishing these goals. Such an analysis might involve certain kinds

---

[5] See footnote 1.

of information feedback, staff help, changes in policy or procedure, equipment and manpower needs.

These tactics may appear to be cumbersome and time-consuming. However, they are based on the well-supported conviction that time spent initially in obtaining identification and commitment to standards and goals will be more than compensated by time saved in solving problems and getting the work out. Except for times of crisis when major adjustments will be required, the process will take little more time than is typically utilized by other strategies.

Naturally there will be difficulties, disagreements and conflict in this process, but management will not be passive or permissive. It will exercise active leadership; and where efforts to resolve conflicts at lower levels are unsuccessful, it will invoke legitimate authority to whatever degree is necessary to establish definite standards and firm limits. The process of capital budgeting, for example, is one in which top management will play a strong role for reasons that will be obvious to all. Here the expectation would be that management will impose limits and make allocations after considering requests from lower levels.

COMMITMENT

When members of an organization are committed to the organization's goals, surveillance in the usual sense becomes largely unnecessary. The problem is not one of obtaining passive compliance but of enabling all parts of the organization to achieve the goals to which they are committed. Each unit down to the individual level has a degree of control over its own fate. The total process, from the initial exploration of reality to the solution of problems arising in the day-to-day attempt to meet goals and standards, provides ample opportunity for intrinsic rewards and for the motivational effects of intrinsic punishments arising from mistakes and failures.

Naturally the development of such strategy is an evolutionary process. It would be foolhardy to attempt to shift from a conventional strategy to this one quickly or to involve all managerial control systems at once. Small-scale pilot experiments within subsystems of an appropriate size are likely to be a more effective way of testing such a strategy. Of course, in a small organization the approach can be companywide.

(I am referring to this type of control system as *organic*, as contrasted to *mechanical*. An organic control system itself is a social invention developed out of an analysis of a particular situation, which itself evolves out of the needs of individuals and subsystems affected by the data, and gathered and transmitted to the relevant systems under conditions of trust and openness.)

The research on performance appraisal in one of the units of the

General Electric Company provides an illustration of this process. It substantiated certain theoretical predictions concerning the threat involved in the administration of performance appraisals and the consequence of side effects.[6]

As a result of these findings, a test of a different strategy has been undertaken on a pilot basis. The alternative strategy is essentially similar to that described above in that it is based on organic conceptions of cause and effect. The tactics are called *work planning,* and they are undertaken by a given manager with individual subordinates. Joint planning is undertaken periodically in the attempt to establish standards and goals for a prescribed period. Emphasis is placed on open communications, mutual trust and support, and the desirability of commitment. The information feedback loop is to the subordinate, and he in turn discusses with his superior where he stands and seeks help as needed in accomplishing the jointly agreed on objectives.

In this case a careful test is being made of results by adopting the new strategy with one group of managers while maintaining the original and more conventional one with another comparable group of managers. Thus the differences can be compared and modifications made as necessary in the new strategy before consideration is given to a wider use of it.

Sometimes the intuitive style of a manager leads him to adopt such a strategy in a crisis situation and thus to bring about a major change in a relatively short space of time. Such an example is reported by Robert Guest in an automobile assembly plant.[7] This plant had been consistently the lowest of six comparable plants in the measures typically applied to performance within the company. The manager of the plant had resorted to pressure in order to improve the situation. His strategy was a typical mechanical one that emphasized extrinsic punishment. The situation went from bad to worse, and higher management eventually replaced the manager with another man.

The new manager was given freedom by higher management to approach the problem in his own way. His intuitive managerial style led him to begin by attempting to remove the pressure from the organization. In an open manner he communicated to the organization his view of reality and of the necessity for drastic change in order to achieve a successful competitive level. He indicated his trust and confidence, and his desire to be supportive, by asking for help. At all levels he asked for an analysis of problems and restraining forces and offered full managerial support in solving them.

---

[6] E. Kay, H. H. Meyer, and J. R. P. French, Jr., "Effects of Threat in a Performance Appraisal Interview," *Journal of Applied Psychology,* vol. 49, no. 5 (1965), pp. 311–17; and H. H. Meyer, E. Kay, and J. R. P. French, Jr., "Split Roles in Performance Appraisal," *Harvard Business Review,* January-February 1965, pp. 123–29.

[7] R. Guest, *Organizational Change* (Homewood Ill.: Irwin-Dorsey, 1962).

It took four years, but at the end of that time this plant was at the top of the six plants in terms of the measures utilized, rather than at the bottom.

One final example occurred a few years ago in a large oil company where top management recognized that a variety of external economic forces bearing on the organization required very substantial increases in organizational efficiency if the organization's competitive position were to be maintained.

The president of this company had been working consistently for some time with his intuitive style along lines that had built a fair degree of mutual trust and support in the organization. In the face of this crisis he undertook first to communicate to the whole organization as openly as possible his view of the reality. He said specifically that he did not wish to impose specific standards or to use pressure to improve performance. Instead, he asked each unit of the organization to examine carefully its own performance and to adopt whatever procedures seemed appropriate to achieve improvement. He indicated that the improvement would need to be substantial, but he did not set a figure on it.

In addition, he promised top management's support in every conceivable way. One specific tactic was to ask each of his key executives to go to a major subsystem and offer help and support. However, in order to ensure as much autonomy as possible in the analysis and planning within the subsystems; each executive was asked to go to a subsystem whose tasks and responsibilities lay outside his own responsibility and competence. Thus the executive would be less likely to attempt to impose his own analysis and prescription on the organizational unit he visited.

A variety of other tactics were utilized, and at the end of a year the president was able to report to his organization that its accomplishments were more than satisfactory.

It is interesting to note that another oil company facing essentially the same pressures elected to follow a more conventional strategy that included the imposition of certain specific standards of manpower and cost reduction on all units of the organization. At the end of the year this company had achieved only about half the improvement specified by the original goals.

STUDENT REVIEW QUESTIONS

1. What problems with management control systems are encountered in many organizations?
2. What should be the objectives of a management controls system?
3. What does McGregor mean by the statement, ". . . noncompliance (with management control systems) tends to appear in the presence of perceived threat"?

4. What does the author say about "management by exception"?
5. What is the author's interpretation of "commitment," and what are the advantages to the organization of such "commitment"? How is this "commitment" achieved within an organization, according to McGregor?
6. Do nonprofit organizations need management control systems?

24. Motivation and Coordination in Management Control Systems[*]

CHARLES T. HORNGREN

How do you judge the effectiveness and efficiency of a management control system? Present criteria often concentrate on the minimization of errors, fraud and waste. They focus on physical control and information handling systems—not on management control systems *in toto.* This paper raises a set of questions that both managers and specialists should ask, in addition to the traditional ones, when evaluating a particular system.

The job of a management control system is to help management attain the harmony of goals (effectiveness) and the optimum acquisition and utilization of resources (efficiency).[1] This is essentially coordination, which, in turn, involves problems of motivation. Motivation permeates the questions we are about to raise.[2]

---

[*] Charles T. Horngren, "Motivation and Coordination in Management Control Systems," *Management Accounting*, May 1967. © 1967 by National Association of Accountants. Reprinted by permission.

[1] Robert N. Anthony, *Planning and Control Systems: A Framework for Analysis* (Boston: Harvard Business School, 1965), pp. 5, 16–17, 27–28.

[2] The major objective of this article is to underscore and make explicit the probable impact of a system on managers' behavior—without getting entangled in disputes about terminology and embroiled in attempts to identify singular cause and effect relationships among the joint effects of the accounting system, management attitudes, styles of leadership, selection of goals, and so forth. Therefore, I have combed the accounting and business literature, not the psychological literature, to gather examples of behavior which was apparently sparked directly by the existing control system. Many recent articles have ably examined the psychological literature as it relates to accounting. For example, see Selwyn Becker and David Green, Jr., "Budgting and Employee Behavior," *Journal of Business*, October 1962, pp. 392–402, and George J. Benston, "The Role of the Firm's Accounting System for Motivation," *Accounting Review*, April 1962, pp. 347–55. Also see the *Journal of Business*, April 1964 for a reply by Andrew C. Stedry to the Becker and Green article, plus a rejoinder to that reply.

GOAL-SETTING

Does your system provide a global emphasis, so that all major goals and their interrelationships are considered insofar as possible when managers act? Expressed another way, does your system specify its goals and sub-goals to encourage behavior that blends with top management goals?

Multiple Goals. The aim is to get sub-goals in congruence, which requires direction and balance. It is fairly easy to assess the direction of each sub-goal by itself; the trouble is that they are interdependent. Moreover, the selection of sub-goals is essentially based on a series of assumptions regarding optimization which must be made at a top planning level.

Overstress on One Goal. Fixation on sub-goals often causes ineffective behavior. The greatest danger is overemphasis on one goal which leads to failure to attain other goals. The most common instance is the short-run maximization of net income or sales which hurts long-run results.

Tools of Coordination. The following practices are illustrations of approaches that have helped coordination:

1. If incentive rewards or punishments are directly dependent on some performance measure, such as sales or contribution to profit, the scheme should be based, at least partially, on some group (global) performance measure, such as total company net income.
2. The goal selection and constraint recognition should be interlocked explicitly. This can be achieved in many ways, from conscious informal management agreement to elaborate comprehensive budgets using linear programming. The point is that this job of goal setting and coordination is so fundamental that it should not be a product of chance or a by-product of the day-to-day extinguishing of business brush fires.
3. Rigid compartmentalization by responsibility or profit centers must be counterbalanced by explicit top management teamwork in seeing that goals harmonize.

STRUCTURE OF ORGANIZATION

Is your system tailored to the organizational structure to strengthen motivation? Is responsibility pinpointed? Are distinctions made between controllable and uncontrollable factors?

Systems and Organization Changes

Ideally the organization itself and its processes must be thoroughly appraised, understood, and altered if necessary, before a system is erected. That is, the design of a system and the design of an organizational structure are really inseparable and interdependent. The point is that the most streamlined system is not a cure-all or substitute for basic organizational ills or management ineptitude. On a practical level, there may be a powerful temptation to separate the design of systems from the design of organizational processes by assuming that the organizational structure is given. But some sad experiences with the hasty installation of computers demonstrate the weakness of such an approach.

In order to maximize efficiency and effectiveness, organizations, subdivide processes and stipulate a hierarchy of managers who are expected to oversee various spheres of responsibility. Some form of a responsibility accounting system usually reflects this process. Responsibility accounting highlights the executive's freedom to make decisions, pinpoints centers of attention and effort, and uses budgets to specify expectations sharply.

Cooperation versus Competition

A fragile balance must be struck between careful delineation of responsibility, on the one hand, and too rigid separation of responsibility, on the other hand. Buck-passing is a pervasive tendency that is suposedly minimized when responsibility is fixed unequivocally.

But often the motivational impact boomerangs; too much falls between the chairs. Managers often wear blinders and concentrate more than ever on their individual worlds. Family cooperation is replaced by intra-company competition.

> *Example:* A president of a large corporation insists that central basic production process making automobile frames. The frames were transfered from the first to the second department via an overhead conveyor system. Because of machine breakdowns in his department, the Department 2 manager requested the Department 1 manager to slow down production. He refused, and the frames had to be removed from the conveyor and stacked to await further processing. A bitter squabble ensued regarding which department should bear the extra labor cost of stacking the frames.

Accounting Records as Motivation Devices

Because the accounting system tallies performance, the records themselves become a direct mechanism of control and motivation. In many cases, particularly where activities are highly routine and the measurement problems are easy, there is a favorable motivational impact from the very act of recording.[3]

---

[3] Peter M. Blau and W. Richard Scott, *Formal Organizations: A Comparative Approach* (San Francisco: Chandler Publishing Company, 1962), p. 178.

Example: A large corporation had difficulty in reducing the volume of errors submitted to its central electronic data processing center by its parts depots. Where all other means failed, the simple step of circulating a report of all depots' individual percentage of errors dramatically reduced the error rate.

But there is also a pitfall here. There can be overdependence on an accounting system as being the prime means of motivation and the final word on the appraisal of performance. Although the system may play a necessary role in coordination and motivation, its many limitations deserve recognition too, particularly in matters of cost allocations and transfer pricing. A common complaint of managers, often marked by tones of discouragement, is that they are being unfairly charged with uncontrollable costs.

Example: A president of a large corporation insists that central basic research costs be fully allocated to all divisions despite objections about uncontrollability. His goal is to force division managers' interest toward such research activity. The basic question is whether the measurement system is the best vehicle for reaching such an objective. Indiscriminate cost allocations may undermine the confidence of the managers in the entire measurement system.

Example: A large decentralized lumber and paper company acquired a small company which manufactured envelopes. Shortly thereafter, the envelope company was instructed to purchase all of its paper needs from a Western paper division at "market" transfer prices. The quality of the paper was inferior to that previously acquired elsewhere. This adversely affected waste and machine speeds.

The paper mill showed a handsome contribution to overall company profit, but the envelope division's performance was poor. Bonuses were awarded to the paper mill managers but not to the envelope division managers because the central management was too far from the underlying activities to evaluate the performance in any way other than by the profit center approach. In this case, the executive had been assigned responsibility without commensurate freedom to manage. He exerted no control over the purchasing function, and his manufacturing function suffered because of inferior raw materials.

The whole idea of decentralization and profit centers is based on the manager's freedom and independence. Unless he has alternatives, unless he can resort to buying and selling outside the company, his so-called profit center is fictitious; it is essentially a cost center in a centralized company. When substantial freedom of choice is not available, the resultant transfer prices are artificial to a point which severely contaminates the rate of return and similar measures of profit performance.

Those who favor the wide use of profit centers often cite the presence of internal friction and competition as a major benefit rather than as a major defect. For instance, exasperating transfer pricing disputes often focus on uneconomic activities which would not be detected by an ordinary cost center system. Profit centers tend to force managers to check outside markets, alternate sources of supply, new processes and alternate materials more frequently than when cost centers are used.

ACQUIRING AND USING RESOURCES

Does your system properly guide managers in the acquisition and ultilization of resources by providing accurate, relevant information?

To be useful, data must be accurate, relevant, material and timely. Here we concentrate on accuracy and relevancy, the two aspects that have the most direct bearings on the motivational influence of a system.

Accurate Recordkeeping. Textbooks do not devote much space to the problems of obtaining accurate source documents. Yet this is easily one of the most pervasive, everlasting problems in collecting information. An accounting system will mean little to management if the recordkeeping function is haphazard.

Accurate recordkeeping is essentially a problem of motivation:

> *Example:* The maintenance crews of a telephone company sometimes would do regular recurring short-term maintenance and repair work on various projects; at other times the same crews would be concerned with huge construction projects—installing or building plant and equipment. The company had weekly performance reports on the regular maintenance work, but loose control over the construction projects. An investigation disclosed that the foremen were encouraging the workmen to boost the time on the construction projects and to understate the time on the regular maintenance projects. The foreman's performance on the latter always looked good. In this case, the correction came in balancing the emphasis between maintenance and construction so that both were budgeted and currently controlled.[4]

Intelligent Analysis of Relevant Data. The accounting system should produce information that leads managers toward correct decisions regarding either evaluation of performance or selection among courses of action. Intelligent analysis of costs is often dependent on explicit distinctions between cost behavior patterns, which are more likely to be achieved via the contribution approach than via traditional methods. The general tendency toward indiscriminate full cost allocations raises analytical dangers.

Central corporate costs are often allocated on the basis of sales dollars because of the lack of any better basis for allocation. Too often, the product or division that is doing the best to better the organization's

---

[4] Marvin A. Griffin, "Operations Research in Budgeting," unpublished doctoral dissertation, The Johns Hopkins University, 1960, p. 128.

fortunes gets the heaviest dose of cost without regard to any possible cause and effect relationships.

The pitfalls of overhead allocation take many forms:

> *Example:* Some department heads have been known to schedule work on older, slower equipment with lower unit depreciation charges rather than on newer, faster equipment with lower variable operating costs but higher unit depreciation charges formulated because of low planned volume.[5]
>
> *Example:* The area of overhead allocation is properly a favorite target for criticism, particularly where sales dollars are used as a base. For instance, small orders tend to generate as much marketing overhead as large orders. Overhead allocation based on sales dollars would err; but allocation based on the number of orders might also be difficult to defend. The resultant unit costs and unit profits must be carefully interpreted.[6]

Emphasis on Cost Behavior.   The foregoing examples demonstrate the importance of knowing the various cost behavior patterns. Intelligent cost analysis cannot be made unless the manager can distinguish between controllable and uncontrollable costs, variable and fixed costs, and separable and joint costs. Moreover, he must be able to interpret unit costs wisely.

ADMINISTRATION OF THE SYSTEM

Do budgets and responsibility accounting and other accounting techniques foster a policed, departmental orientation rather than a positive, overall organizational orientation? Let us ask if the *absence* of such techniques would encourage a broader orientation. The answer to such a question is indeterminate; yet it is doubtful that the lack of a budget would broaden a supervisor's horizons and would make him conscious of the organization as a whole instead of his little departmental sphere.

The *administration* and *communication* of budgetary and other accounting techniques should be distinguished from the techniques themselves. The management control system embraces the techniques and their administration and communication. That is why coordination and motivation have been highlighted in this article.

Every system is marked in some degree by problems of conflicting goals, erroneous source documents, faulty cost analysis, etc. The aim is to reduce the lack of coordination and to increase the proper motivation—to improve systems with the full realization that perfection is unattainable.

---

[5] Robert Beyer, *Profitability Accounting* (New York: The Ronald Press Company, 1963), p. 265.

[6] Marion H. Simpsen, "But the Old Problems Remain," *NAA Bulletin*, February 1964, p. 15.

In many cases of weak systems, the technical aspects of the system are not the culprits. The weaknesses are inept administration, the neglect of communication and education, and the neglect of the motivational impact of the system. The success of a management control system can be affected by both its technical perfection and by other nontechnical factors that influence management behavior.

Summary

Because motivation should be a prominent consideration in designing management control systems, any systems checklists, questionnaires, or criteria should explicitly include an appraisal of the motivational influences of the system under review.

STUDENT REVIEW QUESTIONS

1. Refer to the paper mill example and suggest what changes, if any you would make in the measuring and reporting system to alleviate the problems that have arisen.
2. *a.* What behavioral problems, if any, were created in the example which told of the president of a large corporation insisting that central basic research costs be fully allocated?
   b. What parallels can you draw to a nonprofit organization such as a hospital, a university, or a community service agency?
3. Give an example of how a control system can motivate a manager to behave against the best interests of the organization as a whole.
4. To accept budgeted plans as motivators is to imply that supervisors do not have adequate interest in their job, may even raise questions of a person's integrity and more than likely will cause resentment. Do you agree?
5. Budgets are wonderful vehicles for communication. How does a lack of understanding by supervisors of the language of control systems inhibit goal achievement?